THE GOLDEN BEES

THE
GOLDEN
BEES

The Story of the Bonapartes

THEO ARONSON

NEW YORK GRAPHIC SOCIETY

Publishers, Ltd.

GREENWICH, CONNECTICUT

ACKNOWLEDGMENTS

The author and publisher are indebted to Dodd, Mead & Co. for permission to reprint passages from THE EMPRESS EUGENIE AND HER SON by Edward Legge; to Funk & Wagnalls Co., Inc. for the passages from RECOLLECTIONS OF THE EMPRESS EUGENIE by Augustin Filon; to Harper & Row, Publishers, Inc. for the passages from THE TRAGIC EMPRESS by Maurice Paleologue; to William Heinemann, Ltd. for the passages from MEMOIRS OF THE PRINCE IMPERIAL by Augustin Filon; to Holt, Rinehart and Winston, Inc. for the passages from THE MEMOIRS OF QUEEN HORTENSE; and to John Murray, Ltd. for the passages from THE LETTERS OF QUEEN VICTORIA.

LIBRARY OF CONGRESS CATALOG NUMBER 64-14853

© THEO ARONSON, 1964

FIRST EDITION

PRINTED AND BOUND BY THE BOOK PRESS, BRATTLEBORO, VERMONT, U.S.A.

AUTHOR'S NOTE

In order to accommodate so immense a subject as the history of the Bonaparte family in one book, I have found it necessary to make certain simplifications.

In the first place, I have confined myself to the personal lives of the members of the family; this is a domestic history, not a political one. It is the family—with its eccentricities, vulgarities, and fascinations manifesting themselves in generation after generation—which holds the center of the stage; the great political, economic and military events of the time are heard dimly, as "noises off." Only when some outside event affects the family directly is it explained in any detail; otherwise it is simply mentioned *en passant*.

Secondly, within the family circle itself there have had to be certain shifts of emphasis. For the most part, the more famous characters have been somewhat played down and the lesser-known, but no less intriguing, personalities brought out. This is particularly true of Napoleon I. So much has been written about his stupendous career that I have concentrated on him as a son, brother, husband, father and above all, founder of a dynasty, rather than as a great public figure. The same, to a lesser degree, holds good for Napoleon III. It is with the effect of the two Emperors upon their families rather than with their effect upon the world that I have concerned myself.

I have received a great deal of help during the writing of this book, but my chief debt is to Mr. Brian Roberts. His unfailing interest, advice and encouragement have been invaluable; without them this book would never have been completed. I am indebted also to Dr. Anna Benna of the Haus-Hof-und Staatsarchiv, Vienna; to M. Gilbert Martineau, Conservateur at Longwood, St. Helena; to Dr. Killie Campbell of Durban, South Africa; to Miss A. T. Hadley of the South African State Library; to Miss Elizabeth Dey of the Johannesburg Public Library. I must thank also Mlle. J. Aurousseau, Miss E. H. Berridge, Mrs. C. Champion de Crespigny, Mrs. S. Bartlett, Miss Elizabeth Ross, Mr. Donald MacAndrew, Mr. James Ludovici and Mr. Ronald Duff. I am grateful for all the assistance which I have received in the British Museum and in libararies and newspaper libraries in London, Paris and Vienna. I must thank the South African State Library for tracking down many rare books and the Durban Public Library for making these books available to me. I am grateful to Mrs. Wilma Howes for typing my manuscript so efficiently and, in the face of many upheavals, so uncomplainingly. My final thanks are to those many people, in both Europe and Africa, who have shown me so much kindness during my various journeys in search of the material from which this book has been written.

T.A.

TO MY
MOTHER
AND
FATHER

"To whom then, am I going to leave all this?"
NAPOLEON I

PART ONE

The Years Before

1764–1804

CHAPTER ONE

⚜ ⚜ ⚜

PRINCESS Mathilde Bonaparte, niece of the Great Napoleon, once claimed that had it not been for the achievements of her illustrious uncle, she would probably be selling oranges on the quayside at Ajaccio. The Princess, who could be wrong about some things, was right about this. It was due to Napoleon's genius alone, and to the benefits that were heaped upon his family as a result of this genius, that his niece did not, in fact, spend her girlhood with a basket of oranges hugged to her ample hips. Whatever Napoleon's faults may have been—and they were legion—neglect of his family was not one of them. No founder of a dynasty could have done more for his relations than did Napoleon for his clamorous family.

In this he was typically Corsican. The population of Corsica in the mid-eighteenth century was still rigidly divided into clans; it was an island of fierce family loyalties, of burning family pride, of bloody vendettas which gathered strength from generation to generation. Any slight, real or imagined, had to be revenged. Napoleon in later life claimed that whenever his grandmother needed support in some local misunderstanding, she could be sure of between two to three hundred armed clansmen hurrying to her aid. And when her daughter, Napoleon's mother, was married in the cathedral of Ajaccio in 1764, there were over fifty male cousins on hand to escort her.

This clannishness, this almost primitive sense of kinship, was something which Napoleon never outgrew. It caused him to elevate his relations to positions far beyond their capabilities, and contributed, in no small measure, to his downfall. If he had been a less generous brother, he might have been a more successful ruler. The irony was that this streak of magnanimity, in what could otherwise be a hard and ungenerous nature, was never appreciated. Napoleon's brothers and sisters accepted all that he had to give with singular ingratitude. "My relations," he once exclaimed sourly to Metternich, "have done me more harm than I have done them good."

They owed everything to him. The family into which Napoleon was born on August 15, 1769, was of very limited distinction and of even more limited means. Dedicated Bonapartists have been tireless in their attempts to trace Napoleon's noble origins; there has even been some bland talk of his descent from the emperors of Byzantium. It is to Napoleon's credit that he had no time for this particular form of flattery. "*I am the Rudolf of my race*," he once proclaimed to the Emperor of Austria, referring to Rudolf, founder of the Hapsburg dynasty. And on another occasion he silenced some sycophantic genealogist by claiming that his patent dated back to his first battle and no further. True, on Corsica the Bonapartes were counted amongst the island gentry, but had it not been for Napoleon, it is most unlikely that they would ever have been counted as anything more. Napoleon's claim, in later life, that the Bonapartes had been the Bourbons of Corsica, did not really mean very much.

His father, Carlo Buonaparte, was an advocate; his mother, Letizia Ramolino, a local beauty. Carlo could boast a university education and an uncle who was an archdeacon; Letizia's father had once been inspector-general of the island's happy-go-lucky road system. Carlo had a smattering of culture and a great gloss of manner; Letizia, a becoming modesty and a sizable dowry. Except that they were both young and exceptionally handsome when they married ("Ajaccio's little marvel," they called her), it would have been difficult to find a more dissimilar couple. Where he was idle, easygoing, effervescent, she was industrious, disciplined, withdrawn. Where he was indulgent, trusting, open-handed, she was Spartan, suspicious, almost miserly. Where he squandered his money on embroidered waistcoats and his time on political discussions, she saved by patching and darning, and confined herself to the interests of her home and her family.

Yet their marriage was a happy one. Letizia, for all her strength of character, was enough of a Corsican to identify her own life with the life of her husband; all men had their faults, one simply had to accommodate those faults as best one could. In their twenty years of married life she bore him thirteen children, eight of whom lived. Whatever his shortcomings, Carlo Buonaparte was not lacking in the qualities of a progenitor. If his father had lived, boasted Napoleon on St. Helena, his mother would have been capable of having twenty children.

Of the eight children who survived, five were boys and three, girls. Joseph was the first child, Napoleon the second, Lucien the third, Elisa the fourth, Louis the fifth, Pauline the sixth, Caroline the seventh, and Jérôme, born a few weeks before his father's death, the last. In their youth some of the children were known by other names, but it was by these that they have taken their place in history. An additional child in the house, slightly older than the others, was Letizia's half brother, Joseph Fesch.

Although most of these eight Bonaparte children inherited their father's showy, pleasure-loving characteristics, it was their stern, frugally minded mother who had control of their upbringing. "Her tenderness," remembered Napoleon, "was blended with severity." She seems, in fact, to have been rather more severe than tender, but as she was so scrupulously fair, her children never really resented their frequent punishments. If, in these early days, she had any favorites amongst that turbulent brood, she never let them know it. She scolded or rewarded with strict impartiality. When her husband ("an enlightened man, but too fond of pleasure," said Napoleon) tried to excuse their bad behavior, she would answer firmly, "Don't interfere. It's my business, not yours, to look after the children."

But Carlo Buonaparte was no less of a Corsican than his wife. He, too, knew that his first duties lay with his family. Two months before their second child, Napoleon, was born, Corsica, after years of turmoil, came under the final domination of the French. A good patriot, Carlo had fought as doggedly against the enemy as had any of his countrymen; even Letizia, forsaking the comforts of Ajaccio, had accompanied the men on campaign. Only after all hope of withstanding the superior French forces was gone, did husband and wife return home. Once back at Ajaccio, Carlo, with an eye to the main chance, conveniently turned his back on his pro-Corsican anti-French past and set about ingratiating himself with his new French masters. As a result, he secured for himself the post of *procureur de roi,* and more important, was able to take advantage of the scheme whereby the children of poor Corsican nobles could obtain a free education in France.

The improvement in the father's fortunes brought an improvement in the family's way of life. Carlo added a banqueting room, a library, and a terrace to their home, but it is unlikely that the practical Letizia would have allowed the children free run of these new apartments. She had cleared a large room for their exclusive use, and here her handsome, high-spirited flock spent a great deal of their time. There is no doubt that they kept her busy every minute of every day. "Dullness," notes one of Napoleon's biographers, with a quaintly Victorian turn of phrase, "dwelt not in the Bonaparte household." How could it, when there was a new baby every year or eighteen months and when the second son, on his own subsequent admission, was developing into a "resolute . . . noisy, quarrelsome" little bully who "feared nobody"?

Having, by 1774, become a man of some consequence on the island (he was a member of the Council of Twelve Nobles), Carlo Buonaparte was chosen to go to Versailles to offer congratulations to the new King and Queen of France—Louis XVI and Marie Antoinette. The assignment was very much to his taste. With its gilding and its mirrors and its matchless vistas Versailles was like a dream come true to the romantic Carlo. The visit left him, however, with an even stronger dissatisfaction for his own lot. "He finds nothing to his taste in any of the places where he resides," complains that ardent Bonapartist, Frédéric Masson; "he is satisfied with none of the offices he obtains; he dreams continually of something else: of enterprises which will enrich him, of missions which will bring him glory or profit, of employments which will procure his sons an assured future and mutual support. He wants everything at once; he is importunate, meddlesome; he brings to his desires an anxiety which frustrates them. When he has secured the favors he seeks, he is already tired of them, and neglects what he has for what he may be able to have. . . ." Poor Carlo. If only he had lived long enough to enjoy the fruits of his son's genius.

Already, while still boys, the difference of temperament between Napoleon and his elder brother, Joseph, was becoming apparent. Joseph tells that one day, while the two of them were still at school in Corsica, he and Napoleon were placed in opposite groups in the schoolroom. Above Joseph's group hung the flag of Rome; above Napoleon's the flag of Carthage. Napoleon, furious at being put under the banner of a conquered people, insisted that Joseph change places with him, and Joseph, always good-natured, obliged. Thus, when the time came for Carlo Buonaparte to take advantage of a free French education for his two eldest sons, he decided that the mild-mannered Joseph should enter the Church and the fiery Napoleon, the Army. In 1778, when Joseph was ten and Napoleon, nine, they crossed to France and began their education at the college at Autun.

From the time of this first family separation until fifteen years later, when the entire Bonaparte family left Corsica for France, the bonds between the various members of the family remained as taut as ever.

♔　♔　♔

To follow the comings and goings of the different Bonaparte children between Corsica and the mainland is interesting mainly in the glimpses it gives of their rapidly developing characters. The most significant development of all, of course, was in the personality of Napoleon. Slowly, but ever more surely, he began to oust his brother Joseph from first place amongst the children. "Joseph's character," said one of the masters at Autun, "was gentle, engaging, grateful; he loved his comrades and protected those who were being teased by others. In him I never saw any germs of ambition." Joseph was as amiable, it seemed, as Napoleon was imperious. When, after a few months, Napoleon left Autun to continue his studies at the military school of Brienne, Joseph wept piteously, while Napoleon allowed only one tear to trickle down his own cheek. There was more grief in that one tear, claimed a master who witnessed the scene of parting, than in all Joseph's copious flood.

And when, a few years later, Joseph told his father that he would prefer a career in the Army to the one in the Church for which he was being trained, it is significant that his father promised to consult Napoleon on the matter. Napoleon, although only fifteen years old at the time, knew his own mind perfectly. In a precocious letter written to an uncle, he outlined, at considerable length, his reasons for thinking that Joseph would be totally unsuited for a military career. "Certainly my brother would make an excellent garrison officer," he wrote condescendingly, "he is cheerful and good-looking, the kind of boy who will come in for plenty of foolish flattery; in fact, he has the talent for getting on well in society. But what if it comes to fighting?" His brother has already, sighs Napoleon, shown "some signs of extravagance and frivolity. We shall therefore make a last effort to get him to stick to a clerical career; and failing that, my dear father will take him back to Corsica with him, and keep an eye on him, and try to turn him into a lawyer."

And this is exactly what his father did. But he was not able to keep an eye on Joseph for long, for by now Carlo Buonaparte was seriously ill. Although only thirty-eight years of age, he was subject to the most agonizing attacks of pain in his stomach, and it was decided that he should return to France to consult a doctor. Letizia borrowed some money from the governor of the island (Carlo, as usual, had squandered the little they had to spare), and accompanied by Joseph and Letizia's half brother, young Fesch, Carlo set off for France. On reaching the mainland, he was advised to make for the celebrated medical center of Montpellier. He never left it. On February 24, 1785, he died of cancer of the stomach. The faithful Joseph was with him to the end.

If, in the years ahead, Letizia's iron characteristics, manifesting themselves in her son Napoleon, were to make the family famous, it would be her husband's traits that were to prove more typical of future Bonapartes. In generation after generation the indolence, the vivacity, and the extravagance of Carlo Buonaparte would be repeated, so that long after the Napoleonic blaze had been quenched, the Bonaparte flame would burn on, warmly, luxuriantly, even, at times, brilliantly.

Years after Carlo's death, during the First Empire, the Municipal Council of Montpellier, hoping to win the approval of Napoleon, suggested raising a column in memory of his father. The Emperor refused to sanction the project. "Let us leave the ashes of the dead alone," he said brusquely, "I have also lost my grandfather and my great-grandfather. Why should nothing be done for them?"

With Carlo Buonaparte dead, Napoleon assumed his responsibilities with regard to Joseph. In spite of the fact that Joseph was now the nominal head of the family, it was Napoleon who had to "keep an eye on him and try to turn him into a lawyer." He set to it with a will. By begging grants and by demanding long overdue subsidies on some scheme of his late father's, Napoleon was able to send Joseph off to Italy to study law. Once Carlo was dead, there was never a moment's doubt as to who was in fact the head of the family.

This assertiveness on Napoleon's part was in no way resented by the placid Joseph; indeed, with his tendency to shirk responsibility, Joseph was only too pleased to leave things to this busybody of a younger brother. Joseph talks of his "great happiness" on the occasion of Napoleon's arrival home on furlough, while Napoleon never quite outgrew his early affection for his elder brother. "I love no one, no, not even my brothers," Napoleon once said in later life; and then added, "Joseph, perhaps a little; and if I do love him, it is from habit, and because he is my elder."

At the time of Carlo Buonaparte's death, Lucien, his third son, had already joined Napoleon at the military college at Brienne. At nine years of age Lucien was beginning to reveal characteristics quite different from those of his flaccid brother Joseph or his purposeful brother Napoleon. Five years younger than Napoleon, he had grown up while his two elder brothers were away from home. The result, of course, was that he had been thoroughly spoiled. He was a bright, quick-witted boy, with much of his father's charm and very little of his mother's restraint. Although willful and self-assured, he had a very loving heart. His widowed mother adored him.

When this cocksure creature joined his brother Napoleon at Brienne, he more than met his match. Already Napoleon was beginning to assume a somewhat paternal, patronizing attitude towards his brothers, and Lucien discovered that it took more than charm to get his way with this hard-eyed young soldier. The letter which Napoleon wrote to an uncle, announcing Lucien's arrival at the college, is characteristic. "Lucien is nine years old and three feet six inches in height. He is now in the sixth class in Latin, and is going to go through the full course. He shows lots of ability and willingness. I do hope he will turn out well. His health is good. He is big, quick and lively, and so far, is well thought of. He knows French very well and has forgotten his Italian entirely. He will write you a note himself on the back of this. I won't help him for I want you to see how well he writes. I do hope he will write to you oftener after this than he did when he was at Autun. . . ."

For all Napoleon's rather formal manner, he was fond of his young brother Lucien. The affection was not reciprocated. Lucien, in his memoirs, makes it clear that he took a violent dislike to his brother from the very start. It was an antipathy which he was never to outgrow.

Lucien had not been at Brienne two years before he suddenly decided that he wanted to be a priest. Given his character, it was an odd decision. It meant relinquishing his military scholarship and endeavoring to get one to a seminary instead. Napoleon's views on this waywardness on the part of his brother can be imagined, but Letizia, always indulgent where Lucien was concerned, let him have his way. The matter was resolved by Lucien's not being able to obtain the necessary scholarship and by his realization that he had no vocation for the priesthood after all. For his own sake, and for the sake of the Church, it was as well. He returned to Corsica, where he spent the next few years meddling in island politics. A scintillating, if somewhat undisciplined speaker, it would not be long before his impulsive tongue would get his entire family into trouble.

Of all the Bonaparte children, the one who most closely resembled Napoleon was Elisa, the eldest girl. Not only did she look like him—she had the same strong features, the same intense eyes—but she had something of his proud, independent quality as well. Unlike her sisters, Pauline and Caroline, she was a plain girl, and unlike them, an educated one. In fact, her more scatterbrained brothers and sisters considered her to be something of a bluestocking. In her case, too, her parents had been able to take advantage of the bounty of the King of France, and had managed to place her at the famous girls' school of St. Cyr. At this school for noblemen's daughters she picked up all sorts of aristocratic mannerisms, which she was to find something of an embarrassment in the revolutionary years which lay ahead.

There is a story of a visit which the young Napoleon paid to his sister at St. Cyr which gives an excellent glimpse of his character at the time. Accompanied by some friends of his parents, he arrived at the convent to find his sister Elisa in tears. It appeared that a farewell party was being given for one of the girls and that Elisa had not had enough money to make her contribution towards the expenses. Napoleon immediately felt in his pocket, and remembering that there was nothing there, blushed and looked away. Tactfully and without hesitation, one of the women in the party gave Elisa the money she needed. When the visit was over and they were all in the carriage once more, Napoleon suddenly burst into a torrent of abuse against such establishments as St. Cyr and his own military school. So violent was his language that one of the adults told him to keep quiet. For a few moments, seething with rage, he stared out the carriage window, but before long he was off again. "Silence!" shouted his exasperated companion, "it ill becomes you who are educated at the King's expense to talk like this." At this Napoleon almost choked with anger.

"I am not educated at the King's expense," he hissed. "I am educated at the expense of the state."

"A nice distinction," was the scoffing reply.

Controlling himself with difficulty, Napoleon announced with great emphasis that "if he were the sovereign," matters would be changed. And when, some fifteen years later, he did become sovereign, he made those changes.

One did not lightly humiliate Napoleon or a member of his family; humiliations were something he never forgot.

The fourth Bonaparte boy was Louis. When he was twelve, Napoleon, who had been home to Corsica on furlough, took Louis back with him to France. By now Napoleon, having graduated from military school, was with his regiment at Auxonne, and it was here that he and Louis shared an apartment. As Louis had been unable to obtain a scholarship, Napoleon supported him out of his own pay and undertook the boy's education himself. It was no easy task. The two of them lived in a wretchedly furnished little room, sleeping on hard mattresses and eating very little other than broth cooked by the elder brother. They never entered a restaurant. Yet so strongly developed was Napoleon's sense of responsibility towards his family that he never resented having to support and educate his brother. On the contrary, he was very proud of him.

"Louis is working hard and is learning to write French," reported Napoleon to his brother Joseph. "I am teaching him mathematics and geography. He is also reading history. He will do very well. All the women here are in love with him. He has developed a slightly French manner, both charming and fashionable; he knows how to behave, bows most gracefully, and asks the right questions with all the solemnity and poise of a man of thirty. I have no doubt that he is going to be the most presentable of the four of us . . . ."

Unlike his more rebellious brother Lucien, Louis was very grateful for Napoleon's goodness towards him. Indeed, he worshiped his elder brother. The fact that Louis, so alert and affectionate in these days, was to become so morose and embittered in later life, might well have had something to do with this early passion he harbored for Napoleon. He loved his brother, the Empress Josephine was to say in years to come, "as a lover loves his mistress." The theory that Louis Bonaparte was a suppressed homosexual is probably well founded. But at this stage at Auxonne he was still a cheerful, well-behaved little boy, wide-eyed with admiration for his Spartan, sensible, hard-working brother.

The three remaining children, Pauline, Caroline, and Jérôme, were too young to leave Corsica for France during this period. It was thus during Napoleon's frequent and extraordinarily long furloughs that he was able to get to know something more of them. Like all the Bonaparte children, they were handsome and high-spirited, and already at this tender age Pauline was beginning to reveal all the flirtatiousness, Caroline, all the selfishness, and Jérôme, all the frivolity which was to characterize them in later life. If at this stage Napoleon had a favorite amongst them, it was the pretty little Pauline. Even in these childhood years she had the ability to win hearts; the ability to break them would come later.

Widowhood, in the meantime, had revealed all the strength of Letizia Buonaparte's character. Having lost her husband when she was thirty-five, she turned her back on the sexual side of life and devoted herself entirely to her duties as a mother. In the days when her husband had been friendly with the new French masters of Corsica, the family had been moderately wealthy, but now his death brought a return to the impecuniousness of their early married life. Uncomplainingly, Letizia set about making ends meet. So weighed down was she with household duties that she even had to ask her confessor for a dispensation from churchgoing. "Losses, privations, fatigues, she sustained and faced them all," remembered Napoleon in later life. "She had the head of a man on the body of a woman."

These lessons in drudgery and poverty were never lost on Letizia. Always careful with money, her thriftiness now turned to miserliness, her miserliness, to avarice. When, in years to come, Napoleon would chide her for her penny-pinching, she would say, in that quiet, cynical way: "If ever all of you fall on my hands again, you will thank me for what I am doing now." Time was to prove her right.

But they had more to thank her for than that. They owed her so much for those years of unselfish toil and for that love which she so unstintingly but undemonstratively lavished on them. "To the manner in which she formed me at an early age," admitted Napoleon, "I principally owe my subsequent elevation."

It is a pity that of her eight children, Napoleon would be the only one to inherit her sense of discipline and her capacity for hard work.

       ✿   ✿   ✿

The French Revolution had broken out in 1789. This whirlwind, which was to sweep the Bonapartes to the pinnacles of power, barely ruffled their family life during its early years. Napoleon's sympathies were all with the revolutionaries at first, and he had hopes of Corsica's winning back her independence during the course of this upheaval. He wrote long letters to his brothers, keeping them informed of the latest developments, and whenever he got back to Corsica, he would team up with the easygoing Joseph and the hotheaded Lucien to conspire about the island's future. Although Joseph fell in easily enough with all Napoleon's plans, Lucien proved more difficult. That first violent antipathy which Lucien had felt on joining Napoleon at Brienne had never left him; headstrong himself, he bitterly resented his brother's dictatorial methods.

There was just no arguing with him, complained Lucien. Napoleon took offense at the slightest criticism and blazed up at the least opposition. Even Joseph never dared to question his brother's actions. Not only did Lucien find Napoleon difficult to deal with, but, better than the others, he seemed to understand his brother's complex character. A letter which Lucien wrote to Joseph at about this time reveals an extraordinary perception for an eighteen-year-old—even a Bonaparte.

"I have always felt in my dealings with Napoleon," he told Joseph, "that he is actuated by an ambition which, though not wholly selfish, weakens his enthusiasm for the public good. I am convinced that, if he were subject to no restrictions, he would be a dangerous man. He seems to me to have a strong liking for tyrannical methods; if he were king, he would be a tyrant, and his name, for posterity and in the ears of sensitive patriots, would be a name of horror.

"I see signs (and not for the first time) that, in a revolution, Napoleon would try to ride the waves; he is quite capable of playing turncoat to serve his personal interest. . . ."

These were prophetic words, and the sentence which followed was no less prophetic.

"One day I shall tell him to his face exactly what I think of him, for my mind is far too firmly made up to permit of my following any ideas other than my own. . . ."

This sentiment might almost be considered the *leitmotiv* running through the lives of Napoleon and his brother Lucien.

In the summer of 1792 a decree closing the royal schools presented yet another family problem. Elisa, the eldest girl, had to be brought home from St. Cyr. The Revolution having taken a somewhat more bloodthirsty turn by now, the removal of Elisa from this undeniably aristocratic establishment was a rather hazardous undertaking. It was Napoleon, of course, who was entrusted with the mission. The vehicle carrying brother and sister was stopped several times on the road from St. Cyr to Paris, and even at their shabby hotel in the capital they were frequently asked to show their papers. Napoleon's uniform protected him from too much questioning, but the fact that Elisa was from St. Cyr always aroused suspicions. Fortunately, with her olive complexion and her somewhat masculine features, Elisa did not look in the least aristocratic; if Pauline, Napoleon's second sister, with her elegantly feminine air, had been with him, things would probably not have gone nearly so well. Again, on the road from Paris to Toulon their carriage was stopped time after time by groups of revolutionaries, demanding their passports and insisting on their shouting, *"Vive la nation!"* It was a cry which Napoleon could still echo with enthusiasm. When asked if they were aristocrats, he would reply that as Corsicans they had, on the contrary, always fought for liberty. At Marseilles, where Elisa discarded her simple St. Cyr headdress for a feathered hat, they were once more accused of being aristocrats. "We are no more aristocrats than you are!" shouted Napoleon, taking care to fling away the offending hat. Brother and sister reached Ajaccio, unharmed, in October.

Here, over the months, the situation had been changing. It was becoming increasingly apparent that if Corsica was to win her independence from France, it would mean siding with Britain, France's enemy. And Letizia's children had become too closely associated with France for that. Her three eldest sons, Joseph, Napoleon, and Lucien, therefore forsook their long-cherished dreams of Corsican independence and joined the pro-French faction. Early in 1793 the irrepressible Lucien, addressing the Revolutionary Club in Toulon, attacked the anti-French party with such effect that the Republican government ordered the arrest of its leader. "I've given our enemies a knockout blow," bragged Lucien in a letter to his brothers. "You didn't expect that, did you?"

They did not, and as a result of Lucien's speech, a vendetta was sworn against the Bonaparte family. The only thing to be done now was for them to get out of Corsica as quickly as possible. "Prepare yourselves," ordered Napoleon. "This country is not for us." Joseph had already left Ajaccio to join the French partisans on another part of the island; Napoleon followed soon afterwards. Leaving her two youngest children, Caroline and Jérôme, in the care of her mother, Letizia fled with Elisa, Louis, and Pauline to join her sons at Calvi, in the north. It was from here that they all (the two youngest had by now rejoined Letizia) set sail for France on June 11, 1793.

They landed at Toulon two days later, there to be welcomed by the smug, the smiling, the disarmingly unashamed instigator of this flight for their lives—the eighteen-year-old Lucien.

♔　　♔　　♔

When the Bonaparte family struggled ashore at Toulon on that summer morning, they brought to France very little other than their undoubted talent. They were all desperately poor, and all, with the exception of Napoleon, without qualifications for earning a living. Joseph had not the necessary degree to practice law in France; Lucien had never worked; Elisa, Louis, Pauline, Caroline and Jérôme were all too young to contribute to their own keep. Napoleon established them as cheaply as he could in a house on the outskirts of the town and hurried off to rejoin his regiment. For three months he unhesitatingly and uncomplainingly supported his entire family on his pay. In September he got Joseph a job as a war commissioner, and soon after, arranged for Lucien to become a supervisor of army supplies. As a result, Letizia and her brood were able to move into slightly better lodgings in Marseilles.

There is a description of Napoleon written by a young girl who knew him during these bleak years; as she was to know him, years hence, in the full flush of his power, the picture is doubly interesting. "At this period of his life," wrote Laure Permon, afterwards Madame Junot, "Napoleon was so plain, he took so little care of himself, that his uncombed and unpowdered hair gave him a disagreeable appearance. I can still see him, entering the court of the Hôtel de la Tranquillité, crossing it with awkward and uncertain steps, a miserable round hat pulled down over his eyes, and letting escape his two *oreilles de chien*, which fell upon his iron-gray redingote; his hands long, thin, and black without gloves, which, he said, were a useless expense; wearing boots ill-made and unpolished; his whole appearance, with his yellow complexion and his thinness, giving him a sickly air. . . ."

And then, quite suddenly, his spectacular rise to fame began. In August of the same year he published a political pamphlet entitled *Le Souper de Beaucaire;* its publication attracted immediate attention in certain military circles. A few weeks later he was put in command of the artillery at the siege of Toulon. There, his magnificent contribution towards the defeat of the English earned him promotion to brigadier-general. And finally, in 1795, by a display of ruthless efficiency, he saved the Government from an attack by the insurgent National Guard. This achievement, which was to go down in history as the glorious 13 Vendémiaire (or, in Carlyle's phrase, the "whiff of grapeshot") established Napoleon as a man of consequence overnight. Within three weeks he was promoted to Commander-in-Chief of the Army of the Interior.

His first thoughts on gaining this lucrative post were for his relations. His family, he now declared, would lack for nothing. And he was as good as his word. With customary thoroughness he set about improving the Bonaparte fortunes.

The family, in fact, had grown somewhat since its arrival in France two years before. In 1794 Joseph, the eldest son, had married Julie Clary, the daughter of a silk merchant in Marseilles. She was a plain girl, but she was rich. Her homely face and slightly misshapen body were more than offset, in the eyes of the handsome, graceful Joseph, by her considerable fortune. Letizia was delighted with the match, for Julie, besides being rich, was a sweet-natured, sensible girl, and one who would love her husband devotedly. Even Napoleon was satisfied. There was, indeed, a short period when it seemed as though he might follow his brother's example. Julie Clary had a sister called Désirée, a sixteen-year-old as pretty as her sister was plain, and it was understood that she and Napoleon would one day marry. The scheme came to nothing, however, and

Désirée, instead of becoming Empress of the French, married Marshal Bernadotte and became Queen of Sweden. The thought of Joseph's successful marriage to Julie would sometimes engulf the young Napoleon in a wave of bittersweet envy. "How lucky he is, *ce coquin de Joseph*," he would say with a sigh.

In these early days Napoleon was still genuinely fond of his brother Joseph. Exasperation with his failure to fulfill Napoleon's grandiose expectations of him would come later. "In what ever position fortune may place you," he wrote to him in this period, "you know well, *mon ami*, that you could not have a better friend than myself, one to whom you are dearer, and who wishes more sincerely for your happiness. Life is a slight dream that vanishes. If you go away and think it will be for some time, send me your portrait; we have lived so many years together, so closely united, that our hearts are mingled, and you know better than anyone how entirely mine is yours . . . ."

When success did come to Napoleon, he showered his elder brother with favors. He saw that Joseph was awarded a consulship, he loaded him with letters of introduction, he aided and advised him on financial matters. "My only regret," he wrote to him, "is that I am so far away from you as to be cut off from your society."

With Lucien, of course, things had not gone nearly so smoothly. Although the least good-looking of the Bonaparte brothers (he was short-sighted, gangling, and slightly stooped), Lucien could be very attractive to women. His smile was dazzling, and his charm, when he chose to exercise it, could be overwhelming. The result was that he, too, had got married since his arrival in France. His bride, however, was as much a liability to the family as Joseph's was an asset. Her name was Christine Boyer. She was a dark, pretty, even-tempered little creature, but she was two years older than Lucien, completely illiterate, and very poor. With typical impulsiveness Lucien had faked his birth certificate (he was still a minor at the time), and had married her without bothering to inform his family. In his memoirs Lucien claimed that he felt morally obliged to marry Christine, as, after a particularly eloquent speech on the subject of equality, made of course by himself, her father had stood up and, in front of a large audience, had tackled him on the subject of his daughter. If, shouted M. Boyer, we were all equal, why did Lucien, who was pressing his attentions on his daughter, not marry her?

When Napoleon heard of Lucien's marriage, he was furious, especially as he was doing his utmost to build up the family's position, both financially and socially. Letizia, however, on meeting the modest, well-meaning girl, resigned herself to the match. No sooner had Lucien rounded off this escapade than he became involved in another. His departure from Corsica had meant no lessening of his political activities, and a few months after his marriage he was arrested and jailed. As usual, it was Napoleon who got him out of trouble. Lucien emerged, slightly crestfallen, from a fortnight in prison, and when he visited his mother in Marseilles, she found him unusually depressed. Lucien was, and would always be, her favorite son; the quicksilver quality of his mind and his infectious eloquence appealed to the strong vein of romanticism running through her practical nature; he was so like his father at the same age.

For all the anxiety which Lucien had caused him, Napoleon did not neglect him after 13 Vendémiaire. He had his brother appointed a commissioner with the Army of the North and had him given a temporary post as assistant to Fréron, Commissioner-Extraordinary for Southern France.

Letizia naturally moved out of her humble rooms into a more spacious apartment, and every post brought gifts from Napoleon for herself and his three sisters. In their new low-necked, high-waisted muslin dresses, the three sisters of the new Commander of the Army of the Interior began to attract considerable attention. Elisa, who for all her cultural pretentions had come in for a generous share of the Bonaparte sensuousness, and Pauline, who had come in for little else, were both eagerly sought after, and even the thirteen-year-old Caroline did not go unnoticed. Behind a pretty face this youngest daughter of Letizia was beginning to reveal a stubbornness and a tempestuousness not unlike those of her brother Lucien. The behavior of the Bonaparte girls, in fact, seems to have become something of a talking point at this time. Firm in so many ways, Letizia seems to have been not nearly firm enough with her daughters. "These young ladies showed that they had not been brought up in the severity of a very scrupulous morality," wrote someone who knew them in later life, "and the unpleasant anecdotes, imprudently repeated by certain Provençals, always militated against the interests of all Provence, so far as the Emperor was concerned."

"Opinion at Marseilles was not favorable to them," noted a frequent visitor to the house. "It attributed to them gallant and even scandalous adventures."

Louis, now seventeen years old, but no less infatuated by Napoleon, was appointed his aide-de-camp and personal secretary. The eleven-year-old Jérôme, Letizia's youngest child, was bundled off to a good school in Paris. Napoleon's avowal that he lived only for what happiness he could give his family was being borne out.

♔   ♔

It was at this point that the fifteen-year-old Pauline embarked on the first love affair in what was to be a lifetime devoted to love affairs. Lucien and his new chief, Fréron, the Commissioner-Extraordinary for Southern France, had arrived in Marseilles. At forty years of age the cynical Fréron, with his monocle, his powdered hair, and his gold-headed cane, was irresistible to women, particularly one so naïve and ill-educated as Pauline. Less empty heads than hers had been turned by his drawling voice and silken manner, and a verse from that fluent pen could melt the hardest heart. Not that Fréron had any need to bring his many charms into play to win the love of the amorous Pauline; the mere sight of him was enough. She fell passionately in love, and he, flattered by the adoration of this faunlike adolescent, led her on. Although Fréron was not actually on the lookout for a wife (he had a perfectly good mistress and two children in Paris), so unrestrainedly did Pauline throw herself at him that he began to think seriously of marrying her. Her flowerlike freshness appealed to his jaded senses, and her brother's prospects appealed to his cupidity. At forty he was having some difficulty in keeping up with this new, young revolutionary world; it might be as well to hitch his wagon to this rising star. Dexterously, and not without ardor, he set about making love to the ingenuous creature.

The affair alarmed Letizia, and she appealed to Napoleon. He, displaying a cynicism to equal Fréron's, assured his mother that he had no objection to the match provided Pauline's suitor were wealthy. When he heard that he was not (and by then he had heard some of the less savory details of Fréron's private life as well), he encouraged Letizia to withhold her consent. This immediately split the hot-blooded family into two factors. Lucien, who had not forgiven Napoleon for disapproving of his illiterate wife, Christine, and Elisa, who saw in Fréron an echo of her more gracious days at St. Cyr, sided with the almost hysterical Pauline, while Letizia and Napoleon (Joseph and his wife Julie were away at the time) opposed the match.

And so matters rested until a few weeks later, when Napoleon's first astounding success with the Army in Italy made all Europe ring with his name. There was no room in the family now for a tired old roué like

Fréron, and Letizia was told that she must forbid the marriage. She did, and Pauline was packed off into the country in a state of black depression, from which she seems very quickly to have recovered. Napoleon's instructions on the matter of Pauline's marriage were remarkable for their new dictatorial ring.

"It is not my intention," he informed his elder brother curtly, "that she shall marry Fréron." There was no doubt that Napoleon was now the head of the family.

CHAPTER TWO

☙ ☙ ☙

It was a far cry from the rough and tumble of the various Bonaparte households to the gilded salons in which Josephine de Beauharnais and her circle passed their leisurely days; but these were extraordinary times, and the two worlds were about to collide.

Soon after Napoleon's triumph of 13 Vendémiaire, all civilians in Paris were ordered to hand over their weapons. One morning a boy of fourteen, Eugène de Beauharnais, called at Napoleon's headquarters to ask whether he might keep the sword which had belonged to his father, the Vicomte de Beauharnais. The boy told Napoleon that his father had been a noble who had served with the Revolutionary Army, and that he had been guillotined during the Reign of Terror. Napoleon, himself the most devoted of sons, had a high regard for filial loyalty in others, and impressed by this and by the boy's eloquence, allowed him to keep the sword. A day or two later the boy's mother, Josephine de Beauharnais, called to thank Napoleon for his generosity towards her son.

To say that Napoleon fell for the seductive widow on sight might be an exaggeration, but it is true that before many weeks had passed, he was head over heels in love with her.

Josephine de Beauharnais had been born on the tropical island of Martinique, the eldest daughter of an aristocratic but impoverished sugar planter. At sixteen she had come to France to marry the nineteen-year-old Alexandre de Beauharnais, and by him she had had two children, Eugène, born in 1781, and Hortense, born two years later. The marriage had not been a happy one, and the young couple had soon drifted apart. It was the Revolution which had united them once more, for despite the fact that Beauharnais was a liberal aristocrat who had fought with the Revolutionary Army, they were both arrested and thrown into prison. He was tried, condemned, and executed, but she, by a set of fortunate circumstances, was allowed to go free. Friendless in Revolutionary Paris at the age of thirty-one, with two children to support, Josephine had to keep her head above water as best she could. There was, for a woman of her somewhat limited intelligence and generous physical attractions, only one way to do this, and understandably, she chose it. That there is any truth in the rumors that she gave herself to all and sundry at this period is doubtful, but she did become the mistress of Barras, one of the leading members of the government of the day. This liaison with Barras introduced her into the worldly, well-dressed, happy-go-lucky milieu of which he was master; it was a milieu in which the *soigné* Josephine felt admirably at home.

Josephine de Beauharnais was one of those women who, without being beautiful, give off an aura of beauty. Taken feature for feature, there was nothing exceptional about her; even the most flattering portraits show a sophisticated, moderately attractive woman, nothing more. Yet to her contemporaries she was beautiful. The sweetness of her smile, the softness of her expression, the gracefulness of her manner, the abandon of her movements, the elegance of her clothes, all combined to give her person a radiance indistinguishable from beauty. And to these physical attractions she added social ones; her tact, her good humor, her unfeigned kindness, disarmed even the most cynical; strangers, on their guard when they met her, came away enchanted. She was the personification of grace.

But there was not much more to her than this. She was a shallow, idle, irresolute creature, all curves and no corners, all froth and no substance. The line she took was always the one of least resistance; faced with a problem, she would evade it; confronted with an accusation, she would defend herself with tears. Well-intentioned and good-hearted, Josephine de Beauharnais completely lacked force of character.

And as men of strong personalities are often attracted by their mental and physical opposites, so was Napoleon attracted to Josephine. He had never met anyone like her. The more he saw of her, the more impressed he was by her languidly aristocratic air. In her gauzy dresses and her cashmere shawls, she was utterly unlike any of the women he had known hitherto, for despite the fact that he was now the hero of the hour, Napoleon was still a gauche, badly dressed little Corsican, painfully ill at ease in nonmilitary society. "I was not indifferent to the charms of women," he admitted on St. Helena, "but up to this time they had not spoiled me; and my disposition made me shy in their company. Madame de Beauharnais was the first who gave me reassurance." Josephine, to whom this reassuring of men was almost second nature, gave him, it seems, rather more than that.

"I awake all filled with you," wrote the infatuated Napoleon one morning in December 1795. "Your image, and the intoxicating pleasures of last night, allow my senses no rest. Sweet and matchless Josephine, how strangely you work upon my heart! Are you angry with me? Are you unhappy? Are you upset? . . . My soul is broken with grief, and my love for you forbids repose. But how can I rest any more, when I yield to the feeling that masters my inmost self, when I quaff from your lips and from your heart a scorching flame? Yes! One night has taught me how far your portrait falls short of yourself! You start at midday: in three hours I shall see you again. Till then, a thousand kisses, *mio dolce amor:* but give me none back, for they set my blood on fire."

Napoleon, without a shadow of doubt, was in love. And Josephine? She, indeed, was hardly even attracted to him. She was no doubt flattered by the vehement attentions of this youth (he was six years younger than she), and so passive was her nature that she did nothing to check his mounting passion. When he suggested marriage to her, she consented. The proposed match must have surprised and amused her more sophisticated friends. It was easy enough to see why the "funny little Corsican," as Josephine herself called him, should wish to ally himself to this seductive Creole with her well-bred airs, but Josephine's reasons for marriage seemed more obscure. She was up to her neck in debts, but then Napoleon was not rich; her youth was slipping by, but she was by no means old or unattractive. Perhaps, in her simple-minded way, she recognized that Napoleon's qualities—his enthusiasm, his energy, his efficiency—would make an excellent foil for her own nonchalance; perhaps his very aggressiveness attracted this most feminine of women. Utterly without security as she was, marriage to this popular young general was at least a chance worth taking; who knew but that this ambitious soldier might not turn out to be a success after all?

They were married at a Registry office on March 9, 1796. Josephine lopped four years off her age; Napoleon added two to his. Barras, glad to see her taken off his hands, was a witness. They returned to Josephine's house in the Rue Chantereine, where, in her chic many-mirrored bedroom, her dog Fortuné bit the ardent young husband in the leg.

♛   ♛   ♛

Their respective families had still to be reconciled to the match. Josephine's two children had been against it from the start; Napoleon's family did not even know about it.

Josephine's eldest child, Eugène de Beauharnais, whose unwillingness to part with his father's sword had impressed Napoleon so much, was won over fairly easily. An easygoing boy with military daydreams of his own, he could not for long resist the attentions of this brilliant young general. His sister, Hortense, proved less amenable. She had first met

Napoleon at a dinner party given by Barras. "At table I found myself placed between my mother and a general who, so as to talk with her, kept on leaning forward with so much vivacity and perseverence that he tired me out and forced me to sit back. Therefore, in spite of myself, I had to study his face, which was good-looking, strongly expressive, but remarkably pale. He talked animatedly, and seemed entirely taken up with my mother."

These "marked attentions" on the part of Napoleon towards her mother alarmed Hortense, for being thirteen years of age at the time, she was determined that her mother should not marry again. Whenever Napoleon visited Josephine after this, Hortense made a point of cold-shouldering him. He tried kindness, he tried teasing, but it was no use. When Hortense, who shed tears with the same abandon as her mother, begged her not to marry again, Josephine made some characteristically evasive reply and joined in the crying. "But the General," noted the heart-broken little girl, "had already more influence than I."

It was typical of Josephine that she should commission someone else to break the news of her marriage to Hortense. It was left to Madame Campan, the headmistress of Hortense's school, to tell the girl the tidings. In vain did Madame Campan stress the suitability of the match; in vain did she point the advantages it would afford Hortense's brother; her pupil would not be reconciled. And when the news of Napoleon's first victories in Italy began flooding the newspapers, Madame Campan became almost hysterical with enthusiasm for the girl's stepfather. "Do you realize that your mother has united her fate to that of a most remarkable man?" she cried. "What gifts! What valor! Fresh conquests at every moment."

"Madame," replied Hortense, with a neat turn of phrase, "I will give him credit for all his other conquests, but I will never forgive him for having conquered my mother." Madame Campan, delighted at her pupil's sharp reply, repeated the *mot*, and it was soon being tittered about all over Paris.

When the long-suffering Madame Campan finally did prevail upon the girl to write to her stepfather, Hortense's letter was remarkable only for its brevity and its churlishness. "I have been told of your marriage with my mother. What surprises me is that you, whom I have so often heard speak badly of women, should have made up your mind to marry one."

Napoleon's answer to this display of childish ill humor was, on Hortense's own admission, full of "kind phrases." The pity of it was that Napoleon's handwriting was so bad that it was not until several years later, when he was already First Consul, that Hortense was able to get it deciphered by one of his patient secretaries. And she had long since been reconciled by then.

Compared with the reaction of the Bonapartes to Napoleon's marriage, Hortense's reception of the news might almost be considered sanguine.

Going against all the traditions of his native Corsica, displaying, for once in his life, a total disregard of his family, Napoleon married Josephine without telling any of them anything about it. Realizing that the widowed, worldly, extravagant Josephine would never be acceptable to his mother, and being far too much in love to care anyway, he settled for a *fait accompli* instead of a series of family harangues. Josephine had met only two of the Bonaparte brothers by the time she married—the rebellious Lucien, whom she had seen at some of Barras's receptions, and the devoted Louis, who was still acting as her husband's aide-de-camp. Napoleon had packed both brothers off into the country just before the wedding, with the result that no member of his family had been able to act as witness.

Forty-eight hours after the ceremony Napoleon was on his way south to take command of the Army of Italy. En route, he stopped over for a few days with his family at Marseilles. He brought with him a letter from Josephine to Letizia. It was an impersonal, conventional little note, and Letizia's reply, drawn up after several family conferences, was no less correct. "I have received your letter, Madame," ran Letizia's answer. "It could not, of course, add anything to the charming picture I had already formed of you in my mind. My son has already made me aware of his happiness; from that moment you possessed not only my consent but my approval. All that is wanting now to my happiness is the pleasure of seeing you . . . ."

The formal honeyed phrases gave no indication whatsoever of the tempestuous background against which they were written. Napoleon had arrived at Marseilles in the middle of his sister Pauline's torrid affair with the middle-aged Fréron. As Fréron knew Josephine, he lost no time in acquainting the family with a wealth of picturesque detail concerning her past. Letizia, who anyway considered Josephine to be "an old woman with grown up children," was shocked that her son should have married such a creature, while the lovesick Pauline, enthusiastically seconded by Lucien and Elisa, wanted to know in what way Napoleon considered the middle-aged roué Fréron inferior to the middle-aged courtesan Josephine. Even Joseph, ordinarily too astute to bite the hand that fed him, objected to the match. He had hoped that Napoleon would marry his sister-in-law, Désirée Clary, so that the source from which they all drew their benefits would be retained well within the family circle. An impoverished but extravagant widow with two children of her own to support was going to mean a serious drain on that golden stream.

At loggerheads over everything else, the Bonaparte family would always be united in their opposition to Josephine.

The infatuated Napoleon drove off to Italy and the family immediately began their vendetta against his wife. It was Pauline, still pale with love for Fréron, who made the first thrust. Josephine, she claimed, had set Napoleon against Fréron. "In fact," she informed her aging lover, "she's written to her husband that I should demean myself by marrying you, and that she hopes to prevent our marriage." Lucien, who all along had championed Fréron against Napoleon, now waited for the opportunity to attack Josephine as well. When Napoleon ordered him to take up his post with the Army of the North (Lucien had been hanging around Paris for weeks without leave), he complained that it was because Josephine objected to his friendship with Fréron that Napoleon had ordered him to leave Paris. Unable to disobey his brother's command, he set off for the Army, taking his wife, Christine, with him; when she had a miscarriage en route, he claimed that it would never have happened had not Napoleon, egged on by Josephine, forced them to travel at that critical time.

Arriving at Marseilles on a visit to his family a few weeks later, Lucien was presented with a further opportunity for a stab at Napoleon and Josephine. His sister Elisa had recently had a proposal of marriage. Now twenty years of age, the serious, somewhat masculine Elisa was developing, says Frédéric Masson, into "one of those strange beings, who, without possessing the qualities of the other sex, had lost the charms of her own." Her admirer was a Corsican named Felix Bacciochi. That Bacciochi was a thirty-five-year-old nonentity of no more than modest means was bad enough; what would really discredit him in the eyes of Napoleon was that he had fought with the pro-English, anti-French faction in Corsica in 1793. The certainty that Napoleon would reject Bacciochi as a brother-in-law was enough to make Lucien take him up. Letizia was in favor of the match. At twenty, Elisa, who had her full share of the hot Bonaparte blood, was far too old to be unmarried, and Bacciochi had those dependable qualities so sadly lacking—with one notable exception—in Letizia's own sons. She wrote off to Napoleon for his consent, but before he had time to reply, Lucien had persuaded her to allow the marriage to take place. When Napoleon's answer did arrive, it was an unequivocal refusal. By then the spiteful Lucien was satisfied.

A further irritant for Napoleon was supplied by Jérôme, the youngest of the family. Napoleon had enrolled him at a fashionable school in Paris, but no sooner had he arrived there than he complained that he was homesick and wanted to come back. Letizia, softer-hearted now than she had been in the days of struggle, wanted to let him have his way. Napoleon was furious, and insisted that Jérôme remain where he was. It was the first, but by no means the last, time that the wayward Jérôme was to exasperate his eldest brother.

If Lucien imagined that any of these family maneuverings would worry Josephine, it proved how little he knew her. Far from resenting Napoleon's relations, she hardly gave them a thought. It was very seldom, in fact, that she thought about Napoleon himself. While he, in one spectacular victory after another, was forcing the Austrian armies back across Italy until his name became a household word throughout Europe, Josephine was amusing herself in Paris, too busy even to write him a few lines. Yet such a torrent of love letters poured from him to her that one wonders how he ever found time to win those resounding victories. Day after day his couriers went galloping along the white roads to Paris with yet another parcel of passionate letters for their general's wife; sometimes they were instructed to remain in Paris for a few hours only before careering back with an answer. Often she did not even bother to reply.

"I have not passed a day without loving you," ran one of his more restrained outpourings. "I have not passed a night without pressing you in my arms, I have not taken a cup of tea without cursing glory and ambition that keep me far from the soul of my life. In the midst of work, at the head of my troops, while inspecting the camps, only my adorable Josephine is in my heart, fills my spirit, absorbs my thoughts. . . ."

Once he had achieved his first military successes, he was determined that Josephine should join him in Italy. "You will come, won't you?" he begged. "You will be here by my side, on my heart, in my arms, on my mouth. Take wings. Come, come. . . ." Time and again he implored her to start out for Italy, time and again she delayed her departure. The prospect of the long jolting journey appalled her, and anyway, she had made a new friend, a dashing, dark-haired subaltern by the name of Hippolyte Charles. She sent a message to Napoleon, saying that she was pregnant and could not possibly undertake the journey; he answered by saying that he was "dying to see how (she) carried her child."

In May, Joseph arrived in Paris. He brought Josephine yet another letter from his besotted brother. "My sweetheart. My brother will give you this letter. I have the greatest affection for him. I hope he will gain your own. He deserves it. Nature has given him a gentle, equable, and unvaryingly good character. He is full of good qualities. I am writing to Barras to have him appointed consul in one of the Italian ports. He wishes to live with his little wife far removed from the tumult of great events . . . ."

If this was indeed what Joseph wanted, then Napoleon would have done better to have remembered it in years to come.

Finally, towards the end of June, Josephine, who was not pregnant after all, set out to join her husband in Milan. In her coach traveled her brother-in-law Joseph, one of Napoleon's staff officers, Junot, and the amusing Hippolyte Charles. Whether it was true that Josephine shared her bed with Hippolyte Charles during the night stops, one does not know; nor can one be sure that Joseph was obliged to sleep alone because of a rather painful reminder of his recent stay in Paris.

Josephine was reunited with Napoleon just over one month later.

  ♔ ♔ ♔

In the summer of 1797 Napoleon assembled almost all his family at the castle of Mombello, a few miles outside Milan. If evidence were needed that the Bonaparte clan had risen in the world, the impressive, almost regal atmosphere which now surrounded them supplied it. Whether conferring with his brilliantly uniformed staff in one of the palatial rooms, or whether granting audiences in the vast tent set up in the garden, Napoleon seemed emperor already, in all but name. And if he wanted to play the emperor, Josephine was more than capable of playing the empress; no one could queen it better than she. In her chic Paris clothes she floated through the great rooms of the castle, smiling her sweet smile and nodding her carefully coiffured head. And all the while, with dark, hard eyes, the Bonapartes watched her.

The handsome Letizia, with her finely chiseled features and her ramrod back, watched most closely of all. Napoleon's wife represented almost everything she disliked in a woman—indolence, extravagance, fickleness. And as far as Letizia's eagle eye could make out, Josephine did not even fulfill the most basic wifely qualification; she showed no signs of bearing Napoleon a child. This, by Letizia's reasoning, would be the unforgivable failing.

Josephine tried her best to make herself agreeable to this unsmiling matriarch; she "showed herself," said Napoleon, "a most dutiful daughter-in-law; she overwhelmed my mother with attentions and kindnesses . . . ." But it was all to no purpose. Letizia, ashamed of her own faulty French and of her lack of social grace, remained impervious to her daughter-in-law's charms.

Joseph did not allow himself to look nearly so disapproving. Knowing how passionately his brother loved Josephine, he saw no advantage in siding openly with the rest of the family against her; it would be better if he and his submissive wife, Julie, minded their own business and accepted whatever Napoleon felt inclined to offer. Their reticence was richly rewarded; Joseph was appointed French ambassador to Rome.

Elisa, too, had every reason to make herself as agreeable as possible. Knowing how strongly Napoleon disapproved of her recent marriage to Bacciochi, she needed all the support she could muster; even so, she found it difficult to be more than polite to Josephine. To her great relief Napoleon accepted the marriage quite calmly. Although acquaintance did not improve his opinion of Bacciochi, he gave his sister a dowry of forty thousand francs and wangled a military command in Corsica for her husband. On one thing he did insist, however, and that was their previous civil marriage be followed by a religious ceremony at Mombello. As Napoleon rose to a position of power in the world, so did he begin to pay lip service to the world's other established powers.

Louis, the fifth Bonaparte child and, at this stage, Napoleon's favorite brother, seemed to resent Josephine rather less than the others. It might have been that he was better mannered, or simply that he was too self-obsessed to be bothered with these family squabbles. At nineteen Louis's character was undergoing a change. Hitherto, he had been Napoleon's devoted pupil, and as his aide-de-camp during this Italian campaign he had acquitted himself very well. "This brave young man," Napoleon had written to the Minister for War, "deserves all the consideration that you may be so good as to show him." But at about this time, Louis had begun to lose his taste for soldiering, and with it he lost the cheerfulness and the willingness to please which had so endeared him to Napoleon. He became quieter, graver, gloomier. He often forsook the brilliant circle at Mombello and went for long solitary walks. His health became his chief preoccupation, and from now on he was never happier than when consulting his doctors about the vague pains which plagued but never actually incapacitated him. He lost touch with his military friends and cultivated the society of young unknown writers;

he conducted these new friendships earnestly and jealously. His character, which had once seemed so open and uncomplicated, now became shuttered, introvert, enigmatic. But at Mombello, Josephine was grateful for his presence, for if he was not actually friendly towards her, he was at least polite.

One could not say as much for Pauline, the sixth Bonaparte. She, of them all, caused Josephine the most distress. At seventeen Pauline had more than the Bonaparte good looks; she was radiantly beautiful. Gray-eyed, chestnut-haired, with a flawlessly white skin and a soft, seductive body, Pauline was already setting the hearts of Napoleon's young officers aflutter. But for all her dewy freshness, when set beside the *soigné* Josephine she seemed countrified, almost gauche. To mask her jealousy of her polished sister-in-law, Pauline behaved outrageously; she giggled incessantly, she flirted with the officers, she repeated their smutty gossip (a great deal of which concerned her brother's wife), and when Josephine's back was turned, she ran her tongue out at her.

Napoleon very wisely decided that the best thing to do with this badly behaved, hot-blooded little girl was to marry her off as quickly as possible. He decided to do it there and then. There was a husband to hand in the person of General Leclerc, a twenty-five-year-old friend of Napoleon's who happened to be both handsome and rich. Pauline, who had by now overcome her infatuation for Fréron, seemed willing enough, and she and Leclerc were married with a nuptial Mass in the castle oratory. The ceremony was followed by a benediction for Elisa and Bacciochi.

Caroline, at fifteen, was too young to cause any serious trouble. She shared her sister Pauline's envy of Josephine's accomplishments, and joined in her giggles at Josephine's expense.

Also at Mombello was the man whom Caroline would one day marry. In an era of exceptionally handsome men, Joachim Murat was the most handsome of them all. Magnificently built, superbly uniformed, his fellow cavalrymen called him, very appropriately, "Franconi," after a renowned circus master. His passion for soldiering was equaled only by his passion for love-making; for fearlessness on the battlefield and prowess in bed, Joachim Murat had no rival. At thirty years of age, despite his crowded career, he still retained an almost boyish enthusiasm for life. And at Mombello even he, although not yet a member of the family, slandered Josephine by hinting to his fellow officers that he had seduced her in Paris the year before.

Jérôme, the youngest child, who had recently been forced by Napoleon to remain at school, now joined his family at Mombello during the holidays. At thirteen years of age he was already showing signs of becoming the best-looking and the most frivolous of the Bonaparte boys. Jaunty, insouciant, and quick-witted, he was known by his friends as Fifi. A story goes that one evening, when the young Jérôme and his friends were strolling through the streets of Marseilles, they were stopped by a sentry. Noticing that the boys were not sporting the compulsory tricolor cockades, the sentry asked, "Little citizens, why aren't you showing cockades?"

"Because," answered Jérôme glibly, "we wear them in our hearts."

Only Lucien, the intelligent, ill-tempered, incorrigible black sheep of the family, was absent. He was still smarting under Napoleon's outspoken disapproval of his marriage to the simple Christine and of his friendship with the dissolute Fréron. He had not been with the Army of the North for more than a few weeks before he was begging the War Minister to allow him to return to Marseilles. The War Minister referred the matter to Napoleon, and he, considering Marseilles far too explosive a city for someone of Lucien's temperament ("This young man has a certain amount of talent, but at the same time a very ill-balanced mind"), had him posted to Corsica instead. This suited the ambitious Lucien not at all, but he had the good sense to lie low for the moment. Having plenty of time on his hands, he set about teaching his wife Christine how to write; and not only *how* to write, but *what* to write. "Do not despise us because we are poor," she wrote prettily in her first letter to Napoleon, "for after all, you are our brother." Her letter had the desired effect, and Lucien was appointed French commissioner at a very handsome salary.

Josephine had at least one ally in the person of her son, Eugène. Napoleon had recently sent for him and made him one of his aides-de-camp. Now sixteen years of age, Eugène, like his mother, was notable less for physical beauty than for an attractiveness of manner. And like her, he had a certain suppleness of temperament which was to stand him in very good stead in the years ahead. "Eugène," wrote one of Napoleon's secretaries, who first met him at this time, "had an excellent heart, a manly courage, a prepossessing exterior, with an obliging and amiable temper." Although Josephine's daughter, Hortense, could not be present, Napoleon did not forget her, and "the hundred pretty things" which he had promised her in a postscript to that illegible letter began arriving in a steady stream at Madame Campan's school. And with the arrival of dozens of these jeweled and enameled trinkets from Italy, Hortense's very feminine heart began to warm towards her stepfather.

The Bonaparte family left Mombello after a stay of two weeks. It must have been the longest fortnight of Josephine's life. If it had done nothing else, their stay had confirmed their resentment against Napoleon's wife; from now on there would not even be a show of friendliness towards her. She, in turn, would always refer to them as "those monsters." The breach between the Bonapartes and the Beauharnais was acknowledged; it was a breach which would long outlast the present generation.

♚   ♚   ♚

The Italian campaign successfully concluded, Napoleon returned to Paris in triumph. In his wake trailed his equally triumphant family. Napoleon and Josephine settled down in her house in the Rue Chantereine (now renamed the Rue de la Victoire in his honor), where Napoleon did his best to avoid the crowds which all day hung about the gates in the hope of seeing him. They would gather as eagerly to see him if he were going to the scaffold, he remarked cynically.

Joseph's spell as French ambassador to Rome had been extremely brief. Within a few months a riot had driven him, his wife, Julie, and his younger sister, Caroline, back to Paris. Here, displaying a talent for good living which far outstripped his talent for diplomacy, he bought himself two magnificent houses: a town house in the Rue de Rocher and a country place at Mortefontaine, near Chantilly. Caroline's presence in Paris allowed Napoleon to do something about his youngest sister's badly neglected education; with customary firmness he packed her off to join Josephine's daughter, Hortense, at Madame Campan's school. "I counted on finding a real friend in Caroline Bonaparte," wrote Hortense with charming naïveté, blaming her subsequent disillusionment on Napoleon. Her stepfather, she claimed, made the mistake of always holding her up as an example to Caroline. In vain did the sweet-natured but possibly patronizing Hortense try to help the disgruntled girl; the spiteful Caroline repaid her kindness by complaining to Napoleon that Hortense was showing off at her expense. The Bonaparte vendetta was being extended to the second generation.

Louis Bonaparte, limping slightly from a real or an imagined ailment and growing moodier by the day, used sometimes to visit the two girls at Madame Campan's. "He seemed particularly interested in me," noted Hortense in some alarm, adding that there was something about his bearing that she mistrusted. Of a generous, sunny disposition herself, she disliked Louis's withdrawn, melancholy temperament. If he was showing some interest in Hortense at this time, she certainly was not returning it. In a rare burst of girlish confidence, Caroline now revealed to Hortense that she was in love with the dashing Joachim Murat, and that was why she had insisted on coming to Paris with her brother Joseph and his wife. "Her confidence," said Hortense, who herself harbored hopes of being allowed to marry a man she loved, "touched me."

Before long, Madame Letizia joined Joseph and Julie in Paris. The change in the family's fortunes brought no diminution of Letizia's deep-rooted parsimony. While her children paraded their new finery, their mother stuck to her old clothes; when the extravagant Pauline teased her for her miserliness, she countered by calling her daughter a spendthrift and telling her to be quiet. She had to save, she claimed, for her sons. They were not all in what she called "settled positions" yet. At Pauline's age it was natural to think of pleasure; *she* had more serious matters to consider. "I do not want Bonaparte to have cause for complaint. You take advantage of his good nature."

It was not long before Lucien, whom Napoleon had made French commissioner in Corsica, was also back in Paris. Unable to keep out of politics, he had managed to get himself elected as Corsican deputy to the Council of Five Hundred. The fact that he was far too young to stand for election (he was twenty-three, and a candidate had to be at least twenty-five) was conveniently glossed over, and he took his seat in April 1798. Never one to hang back, he was soon one of the most voluble members of the assembly. Nor were his frequent speeches mere verbiage; buried under the florid phraseology and the classical allusions was a lot of good sense. Lucien could be foolish, but he was no fool. His listeners began to take this ardent young man more seriously, and before the year was out he had become a real force in the Council of Five Hundred. His position was soon to stand his brother Napoleon in very good stead. Like Joseph, Lucien bought himself a town and a country house, and although he could not match his brother's qualities as a host, his estate at Plessis was equal to Joseph's in magnificence.

Elisa and her husband, Bacciochi, whom she was now beginning to despise for his dough-like dependability, seemed to spend as much time in Paris as in Corsica; they were always staying for a month or two in one of Elisa's brother's new homes. Her newly married sister Pauline could also boast a couple of houses in France; one in the Rue de la Victoire, on which Napoleon and Josephine had their home, the other at Montgobert. Like Elisa, Pauline found her husband Leclerc deadly dull, but unlike Elisa, she had no difficulty whatsoever in attracting other, more vivacious men.

Already, after only a few weeks in the capital, she was earning a reputation for herself in Parisian society. Her seductive beauty, her suggestive clothes, her admirers without number, were widely discussed. "She was still fresh on her arrival in Paris from Milan," noted a friend, "but this freshness was of short duration; by the time she had lived a year in Paris, she began to be a very different person. . . ."

Life on the Rue de la Victoire did not suit Napoleon. He was restless. Eager to sustain the reputation he had won in Italy, he longed for another campaign. "I don't want to stay here," he complained. "Already my glory is gone. This little Europe doesn't supply enough of it. One must go to the East. All *les grandes gloires* emanate from there." The Government, uneasy about those near-hysterical crowds thronging the approaches to Napoleon's house, let him have his way, and in 1798 he set off to conquer Egypt. He took his brother Louis and his stepson, Eugène, with him, but left Josephine at home; there was a plan that she might join him later.

While Napoleon won victory after victory in the Near East, Josephine sustained defeat after defeat at the hands of the Bonapartes. Unfortunately, she supplied her enemies with plenty of ammunition. No sooner had her husband set sail for Egypt than she began spending money and keeping company with the dapper Hippolyte Charles once more. Napoleon, certain of her extravagance and suspecting her infidelity, had asked Joseph to keep an eye on her; he had even entrusted her allowance to his brother. Josephine, resenting Joseph's ever-watchful presence, referred to him as a "vile, abominable creature," and claimed that he had told one of her friends that he would not rest until he had broken up her marriage. To get away from the cold snakelike stares of the family, Josephine bought herself a house in the country; it was called La Malmaison. Here, far removed from the clamor of Paris, she was able to devote her days to the garden and her nights to the scintillating Hippolyte Charles. In the evenings these two would stroll arm in arm under the great trees, Josephine's filmy dresses glowing white in the moonlight. Those who did not know that Eugène was with his stepfather in Egypt assumed that the young man was Josephine's son: The Bonapartes knew better, and they lost no time in letting their brother know the identity of Josephine's frequent guest.

Bourrienne, Napoleon's secretary, was with him in Egypt on the day that he heard about Josephine's unfaithfulness. He had never seen

Napoleon more upset. "There was something convulsive in his features, something wild in his looks, and he several times struck himself on the head."

"Josephine!" shouted Napoleon to the startled Bourrienne, "To deceive me like that! . . . She! Woe betide them! I'll exterminate that race of whippersnappers and fops! . . . As for her, divorce! Yes, divorce! A public, resounding divorce! . . . I must write! I know all! Divorce must part us forever! I will not be the butt of every loafer in Paris! I shall write to Joseph: he will procure a divorce!"

And write to Joseph he did. It was a sad, disillusioned letter. In it he spoke of his "domestic trouble" and assured Joseph that he alone remained dear to him. "I am tired of human beings: I need solitude and isolation. Greatness bores me, my feelings are dried up, *la gloire* has lost its taste. At twenty-nine I have exhausted everything: there remains nothing for me but to become a complete egotist . . . I have nothing more to live for. Adieu, my one friend."

There is no doubt that Josephine's infidelities caused Napoleon a deep hurt, from which he never quite recovered, but one must remember that his own private life in Egypt was far from blameless. While in Cairo he saw, and was attracted to, the wife of a certain Lieutenant Fourés. He promptly dispatched Fourés to France with messages for the Directory and installed his wife as his mistress. For a time he even considered divorcing Josephine and marrying Madame Fourés, provided she could bear him a child. "But the little idiot doesn't know how to have one," he complained, to which she replied that the fault certainly did not lie with her. This seems to be one of the first occasions on which some doubt was expressed on Napoleon's ability to father a child. He had been married to Josephine for three years now, and there was still no sign of her becoming pregnant. The fact that she had already borne two children vindicated her somewhat, and her sharp rejoinder, "Perhaps it is you," when Napoleon asked her why she had not yet given him a son, seemed more than justified. When her sister-in-law, Elisa, asked the same question and Josephine again pointed out that she already had two children, the sour-tongued Elisa said smilingly, "But, sister, you were much younger then." This, in fact, was what was beginning to worry Josephine. She was now thirty-six years old; it was sixteen years since she had given birth to Hortense, and for all her visits to Plombières, whose waters were said to have a rejuvenating effect on the genital organs, she seemed unable to conceive. And she knew very well that the Bonapartes were citing her continued infertility as yet another reason for Napoleon to divorce her. If she could not give her husband a son, she doubted if she could maintain her hold over him.

From Egypt the loyal Eugène wrote his mother, warning her that Napoleon had heard of her infidelities (he himself, said Eugène, would like to believe that it was all gossip invented by her enemies), but his letter was captured by the British and never reached her. A second warning was sent, this time by Napoleon himself, through his brother Louis, whom Napoleon was sending back to France with some trophies. "I am asking Louis to give my wife some good advice," he told Joseph. Joseph, of course, saw to it that the good advice was never delivered.

In October 1799, after an absence of almost one and a half years, Napoleon landed in the South of France. Through skillful propaganda he had managed to present his somewhat inconclusive Near Eastern campaign as a tremendous triumph, and he returned to France a hero once more. Eugène wrote from the south to tell his mother of Napoleon's arrival. Knowing that his brothers would try to reach him first in order to slander her, Josephine, for once in her life, sprang into instant action. She hurried away from the dinner party at which she had heard the news, threw herself into her traveling carriage, dashed to Madame Campan's to pick up Hortense (two weeping women would be better than one, she reckoned), and then drove as fast as she could for the coast. All along the route they had chosen—the Burgundy road—the two jolting women noticed the triumphal arches being erected in Napoleon's honor; surely they must be on the right road.

In the meantime Napoleon's brothers, Joseph, Lucien, and Louis, with Pauline's husband, Leclerc, had acted even more swiftly; they were already thundering south, three hours ahead of Josephine. The two coaches careered down the Burgundy road while Napoleon rolled triumphantly up the other route to Paris. It was only when Josephine reached Lyons that she realized her mistake; by then Napoleon was almost back in Paris, with his brothers, who had also discovered the error, close behind. Sick with apprehension and now days late, she turned back to Paris.

Napoleon arrived at the Rue de la Victoire to find the house empty. It was not empty for long. Letizia and Pauline hurried over to greet him, and a few hours later his brothers, exhausted but victorious, tumbled out of their coach. The fact that Josephine was not even there to welcome him home seemed to confirm all the slander that his family was now pouring into his ears. He was determined to break with her.

She arrived home on the evening of the third day after his return.

The house was as quiet as the grave; Napoleon had already gone to bed. She hurried upstairs and knocked at the door of his room, but he refused to open it to her. All night long she remained outside his closed door, knocking, pleading, crying. At the suggestion of an astute maid, she sent for Eugène and Hortense, and the three of them stood there in the half-light, begging him to open the door. Finally, because tears never failed to move Napoleon, he opened it. They could see that his own face was creased with crying. The children returned downstairs and Napoleon, helping the limp Josephine to her feet, led her into his room. Once more he closed the door.

Early the following morning Lucien, with a spring in his step and a confident smile on his face, arrived to see his brother. He was told that Napoleon was not up yet. He knocked on the bedroom door, and his brother shouted to him to come in. He did. In the room he saw Napoleon and Josephine in bed together. Stammering with rage and confusion, he greeted his sister-in-law and hurried away to tell his family the news. The Bonapartes had reckoned without Josephine's trump card.

♚ ♚ ♚

During Napoleon's absence in Egypt his brothers Joseph and Lucien had not confined their scheming to Josephine's downfall. France herself was in a state of political turmoil, and the Bonapartes were working actively for the overthrow of the Government. If France were to be saved from another revolution, they reckoned, the present irresolute government would have to be replaced by another, more purposeful one. And when Napoleon, who had doubtless been kept informed of his brothers' plans, returned to France, they decided that the time was ripe for action. Napoleon hoped to institute his new order by legitimate means, and in this determination he rode out to Saint-Cloud at the head of his troops to address the Council of Elders and the Council of Five Hundred. Both Joseph, who had friends in the Council of Elders, and Lucien, who was now President of the Council of Five Hundred, had prepared the ground fairly thoroughly; a persuasive speech by Napoleon should have been enough to overthrow the existing regime. But it was not as easy as that. In the first place Napoleon was no orator, and his long-winded appeal to the Council of Elders trailed off inconclusively; in the second place civilian disorder unnerved him, and his arrival in the Council of Five Hundred was greeted with shouts of "Down with the traitor!" and

"Outlaw!" It was Lucien who saved the day. When the excited assembly urged him to put the motion of Napoleon's outlawry to the vote, Lucien ripped off his toga and resigned as President of the Council. Making for the courtyard, to which the flustered Napoleon had already withdrawn, Lucien leaped onto a horse and addressed the troops. He urged them to "march against the traitors who were in the pay of England," and swore that he himself would stab his brother Napoleon in the heart if he in any way tampered with the liberties of France. Led by Murat and Leclerc (it was all very much a family affair), the troops poured into the hall with bayonets fixed. The terrified deputies fled, helter-skelter, into the garden, and it was not until nine o'clock that evening that a few of the more pliant ones were rounded up and coaxed into voting for a change of government. The Directory was abolished and replaced by a consulate of three. The consuls were Sieyès, Ducos, and Napoleon, with Napoleon, of course, as First Consul. It had needed a *coup d'état*, after all, to make him master of France.

Napoleon's mother and his sister Pauline were at the theater when they heard the news of the *coup d'état*. Earlier that day Madame Letizia had refused to join her daughter-in-law, Josephine, during these hours of uncertainty. "I should never go there to find the comfort I need," she said proudly. "I should go to Julie (Joseph's wife) or Christine (Lucien's wife)—in their homes I see my sons happy. But the other! No!" Now, at the theater, when they heard that Napoleon's life had been in danger that day, Pauline let out a piercing scream and could only be calmed by a sharp word from her mother. Anxious for more definite news, they hurried from the theater. As things were, the only person who could possibly know about the day's events was Josephine, so Letizia was forced to swallow her pride and make for the Rue de la Victoire. And it was here, with the despised Josephine, that she heard that her thirty-year-old son was now the ruler of France.

Josephine's daughter, Hortense, and Napoleon's sister Caroline heard the news in a rather more dramatic fashion. At midnight four young grenadiers came galloping down the street in which stood Madame Campan's school for girls. Dismounting boisterously from their horses, they pounded on the doors of the darkened house. They had been sent by Joachim Murat to break the news of the *coup d'état* to Napoleon's sister and stepdaughter. Madame Campan was understandably annoyed at this display of boorishness, but the knowing young Caroline read it as proof of Murat's love.

Napoleon, by this time, was the calmest of them all. "At three o'clock in the morning," writes his secretary Bourrienne, "I accompanied Bonaparte in his carriage to Paris. Absorbed in his reflections, he did not utter a single word during the journey." Only when he reached home did he break his silence. "Tomorrow," he said brusquely to Josephine, "we sleep in the Luxembourg."

CHAPTER THREE

❧ ❧ ❧

THIS squabbling, self-seeking, pleasure-loving, handsome, high-spirited, talented brood of Bonapartes was now suddenly projected into the position of first family of France. And, as on every previous occasion when Napoleon had hoisted himself a little higher in the world, he heaped them with honors.

He and Josephine moved first to the Luxembourg, and then, gaining confidence, into the palace of the Tuileries. On taking up residence, he ordered that the caps of liberty, painted on the palace walls by ardent revolutionaries a few years before, be washed out, and that two trees of liberty planted in the courtyard, be chopped down. "I won't have any such fooleries," he snapped. Ignoring the inscription cut into one of the palace gateways; "*10 August 1792, Royalty in France is abolished; and shall never again be established!*" Napoleon began organizing something very like a court. His hitherto haphazard daily life became more regimented; Josephine's clothes became more brilliant but less seductive; their circle was chosen with more care. They began to assume the formal, slightly aloof air of royalty. "It was not exactly a court," wrote a certain Russian princess, "but it was no longer a camp."

During this transition period from camp to court, from soldier to emperor, Napoleon still looked very much the soldier. Constant, who was to become famous as Napoleon's valet, joined his service at about this time, and he has left a vivid picture of his master in these days before he became the stout, strutting conqueror of Europe. Although no longer the shabby creature described by Laure Permon a few years before, Napoleon was still a far from imposing figure. He was extremely thin, with a sallow, almost copper-colored complexion and fine chestnut hair already receding from his broad forehead. His features, taken singly, were quite handsome, but put together, the "effect of his physiognomy was hardly an agreeable one." He was short, not more than five feet six inches in height, with a head far too large for his scraggy body; if angry or worried, he had a way of biting his nails or shrugging his right shoulder. It was for his eyes, his "fine blue eyes," that his face was chiefly remarkable. Sometimes gentle, almost caressing, they could suddenly become hard and forbidding; more than any other man's they seemed to "depict the divers emotions which stirred him."

Constant's description of Napoleon's wife was almost lyrical. Josephine's every movement, he says, was a delight; she almost floated as she walked. Even in these early days, wearing a simple red handkerchief tied, Creole-style, around her head, she carried herself like a queen. "If she smiled, involuntarily one smiled too, just as one became sad if she showed signs of grief." As Napoleon's eyes were his most compelling feature, so, in a different way, were Josephine's. Hers were deep blue, with large, almond-shaped lids and long sweeping lashes; "When thus dreamily she gazed at you," reports young Constant breathlessly, "you felt drawn towards her as by a resistless force."

Josephine's warmth, her elegance, her matchless social accomplishments, were invaluable to Napoleon at this time; he was trying very hard to reconcile the new Republican personalities with the old pre-Revolutionary society, and these two worlds seemed to fuse in the person of Josephine. For all the chic of her flimsy neo-Grecian clothes and the ease of her manner, something of the *ancien régime* seemed to emanate from her. When set beside Napoleon's boisterous brothers and sisters, she was an aristocrat to the very finger tips.

When Napoleon took up residence in the Tuileries in 1800, he invited his mother to come and live with Josephine and himself. Unhesitatingly, she declined. Life in the home of the easygoing Joseph and the unsophisticated Julie was far more to her taste than the splendid ceremonial surrounding Napoleon and Josephine. Indeed, she looked upon her son's sudden elevation with some cynicism and considerable apprehension; it was all very well, she used to say, "*Pourvu que ça dure.*" But while it did last, Letizia decided to make the most of it. Obsessed by the fear that the family might one day fall again on hard times, Letizia saved as carefully now as ever she had done in the early days of her widowhood. As fast as her children squandered their new fortunes, she nursed and enlarged hers; she had investments in almost every country in Europe. Unlike her gregarious children, she moved about very little in society; "her shyness," says a friend, "was always a hindrance to her in society as well as her permanent difficulty in expressing herself in French." And her only concern with politics was to press the claims of her various Corsican relations. In this she could be every bit as imperious as Napoleon; the welfare of her family was far and away her chief interest in life.

In the scattering about of family honors after the *coup d'état*, Joseph, as usual, had come off best. Napoleon made him a member of the new Corps Législatif, as well as ambassador extraordinary for the peace negotiations with America. Joseph was now able to indulge his taste for luxurious living to the full. Always a good host, his estate at Morte-fontaine became renowned for the sumptuousness and stylishness of its fetes. Laure Permon, now Madame Junot, paid several visits to Morte-fontaine, and she had nothing but praise for the brilliance of the entertainments and the charm of the host. "A perfect ease and liberty," she says, "gave charms to the passing hour"; but what "filled the measure of enjoyment" was the genuinely warm reception accorded by the master of the house. The element of laziness in Joseph's character made him the pleasantest and most relaxing of companions; he was very much his father's son.

Joseph's wife, Julie, the silk merchant's daughter from Marseilles, had neither her husband's good looks nor his smooth sociability, but she had more commendable virtues. "Madame Joseph Bonaparte was an angel of goodness. . ." enthused Madame Junot. "Her unalterable kindness, her active charity, gained her the love of everyone." So genuine, in fact, was Julie's good-heartedness, that she never allowed herself to be drawn into the family quarrel against Josephine. And that was indeed an achievement. Let the Bonapartes rave against Napoleon's wife as much as they pleased; the amiable Julie very wisely kept silent. She was thus able, noted Madame Junot with just a hint of malice, "easily to determine what part to take when fortune smiled on Josephine."

It was at Mortefontaine that this always simmering Bonaparte-Beauharnais feud once came to the boil. The entire family, including Letizia and Josephine, had been invited there for several days. The first afternoon had passed pleasantly enough with the guests strolling through Joseph's magnificent gardens, but when the host announced that he intended taking his mother in to dinner and that she would be sitting on his right, with Josephine on his left, Napoleon objected to the arrangement. On no account would he allow Josephine to take second place. Joseph remained firm, but as he was about to lead Letizia in to dinner, with Lucien and Josephine following, Napoleon suddenly shot forward, snatched his wife's arm, and pushed his way past Joseph and his mother. He plunked himself down at the table with Josephine at his right and one of her ladies at his left. "The company," says the poor lady in waiting, "were all greatly embarrassed," particularly Julie, who, although hostess, found herself placed at the bottom of the table. The brothers were furious, Josephine looked wretched, and the lady in waiting felt extremely conspicuous as Napoleon addressed not a single word to his family and spent the entire meal speaking to her.

In the round of family promotions, Lucien, in spite of all the trouble he had caused Napoleon, was created Minister of the Interior. He promptly used his position to make more trouble. Having little taste for administrative routine, he left day-to-day work to his subordinates and concentrated on the more rewarding aspects of the job. He cultivated the society of such journalists and writers as came his way, and was soon the center of a lively but outspoken circle. His house at Plessis, in fact, became the gathering place for critics of the First Consul's policy. It was not long before reports of these indiscretions reached Napoleon's ears, and the hot-headed young man was told to watch his step. The warning was ignored.

His wife, Christine Boyer, did not have her husband's talent, but like her sister-in-law Julie, she had a good heart, and unlike her, a good figure. More than any other member of the family, Christine found this sudden accession to wealth and power unnerving; "all this grand display alarmed her," said a friend. There was one circumstance, however, from which she could draw comfort: the formidable Napoleon, appreciating the sweetness and simplicity of his sister-in-law's nature, was always very good to her.

Elisa and the phlegmatic Bacciochi were now brought to Paris. The move did nothing to improve their domestic relations. Elisa, who rather fancied herself as a patroness of the arts, considered her husband hopelessly uncultivated, and treated him with open contempt. Beside what she imagined to be her deep cultural interests, her husband's ability to play the violin seemed a paltry accomplishment indeed. So constantly did he air this accomplishment, complained Lucien, "that he ends by getting on the nerves both of his innocent instrument and his hearers." Elisa did not allow her dissatisfaction with Bacciochi to stop at open contempt; a true Bonaparte, she began to cast about for more rewarding male company. Although the plainest of Letizia's daughters, she knew how to make the most of her good features (she had lovely eyes), and few men, after all, would spurn Napoleon's sister. In Louis de' Fontanes, the eminent littérateur of the day, Elisa felt that she had found a companion worthy of her own abilities. She would be his Egeria, she claimed, while he, through his association with her, attained undreamed of heights in public life. Her salon was crowded with all the most notable men of letters who found it easy to turn a deaf ear when the First Consul's sister aired her forthright if ill-considered views on the arts. "Elisa's house," wrote one of her more naïve guests, "is a tribunal to which authors come to be judged";

rather, was it a fount at which artists came to seek favors. In her extraordinarily affected clothes ("her toilette was a medley of the Jewish, Greek, Roman—of everything, in short, except good French taste," noted one observer), Elisa aspired to the role of one of the great patronesses of the seventeenth and eighteenth centuries. "I always thought her," says Madame Junot tartly, "the most disagreeable woman I ever met."

Elisa's presence in Paris meant that she and her brother Lucien, who had always been allies, could team up once more. Shrewd, ambitious, and independent, they made a redoubtable couple.

The fourth Bonaparte boy, Louis, at twenty-one, was created a colonel in the Fifth Dragoons. This excellent if unearned promotion in no way affected his now habitual melancholy. Tall and good-looking, with polished manners and a good brain, he could have been the most attractive of the brothers. But his hypochondria gave him the appearance of an old man before his time; "this rendered him," says a friend, "morose in appearance and miserable in reality."

Pauline's husband Leclerc was likewise promoted; he became a divisional commander with the Army of Italy. He and Pauline were no better suited than Elisa and Bacciochi. The well-meaning young man adored his butterfly wife, but she seems to have felt nothing for her *petit Leclerc*, as she called him. A physical likeness to Napoleon caused the admiring Leclerc to imitate him in every detail; he clasped his hands behind his back, he paced about with quick, short steps, he spoke in terse, jerky sentences. He even, it was said, affected the gray overcoat and the famous hat. *"Le Bonaparte blond,"* they called him, and he was immensely flattered.

Pauline had been stranded with a disciple when what she needed was a master. Leclerc had not the faintest idea of how to handle this hoydenish, flirtatious, thoroughly spoiled little creature. As a result, she became still more spoiled. Her beauty alone won her enough adulation to turn a less foolish head. Even her enemies had to concede this beauty. "Madame Leclerc was unquestionably the loveliest woman I ever saw," admitted one of Josephine's friends. "Neither jealousy nor envy, which are so quick at discovering a fault in whatever claims general admiration, has ever succeeded in discovering the slightest blemish in that beautiful countenance, which was combined in the same person with the most elegant, the most perfect shape, and the most captivating gracefulness of manners. It was quite impossible to criticize her outward appearance. . . ." But for those who were envious of Pauline's good looks, continued the

writer with more relish, there was an "ample field for revenge in descant-
ing upon the mental defects, the temper and conduct of Madame Leclerc." And even that passionate royalist, the Countess de Boigne, who
despised the lot of them, Josephine included, admits that Pauline was the
most "ravishing beauty" on whom she had ever set eyes. What intrigued
the Countess was how Pauline, with her notorious reputation, managed
to retain her air of "candid maidenhood."

Caroline, the youngest daughter, was not old enough to benefit from
this latest round of family treats. She was still a pupil at Madame
Campan's. Although not nearly so striking as her sister Pauline, she was a
pretty girl, with good teeth, bright eyes, and a skin resembling "white
satin seen through glass." Like Napoleon, she had a head too large for her
stocky body, and like him, she had exquisitely small hands and feet. "As a
young girl Caroline was charming," says Madame Junot, adding significantly, "I have never seen her appear to so much advantage since." In
these early days her pride and ambition, which were in no small manner
to contribute to Napoleon's downfall, were still lying dormant.

The fifteen-year-old Jérôme was now allowed to leave school, where
he seems to have learned nothing, and was brought to live with Napoleon
and Josephine at the Tuileries. Just as Napoleon had always held up
Josephine's daughter, Hortense, as an example to his sister Caroline, so
did the Bonapartes present Josephine's son, Eugène, as a model for Jérôme
to follow. As Jérôme knew that they all hated Eugène anyway, and as
he had not the slightest interest in attaining Eugène's high standards himself, he ignored their lectures. Of all the Bonapartes, Jérôme seems to have
inherited most of his father's happy-go-lucky characteristics, and being
the youngest, the family usually let him have his way. Napoleon was
the only one who ever tried to curb him. He found him self-willed and
"obstinately set on bad objects," he once complained. Madame Letizia
seemed to have spoiled him so much that he doubted whether he could
ever repair the damage. If Napoleon imagined that bringing Jérôme to live
under his wing at the Tuileries would instill some sense of responsibility
in him, he was to be sadly disillusioned. He squandered money ("I only
care for beautiful things," he claimed airily), he frittered away his time
on frivolities, he even became embroiled in a duel. His few achievements
seem to have been of the most ephemeral variety; a member of the
audience at one of the Malmaison theatricals found *Hortense delicieuse!
M. Bourrienne parfait! Jérôme unique!*"

As the Consulate got under way, there also began that series of marriages which were to prove, in one way or another, so disastrous for the family.

   ♔ ♔ ♔

  The first of these marriages was between the seventeen-year-old Caroline and the thirty-two-year-old Joachim Murat. Caroline had been eager to marry the magnificent Murat for years, and he himself was more than willing to hitch his wagon to the Bonaparte star. Letizia approved of the match, and so did Joseph, Lucien, and Elisa. Only Napoleon opposed it. There seem to have been several reasons for his disapproval. Now that he was standing on the very steps of a throne, there was every chance that Caroline would be able to land something better than an innkeeper's son; Murat's reputation as a lover, moreover, was notorious, and Napoleon had not forgotten that, at Mombello, Murat had hinted at something between Josephine and himself. As a soldier Napoleon valued Murat enormously (he "would have sabered the Eternal Father himself," joked Josephine) but he did not favor him as a brother-in-law. His opposition immediately united the rest of the family against him. Added to Caroline's determination—and she had a will of iron—were Letizia's entreaties, Joseph's arguments, and Lucien's outbursts; even Josephine, for reasons quite different from those of the Bonapartes, applauded the match. She was fond of the flamboyant Murat, and he of her, and she imagined that by encouraging him to marry into the family, she would have a friend in the enemy camp. Supported by Eugène and Hortense (the loyalty of these two good-natured young people to their mother was unquestioning) Josephine begged Napoleon to let the marriage take place. He, regarding her insistence as proof that she herself had no interest in Murat, and being far more interested in starting a second Italian campaign, gave his permission. "Well, Bourrienne," he afterwards said to his secretary, "you ought to be satisfied—for my part I am; all things considered, Murat suits my sister, and then they cannot say that I am proud, that I seek grand alliances. . . . Besides, I am pleased that my wife takes an interest in the marriage; you are aware of my reasons. Since it it settled, I must hasten the business. We have no time to lose. If I must go to Italy, I wish to take Murat with us—I must strike a decisive blow there—come tomorrow."

  "Caroline Bonaparte married," Madame Junot found it necessary to point out, "with a reputation as pure and as fresh as her complexion and the roses of her cheeks." On Murat's looks she was less complimentary. A man, she says, is not necessarily handsome because he is large and always "dressed for a carnival"; take away the boisterous curls, the ostrich plumes, and the dazzlement of gold embroidery, and one is left with an undistinguished, almost "mongrel" face. The passionate Caroline, however, seems not to have minded her husband's "lack of nobleness," and they were married at her brother Joseph's estate at Mortefontaine.

Their marriage, during the first years at any rate, was a happy one. It was the second in this particular wave of family marriages which was to prove so unfortunate from the start.

    ♛   ♛   ♛

Napoleon's lightning campaign in Italy ended with his well-publicized victory at Marengo. Again he returned home through what must have seemed a forest of triumphal arches, and as usual, he lost no time in consolidating his position. Within the following eighteen months he had introduced his Code Civil, signed the Concordat with the Pope, made peace with Austria, England, Spain, and Holland, arranged treaties with Russia, Prussia, Bavaria, and Turkey, and been declared Consul for life.

This new life consulship brought into the open something which had been troubling his family for years: the rights of succession. That there were, in fact, no "rights" of succession at this stage seems not to have bothered the Bonapartes unduly; they knew Napoleon better than that. An attempt on his life on the way to the opera one evening made the question more pressing still; something had to be done about an heir to Napoleon.

It was becoming increasingly unlikely that Josephine would provide one. She and Napoleon, according to his valet, Constant, still shared a bed, but despite frequent visits to Plombières, with its sterility-curing waters, Josephine remained childless. The fault, she steadily maintained, was Napoleon's. On one occasion, as she was again setting out for Plombières, the wily Lucien drew her aside and suggested that as Napoleon could not give her a child, she conceive one by another man; or if the fault did indeed lie with her, that she allow Napoleon to have a child by another woman and adopt it as her own. It was essential, he said, to secure a hereditary successor. Josephine knew her brother-in-law far too well to be taken in by this ostensibly unselfish scheme. If she did commit adultery, Lucien would lose no time in letting Napoleon know about it, and if she did admit sterility, Lucien would encourage Napoleon to test his own fertility with someone else. Josephine's hold over Napoleon was tenuous enough without putting it to such a test.

Ever since his return from Egypt Napoleon's attitude towards Josephine had been different. Her nonchalance, her lack of response to his ardent wooing, and, more than anything, her affair with Hippolyte Charles, had killed his love for her. He was still physically attracted to her, and in spite of her shallowness, her weaknesses, and her appalling debts, she would always be very dear to him. She had a way of smoothing his path, of being able to amuse and divert and calm him; she was the one person, it was said, who could sometimes make him change his mind. "Josephine possessed an exact knowledge of all the intricacies of my character," he said, "and with it, an admirable tact." Once her affair with Hippolyte Charles was over, Josephine's name was never again coupled with that of any man other than her husband. But the realization of her love for him came too late; she was now the pursuer, he, the philanderer. Although he tried very hard to keep the knowledge of his infidelities from her (he was too fond of her to hurt her, and he could not stand the sight of her in tears), she usually found out. And added to her jealousy was the fear that one of his loves might have a child by him, and that she, whom he no longer loved, would be cast aside.

She now hit upon a way by which she could provide him with an heir in whom would be mingled both his blood and hers.

Of Napoleon's four brothers—the urbane Joseph, the fiery Lucien, the moody Louis, and the flighty Jérôme—Josephine considered Louis the least objectionable. Unlike the others, he at least treated her with politeness. She now decided that Louis should marry her daughter, Hortense, and that Napoleon should adopt their eldest son as his heir. With all the tact, tears, and powers of persuasion for which she was famous, Josephine set about achieving her ambition.

Napoleon seemed to be quite agreeable. "We may never have children," he admitted. "I brought up Louis and look upon him as a son. Your daughter is what you cherish most on earth. Their children will be ours. We will adopt them, and this adoption will console us for not having any of our own." Josephine was overjoyed, and set about telling Hortense. But as in the case of her own marriage to Napoleon, Josephine could not bear to break the news to Hortense herself. She made Napoleon's secretary, Bourrienne, do it. Hortense, who had always made a point of showing her "aversion to marriages of expediency," was struck dumb by this proposal. She promised to give her answer at the end of a week. Her brother Eugène, the only person to whom she could have turned for comfort and advice, was with his regiment at Lyons. She must have known, however, what his advice was likely to be. Once, when she had been bubbling on about marrying for love, he had warned her not to delude herself. The higher they rose in life, he said, the less opportunity they would have of choosing their own partners. She would have to marry to suit Napoleon's plans; it would be best to forget her dream of an "impossible bliss."

Of all the persons who made up Napoleon's family circle, Hortense de Beauharnais was undoubtedly the most attractive. Fair-haired, blue-eyed, fresh-complexioned, with a figure as "slender as a palm tree," she had all her mother's grace and much of her suavity of manner. To these inherited traits she added others notably lacking in Josephine's character: intelligence, wit, vivacity, and just enough malice to be amusing without ever being unkind. Where Josephine's personality was a negative one, Hortense's was more positive; by no means an intellectual, she was talented, sensible, and well educated. And in spite of a good deal of unhappiness and disillusionment which she was to experience during her lifetime, she always retained a touching idealism.

Hortense's objections to her marriage with Louis were washed away by Josephine's tears. In fact, from the day that the news was first broken to Hortense until the day of her marriage—and for a few days thereafter—Josephine seems to have been continuously in tears. "You know, my darling, that all the Bonapartes hate me," she sobbed. "They want to separate me from your stepfather. They want him to divorce me. And you, only you, can save me. The day you become Madame Louis, they will no longer dare to do anything against me."

What could the devoted, sweet-natured, pliant Hortense do? She consented, and her sacrifice was rewarded by yet another flood of her mother's tears.

Once the matter was decided (Louis had raised no objections), Napoleon was in a hurry to get it over with. At the ceremony the entire Bonaparte family, with the exception of Pauline, who was out of the country, bore steely-eyed witness to this flowering of Josephine's schemes. Letizia, in fact, referred to it as a triumph of a strange family over her own. The fair-haired Hortense, wearing a simple white dress and a single string of pearls (at the last moment she had recoiled from the idea of wearing the elaborate dress which Josephine had given her), was married to the dark, handsome, melancholy-eyed Louis. Napoleon took the opportunity of getting the marriage of Caroline and Joachim Murat blessed at the same time; their previous ceremony had been a civil one only. This double wedding upset Hortense; Caroline and her husband were so radiantly happy, she was afraid that "all the happiness lay on one side, all the unhappiness on the other."

Lucien made sure that whatever chance of happiness there might have been in the match was jeopardized by whispering to Louis that Napoleon was Hortense's lover. It was a slander which the brooding, suspicious, sexually maladjusted Louis would never be able to get out of his mind.

♛   ♛   ♛

Lucien's matrimonial affairs were the next to claim Napoleon's attention. They provided the climax to years of worsening relations between Napoleon and himself. It seemed that as Minister of the Interior Lucien had been using his official position to feather his own nest, and that his misconduct was beginning to be talked about. As Napoleon was doing his utmost to clothe his family in some sort of respectability at this time, he was furious with Lucien. His brother's private life, too, was giving cause for talk. On one occasion when Napoleon was visiting Lucien's country estate, he was treated to an amateur theatrical performance in which both Elisa and Lucien appeared in the scantiest of costumes. As Elisa was aggressively plain and Lucien singularly graceless, it could not have been a pretty sight. This, however, was not what bothered Napoleon. "It's a scandal!" he shouted to the startled company. "What! When I am trying to restore purity of manners, my brother and sister must exhibit themselves on a platform, almost nude. It's an insult!"

The publishing of a pamphlet entitled *Parallèle entre César, Cromwell, et Bonaparte*, which supported, rather too early in the day, the theory that the position of First Consul should be made permanent and hereditary, caused Napoleon quite a different sort of embarrassment. When he discovered, through the vigilance of his sinister Minister of Police Fouché, that Lucien was the author, his anger knew no bounds. Letizia, on hearing that Napoleon was annoyed with her favorite son, Lucien, immediately assumed that Josephine was behind it all; encouraged by Lucien, she decided that Josephine and Fouché were in league against him. She drove at once to the Tuileries and demanded an audience with Napoleon. There, in Josephine's presence, and with a face like thunder, she wanted to know why the police were doing nothing about these slanders against Lucien. Napoleon promised that he would instruct the police to proceed against the offenders. But Letizia, confident that she knew who the offenders were, turned her cold black eyes on Josephine. "And you," she said calmly to the now sobbing Josephine, "will you warn your friend Fouché that I am quite capable of making anyone who slanders my sons regret it?"

Letizia's championing of Lucien did nothing to soften Napoleon's anger against him. He decided that his headstrong brother must be sent out of the country for a few months. Two days later, during a card evening at the Tuileries, Napoleon beckoned to Lucien to join him in the next room. They remained there for over an hour. When they emerged, Napoleon's face was flushed with anger, while Lucien's was stiff with affected gaiety. Lucien announced that he was resigning as Minister of the Interior to go to Spain as ambassador. Elisa's husband Bacciochi, who was his secretary, was to go with him. Josephine hurried to Elisa's side, but Elisa, who had been sitting apart all evening, turned her back and hurried out. The Bonapartes considered Lucien's exile to be yet another triumph for the detestable Josephine.

That same year Lucien's wife, Christine Boyer, had died rather unexpectedly. Although Lucien was fond of this good-hearted woman whom he had married in humbler days, he wasted no time on vain regrets. On arriving in Spain, he very quickly acquired a mistress.

Lucien remained at his new post for six months. During this time he managed to amass a small fortune ("I am loaded with favors," he reported to his brother) and to think up yet another scheme whereby Napoleon could secure an heir. His brother should divorce Josephine and marry the Infanta Isabella. Napoleon would not hear of it. Why, he said, should he discard Josephine merely because he had been successful? Had he failed to make himself master of France and been imprisoned, she would never have deserted him. Besides, he added, running more true to form, "If I did think of another marriage, I would not seek an alliance with a royal house that has begun its decline."

Napoleon's annoyance over his brother's impulsively drawn up peace treaty between Spain and Portugal brought Lucien back to France in a huff. Once home, he promptly fell in love with a married woman by the name of Alexandrine Jouberthon. Napoleon, who had been fond of Lucien's unpretentious wife and who thought nothing of his affair with Alexandrine, now turned his attention to a second marriage for his brother. Lucien, without a wife, was a valuable pawn in Napoleon's political game; for all the rebelliousness of his temperament, Lucien was an intelligent and talented man—Napoleon could organize a brilliant match for him.

He should have known Lucien better than that. Alexandrine Jouber-thon, whose husband had deserted her and gone off to San Domingo, was installed at Plessis, Lucien's country place. Elisa, who had been acting as hostess for her brother since his wife's death, now refused to play second fiddle to Lucien's new mistress. But she was kept informed by Fontanes, who wrote: "The lady is lovely; as gay as she is beautiful, and as greedy as she is gay." With her mane of red hair and her bold blue eyes, Alexandrine was a long way from being, as Lucien claimed, the most virtuous woman in the world, but he was violently in love with her. Not content to remain buried in the country ("She wants the fuss, notoriety, all the advantages of an open affair," reported Fontanes), Alexandrine accompanied Lucien to Paris, and there, in May 1803, she gave birth to a son. The following day she and Lucien were secretly married. "Because of a political obstacle of an absolute kind," wrote the priest who married them, they could not "make a public declaration of their marriage." The political obstacle was not the only one; more serious was the fact that no one seemed to know whether M. Jouberthon was alive or dead. It would be as well to keep the whole thing secret at this stage.

As chance would have it, Napoleon chose this very moment to suggest a spectacular marriage for his brother Lucien. This was to be Napoleon's most ambitious matrimonial project to date; the suggested bride was no less a person than the Queen of Etruria. True, she was only a newly created queen, a widow, and incredibly ugly, but she was, after all, the daughter of the King of Spain. To Napoleon's surprise, Lucien gave an evasive answer; but the Queen had been widowed for a mere forty-eight hours, so there would be plenty of time for Lucien to come round to his brother's way of thinking. Napoleon granted his brother another lucrative post (Lucien had turned his Spanish presents into cash) and decided to bide his time.

It was some months later that he heard about Lucien's secret marriage. This time every member of the family was treated to a tirade against Lucien. The marriage was a crime against France, he ranted; Lucien's child was a bastard; he would have the marriage annulled. "What!" he shouted to Hortense and Caroline when he heard that they had received Lucien's wife. "I try to restore morality, and a woman like that is brought into my family!"

Letizia, of course, sided with Lucien, but she very wisely advised him to lie low. If he showed moderation, she said, Napoleon's brotherly feelings and sense of justice would reassert themselves. He "knows quite well that, situated as you are, he has no more right to ask you to marry to please him than you would have to ask him to marry to please you."

A family quarrel could not be complete without a thrust at Josephine. "Do all the women who use that name (Bonaparte) confer as much honor on it as Christine or Alexandrine?" Lucien asked Joseph. Josephine, in fact, was pleading Lucien's case, but Napoleon was adamant; Lucien must renounce Alexandrine or leave France. To his credit, Lucien refused to break with her. "We are one," he wrote to Joseph, "my wife, my son, my daughters, and I." When Letizia came to the Tuileries to beg Napoleon to reconsider his decision, he remained firm, and Lucien, his heart brim full of bitterness, was obliged to leave for Italy.

"That's done," sighed Napoleon to Josephine when it was all over. "I've broken with Lucien and ordered him from my presence." The gentle Josephine tried to soothe him. "You are a good woman to plead for him," said Napoleon, taking her in his arms. "It is hard, though, to find such opposition in one's own family. . . . Must I rely on myself alone? Well, I will suffice to myself alone—and you, Josephine—you will be my comfort always."

⚜ ⚜ ⚜

Pauline's second marriage was the next one to infuriate Napoleon.

The island of San Domingo had been lost to France during the Revolution, when the local Negroes had fought for and gained their independence. Napoleon, determined that the island should become French once more, mounted a combined naval and military expedition to reconquer it. As commander-in-chief of the expedition he chose Pauline's husband, the *petit Leclerc*. In this he revealed once again, and in spite of all the evidence to the contrary, his pathetic faith in the abilities of the members of his family. "Here are your instructions," he said brusquely to Leclerc. "Now is your chance; go, and get rich, and trouble me no more with your continued importunities for money."

Leclerc was none too eager to accept the appointment ("If I succeed, no glory will rebound on me. . . . If I fail, the responsibility will be mine alone," he remarked shrewdly); but he dared not refuse.

The frivolous Pauline, whom Napoleon insisted accompany her husband, was horrified at the idea. "How can my brother be so hard-hearted, so wicked, as to send me into exile among the savages and serpents?" she sobbed. "I shall die before I get there."

The kindly Madame Junot tried to console the almost hysterical girl. Stroking her hand, she spoke as one would to a child, telling her that she would be queen of the island, that she would ride in a palanquin, that slaves would carry out her slightest wish, that she would stroll through groves of sweet-scented orange trees. To crown it all, she told her that she would look exquisite in Creole costume. "As I advanced my arguments, Madame Leclerc's sobs became less and less hysterical. She still wept, but her tears were not unbecoming. 'You really think, Laurette,' said she, 'that I shall look pretty, prettier than usual, in a Creole turban, a short waist, and a petticoat of striped muslin?' " On being assured that she would, Pauline rang for her maid. "Bring me all the bandannas in the house," she commanded excitedly. When they arrived, she and Laure Junot chose the prettiest and began arranging them on Pauline's beautiful head. Looking at herself in the glass, Pauline cried: "Laurette, you know my dear, how I love you. You must come to San Domingo—you will be next to myself in rank. I shall be queen, as you told me just now, and you shall be vice-queen. I will talk to Bonaparte about it . . . we will give balls and parties of pleasure amongst those beautiful mountains. Junot shall be the commander of the capital. What is its name? I will tell Leclerc that I expect him to give a fete every day. . . ."

As it turned out, the expedition was a complete fiasco. No sooner had Leclerc subdued the island than an epidemic of yellow fever broke out, killing almost forty thousand people. Then the formerly pro-French Negroes deserted, reducing Leclerc's already depleted force to a mere two thousand men. He tried to persuade Pauline to return to France, but she, showing unexpected courage (or perhaps a complete unawareness of the gravity of the situation), refused to leave him. "You may be afraid, you others," she shouted gaily to her terrified attendants, "but I, I am the sister of Bonaparte, and have no fear." That was all very well, but it needed considerably more than a show of courage to save the swiftly crumbling expedition.

On November 1 Leclerc died of yellow fever. The emotional Pauline was thrown into a paroxysm of grief. She cut off her hair and had it placed in her husband's coffin; she had his heart put in an urn on which were inscribed words to the effect that her own love was buried beside the heart. Then, with the lead coffin in the ship's hold, she sailed back to France.

Another coffin, containing the remains of someone else who had once been closely associated with Pauline, remained on the island. In it was the body of her first love, Fréron. The years had been hard on poor Fréron. From his position as darling of the Paris salons he had slipped to the prefectship of southern San Domingo, and it was here that he, too, succumbed to yellow fever. While Pauline sailed back in state to Paris, he was buried in an unmarked grave on that far-away island.

Pauline arrived back in France on New Year's Day, 1803. "I have reached Toulon after a frightful voyage and in miserable health which, however, is but the least of my troubles," she wrote to Napoleon. "I have brought with me the remains of my poor Leclerc; pity your poor Paulette who is most unhappy."

She did not remain unhappy for long. Napoleon had taken advantage of Leclerc's death to plunge the consular court into something very like royal mourning, but he had a hard time making the chief mourner observe it. Before many weeks had passed, Pauline, looking charming in black, was the talk of all Paris once more. The only thing to do with this flirtatious widow was to find her another husband as soon as possible.

Luckily, there arrived in Paris at this time the Italian Prince Camillo Borghese. He was almost completely uneducated, but this shortcoming was more than compensated for by his almost unbelievable wealth. He was also young, attractive, and amiable. An alliance between the noble Borgheses and the powerful Bonapartes appealed to both families. The Bonapartes were, after all, an Italian family. "When the marriage of my sister Pauline with Prince Borghese was announced," said Napoleon years afterwards, "there was only one voice, at Rome and in Tuscany, in this family and all its connections: *C'est bien! C'est entre nous, c'est une de nos familles!*" Pauline, of course, was almost delirious at the idea of becoming a real princess; what a shot in the eye for Josephine that would be!

For once it seemed as though everyone concerned was going to be satisfied. But in the flurry of preparations, Pauline had quite forgotten that Napoleon, with his new passion for a show of public decency, had revived the pre-Revolutionary regulation imposing one year and six weeks of mourning for a husband. Pauline could not possibly wait that long, and when Napoleon was consulted on the matter, he agreed to waive the six weeks, but no more.

Letizia, however, knew her daughter, and encouraged by Joseph and Lucien, allowed her to marry Prince Borghese in secret several months before the end of the prescribed period of mourning. Once more the truth of a family marriage had to be kept from Napoleon. Unsuspecting, Napoleon went ahead with his plans for Pauline's marriage in November; it was not until two weeks before the set date that his family admitted that the November ceremony would have to be a civil one only, as Pauline and Borghese had already been married by the Church.

There was only one way in which Napoleon, enraged at this latest display of his family's duplicity, could punish Pauline. He refused to attend the civil ceremony. His absence robbed the occasion of any of its intended brilliance, and Pauline's November marriage was almost as secret as the August one had been. Still, there were compensations, chief amongst them the famous Borghese diamonds, which now came into Pauline's possession. She had ample opportunity to air them in the round of farewell calls which she was required to pay before leaving for Italy. Of these, the most important was the visit to Josephine (Napoleon was still away at Boulogne), and Pauline was determined to spare nothing in her efforts to outshine her detested sister-in-law. In a carriage drawn by six superb horses and attended by liveried outriders carrying flaming torches (nothing like it had been seen since before the Revolution), she swept up the driveway to the palace of Saint-Cloud. There were gasps of admiration as she alighted. Her dress was of rich green velvet, and she was ablaze with diamonds. With every turn of that lovely head, every flutter of those little hands, every rise and fall of those celebrated milk-white breasts, her jewels flashed out. The effect was breath-taking.

But Josephine was more than ready for her. Having found out exactly what shade of green Pauline would be wearing, Josephine had had her salon entirely redecorated in a particularly unsympathetic shade of blue. It was impossible to avoid it, and the result, as far as Pauline was concerned, was disastrous. Josephine's own dress was an extremely simple but expensive creation of Indian muslin; it was bordered with a single strand of gold thread and caught at the shoulders by two small gold clasps. She wore no jewelry whatsoever. As she moved forward in her elegant, effortless way to greet her glittering sister-in-law, there was not a moment's doubt as to who had triumphed.

♔　　♔　　♔

Jérôme, the only remaining unmarried Bonaparte, made the most disastrous match of all.

In an attempt to strengthen his youngest brother's somewhat flaccid personality, Napoleon decided that Jérôme must join the Navy. Jérôme was horrified at the idea at first, but once he had joined the service, he discovered that his senior officers treated him with extraordinary solicitude, and he began to enjoy himself. In vain did Napoleon bombard both Jérôme and his superiors with instructions for turning the youngster into an efficient sailor; Jérôme went his own sweet, smiling way and his superiors sent back glowing reports to the First Consul. "Let me be told that you are as active as a very cabin boy," instructed Napoleon on one occasion. "Don't allow anyone to do your work for you. Seek every chance of distinguishing yourself. . . ." He might have saved his breath. Jérôme devoted himself to choosing uniforms (he arrived at San Domingo in a uniform of a captain in the Berchiny Hussars), to spending money, and to remaining in port as long as he possibly could. At none of these eccentricities did his superiors allow themselves to be ruffled. The young Jérôme was impregnated, reported an Admiral blandly to Napoleon, "with the noble ambition of making his name as famous in the Navy as it is already in the annals of war and politics." It is most unlikely that Napoleon was taken in.

It was after a cruise in the West Indies in 1803 that Jérôme, who was about to return to France, learned that British ships were on the lookout for him. To return home on a French vessel would be an invitation to capture (the British fleet was blockading the coast of France), so he decided to make for North America and sail from there in a neutral ship. He promptly took passage from Martinique on an American vessel, and landed at Norfolk, Virginia, on July, 20. This was the first occasion on which a Bonaparte visited the country which was to see so much of the family during the coming century and a half. Fortunately, the behavior of subsequent guests would not be quite so reprehensible.

Jérôme first instructed Pichon, the French consul-general in Washington, to charter a vessel, at vast expense, to take him back to France. Then he ignored the waiting ship and traveled to Baltimore, where an American adventurer whom he had met in the West Indies owned a hotel. When it was discovered that the self-assured, well-mannered, wildly extravagant young Frenchman was none other than the brother of the First Consul of France, every door in Baltimore was thrown open to him. In vain did poor Consul-General Pichon, half demented with the responsibility of looking after Napoleon's brother, warn Jérôme about the dangers of keeping bad company. "I have sufficient discernment, I think, to choose the society which is fitting for me," replied the nineteen-year-old youth sharply.

It was during this social whirl in Baltimore that Jérôme met and fell in love with an eighteen-year-old girl named Elizabeth Patterson. Exactly how they met is uncertain. One story is that during a reception the lovely

Elizabeth found herself caught up by a gold chain which formed part of Jérôme's flamboyant uniform; as the charming young man disentangled her, she was reminded of a prophecy that she would one day be a great lady in France. Another theory is that they met at the races; it was Elizabeth's clothes that seemed to be the more notable on this occasion— the sight of her in a buff silk dress and a black plumed hat was enough to set young Jérôme afire. But however they met, there is no doubt that before many weeks had passed, they were determined to marry.

Elizabeth Patterson was the daughter of one of Baltimore's most prosperous citizens, a man, according to no less a judge than Thomas Jefferson, "of great worth and of great respectability," whose social standing was "the first in the United States." This might, of course, have been an exaggeration on the part of the President of the United States, who wrote it for Napoleon's benefit, but there is no doubt that William Patterson was a man of considerable wealth and position. His daughter, according to her first biographer, was the "belle of Baltimore—the most beautiful woman in a city always famous for its beautiful women." Her beauty, in fact, seems to have been exceptional, although the mildness of her expression and the delicacy of her features did somewhat belie the rock-like qualities of her character. Even at eighteen she revealed enough ambition, love of pleasure, and strength of will to match any Bonaparte. "Like all young persons in this country," wrote the jaundiced Pichon, "(she) has had an education limited to very little."

Her lack of education in no way discouraged the infatuated Jérôme; indeed, he was a poor judge. He prevailed on his friend the Spanish ambassador to ask Mr. Patterson, on his behalf, for his daughter's hand. Her answer left no room for doubt. She "would rather be the wife of Jérôme Bonaparte for one hour than wife of any other man for life," she declared fervently. Her choice of phrase, if dramatic, was unfortunate and somewhat prophetic.

When Jérôme broke the news of his intended marriage to Pichon, the poor man vainly pointed out that Jérôme was under age, and that a marriage without his mother's consent would be null and void. Jérôme ignored his frenzied warnings and went ahead with his plans. It was at this stage that Mr. Patterson, having second thoughts on the matter, decided not to allow the marriage to take place and sent Elizabeth off on a holiday. An anonymous letter, referring to Jérôme as "the most profligate young man of the age," might have had something to do with Mr. Patterson's decision. Jérôme wrote to tell Pichon that after mature reflection, he had broken his engagement, and Pichon, almost delirious with relief, lent him the $5,000 he asked for. Miss Patterson promptly returned to Baltimore, and her father, realizing that her love for Jérôme had withstood the separation, agreed to the match.

On Christmas Eve, 1803, Jérôme Bonaparte and Elizabeth Patterson were married. Mr. Patterson, suspecting future trouble, made sure that they attended a civil as well as a religious ceremony. Jerome was resplendent in purple satin, gold embroidery, and diamond buckles; his bride, according to one disapproving witness, wore so little that her entire costume could have fitted into his pocket. Beneath her almost transparent dress, he noted, "she wore but a single garment."

The anguished Pichon had now to break the news to Napoleon. At the same time Elizabeth's father sent his son Robert to France to give the Patterson version of the affair. The American ambassador in Paris left Robert Patterson in no doubt as to Napoleon's feelings on the matter, and advised both him and Jérôme to steer clear of the First Consul. The rest of the family, of course, sided with Jérôme, and in a cool speech Lucien assured Robert Patterson that Napoleon would soon come round to their way of thinking. "Our present earnest wish is that Jérôme may remain where he now is, and take the proper steps to become, as soon as possible, a citizen of the United States," pronounced Lucien. Joseph, too, was all sympathy for his headstrong young brother. His entire resources, he assured Jérôme, were at his disposal; he was only too ready to share everything with him. Jérôme's wife, he felt sure, possessed all the qualities necessary to promote his brother's future happiness. But Joseph, never forgetting on which side his bread was buttered, took care to add that Jérôme's wife would have no more affectionate brother than himself *once she had been acknowledged by the chief of the family.*

Napoleon's reaction was much more to the point. Jérôme was to be refused any money whatsoever; he was to be put aboard a French frigate as soon as possible; the young person with whom he had "connected himself" was to be forbidden access to the ship; and in the event of her managing to get aboard, she was not to be allowed to set foot on French soil. "I will receive Jérôme," wrote Napoleon, "if he leaves the young person in America and comes hither to associate himself with my fortunes."

This refusal on the part of Napoleon to acknowledge Jérôme's wife, who, unlike Lucien's wife, Alexandrine, was a young girl of good family and spotless reputation, was an example of his increasing snobbishness.

Jérôme, imagining that the sight of his wife's lovely face and, if necessary, her copious tears, would melt Napoleon's heart, managed to get her aboard a ship, and together they sailed for France. At the same time Napoleon issued a decree declaring Jérôme's marriage null and any offspring from it illegitimate. When the couple reached Lisbon, Elizabeth was not allowed to land, and Napoleon's consul-general came aboard to ask what he could do for "Miss Patterson."

"Tell your master," replied Elizabeth, with a typical show of spirit, "that Madame Bonaparte is ambitious and demands her rights. . . ."

Napoleon had given orders for Jérôme to join him in Milan, and Jérôme, hoping to change his brother's mind, set off alone to meet him. En route he bumped into Madame Junot (her husband had just been appointed ambassador to Portugal), into whose attentive ears he poured his troubles. Just as Napoleon had become reconciled to Lucien's first wife, *cette bonne Christine*, claimed Jérôme, so would he come to accept the beautiful Elizabeth. Junot, who understood Napoleon better, advised the young man to do as his brother wished. "I am determined not to yield," declared Jérôme stoutly. "Strong in the goodness of my cause, I will take no action that I will afterwards repent."

But he did yield. Faced with the iron-willed Napoleon, Jérôme's resolution crumbled. Accused by his brother of being the first member of the family to "desert his post" (he was neither the first, nor would he be the last), Jérôme forgot all his carefully prepared arguments. When Napoleon assured him that, provided he broke with Elizabeth, he would ignore his little "love affair" and receive him into his good graces once more, Jérôme acquiesced. Elizabeth Patterson was repudiated and Jérôme returned meekly to the fold.

Elizabeth, disgusted at Jérôme's lack of spirit, sailed for England. There, in Camberwell, on July 7, 1805, she gave birth to a son. He was named Jérôme Napoleon, and was to become the founder of the American branch of the Bonaparte family. Elizabeth Patterson now faded from the Napoleonic scene, to reappear, years later, when the Bonapartes themselves had been rejected, to dazzle Europe with her wit, her talent, and her enduring beauty. Except for one brief, embarrasing encounter, she never set eyes on Jérôme again.

A few months before her son, Jérôme Napoleon, was born, his uncle Napoleon, amidst scenes of theatrical splendor, crowned himself Emperor of the French.

PART TWO

The First Empire

1804–1815

CHAPTER FOUR

❦ ❦ ❦

ON May 18, 1804, Napoleon Bonaparte was proclaimed Emperor of the French. And from that momentous day until his coronation some six months later, his family was in a state of almost continuous ferment.

It started on the very evening of the proclamation. Napoleon had invited all the members of his family who were in Paris to a state dinner at the Tuileries. A few minutes before Napoleon and Josephine made their appearance, the Governor of the Palace came to inform the assembled relations that the Emperor had decided to create his brothers Joseph and Louis Princes of the Empire. Lucien and Jérôme, who were both out of the country and whose unsuitable marriages still rankled with their brother, were denied any titles; his mother, who was in Italy comforting her beloved Lucien, was likewise ignored. Murat, Caroline's husband, was made a marshal, while Bacciochi, Elisa's husband, got nothing. This meant that whereas Joseph's wife, Julie, and Louis's wife, Hortense, became princesses, Napoleon's sisters Elisa and Caroline did not. Pauline, of course, by her marriage to Prince Borghese, was now a princess in her own right. The indignation of Elisa and Caroline, on realizing that Josephine was now an empress, and her daughter Hortense, a princess, can be imagined. And when Napoleon and Josephine made their entrance— he pleased as Punch and she as gracious as if she had been born royal—the two sisters could hardly contain their anger.

The day had been hot and sultry, with the promise of thunder, and as the family went in to dinner, the long expected storm broke. The atmosphere at table, reported one of Josephine's ladies, was no less thundery in than out. Napoleon seemed to take a savage delight in addressing Hortense as "princess" every few minutes, with the result that Caroline became too annoyed even to eat. She downed several glasses of water in an effort to control herself, but it was no use; the next time Napoleon called Josephine's daughter princess, Caroline burst into tears. Elisa, who had a better grip on her emotions, resorted to shafts of biting sarcasm and long haughty silences.

The following day there was a violent quarrel between Napoleon and his sisters. Caroline, whose voice could be heard outside the room, demanded to know why she and her sisters were to be "condemned to obscurity and contempt while *strangers* were to be loaded with honors and dignity." Napoleon, who was quite capable of shouting even his sisters down, assured her several times that he was master, and that he would distribute honors as he pleased. Neither tears, nor taunts, nor reproaches could soften his attitude. "To listen to you," he shouted to the almost hysterical women, "one would think that I had robbed my family of the heritage of the late king, our father." At this, Caroline, overcome with rage, fainted dead away. When she came round, Napoleon, feeling somewhat contrite, promised that he would do something for her.

A few days later it was decreed that Elisa and Caroline would henceforth bear the title of "Imperial Highness." This however, led to further complications. As a princess, Caroline could now enter the newly created throne room, whereas her husband, Murat, as a mere marshal, could not. Murat was extremely annoyed at this arrangement (he was once turned back at the very door of the room), and the iron-willed Caroline did not rest until it had been altered.

But what infuriated the Bonapartes most was the new status of their archenemy, Josephine. They were determined that although she had been proclaimed an empress, she would not be crowned one. From now on they were untiring in their efforts to get Napoleon to divorce her. Even Joseph, who, as the eldest Bonaparte, had some chance of inheriting Napoleon's crown if Josephine remained childless, urged his brother to break with her. The coming coronation, which was to be performed by the Pope himself, would provide an excellent excuse for Napoleon to take a more illustrious, or at least a more fertile, bride. Joseph's arguments carried more weight with Napoleon than did his sisters' shrill tirades. He was fond of Joseph, and in spite of his brother's lackadaisicalness, he valued his opinion. Josephine's scheme whereby Napoleon would adopt the eldest son of Louis and Hortense was also vigorously opposed by the family. Encouraged by his brothers and sisters, the surly Louis now refused to allow Napoleon to adopt his boy; this refusal weakened Josephine's position considerably.

But it was Caroline Murat, beginning now to reveal all the characteristics of selfishness, spitefulness, and downright treachery for which she would become notorious, who took the most positive step towards having Josephine superseded. She introduced into the court a certain Madame Duchâtel, who, being young, attractive, and ambitious, very soon caught the Emperor's eye. As Madame Duchâtel had something of Josephine's quality, Caroline hoped she would supplant Josephine in Napoleon's affections. Although the Empress suspected that Madame

Duchâtel had become Napoleon's mistress, she had no proof, and for a while she listened to those who advised her against openly accusing her husband of infidelity. To antagonize the Emperor would be to play right into the Murats' hands. But Josephine lacked the necessary subtlety for this sort of situation; when she next suspected that Napoleon and his mistress were together, she surprised them in his bedroom. Napoleon was furious. Madame Duchâtel fled the room, leaving Josephine, who had quickly been reduced to tears, to her husband's anger. Striding up and down the room, smashing the furniture to pieces with savage kicks, he shouted that he was sick and tired of her spying, that he was determined to throw her out, that he was going to marry a woman capable of giving him children. She was to leave the palace immediately, he thundered.

He sent for Eugène Beauharnais and told him that he intended divorcing his mother and that he was to take her away at once. He would compensate Eugène he said, for his loss of position. The modest Eugène refused Napoleon's offer and said that he asked for nothing more than to be allowed to devote his life to looking after his mother. He would sacrifice his own opportunities for her comfort, he claimed. As always, when confronted by the members of the Beauharnais family—be it Josephine, Eugène or Hortense—Napoleon was disarmed by their unselfishness and their pliancy. None of them had ever asked any favors of him; none had ever opposed his wishes. They were so very different from his own grasping, carping, ambitious brothers and sisters. Napoleon listened to Eugène's resolution in silence, and then dismissed him. When Eugène told his sister Hortense the news, she very wisely decided not to intervene. "If there be any chance at all of setting the matter right," she said, "it is the influence over Bonaparte of my mother's tears and her gentleness. Believe me, it is better to leave them to themselves. . . ."

Hortense was right. Josephine's tears again won the day. "I have not the courage to come to a final resolution," sighed Napoleon to his wife, "and if you let me see that you are too deeply afflicted . . . I feel that I shall never have the strength to oblige you to leave me." But he went on to tell her that she might yet one day be obliged to resign herself to "the interests of my policy," and that she should spare him the difficulties of a painful separation.

A few weeks before the coronation Napoleon, during an interview with one of his councilors of state, summed up his attitude to these family squabbles in his usual frank and staccato manner. "They are jealous of my wife, of Eugène, of Hortense, of everyone about me," he said. "Well, my wife has diamonds and debts, that's all. Eugène has not twenty thousand francs a year. I like those children because they're always eager to please me. If a gun is fired, it's Eugène who goes to see what's happening. If I have a ditch to cross, it's he who gives me a hand. . . . I love Hortense; yes, I love her. She and her brother always take my side, even against their mother, when she flares up over a wench or some such trumpery. They say: 'Well, he's a young man! You are in the wrong. He has plenty to put up with. We have plenty to thank him for.' If Hortense were to ask for me while I was in council, I should go out and see her. If Madame Murat were asking for me, I shouldn't go. . . . My wife is a good-natured woman who does them no harm. All she wants is to play the empress a little, to have diamonds, handsome gowns, the trumpery of her age. Yes, she shall be crowned! She shall be crowned, if it should cost me two hundred thousand men!"

When, in his brusque way, Napoleon came to tell Josephine that she, as well as he, would be both consecrated and crowned by the Pope, and that she had better prepare herself for the great day, her relief and joy were boundless. This, surely, would secure her position; it would be impossible for Napoleon to divorce her now.

On the morning of the day before the coronation, Madame Junot was invited to breakfast with the Empress. She found Josephine in a most cheerful mood. Napoleon had made his wife try on her crown just before breakfast, and her eyes now spilled over with tears of joy as she told her guest about it. She also told Madame Junot how disappointed she had been at Napoleon's refusal to listen to her pleas on behalf of the exiled Lucien. "I wished to make tomorrow a day of grace," she told her companion, "but Bonaparte impatiently rejected my suit, and I was compelled to be silent. I wanted to prove to Lucien that I can return good for evil." Despite this disappointment, Madame Junot thought the Empress in "excellent spirits," with "no gloomy presentiments either as regards herself or Napoleon."

There was still one gap in her defenses, and as it was a huge one, she lost no time in breaching it. She and Napoleon had never been married by the Church. Although he had insisted on religious as well as civil ceremonies for his sisters' weddings, Napoleon had never suggested that his own marriage be blessed by the Church. Josephine had always assumed that he hoped thereby to be able to divorce her more easily. When the Pope arrived in France, Josephine confessed to him that her marriage had been a civil one only, and His Holiness very understandably insisted that she and Napoleon be properly married as soon as possible. He could hardly be expected to officiate at the coronation of a couple who were living, as far as he was concerned, in sin. So, secretly, on the eve of the coronation, before a hastily erected altar in the Emperor's study, and with only two aides-de-camp to witness it, Napoleon and Josephine were married. Josephine's state of "delight and satisfaction," says one of her ladies, was plain for all to see.

⚜ ⚜ ⚜

At noon on the morning of December 2, 1804, Napoleon and Josephine came to the cathedral of Notre Dame for their coronation.

Murat, bearing the crown on a velvet cushion, led the Imperial family into the crowded, garishly decorated cathedral. Behind him walked Josephine, her face expertly enameled by the painter Isabey, her white richly embroidered dress worn with all the grace and assurance of which she alone was capable. For all her forty-one years, she looked, they say, no more than twenty-five that day. Her heavy velvet mantle was carried by her daughter, Hortense; her sisters-in-law, Elisa, Pauline, and Caroline; and Joseph's wife, Julie. Hortense and Julie alone carried it with a good grace (although Joseph considered "such a duty painful for a virtuous woman"), while Elisa, Pauline, and Caroline scarcely bothered to conceal their resentment. There had been endless bickerings between Napoleon and his family about this carrying of Josephine's train; at one stage Joseph had threatened to give up everything and retire to Germany rather than let his wife, Julie, demean herself thus. When Napoleon remained firm, Joseph, of course, gave in. His protesting sisters would only consent to carry it if they, in turn, could have their own trains borne by their respective chamberlains and if the phrase *bear the cloak* was substituted for *carry the train*. This Napoleon allowed. It was thus a very disgruntled little group who trailed in the wake of the smiling, slowly pacing Empress.

Napoleon walked behind, followed by his brothers Joseph and Louis. His body seemed too puny to support his robes of state. "They seemed," said an eyewitness, "almost to crush him; his slight frame collapsed under the enormous mantle of ermine." He wore on his head a simple laurel wreath; his face was pale, and his expression, "stern and somewhat distressed." His brothers seemed more at ease in their short velvet cloaks and their lavishly plumed hats. "If only," Napoleon had said to Joseph earlier on that day, "our father could see us now."

The length of the coronation ceremony seemed to tire the noto-

67

riously impatient Emperor. Several times he was caught stifling a yawn. When the Pope solemnly anointed him on the head and the hands, the watching Madame Junot was convinced that his only thoughts were of wiping off the oil. When it came to the moment of crowning, Napoleon, by previous arrangement with the Pope, placed the imperial crown upon his own brow. Although the crown suited him no better than did his cumbersome robes, he looked, says Madame Junot, "really handsome, and his countenance was illuminated by an expression" almost impossible to describe. As he placed the crown on his head, a little stone, no bigger than a nut, fell down from the roof and bounced off his shoulder. But by no change of expression or movement of his body did he reveal that he had felt it strike him.

It was now Josephine's turn to receive her crown. As no queen had been crowned in France for two centuries (the last had been Marie de Médicis, and that was because of the likelihood of her becoming regent), it was indeed a triumph for Josephine. "A general movement of admiration was noticeable at the moment when the Empress was crowned," writes Madame de Rémusat, one of her ladies. "She was so unaffected, so graceful, as she advanced towards the altar; she knelt down with such simple elegance, that all eyes were delighted with the picture she presented."

"I have had the honor of being presented to many *real* princesses . . ." agreed another spectator, "but I never saw one who, to my eyes, presented so perfect a personification of elegance and majesty."

Josephine knelt before Napoleon. By now, of course, there were tears in her eyes. Napoleon took her small crown, placed it first on his own head, and then set it upon hers. As he crowned his wife, his manner seemed almost playful. He placed it very carefully over the tiara of diamonds which she already wore, then took it off, and then replaced it. It was as if he were trying to tell her that she should wear it gracefully and lightly. The two of them seemed to "enjoy one of those fleeting moments of pure felicity which are unique in a lifetime; and serve to fill up a lustrum of years."

Her felicity was short-lived. As she turned from the altar to go back to her throne, the three Bonaparte sisters, livid with a blend of rage and envy, refused to lift her train. The unexpected weight of velvet dragging at her shoulders caused her to stumble, and although she quickly regained her balance, she was unable to move forward. Napoleon, noticing this, rapped out a few sharp words to his sisters, and they hastily lifted the mantle and moved forward. As the Emperor and Empress regained their thrones, the cathedral echoed and re-echoed with magnificent *vivats*.

At the close of the ceremony, Napoleon, walking in solemn procession towards the door of the cathedral, suddenly wanted to attract the attention of one of the cardinals preceding him. Impatiently and quite unself-consciously, he prodded him in the back with his scepter.

That evening the Emperor was in the best of spirits. Although he and Josephine dined alone together, he insisted that she wear her crown during the meal, and complimented her several times on the charm with which she wore it. After dinner he moved amongst his brilliant court, critically inspecting the women's dresses and saying some flattering thing to each. He was not usually so complimentary. "You owe it to me, mesdames," he said smilingly this evening, "that you all look so charming." One woman whom he did not consider to look so charming was Madame Junot. Although she had been very much in the background during the coronation ceremony, the eagle-eyed Napoleon had noticed exactly what she had been wearing. She had chosen a dark dress in order to show off her jewelry. Napoleon hated dark colors (Josephine tried to wear white as often as possible), and when next he saw Madame Junot, he left her in no doubt as to his views on her choice of costume.

In evidence everywhere during this magnificent day was the new emblem which Napoleon had chosen to replace the fleur-de-lis of the Bourbons. It appears to have been the cypher of one of the ancient kings of France. Embroidered on dresses, sewn onto mantles, woven into carpets, worked into hangings, mounted onto metal, painted onto coats of arms, swarming across every available surface in palace, cathedral, and processional way, were thousands upon thousands of glittering golden bees.

♛   ♛   ♛

"The French Empire," Napoleon once said complacently, "will become the mother country of the other sovereignties of Europe. I intend that each of the kings shall be obliged to build a large palace for his own use in Paris, and that, on the coronation of the Emperor of the French, these kings shall come to Paris, and grace by their presence that imposing ceremony to which they will render homage."

This was all very well, but who was this future Emperor to be? The present Emperor had no direct heir. At the time of the coronation it was decreed that in the event of Napoleon's having no sons, the succession would pass first to Joseph's sons and then to Louis's sons. The Emperor was also given the power to adopt, as his successor, any one of his brothers' sons whom he might choose. It was an odd situation whereby both Joseph (although the eldest in the family) and Louis were to be passed over in favor of their sons; but then, Napoleon had found himself in a predicament without precedent. "Everything," says Masson, "is singular and strange; all is illogical and illegal; everything, in this constitution of heredity, will be contrary to monarchical laws, and even more so, to the laws of common sense."

As Joseph was older than Napoleon, and as he had only two daughters, it seemed unlikely that his branch of the family would succeed. Louis and Hortense had two sons at this time, Napoleon-Charles and Napoleon-Louis; a third was born in 1808.

Napoleon still hoped to adopt Louis's eldest son, Napoleon-Charles; but Louis, becoming more difficult by the day, was determined that he should not. He still half believed the rumor that Napoleon might be the boy's father, and consequently made a point of calling his son Charles and not Napoleon. He also resented the fact that the boy's adoption by Napoleon would elevate him to a loftier position than he himself held. Napoleon, in fact, was extremely fond of young Napoleon-Charles. Whenever Hortense took him to the Tuileries to visit his grandmother, Josephine, Napoleon would snatch him up and play with him. Like so many tyrants, he adored children. He would seat the little boy on his lap and treat him to sips of wine or handfuls of lentils from the table. As Napoleon's gestures of affection were often of the most sadistic nature (his valets, his secretaries, and even his generals were subjected to the most violent pinchings and ear pullings), little Napoleon-Charles was often reduced to tears by Napoleon's rough handling. But he was fond of his uncle and would run to him with arms outstretched when he saw him.

"Whose garden is that?" Napoleon would ask, pointing out of the window.

"Uncle's," would be the boy's answer.

"After me," the Emperor would say, "it will be for you."

One day Caroline Murat brought her children, including her eldest son, Achille, to the Tuileries to visit their uncle. Napoleon, sitting in the middle of the noisy group with the young Napoleon-Charles on his knee, leaned down to the little boy and said: "Did you know, baby, that you run the risk of being a king one day?"

"And Achille?" demanded Caroline, flushing with anger.

"Oh, Achille will make a good soldier," answered Napoleon airily. "Take my advice, you poor little thing," he continued teasingly, addressing the baby. "If you want to live, never accept anything to eat from one of your cousins."

Caroline was furious, particularly as she did in fact have ambitions for securing the throne for her own branch of the family. Unfortunately for them, Napoleon did not like the Murat children nearly as well as he did Hortense's boys. Once, when he was pinching young Achille's ears with his usual vigor, the boy, in considerable pain, wrenched himself free, and striking his uncle with his fists, shouted; "You are a wretch, a wicked wretch!" Napoleon, hating insubordination, answered by slapping the child across the cheek and slamming out of the room. He left too quickly for Caroline to stage her usual fainting fit, but not before he had called her *"une mijaurée,"* and accused both her and Murat of spoiling their children. The scene reflects little credit on any of its actors.

A few weeks after the coronation Napoleon sent for Louis and Hortense. It was imperative, he told them, that he adopt young Napoleon-Charles and name him King of Italy, with the title of Napoleon II. He would allow Louis to be regent until the boy was of age. Louis refused. "My husband," writes Hortense, "replied that he would never consent to his son holding a higher rank than his own." Napoleon tried threats, he tried tantrums, he tried reason, he tried cajolery, but Louis remained obstinate. Hortense said nothing; she knew that in the end it was always her mother, Josephine, who suffered from these scenes. "The Emperor's constantly impatient manner seemed to reproach her with the misfortune of her childlessness," she wrote.

Napoleon had already offered the crown of Italy to Joseph, but as in his case it would have entailed giving up all claim to the French succession, Joseph had refused. He then tried to get Lucien to abandon his second wife, Alexandrine, and accept the crown, but Lucien was not to be tempted. Finally, disgusted with this "family that bore so little of the burden and assisted him so little in his labors," he accepted the crown for himself. He and Josephine traveled to Milan for a further round of grandiose ceremonies.

In order to teach his own stubborn family a lesson, Napoleon now decided to elevate his stepson, Eugène de Beauharnais. It must have been a relief to turn his attention from his own discontented brothers and sisters to this honest, self-effacing young man. "Prince Eugène," said one of Josephine's ladies, "did not lack personal attractions. His figure was graceful; he was skilled in all bodily exercises; and he inherited from his father that fine manner of an old French gentleman. . . . To these advantages he added simplicity and kind-heartedness; he was neither vain nor presumptuous; he was sincere without being indiscreet, and could be silent when silence was necessary. Prince Eugène had not much natural talent; his imagination was not vivid, and his feelings were not keen. He was always obedient to his stepfather. . . ."

Before leaving for Milan, Napoleon made an announcement, in the most flowery possible terms, of Eugène's promotion to Vice-Chancellor of State. "Among all the acts of our sovereignty, there is not one more gratifying to our heart. Brought up by our care from childhood, he has proved himself worthy of emulating and, with the help of God, of someday surpassing, the examples and the lessons that we have given him. . . ." That the sunny, complacent, well-intentioned Eugène would try his best to emulate his stepfather was quite likely; that he would ever surpass his "examples and lessons" was extremely doubtful. The Bonapartes looked upon it as an act of adoption and as a further triumph for Josephine. The stronger Eugène's position, they realized, the more secure hers.

Some months later Napoleon proclaimed Eugène Viceroy of Italy, and the following year adopted him as his son. Eugène now became an Imperial and Royal Highness, taking precedence of Joseph and Louis. He was designated successor to the throne of Italy, after Napoleon. That was a shot in the eye for the Bonapartes indeed.

It was at about this time that Napoleon made an extraordinary proposition to Josephine. By now the chances of her having a child were extremely remote. Neither gallons of spa water nor countless treatments by Corvisart, the imperial physician, could cure her infertility. She still maintained, of course, that the fault lay with Napoleon, not her. "*Bon-a-parte est bon-a-rien*" is a *mot* which she was supposed to have circulated about her husband's sterility. And it was said that she spread a more intimate rumor than this. One night at Saint-Cloud, when Napoleon had just given proof of his manhood to Caroline's protégée, Madame Duchâtel, the lady suddenly burst out laughing. "And the Empress," she whispered in answer to the puzzled Napoleon, "said it was like water!"

The story might or might not be true, but the Imperial couple remained childless. Napoleon now hit upon a remedy. He suggested to Josephine that she feign pregnancy, that he have a child by some other woman, and that she then acknowledge the child as her own. The whole Machiavellian scheme would be carried out in the strictest secrecy.

Josephine, ready to grasp at any straw, agreed. Napoleon now approached his doctor, Corvisart, to get him to play his part in the deception. "I want you," he said to Corvisart, "as a witness of the pretended confinement of the Empress, to do all that would be necessary to give the device every appearance of reality." Corvisart, quite naturally, refused to have anything to do with the dishonorable project, and Napoleon was obliged to drop it. It was only years later, after the divorce of Josephine and the birth of Napoleon's son, that Corvisart repeated the story.

Napoleon might have divorced Josephine more readily if he could have been sure that he was capable of producing an heir. It was true that some of his mistresses had had children, but with such women the paternity of their offspring was always in doubt. These adventures of Napoleon's, whether one-night affairs or more durable liaisons, always upset Josephine. Not only did she live in dread of one of these women being able to furnish undeniable proof of Napoleon's fertility, but Napoleon's own sense of guilt took the form of an added aggressiveness towards his wife. Furthermore, she loved him, and was genuinely jealous of his other loves. When she reproached him for his behavior—for she never learned that the best way to deal with these affairs was to let them run their course—he would answer her complaints with a fine display of temper. "I am not an ordinary man," he would shout, "and the laws of morals and of custom were never made for me!" It was her place to submit to all his fancies; she should realize that it was quite natural for him to amuse himself in this way. "I have a right to answer all your complaints by an eternal *moi*. I am a person apart. I will not be dictated to by anyone."

"She troubles herself a great deal more than is necessary," he would say to one of her friends when the storm had passed. "Josephine is always afraid that I will fall seriously in love. Does she not know, then, that I am not made for love? . . . What do these fancies, into which my affections do not enter, matter to her?"

And when that particular amour was over, he would return again to this woman whose soothing, malleable, soft-voiced presence was such a balm to his own restless, passionate spirit. There were those who claimed that Josephine was his good genius, that while he remained married to her, his luck would hold. Perhaps they were right, perhaps he should keep her always by his side and overlook the fact of their childlessness. But at other times his failure to produce an heir filled him with an overwhelming sense of despair.

"To whom, then," he sighed one day to his valet Constant, "am I going to leave all this?"

♣ ♣ ♣

In September, 1805, Napoleon left Paris to face the new coalition formed between England, Austria, Sweden, and Prussia. As always, he struck swiftly and ruthlessly. He routed the Austrian army in Ulm in October, and on December 2, the first anniversary of his coronation, he defeated the combined Russo-Austrian army at Austerlitz. This resounding victory at Austerlitz did more than strengthen his position as Emperor of the French, it made him the undoubted master of Europe. He could now begin to realize his dreams of a great French Empire spreading across the Continent.

It was his family, of course, who reaped the benefits from his most recent aggrandizement. He either made his relations kings and queens, or else allied them to existing royal houses. The first round went to the Beauharnais faction. The King and Queen of Bavaria had a pretty seventeen-year-old daughter called Augusta. The fact that she was already engaged to be married bothered Napoleon not at all; he suggested that she break her engagement and marry the twenty-five-year-old Eugène de Beauharnais. The King and Queen of Bavaria, imagining that they were being fobbed off with a Beauharnais when what they really wanted was a Bonaparte, raised objections. These Napoleon stifled by assuring the King that he planned to make Eugène King of Italy, and by all but making love to the Queen. It was at this stage that he formally adopted Eugène as his son, creating him Prince Eugène of France, and making him Viceroy of Italy for life. On the last day of 1805 he sat down to inform Eugène of his plans. "Here I am at Munich," he wrote. "I have arranged your marriage with Princess Augusta, and it has been announced in the papers. The Princess came to see me this morning, and I had a long talk with her. She is very pretty. I am enclosing a portrait of her on a cup; but it doesn't do her justice. . . ."

The match between the Prince Eugène and the Princess Augusta was surprisingly successful—a *mariage de convenance* which matured into a partnership of love. Eugène "possessed in perfection," says Madame de Rémusat, "those qualities which make the happiness of home life— sweet temper, and that natural cheerfulness which rises above every ill, and was perhaps due to the fact that he was never profoundly moved by anything. When, however, indifference towards the interests of other people is also displayed in one's own personal troubles, it may fairly be called philosophy." This happy union between Eugène and Augusta was to provide the world with several sovereigns, among them an Empress of Brazil, a Queen of Sweden, and a Consort of the Queen of Portugal.

The Murats, of course, were furious about the affair. When Joachim Murat heard that Napoleon had adopted Eugène and that Josephine's son would now take precedence of him, he smashed his sword in a fit of temper. Caroline, whose anger was always diverted into more practical channels, incited Napoleon to divorce Josephine and marry the young Princess Augusta himself. Napoleon ignored their jealous reactions and insisted that they attend the wedding. They did so, reports Hortense, with the worst grace in the world. So incensed, in fact, was Caroline at having to play second fiddle to Princess Augusta at Munich, that she feigned illness and kept away from as many of the ceremonies as possible. They suffered further mortification when Napoleon arranged for Stéphanie de Beauharnais, a cousin of Josephine's, to marry Princess Augusta's rejected suitor, the Grand Duke of Baden. Napoleon, in a capricious mood, commanded that Stéphanie rank immediately after the Empress, thus giving her precedence over the rest of the family. Stéphanie, who until her marriage had been something of a poor relation at court, now completely lost her head; with the Emperor to back her up, she took every opportunity of insulting his sisters. She even refused to consummate her marriage, preferring to spend her wedding night with a girl friend rather than the poor Duke of Baden. Josephine, who certainly had no love for Napoleon's sisters or any special regard for the Duke of Baden, realized that Stéphanie was going too far, and gave her a sharp talking to. Finally Napoleon, tiring of the squabbling which his own perversity had produced, packed her and her husband off to Baden.

He now turned his attention to his blood relations. His mother, who, owing to her championship of the stubborn Lucien, had been ignored at the inauguration of the Empire, was subsequently given the title of *Son Altesse Impériale Madame la Mère de l'Empereur*. She seems, in fact, to have been very anxious about this delay in the granting of her title. "Your mother is ambitious for a title, a settled position," wrote Letizia's half brother Joseph Fesch (he was now a cardinal). "She was distressed that whereas some already called her 'Majesty' and 'Empress Mother,' others addressed her merely as 'Imperial Highness.'" Napoleon, disregarding this hint that she would like to be known as the Empress Mother and be addressed as "your Majesty," revived the old Bourbon title of "Madame," and obliged Letizia to be content with this. From now

75

on she became known as Madame Mère. Her official place was to be at the Emperor's right hand, taking precedence over the princes, while the Empress, on his left, would take precedence over the princesses.

Letizia was installed in a magnificent house in Paris and given the castle of Pont as a country residence. In spite of the enormous allowance granted her by Napoleon, she was soon writing to ask for more. "Will you then, Sire," she wrote, "ask yourself if my allowance is large enough when set against the obligations which the position I occupy impose on me; and again if the present method of paying this money is entirely satisfactory."

What exasperated Napoleon was that instead of spending the vast sums he gave her in a manner worthy of her new position, she hoarded most of it. "Well, Signora Letizia, how do you like court life?" he would ask. "You are bored, aren't you? Look at your daughters, they seem born to it. I have given you a beautiful house, a beautiful property, and a million a year to enjoy it all, and you live like a bourgeois in the Rue Saint-Denis!"

"I wish I could see you get through your million a year!" he chided her on another occasion.

"I will spend it on condition you give me two," countered the shrewd old lady.

The next member of the family to be elevated was Joseph. He and his wife now became the King and Queen of Naples. "My intention is that the Bourbons shall cease to reign at Naples," wrote Napoleon tersely to Joseph in January 1806. "I will place on the throne a prince of my family. I offer it to you in the first place; if this does not suit you, it will be given to another." Joseph accepted his brother's imperious offer, and less than a month later entered Naples at the head of a column of French troops. For the two years that he reigned at Naples, Joseph enjoyed considerable popularity. His easygoing disposition, his courtly manners, his interest in the arts, and his love of display were all very much in tune with the Neapolitan character. He retained as many of the officials of the old regime as possible, he refrained from levying any contribution to support the French Army, and he made very few changes in the day-to-day life of the people. He set out to make himself the protector rather than the conqueror of the Neapolitans; he planned to rule as an Italian king, not a lieutenant of the French Empire.

But he was reckoning without Napoleon. Before many weeks had passed, the Emperor began bombarding him with letters of instruction. Napoleon considered Naples a conquered country, and wanted it treated

as such. *"Dans un pays conquis la bonté n'est pas l'humanité,"* he wrote
brusquely. The people should be disarmed, a substantial war contribution
should be levied, and the French Army should be allowed to live
comfortably at the expense of the conquered Neapolitans. He should be
prepared for an insurrection. But Joseph, imagining that he knew better,
remained sanguine. When civil war did erupt, he took fright. "Sire, you
must come to our assistance," he wrote frantically to his brother. "The
state of this country is deplorable. The treasury is empty. Trade does
not exist. The Army is in want of everything and I have no means for
providing it. I am working day and night . . . the enemy is showing
himself at all points on the coast, and the Army is losing heart."

Actually, it was not as bad as that. The French troops managed to
control the insurgents and the British fleet neglected to follow up their
intermittent attacks on the coast. Although civil war dragged on for
some twenty months, it was confined mostly to the mountainous districts.
Naples itself remained calm, and Joseph was able to devote his energies
to the pursuit of luxury once more. "Naples is as tranquil as Paris," Joseph
now wrote to his wife, Julie, still at Mortefontaine. "There is no dis-
content in any class of society; I give an example of moderation and
of economy; I have no luxury; I spend no money on myself; I have neither
mistresses, nor Mignons, nor favorites; no one leads me, and in fact,
everyone is so well-off here that the French officers whom I am obliged
to send away complain because they cannot remain at Naples. Read this,
my good Julie, to Mama and to Caroline, because they are anxious . . .
recall to Mama that, at all the epochs of my life, as an obscure citizen,
as a farmer, as a magistrate, I have always sacrificed with pleasure my
time to my duties."

It is doubtful whether Julie or "Mama," loyal women, but neither of
them fools, believed one word of all this self-righteous nonsense.

It was not until the very end of Joseph's two-year reign that Julie
and their two daughters, Zénaïde and Charlotte, joined him at Naples.
The retiring Julie had no taste for queenship; she preferred to remain at
Mortefontaine, devoting her time to the education of her daughters.
When Napoleon urged her to take her place beside her husband, she
made excuses: the civil war had made Naples too unsafe, her health was
not good, the journey across the Alps would exhaust her, the hot climate
of Naples would not agree with her. Joseph seems to have managed very
well without her company; in spite of all his protestations, a certain
Neapolitan beauty seems to have provided for all his needs, and he for
hers. It was not until Napoleon actually ordered Julie to join her husband

that she set out for Naples. She had hardly arrived when the Emperor moved the two of them off again—this time to mount a still more illustrious throne.

There was no throne for Lucien. Ever since his quarrel with Napoleon over his marriage to Alexandrine, Lucien had been living in exile in Rome. It was an exile of the most sumptuous sort; even the extravagant Joseph, on passing through Rome on his way to his new kingdom at Naples, was amazed at the style in which Lucien lived. In a city studded with superb *palazzi*, Lucien's was one of the most magnificent; in a center famous for its art galleries, Lucien had one of the foremost collections. As a host and as a patron of the arts, there were few to rival him. In spite of Napoleon, he even had a title. In the summer of 1806 he bought the papal property of Canino, and by arrangement with the Pope, became the Prince of Canino. With his wife, the flamboyant but devoted Alexandrine, and his children (including Charlotte and Christine, daughters of his first wife, Christine Boyer), he lived in happy independence of his king-making brother.

But Napoleon was not content to let this state of affairs endure for long. He was determined that Lucien should put his talent for public life to use, but equally determined that Alexandrine should have no share in such a life. He enlisted the help of Letizia and Joseph in an effort to win Lucien round, but his brother remained inflexible. "No matter what arguments I urged him with," reported Joseph to Napoleon, "I could never get from him anything but a declaration that he felt his honor was concerned in not disavowing his wife or any of his children, and that it was impossible for him to disgrace himself in his own eyes."

In the winter of 1807 Napoleon visited northern Italy and arranged to meet Lucien in Mantua. The interview lasted for six hours. Lucien assured his brother that he was prepared to take a more active part in public affairs, while Napoleon promised to make Lucien an Imperial Prince, to arrange a royal match for his eldest daughter Charlotte, and to recognize the daughters of his second marriage as his nieces. He would even consider giving him a crown. In turn Lucien was to divorce Madame Jouberthon (as Napoleon always insisted on calling her) and to disinherit their son, Charles Lucien, who had been born the day before their marriage. Lucien, in whom Napoleon always met his match, refused even to consider these conditions, and the brothers parted. "On leaving the Emperor," noted Napoleon's secretary Méneval, "Lucien was deeply affected, and his face was streaming with tears." When Méneval had escorted Lucien back to his lodgings, Lucien asked him to say good-by to the Emperor for him. "It may be forever," he said dramatically.

Elisa was created hereditary Princess of Piombino. Napoleon's gift of this little principality, not far from Pisa, gratified her immensely. Since the exile of her favorite brother Lucien, life had been rather dull in Paris; her salon, once regarded as the cultural center of the capital, was often half empty. And being saddled with the simple Bacciochi, whom even the family-minded Napoleon could never raise to a position of authority, she suffered the mortification of seeing relatives outrank her. Napoleon's claim that he was now entrusting Piombino to Elisa, "not from fraternal tenderness but from political prudence," was probably true; the least favorite of his sisters, she was, despite her pretensions, the most competent.

"So Elisa is a sovereign princess," sniffed Caroline Murat on hearing the news, "with an army of four privates and a corporal."

Elisa tackled her new task with all her customary vigor. First she arranged for the neighboring republican state of Lucca to come under her control as well, and then, preferring it to Piombino, took up residence there. Considering none of the existing palaces worthy of her, she had a new one built. In it she lived in most magnificent style. "The Court of Lucca," reported the French envoy, "is on a small scale what Saint-Cloud is on a large. I have even found it more brilliant, save in point of numbers, both in costume and ceremony."

She built roads, she drained marshes, she abolished certain taxes, she started a silk industry, she reorganized the judicial system, the police force, and the prisons. "The habit of work has become a passion with me," she wrote to Napoleon; "it takes the place of every other idea, and when I return to my study, I remain there with as much pleasure as at the most brilliant fete. You see, Sire," she added shrewdly, "how your lessons and your paternal counsels can change all ideas and all sentiments."

But true Bonaparte that she was, she was not neglecting her own interests—financial or amorous. Finding her enormous civil list inadequate, she supplemented it by dabbling in various commercial enterprises, including the reopening of the marble quarries at Carrara. For the next few years Europe was flooded with busts of the Emperor, the Imperial family, the marshals, and lesser dignitaries of the Empire—all in Carrara marble. Her love life was no less successful. With Fontanes left behind in Paris, she turned to her husband's secretary, Lespérut. When Napoleon packed him off to Silesia (he had a way of getting rid of his sisters' lovers), she consoled herself with one of her equerries, Cenami. And

Bacciochi? He seems to have been quite happy to leave the business of government in his wife's hands, and was always extremely flattered when approached by some petitioner. "I will mention it to the Princess," he would reply grandly. "I will recommend your affair to her." Far from resenting his wife's lovers, they allowed him all the more time for his own mistresses. In this respect he could prove himself every bit as capable as his wife.

The independence of their private lives did not prevent Elisa's giving birth to a daughter in June 1806. With an eye to pleasing her illustrious brother, she called the child Napoléone. This daughter, who grew up to be even more aggressively masculine than her mother, was to make a dramatic reappearance in the Bonaparte story some twenty-five years later.

Continuing to fill the thrones of Europe with members of his family, Napoleon now made Louis and Hortense King and Queen of Holland. The prospect was not much to the taste of either; Louis feared the damp climate of Holland and was afraid that he might be denied his two-month-long sojourns at various spas, while Hortense dreaded leaving Josephine and resented what was bound to be a disruption of her retired daily life. Hardly had Napoleon offered Louis the Dutch throne (he had made it appear as though the Dutch had requested him to supply them with a Bonaparte prince) than Caroline Murat came bustling round. "I attended the marriage of Prince Eugène at Munich," she told Hortense, "only because the Emperor promised me the crown of Holland. I don't want to remind him of his promise without your consent. Will it be all right if I do so?"

Louis and Hortense assured her that they would be only too happy if she got her way, but Napoleon brushed aside her ambitions and insisted that Louis become king. "Why don't you rise to the situation?" he said chidingly to the depressed Hortense. "Go, reign, and make your people happy. That ought to be some satisfaction for you! I have done something for you that is unknown in any other country. According to the constitution, you will have regency rights, and that's a very flattering distinction. Show yourself worthy of it."

"Oh, Sire," protested Hortense, "it's no use trying to make me over. I will always be a bourgeois at heart—if that is what you call being passionately fond of my own country, my own friends, my own family."

But it was no use, and Louis and Hortense, accompanied by their sons, Napoleon-Charles and Napoleon-Louis, set off for The Hague.

Just as Joseph had tried to be the King of Naples first and the brother of the Emperor second, so Louis endeavored to identify himself with his Dutch subjects to the exclusion of French interests. And like Joseph, he very soon came up against Napoleon's iron will. From the outset Napoleon had warned him that as a Constable of the Empire his first duties lay with France, and before long the Emperor had ordered him to collect a year's taxes in advance and to bring the Dutch army to assist him in his latest campaign. Acting with his usual swiftness, Napoleon routed the Prussian army at Jena, and Louis, whose role in the campaign had been, at best, negative, returned to Holland aureoled in reflected glory.

His return brought little comfort to Hortense. Their marriage was desperately unhappy. Year by year Louis was growing more suspicious of his lovely wife; Lucien's assertion that Hortense had been Napoleon's mistress had made Louis suspect almost every man with whom she came in contact. He saw to it that all the men in their household were unattractive, and Hortense's equerries were always the oldest, ugliest creatures he could find. He denied her all pleasures and surrounded her with a dull, formal, pompous court. Rumors of his selfish treatment reached Napoleon at the front, and he, never too busy to dash off a letter of advice to one of his relations, took Louis to task.

"Your quarrels with the Queen are known to the public," he lectured. "Show in your private life the paternal and soft side of your character, and in your administration the rigor you display at home. You treat your young wife as though she were a regiment. Let her dance as much as she likes; she is just at the age to enjoy it. I have a wife of forty, and from the battlefields I write to her to go to balls; but you expect a young woman in her twenties to live in a cloister, to be like a nurse, forever washing the baby! The trouble is that you have a wife who is too virtuous. If she were a coquette, she would lead you around by the nose. Instead of that her pride is hurt, and she rebels because you have such a poor opinion of her."

He also wrote to Hortense, assuring her that Louis's jealousy was merely proof of his love and that although he could sometimes be a strange man, he was a just one.

It took a domestic tragedy to bring about a temporary reconciliation. In 1807 their eldest son, Napoleon-Charles, died. The death of this five-year-old boy, whom Napoleon had always looked upon as his heir, almost broke Hortense's heart. Josephine came hurrying north to be near her daughter, and was horrified at the numbed, almost apathetic state in which she found Hortense. "The Queen [Hortense] has but one thought," wrote Madame de Rémusat, "the loss she has suffered; she speaks only of one thing, of *him*. Not a tear, but a cold calm, an almost absolute silence about everything, and when she speaks, she wrings everyone's heart. . . ." The death of young Napoleon-Charles revealed an unexpected depth of tenderness in Louis towards his wife. For a few months, after her first deep shock had worn off, they resumed normal marital relations, but the reconciliation did not last long. By the time Hortense gave birth to yet another boy, in April 1808 in Paris, she and Louis had already parted. The cunning Caroline Murat, infuriated at this further link in the chain which bound Napoleon to the Beauharnais family, hinted to Louis that he was not the child's father. Louis, always ready to believe the worst about Hortense, resumed his insulting treatment of her. "It is a consolation to live far from you," he wrote from Holland, "to have nothing to discuss with you, nothing to do with you, nothing to expect from you. If I have anything to fear, at least it is not from you."

Their son was given the name of Charles Louis Napoleon. They were the names of his grandfather, his father, and the Emperor. Of all Napoleon's nephews, this little boy, so puny at birth that he had to be wrapped in cotton-wool, would have the most spectacular career. He would be the one to continue the Napoleonic tradition, to revive the glories of Napoleon's Empire, to establish himself as the heir to Napoleon. This third son of Napoleon's brother Louis and Josephine's daughter, Hortense, was the future Emperor Napoleon III.

    👑   👑   👑

There remained Pauline, Caroline, and Jérôme to be catered for. Of all Napoleon's brothers and sisters, Pauline was the least self-seeking. All she asked of Napoleon was that she be allowed to remain in Paris (life in the Borghese palace in Rome had bored her), that her husband, Prince Borghese, be kept as far away from her as possible (she had found Prince Borghese more boring even than Rome), and that she be left in peace to pursue her one real passion in life—the perfecting of her own beauty. Her magnificent clothes, her brilliant receptions, her countless love affairs served merely to high-light this beauty; the gasps of admiration and the lustful stares were all the reward she ever wanted. "I do not care for crowns," she said, "if I had wished for one, I should have had it; but I left the taste to my relatives."

This might have been good enough for her, but it was not good enough for Napoleon. "The principality of Guastalla being at our disposal," he announced, "we have disposed of it in favor of the Princess Pauline, to enjoy it in full ownership, under the titles of Princess and Duchess of Guastalla." The principality was to be handed down to the "male descendants, legitimate and natural, of our sister Pauline," and in default of these, to anyone whom Napoleon might judge fit. Pauline, in fact, had no descendants; her only son, the six-year-old Dermide Leclerc, had died in 1804, and it was rumored that Borghese was impotent.

At first Pauline was rather amused by the idea of becoming a reigning princess, but when she heard that Guastalla was a state of some six square miles with an impoverished population of three thousand, she quickly changed her mind. Nothing would induce her to live there. "If there had been kingdoms in the air, as in the time of the sylphs," mused Madame Junot, "she might have been enveloped in a pink and blue cloud, nicely perfumed, and sent to reign in those fortunate regions where the scepter of government is a sprig of flowers." But as this was not the time of the sylphs and as even little Guastalla needed something more than a sprig of flowers to control it, Pauline refused to leave Paris. Napoleon promptly offered to incorporate the little state in his own Kingdom of Italy, and to pay Pauline six million francs for it, on the understanding that she could retain the title. She agreed, and the transaction over, resumed her life in Paris.

It was a life of almost legendary luxury. From the first thing in the morning, when a glistening black Negro carried her to her bath of warm milk, to the last thing at night, when her maids helped her out of one of those shimmering pearl-encrusted dresses and put her to sleep between soft scented sheets, Pauline gave herself over to the cult of her beauty. Stories about this obsession with her looks (coupled with her disarming ingenuousness) are endless. She had herself sculptured, almost nude, by Canova, and when one of her ladies protested that she should never have posed with so little on, Pauline's lovely gray eyes widened, and she answered; "Why not? It was not cold. There was a fire in the studio."

On another occasion, when she arrived at some small town on her way to Plombières, she informed her host that a warm milk bath and a cold milk shower must be got ready for her. Her obliging host assured her that he could manage the bath but not the shower. Then there was nothing for it, said Pauline sweetly, but for him to knock a hole in the ceiling of her room; a shower, he must understand, was essential to her health. As she was the Emperor's sister, the long-suffering man had to ruin a perfectly good ceiling and to resign himself to the house smelling like a dairy for several weeks afterwards.

Enamored of every part of her body, Pauline was particularly fond of her feet. Like all the Bonapartes, she had small exquisitely shaped feet which she kept immaculately manicured and seductively perfumed. But even allowing for this, her treatment of them could sometimes be—to say the least—unexpected. When the Duchess des Cars visited her for the first time, she was surprised to find Madame de Chambaudouin, Pauline's maid of honor, stretched full length on her back in front of the Princess's chair. Madame de Chambaudouin was wearing an extremely low-cut dress, and Pauline's feet were gently and almost unconsciously caressing the lady's breasts. When asked by the visitor if she did not find the position uncomfortable, Madame de Chambaudouin replied that on the contrary, she was quite used to it.

The talk turned to theater and when the visitor remarked that she preferred tragedies, Madame de Chambaudouin, her voice atremble from having her "breast set in motion by a foot," cried out, "I adore tragedies, for they elevate the soul." The Duchess des Cars, almost bursting with suppressed laughter, had to cut her visit short and promise to come another time. She called frequently after that, she says, and became quite accustomed to the sight of Pauline's ladies submitting themselves to their mistress's white and wandering feet.

The same indulgent quality characterized Pauline's love affairs. Whoever she wanted, she took. No sooner had she set eyes on a certain young German officer who had come with a message than she had him conducted, by a secret doorway, into a sumptuous underground salon. In the middle of the room was a huge bath. A few minutes later Pauline reappeared, wearing the flimsiest of garments. The velvet cushions of an enormous couch bore witness, as he put it, to the way in which they slaked their passions. When he had satisfied her (she proved herself a very experienced teacher, he afterwards remarked), Pauline rang for her maid, who then prepared the bath. For almost an hour the Princess and the soldier refreshed themselves in the cool, clear water, and then rounded off the day with a light but elegantly prepared meal.

So insatiable was her sexual appetite that at the height of her affair with the handsome Auguste de Forbin ("You won't find such men nowadays," sighed Madame Junot in her old age), her doctors feared that unless she restrained herself, she might injure her health permanently. Her personal physician spoke to Madame Mère about his apprehensions, and she talked Pauline into dismissing Forbin and going to Aix-les-Bains for a cure. Heart-broken but obedient, she set off. She took so much luggage with her that her cortege could easily have been mistaken for the baggage train of a small but well-equipped army. Once there, it needed a sizable mansion to house her ladies and gentlemen, her doctor, her Negro litter-bearers, her servants, her sedan chair, her hammock, her special bath, her dresses, her hats, her parasols, her jewelry, her parrots, her lap dogs. . . .

And yet, for all her weaknesses, for all her frivolous self-obsession, Pauline was a good sister to Napoleon. She never forgot that she owed everything to him, and when his Empire began to crumble, she was one of the very few who stood by him.

Caroline was quite different. "Of all the family, she was perhaps the only one who had not learned to become a princess," writes the ever-observant Madame Junot. "She could not leave off the satirical giggle and sneering of the schoolgirl, while her manners were undignified, and her walk, the most ungraceful possible. But in self-sufficiency she was perfectly the sovereign lady; she spoke of herself and of her person with the highest consideration, and with a contemptuous ridicule of others. . . ." It was soon to become apparent why Madame Junot, always sharp-tongued but seldom downright rude, felt so strongly about the pretensions of Princess Caroline.

After months of tireless scheming on the parts of the Murats, Napoleon gave them the duchies of Berg and Clèves. They had both hoped, of course, for something more than this, but were shrewd enough to accept it and begin working for something better. Murat, resplendent in furs, feathers, and yards of gold braid, went clattering into his new domain, while Caroline remained in Paris to play hostess in that lavish manner so dear to her brother the Emperor's heart. With Hortense away in Holland, Pauline pampering her body at some spa, and the forty-five-year-old Empress getting a little too old to dance, it was Caroline who did most of the imperial entertaining. "The Grand Duchess of Berg lived in great splendor at the Elysée," noted one of Josephine's ladies. "Her beauty was enhanced by the most exquisite toilettes; her pretensions were great, her manners affable when she thought it prudent, and more than affable to men whom she desired to fascinate."

And the men whom she most desired to fascinate at the moment were those who could help further her overweening ambitions. For Caroline had her eye fixed on no less a prize than the Imperial throne. If Napoleon were to be killed in battle, and the chances were by no means remote, Caroline would know exactly what to do. She cultivated the astute Fouché, the suave Talleyrand (he claimed that she had the head of a Cromwell on the shoulders of a pretty woman), and above all, Junot, the Governor of Paris. With both Napoleon and Murat away on the campaign which was to end so brilliantly with the victories of Jena and Auerstädt, Caroline was beginning to put her plan into operation. If Napoleon were to be killed, the succession would pass to Joseph, Louis, or Jérôme. But as none of these three brothers had any influence with the Army, and as the Army would play the dominant role in such a situation, Murat would be the most likely choice. He was immensely popular with the troops, and the fact that he was Napoleon's brother-in-law set him above other equally popular or deserving generals. As Governor of Paris, Junot controlled all the troops in the military district of Paris, and if Caroline could be sure of his cooperation, Murat could be proclaimed Emperor in Paris as soon as the news of Napoleon's death reached the capital.

To win Junot's cooperation, the cold, calculating, insatiably ambitious Caroline seduced him. "She opened all the balls with the Governor of Paris, played whist with the Governor of Paris, rode on horseback with the Governor of Paris, received the Governor of Paris alone in preference to all other persons, until the poor Governor of Paris, who was certainly no angel . . . could no more resist the perpetual seductions which assailed him than the Christian Knights could resist the seductions of the Palace of Armida." The writer is Madame Junot, his wife.

But the Emperor was not killed in battle, and when he returned to Paris, he sent its governor to join the growing colony of his sisters' ex-lovers living in exile in the Iberian Peninsula. His adroit, unscrupulous sister he dismissed as a "little fool."

Napoleon's youngest brother, Jérôme, was made King of Westphalia. Once the Elizabeth Patterson escapade was over and he had again been taken under Napoleon's wing, Jérôme resumed all the carefree, dissolute habits of his bachelorhood. He spent more money, complained Napoleon, than any other prince in Europe. "One cannot imagine," he wrote, "how much this young fellow costs me, and with it all, he only gives me disappointment and is no use in my plans." He referred to him as "that *mauvais sujet*, my brother Jérôme."

In the hope of cementing his fluid character, Napoleon again sent him off to sea, and on his return some months later, gave him command of an army corps in the Prussian campaign. Jérôme seems to have distinguished himself chiefly by his mistakes, his insubordination, and his extravagance, but was nevertheless rewarded with a throne. "Prince Jérôme conducts himself well," reported Napoleon to his brother Joseph. "I am well satisfied with him, and I am much mistaken if there is not that in him to make a man of the very first order. . . ." As was always the case when he judged his relations, Napoleon was "much mistaken."

"My brother," he wrote to Jérôme himself, "I have just signed the peace with Russia and Prussia. You have been recognized as King of Westphalia. This kingdom will include all the states of which you will find the list hereto attached."

Napoleon had given Westphalia a king, and now he set about giving it a queen. He chose, as Jérôme's new bride, Catherine of Württemberg, the daughter of the King of Württemberg. Princess Catherine was twenty-four years of age, some two years older than her proposed husband. Jérôme, on meeting her, considered her "very good-hearted," and said that although she was not beautiful, "*elle n'est pas mal.*" A somewhat more articulate witness of this first meeting found Princess Catherine squat, plain, badly dressed, but with a fresh complexion and a certain dignity of manner. Beside the vivacious, feather-light Jérôme (the elegance of whose satin coat and white plumes had once caused him to be mistaken for the Empress Josephine in a carriage procession), she was dull stuff indeed. And yet it turned out to be a happy marriage. Catherine's qualities of devotion, simplicity, sincerity, and loyalty were excellent foils for her husband's less dependable characteristics. Much to the amazement of those who knew him, Catherine was to love the frivolous Jérôme for the rest of her days. From their union—and it must have seemed highly unlikely at the time—is descended the present pretender to the Imperial throne.

They were married at the Tuileries in August 1807, amidst scenes of breathtaking splendor. Bride and groom both wore white, Jérôme sporting rather more gold embroidery than she. They spent the first few days of their honeymoon in Jérôme's apartment in the Pavillon de Flore, then joined the court at Fontainebleau. There Jérôme, notwithstanding the fact that he had been married for a matter of weeks only, fell in love. The lady was none other than Josephine's niece Stéphanie, Grand Duchess of Baden. Jérôme's passion for her amused the coquettish Stéphanie immensely, and in spite of the anguish of his poor wife, Catherine, she led him on. One evening as Stéphanie and Jérôme were dancing together at a court ball, Catherine, too plump to dance herself, suddenly turned pale, burst into tears, and slid from her chair in a faint. Josephine rushed to her aid while Napoleon sent Jérôme from the room with a sharp word. The following day the Emperor instructed Josephine to speak to her niece, and again Stéphanie was treated to a lecture on her behavior. As she had by now completely lost favor with Napoleon (he had for a long time ignored his own rules with respect to her rank, and she now took her place far behind the members of the Imperial family), she listened attentively to all the Empress had to say. She promised to behave herself in the future, and was true to her word. She cold-shouldered Jérôme, she renewed relations with her husband, and returned to Baden with a good grace at the end of the season.

Not till December 1807 did Jérôme and Catherine leave France and enter their new kingdom. Here they took up residence in the palace of Wilhelmshöhe, now renamed Napoleonshöhe in honor of the Emperor. Some sixty years later another Emperor, Napoleon III, would come to Wilhelmshöhe, but he would come to it, not as a reigning sovereign, but as a political prisoner.

♔   ♔   ♔

On June 14, 1807, Napoleon defeated the Russian Army at Friedland, and eleven days later met Czar Alexander at Tilsit.

A little tented raft had been moored in the middle of the river, and to the sound of trumpets, drums, and cannon, the Emperor of the West and the Emperor of the East were rowed out simultaneously from opposite banks for half an hour's talk on the floating pavilion. Here, during a series of meetings amidst elegant Empire furnishings, the two emperors settled down to divide Europe between them. In a career rich in scenes of splendor, this surely must have been Napoleon's most splendid scene yet; it was, in many ways, the apogee of the First Empire.

Napoleon was now thirty-eight years old. The slender, gauche, eager-eyed, long-haired, sallow-skinned young soldier described by Laure Junot and Constant had given way to the plump, self-assured, stern-eyed, balding, cameo-complexioned conqueror of Europe. A lady in waiting to the Queen of Prussia, who met him at Tilsit, talks of his excessive ugliness, his swollen face, his corpulent body, his great gloomy eyes, and his severe features. "He looks like the incarnation of fate," writes the lady, but then she, like all the Prussian court, loathed him. Perhaps a less biased picture is given by Count Molé in his memoirs. "Napoleon's face, seen at such close quarters, struck me even more forcibly than the idea I had formed of it. I have always believed in faces. His was in keeping with his whole history. His head was superb, and unlike any other. In the depth of his skull, the formation of his splendid forehead, the setting of his eyes, his sculptured lips, the droop at the corners of his mouth, the beautiful proportions of the face, and the regularity of his features, but above all in his glance and his smile—in all this, I thought I could recognize all the qualities which raise a man above his fellows, and make him fit to rule over them."

Whether Napoleon was, in fact, so fit to rule over his fellow men is a matter of conjecture, but what does seem to be beyond question is the unfitness of his brothers and sisters for the task. His brothers were nothing more than gentlemen of leisure; at best Joseph and Lucien could have been accredited as ambassadors to some civilized, politically uncomplicated state. His sisters, as one of their biographers has said, aspired to be sovereigns and remained nothing more than crowned courtesans. This year of Tilsit saw them, as well as Napoleon (for they were merely reflectors of the bright light of his glory), at the apex of their power. Napoleon himself was Emperor of the French and King of Italy; Joseph was King of Naples and soon to become King of Spain; Louis was King of Holland; Jérôme was King of Westphalia; Elisa was hereditary Princess of Piombino and Lucca; Pauline was the Grand Duchess of Guastalla; Caroline was the Grand Duchess of Berg and would soon be Queen of Naples. Fifteen years ago they had been a family of unknown Corsican refugees; now they were the most powerful dynasty on the Continent. The oldest of them was still in his thirties; the youngest, not yet twenty-three.

Like those golden bees which Napoleon had adopted as his emblem, his family now began to swarm into every court in Europe.

CHAPTER FIVE

NAPOLEON's triumphs on the battlefield during these years had been accompanied by triumphs of a more personal nature. He had been able to prove his sexual potency at last. It was his sister Caroline, relentless in her war against Josephine, who had helped furnish him with the proof.

Caroline employed as a "reader" a young woman by the name of Eléonore Dénuelle. She was a tall, dark, bold-eyed girl; her parents were adventurers, and she was married to a no less adventurous captain recently imprisoned for forgery. The shrewd Caroline at once recognized in her the qualities she needed for an experiment she was planning. She arranged for Eléonore to meet her brother Napoleon early in 1806. Eléonore, eminently at home in the role which Caroline had planned for her, played it with gusto; before long she was visiting Napoleon in his secret room at the Tuileries. But whether she saw him there or at the Murats's house, Caroline kept a close watch, to make certain that no other man enjoyed her favors. By the time Eléonore obtained a divorce from her husband in April, she was already pregnant by Napoleon. The Emperor left Paris in September to take command of his Army once more, and on the last day of the year, encamped before the gates of Warsaw, he heard that Eléonore had given birth to a son. The boy was named Charles Léon, and grew up to look very like his illustrious father.

Although Napoleon very quickly tired of Eléonore, he often saw the son. Constant would bring the little boy to the Emperor, and Napoleon would feed him "quantities of sweetmeats," as a reward for his "vivacity and his cleverness."

On New Year's Day 1807 Napoleon drove in triumph into Warsaw. While the carriage horses were being changed just prior to entering the city, one of his generals led two ladies through the crowd towards him. One of them was young, fair-haired, and radiantly lovely. She turned her large blue eyes on the all-conquering Napoleon and welcomed him as the deliverer of her country. He rewarded her pretty speech by presenting her a bouquet which someone had just flung into his carriage, and by promising that they would meet again in Warsaw.

He was as good as his word. But when next they met, he was rather disconcerted to find that the young lady had really meant what she had said about his being the deliverer of her country, and it was in that capacity, and not in any other, that she admired him. Marie Walewska, for that was her name, was a fervent patriot; she was not another Eléonore Dénuelle. Her equally patriotic countrymen, however, realizing that the Emperor's interest in her had nothing to do with her nationality, urged her to put his interest to good use. If Marie Walewska played her cards correctly, Poland might regain her lost domains and become a proud nation once more. Even her aged husband, Count Walewski, encouraged her to gratify the Emperor's wishes. She did, and Napoleon fell head over heels in love with her. Not for ten years, since his early days with Josephine, had he written such ardent love letters. "Marie, my sweet Marie, my first thought is of you, my first desire is to see you again. You will come again, won't you? You promised you would. If you don't, the eagle will fly to you! . . ."

At the same time he was writing to Josephine to tell her that he could not possibly allow her to undertake the journey to Warsaw. "The roads are too bad—unsafe and deep in mud." Yet only a few weeks before he had assured her that she was all he desired, that there was no one to compare with his Josephine, that "*ces nuits-ci sont longues, tout seul.*" It is unlikely that Josephine, who knew him so well, was taken in by his concern for her safe passage.

When Napoleon moved his headquarters to the castle of Finkenstein, on the Vistula, Marie Walewska went with him. He was beginning to refer to her as his "Polish wife," and indeed, it did seem as though their association would prove more durable than his usual affairs. She was quite unlike any of his previous mistresses. Even Constant, who adored Josephine, had to admit that the love of this "angelic woman, with her sweet, unselfish nature," was of the deepest, most disinterested kind. "Her life, like her temper, was always even"; Marie Walewska seems, in fact, to have had something of Josephine's ability to surround Napoleon with that aura of tranquillity and sweetness which his nature craved.

She joined him in Paris the following year, and was with him at Schönbrunn, outside Vienna, the year after. In 1809 he heard that she, too, was pregnant by him; their child was born on May 11 the following year. This boy, christened Alexandre Walewski, was to play a prominent part in the Second Empire under Hortense's son, Napoleon III.

It was during his idyll with the lovely Marie Walewska at Finkenstein that Napoleon heard of the death of Hortense's eldest son, Napoleon-Charles. The news upset him, but not for long. He had been fond of this little boy whom he had hoped to adopt as his heir, but in the flush of his recent triumphs, both military and amorous, he had no time to mourn. He could not, he said, "amuse himself with feelings and regrets like other men"; the loss of this collateral heir, moreover, did not seem quite so important any more. The certainty that he had fathered Eléonore Dénuelle's child (he was only later to hear that Murat, evading Caroline's vigilance, had also enjoyed her favors) and the delights of his love affair with Marie Walewska were reawakening his ideas of divorce. He had, in addition, been so much in royal circles lately that he was beginning to get a taste for it; an incorrigible snob, there now seemed to be no reason why he should not divorce his wife and marry the daughter of some royal house.

But contemplation of divorce was always easier out of Josephine's company than in it. Once back in Paris, he could not bring himself to broach the subject. For all her faults—her debts, her jealousies, and, most important, her childlessness—she suited him so well. Talking to Hortense one day of the beautiful Queen of Prussia, whom he had met at Tilsit, Napoleon said, "She does not compare with my Josephine." And it was true. No legitimate empress, queen, or princess in Europe at the time could match the parvenu Josephine in charm and elegance. And Napoleon, to whom an outward show meant so much, appreciated these qualities afresh each time he returned to her. "On rejoining his wife," noted one of her ladies, "he again felt for her the kind of affection with which she always inspired him, and which often made him uncomfortable, because it embarrassed him when he grieved her."

Anxious not to grieve her, he would approach the subject of divorce obliquely. Talking on one occasion of the death of Hortense's son, he maneuvered the conversation towards the question of his "perhaps one day" being forced to take a wife capable of giving him children. "If such a thing should happen, Josephine, it will be you who will have to help me make the sacrifice. I shall count upon your love to save me all the odium of a forced rupture. You would take the initiative, wouldn't you?"

But Josephine, whose attitude towards the divorce had always been one of passive resistance, refused to fall into his trap. "Sire," she answered calmly, "you are the master, and you shall decide my fate. When you order me to leave the Tuileries, I will obey instantly, but the least you could do would be to order it in a positive manner. I am your wife; I have been crowned by you in the presence of the Pope. Such honors at least demand that they should not be voluntarily renounced. If you divorce me, all France will know that it is you who are driving me out. . . ."

The quiet dignity of her answers would touch him; they even, on occasions, reduced him to tears. But out of his presence she was much less controlled. She confided to Madame Rémusat her fears that Napoleon might one day try to do away with her altogether. Madame de Rémusat, who had no very high opinion of Napoleon, swore that Napoleon would never for a moment have entertained such an idea.

Fouché, the Minister of Police, came one day to tell Josephine that it was her duty to sue for a divorce. "The political future of France," he claimed, "is compromised by a want of heir to the Emperor."

Josephine, suspecting that Fouché had been sent by Napoleon, taxed her husband with it; but he, protesting innocence, rebuked Fouché, and the affair ended with "many caresses." It had been an "excess of zeal" on the part of Fouché, said Napoleon to his wife. "We must not be angry with him for it; it is quite enough that we are determined to reject his advice, and you know well that I could not live without you."

Josephine was not so sure. She knew that not only Fouché but Napoleon's brothers and sisters were all clamoring for him to divorce her. There was a pathetic little scene between Josephine and the young Madame Junot at Malmaison one day. Madame Junot had brought her little daughter to visit the Empress, and Josephine was showing them the plants in her famous hothouse. Despite the steamy, almost tropical atmosphere beneath the glass dome, and despite the fact the flowers were what pleased Josephine most in the world, she shivered and seemed unable to focus her attention on her beloved plants. "It's very cold," she said to her visitor, drawing her shawl closer. It was, realized Madame Junot, "the chill of grief creeping about her heart, like the cold hand of death."

When the little girl had gone scampering off among the bright banks of flowers, Josephine suddenly took hold of her guest's hands and exclaimed; "Madame Junot, I beg you to tell me all that you have heard relating to me. I ask it as an especial favor—you know that they (Napoleon's family) all desire to ruin me and my Hortense and my Eugène. Madame Junot, I again beg as a favor that you will tell me all you know."

The startled Laure Junot knew, in fact, nothing. She assured the trembling Empress that, on her honor, she had not heard the word "divorce" uttered by either Napoleon's mother or his sisters. At the mention of the dreaded word, Josephine burst into tears. "Madame Junot," she said, her lovely voice choking with sobs, "remember what I say to you this day, here, in this hothouse—this place which is now a paradise, but which may soon become a desert to me—remember that this separation will be my death, and it is they who will have killed me."

At this moment the little girl came running back, and the weeping Empress gathered her in her arms "with an almost convulsive emotion."

"You have no idea how much I have suffered when any one of you has brought a child to me!" continued Josephine. "Heaven knows that I am not envious, but in this one case I have felt as if a deadly poison were creeping throught my veins when I have looked upon the fresh and rosy cheeks of a beautiful child, the joy of its mother, but above all, the hope of its father! and I, struck with barrenness, shall be driven in disgrace from the bed of him who has given me a crown. Yet God is my witness that I love him more than my life, and much more than that throne, that crown which he has given me!"

Twenty-five years later Madame Junot remembered that poignant scene as clearly as though it had happened the day before.

If Josephine was tortured by the prospect of a divorce, Napoleon was by no means sanguine about it. M. de Rémusat once witnessed a temporary parting between Napoleon and Josephine. The Empress, as usual, was in tears, and Napoleon, holding her in his arms, seemed unable to tear himself away. They stood locked together for several minutes, and then the Emperor "was overcome by a sort of nervous emotion, which increased to such a degree that he wept uncontrollably, and almost immediately an attack of convulsions ensued, which brought on vomiting." He was helped into a chair and given some orange-flower water (his favorite remedy) to drink, but he continued to cry for a further fifteen minutes. At the end of that time he suddenly stood up, embraced his wife briefly, and shouted out, "Are the carriages ready? Call the suite, and let's go."

On another occasion, when Napoleon and Josephine were dining together at the Tuileries, she noticed that he seemed sad and silent. They parted, after dinner, to prepare for a reception, and while Josephine was dressing, an attendant came to tell her that the Emperor was ill. Wearing her glittering court dress, she hurried to his apartment. There she found him flung across his bed, "suffering from severe spasms and in a highly nervous state." At the sight of her white, anxious face, he burst into tears. He dragged her down onto the bed and disregarding her finery, hugged her to him. Again and again he cried out; "My poor Josephine. I cannot leave you!"

She tried to soothe him. "Sire be calm"; she whispered, "make up your mind what you really want to do, and let us have an end to these scenes."

Instead of calming him, these words seemed to agitate him even more. His behavior became so "excessive" that she advised him to forget the reception and go to bed. He would only do this, he cried, if she came to bed with him. So poor Josephine was obliged to get undressed again and share his bed. His pillow, she said, was wet with his tears, and "the night was passed in alternate fits of tenderness and intervals of uneasy slumber."

By the following morning he was his old imperious, assured, egotistical, and offensively sharp-tongued self.

♔   ♔   ♔

Napoleon now turned his hand to a little more king-making. The throne to be filled on this occasion was the throne of Spain. Napoleon, considering that it was not being very well filled by the slow-witted Charles IV or, after his abdication, by his almost equally incompetent son Ferdinand, invited the Spanish royal family to Bayonne for a conference. Once this unprepossessing family had forgathered, Napoleon, by alternately bullying and coaxing, got them to pass the Spanish crown on to him. Charles IV, his queen, and his queen's lover were rewarded with handsome pensions, and the young Ferdinand brought to France as Napoleon's "guest." The throne could now be presented to one of Napoleon's relations.

To whom was it to go? Lucien, the only one of Napoleon's brothers without a crown, was the obvious choice, but Lucien remained intractable. Murat, whose vigorous campaigning in Spain had made it possible for Napoleon to get control of the crown, imagined that he would get it. He had hoped, similarly, the year before to be given the crown of Poland. His hopes had been dashed when, on arriving for the meeting at Tilsit in an elaborate Polish costume, Napoleon had told him that he looked like a circus master and had sent him back to change into something more restrained. Murat was due, on this occasion, to be disappointed again. Jérôme was out of the running; not even Napoleon could consider sending a Protestant queen-consort to Spain. There remained Joseph, at present King of Naples, and Louis, King of Holland.

Napoleon, with his strong sense of family hierarchy, offered it first to Joseph. Joseph, perfectly happy at Naples, refused. He then wrote to Louis. "Convinced as I am that I shall never secure lasting peace with England until I set the whole of Europe in motion, I have determined to put a French prince on the throne of Spain. The Dutch climate doesn't suit you. . . . I am thinking of you for the throne of Spain. . . . Give me a plain answer. If I appoint you King of Spain, do you accept? Can I count on you?"

Louis refused. The idea of being shifted around like an official disgusted him; as King of Holland his place was with his Dutch subjects, and that was where he intended to remain. Napoleon, who considered the throne one occupied more important than the subjects one ruled over, was surprised at Louis's rejection of his brilliant offer. He turned once more to Joseph; it had ceased now to be a question of preference—he all but ordered his brother to accept the crown of Spain. And Joseph, ever submissive, fell in with his younger brother's wishes. On June 6, 1808, Napoleon proclaimed Joseph King of Spain and the Indies, and five days later Joseph issued his proclamation, describing himself as "Don Joseph, by the grace of God, King of Castille, Aragon, the two Sicilies, Jerusalem, Navarre, Toledo, Valencia, Galicia, Majorca, Minorca, Seville, Cordova, Murcia, Santiago the Algarve, Algeciras, Gibraltar, the Canary Islands, the West and East Indies, the Islands of the Ocean and Terra Firma, Archduke of Austria, Duke of Burgundy, Brabant and Milan, Count of Hapsburg, Tyrol and Barcelona, and Lord of Biscay." Napoleon considered it excessive.

Don Joseph, who was ignorant of the extremely unsettled state of affairs in Spain, entered his new kingdom full of good intentions. As he had tried to be a Neapolitan king in Naples, so would he endeavor to be a Spanish king in Spain. He was soon disillusioned. Whereas the easygoing Neapolitans had welcomed him, the stubborn Spaniards resisted him. No sooner had he set foot in the country than the people rose in revolt against the French and their king. Only by force could he retain this throne. This was not to Joseph's taste at all, and by August he was begging Napoleon to let him return to his former kingdom. But Napoleon remained firm. He ordered more troops to Spain, and when they seemed to be making no headway against the guerrillas, he crossed the Pyrenees and took command himself. All Joseph's dreams of becoming a popular monarch melted before Napoleon's victorious onslaught against his subjects. Spain was now a conquered country, and he, the puppet of its conqueror. He re-entered his capital in the wake of French bayonets. "I blush with shame," he told Napoleon, "in the presence of my so-called subjects. I beg that your Majesty will accept my resignation of all the rights you have given me to the Spanish crown. I shall always prefer honor and probity to power purchased at so dear a price."

Napoleon simply shrugged, and having reinstated his brother, returned to France. From here, and from wherever he happened to be, he flooded Joseph with instructions on how to conduct his campaign against the rebels. When Joseph ventured to point out that by the time Napoleon's orders reached him, the situation had usually changed, the Emperor ignored him. In the spring of 1809 the future Duke of Wellington's invasion of Spain added to poor Joseph's troubles, and although the French managed to check Wellington's advance and restore order for a little while, the situation remained far from satisfactory. Joseph still maintained that he could be King of Spain, "not by force of arms, but through the love of the Spaniards," if only Napoleon would give him a free hand. "Let me," he wrote to his brother, "either be king in a way that befits a brother of Your Majesty, or let me return to Mortefontaine, where the only happiness I shall ask for is to live without humiliations and to die with a peaceful conscience."

Poor Joseph. This suave, easy-tempered, irresolute, luxury-loving man simply could not measure up to Napoleon's exacting standards. Ardent Bonapartists have blamed him for his "weakness" and his "illusions," but the truth is that he was the wrong man in a difficult situation. "The King [Joseph] has sagacity of mind, but he lacks decision," complained Napoleon; "he has courage, but it is the courage of resistance and not of activity." Murat, he said, was an imbecile, but at least, unlike Joseph, he had dash and daring.

"Much has been said, but to no purpose, relative to the weak conduct of Joseph at Naples and in Spain," wrote someone who knew him well. "I know not what he did, or what he could have done at Naples; but this I know, that in Spain he could do no better, because he went there against his inclination and it distressed him exceedingly to be obliged to go to that unhappy country, filled with troubles and dissensions . . . a country where all the good that he did, and I am certain that he did a great deal, was accounted only as a duty performed. . . ."

It was a pity that when the first crack appeared in the towering edifice of Napoleon's Empire, it appeared in the country reigned over by Joseph.

   ♔   ♔   ♔

Napoleon chose the Murats to fill Joseph's vacant throne in Naples. "I intend the King of Naples to reign at Madrid," he informed Joachim Murat. "I wish to give you the Kingdom of Naples or that of Portugal. Let me know immediately what you think about the matter; for it must be settled in a day. . . . If you tell me that you would prefer to remain with me, that is impossible. You have a number of children, and besides, with a wife like yours, you can absent yourself if war calls you back to my side; she is very capable of being at the head of a regency. I will tell you further that the Kingdom of Naples is a much finer one than Portugal, since Sicily will be joined to it; you will then have six million inhabitants."

Murat, choking back his disappointment at not being given the crown of Spain, and shedding, he assured Napoleon, "torrents of tears" of gratitude, chose Naples. When Caroline heard that she was to become a queen at last, she was "beside herself for several hours." Her delirium, however, did not prevent her from making sure that in the event of her husband's death, she would remain Queen and "alone possess the titles and powers of sovereignty." Both husband and wife were somewhat disconcerted to discover that Napoleon expected them to rule their new kingdom from Naples, and not, as they had hoped, from Paris; the Emperor was getting a little tired of Caroline's intrigues.

The Murats entered Naples in the autumn of 1808. They were everything the Neapolitans expected of a royal couple. He was huge, handsome, flashily uniformed, and affably mannered; she was small, pretty, lavishly jeweled, and when she needed to be, overwhelmingly charming. If Naples was pleased with them, they were no less pleased with Naples. The climate was warm, the populace seemed enthusiastic, and from the windows of the sumptuous Palazzo Reale they could look out on one of the loveliest views in the world. True, the panorama was slightly spoiled by the fact that the island of Capri, floating on the far horizon, was in the hands of the British; Murat promptly mounted an expedition and had it recaptured. Capri was unsuccesfully defended by a certain Colonel Lowe; eight years hence, as Sir Hudson Lowe, he would have more success in withstanding the onslaughts of Murat's brother-in-law on another island. Sir Hudson Lowe was to be Napoleon's jailer on St. Helena.

No amount of contemplation of the Bay of Naples, however, could console Murat for the troubles which awaited him in his new kingdom. Joseph had made off with some of the best generals and administrators in Naples, leaving his successor to face his problems with a badly led army and an almost empty treasury. Nor did Napoleon's incessant interfering help. As usual, the new king wanted to be a king, and Napoleon wanted him to be a French prefect. "I am grieved to see how little you are aware of what you owe to me," complained Napoleon. He urged Murat to demand payment of the Neapolitan debt, even at the risk of sacrificing his own "false popularity." He was to find Murat less pliable than Joseph.

If Napoleon imagined that the transfer of Caroline from Paris to Naples would put an end to her scheming, he was mistaken. In her plans for seating her husband on the Imperial throne in the event of Napoleon's death, Caroline now secured two powerful allies. They were none other than those two erstwhile adversaries, Talleyrand and Fouché. This astute pair, realizing that the showy, swaggering Murat would be putty in their experienced fingers, now united to champion his cause. It was even said that Fouché had arranged for relays of horses to be kept ready on the road between Naples and Paris; as soon as there was news of the Emperor's death, Murat—so popular with the Army and the people—would be rushed to the French capital and proclaimed Emperor.

All this heady talk of becoming Emperor, coupled with the fact that he was already a king, quite unbalanced the vain Joachim Murat. He became more and more autocratic. He resented the slightest interference and refused to tolerate even the mildest opposition. Before long, of course, he came up against his equally highhanded and self-opinionated wife. She saw no reason why she should not be given a share in the governing of Naples. When, at the top of her voice, she reminded her husband that Elisa governed Lucca on her own, he, at the top of his, reminded her that he was not another Bacciochi. One Bonaparte meddling in his affairs was enough; he would stand no interference from another.

"We are unable to pay our court to her (the Queen) except for a moment on Mondays only," reported the French ambassador. "The King has exacted this, and he intends to isolate the Queen more every day. . . ."

But Caroline was a woman of endless resource. Foiled in one method, she tried another. If she could not influence her arrogant husband, there were ways of influencing his lieutenants. The view from her bedroom window was so pretty at night; Caroline was willing to share it with anyone who could further her ambitions. The result of these late-night maneuverings was that the government now split into two factions—the Neapolitan party, headed by Murat, and the French party, headed by his wife. Murat's group wanted him to govern as a national king; Caroline's encouraged her to seek a share in the government, and spent a great deal of time carrying tales to Napoleon about Murat. As Murat, the soldier, was far more important to the Emperor than Caroline, the Queen, Napoleon refused to champion her cause.

Having been kept together by a joint ambition all these years, this unscrupulous pair now began to work against each other. Although they never parted company, this rivalry, coupled with their treachery, was to bring the whole assiduously built temple of their ambition crashing about their ears. But not yet: the sweetest moments of Caroline Murat's life still lay ahead.

♔   ♔   ♔

In the summer of 1809 Napoleon, having beaten the Austrians at Wagram, once again had his headquarters in the palace of Schönbrunn, outside Vienna. His apartment was on the first floor; he slept in a vast tapestry-hung chamber, aglitter with gilt and glass and cut crystal, and from its windows he could see the Gloriette, that elegant pavilion crowning the terraced slope behind the palace. Within this golden room he and Marie Walewska once more picked up the threads of their often-interrupted romance, and it was here that he finally made up his mind to divorce Josephine. Strange that it should be in this room that he eventually decided to beget a direct heir; for it was here, almost a quarter of a century later, that this heir, the King of Rome, died.

There were many reasons why Napoleon made up his mind to divorce Josephine at this time. At the height of his power, it seemed more imperative than ever that he establish a dynasty and perpetuate his achievements. For many years he had been concerned that his powers would wane after forty; already he was getting fat and sluggish. He was forty years of age, and time was running out. He now knew for certain that he was not impotent; Eléonore Dénuelle's boy was almost three years old, and in July that year it was confirmed that Marie Walewska was pregnant by him. The death of his brother Louis's eldest son, moreover, had robbed him of a possible heir.

But perhaps one of the most potent reasons was that he now saw the opportunity of allying himself with one of the royal houses of Europe. For all that he had been consecrated by the Pope, and had been regarded as an Emperor for five years, there must have been times when he was very conscious of his own parvenu status. Having proved himself superior to every king in Europe on the battlefield, he wanted to prove himself at least their equal in the drawing room. For all the pomp with which he surrounded himself ("One cannot conceive all that passed through his head in reference to it," said Madame de Rémusat), for all the rigid code he had introduced into the Tuileries, there was something missing when he set himself against these legitimate kings in their long-standing courts. They might be less brilliant, they might be less powerful, but there was an indefinable aura about them which established their superiority. And to Napoleon, any sense of inferiority was unbearable. There was nothing that he could do about the fact of his own humble birth, but he could at least link himself to one of the noblest families in Europe. This alliance would consolidate his position amongst the family of kings, and from it would spring a line of half-royal children. It was a tempting prospect.

A rather extraordinary incident helped him to make his decision. One day, while reviewing his troops in the great courtyard of Schönbrunn Palace, a well-dressed young man approached him. He seemed to be about to present a petition. When asked by one of Napoleon's attendant generals what he wanted, he replied that he wished to speak to Napoleon. He was turned away, but a few seconds later he again approached to within a foot or so of the Emperor. The general, suspicious of the young man's determined air and of the fact that he kept his right hand in his coat pocket, had him arrested. On him was found an enormous kitchen knife. When, after the review, Napoleon was told about the youngster and his knife, he asked to have him brought before him.

"What were you going to do with your knife?" asked the Emperor.

"Kill you," answered the young man.

"Why did you mean to kill me?"

"Because you are the bane of my country."

"Have I done you any harm?"

"Yes. Me and all Germans."

"Who sent you? Who has encouraged you to do this crime?"

"No one," answered the youth calmly. "It is my deep-seated conviction that by killing you I should do the greatest service to my country and to Europe."

Napoleon, thinking him mad, had him examined by his doctor, but the latter pronounced the youth quite sane. He was tried and shot a few days later. His last words were, "Liberty forever! Germany forever! Death to the tyrant!"

The incident seems to have disturbed Napoleon profoundly. He had always considered himself the friend of people such as this youngster; he could not understand why he, the champion of the ordinary man, should have his life threatened by a middle-class boy like this. If he were indeed so much hated by the common people of Europe, might not someone else try to assassinate him? And if someone else were successful, what would become of his life's work, of his great Empire?

Napoleon returned from Schönbrunn towards the end of October 1809. "My mother," writes Hortense, "instead of being delighted, felt her heart sink." Josephine was certain that Napoleon meant to divorce her at last. From the very moment of their meeting she realized that he was preparing her for the blow. They were to have met at Fontainebleau, but she arrived at the palace a little later than he. When he did not come down to meet her carriage, she entered the palace and went in search of him. He was in the library. "Ah, Madame, there you are!" he said brusquely, not looking up from his writing. "It's just as well that you have come, as I was going to start for Saint-Cloud." Josephine began to mumble an apology, but he cut her short and dismissed her.

That night she discovered that the door connecting their private apartments had been blocked up. His subsequent behavior confirmed all her suspicions. He made sure that they were never left alone for a moment; he began paying all sorts of elaborate attention to the members of his own family; he took advantage of the mistress provided for him by Pauline. He became, says Hortense, "unjust and plaguing." And yet he said nothing. Josephine, knowing that her days were numbered, but not wanting to force the issue, suffered "torturing anxieties."

It was at the end of November that he finally broached the subject. By now they were back at the Tuileries. The Emperor and Empress had hardly spoken to each other for days. Josephine came down to dinner on that last day of November wearing a large white hat tied under her chin; its broad brim shadowed her pale face and her tear-ravaged eyes. Not a word was exchanged between them during the meal; the only sounds were the clatter of plates and the occasional nervous tapping of the Emperor's knife against his glass. They ate nothing. Their attendants stood about the room as motionless as statues. Once Napoleon sighed and asked Bausset, a prefect of the palace, what the weather was like. He did not seem to hear the answer.

Having sat at the table for ten minutes, Napoleon rose. Josephine, pressing a handkerchief to her lips to stifle her sobs, followed him into the drawing room. When the coffee was served, the Emperor, not waiting for his wife to pour, helped himself and then handed his cup back to the page. Josephine simply stood there, reports Constant, "in a sort of stupor." Napoleon then signaled the company to leave him alone with the Empress. He closed the door. Bausset and Constant stationed themselves just outside. The silence about the two young men was oppressive. It was suddenly broken by the sound of the Empress's shrieks. The two men rushed towards the closed door, and at that moment the Emperor opened it and said quickly, "Come in, Bausset, and close the door." During the few seconds that the door was ajar, Constant saw

Josephine lying full length on the floor, sobbing bitterly. "No, no, you won't do it," she cried out. "You don't want to kill me!"

When Bausset entered the drawing room, he was asked by Napoleon to carry the hysterical Empress up the private staircase leading to her apartments. As he lifted her, her moans stopped, and he imagined her to have fainted. The private staircase being extremely narrow, Napoleon was obliged to take Josephine's legs while Bausset held her round the waist, with her back resting against his chest and her head lolling on his right shoulder. Holding their immobile burden, the two men stumbled up the steep stairway. Bausset, struggling to keep from tripping over his ceremonial sword, was extremely worried about the state of the unconscious Empress. Suddenly, at a moment when his head was bent close to hers, she whispered; "You're gripping me too tight."

"I then saw," reports the worthy Bausset, "that I had nothing to fear for her health, and that she had not lost consciousness for a moment."

Reaching her apartment, they laid her on a sofa and called for her women.

Throughout this painful scene Bausset had been so worried about the Empress that he had hardly noticed Napoleon. But now that her women had taken over, he followed Napoleon into a small room leading off Josephine's bedroom. The Emperor was in a terrible state. "The interest of France and of my dynasty has done violence to my heart," he blurted out to the embarrassed Bausset. "Divorce has become a binding duty. . . . I am all the more distressed by the scene Josephine has just made because it is three days since she must have learned from Hortense of the unhappy obligation which condemns me to part from her. . . . I pity her with all my soul."

So violent were his feelings that he had to make long pauses between each sentence. His voice, says Bausset, was agitated and choked, and his eyes were filled with tears. "He must have been really beside himself, to enter into so many details with one so remote by station from his counsels and confidence."

The following day the Emperor sent for Hortense. Embarrassed before this admirable young woman whose mother he was about to discard, he affected an abrupt manner. "You have seen your mother," he snapped. "She has spoken to you. My decision is made. It is irrevocable. All France desires a divorce and claims it loudly. I cannot oppose my country's will. So nothing will move me, neither prayers nor tears."

"Sire," answered Hortense, who had not the slightest intention of either praying or crying, "you are free to do as you think fit. No one will try to oppose you. Since your happiness exacts this step, that is enough; we shall know how to sacrifice ourselves. Do not be surprised at my mother's tears; it would have been surprising if, after fifteen years of married life, she shed none. But she will submit, I am convinced; and we shall all go, remembering only the kindness you have shown us."

At this Napoleon's air of reserve crumbled. In a voice thick with emotion, he begged them not to leave him. Her mother would always be his dearest friend, he claimed; her brother Eugéne would continue to be like a son to him; she herself, if only for her children's sake, must never dream of leaving him. Again and again he protested that he was divorcing Josephine for the sake of his country only; "the one way of assuring the future peace of France was to leave his throne to his own child."

"Sire," answered Hortense, "my duty is towards my mother. She will need me. We can no longer live near you. That is a sacrifice we must make. We are prepared to make it."

When Eugène arrived from Italy in answer to Napoleon's summons, the Emperor went through a similar scene with him. Eugène, like Hortense, was eager to make a clean break. Although Eugène stood to lose so much more than Hortense (as Napoleon's adopted son he might have become Emperor, or at least King of Italy), he told Napoleon that he wanted to start life afresh, "far from the court and its intrigues." But the Emperor would not hear of it. He wanted all three of them to remain close to him. "I need you," he said to Eugène. "Your sister cannot leave me either. She owes that to her children, my own nephews. Nor does her mother wish it either. . . . Stay with me unless you wish it said that the Empress was repudiated and abandoned, and that perhaps she deserved it."

His arguments, which had already won over the weak-willed Josephine, now convinced her children as well. They decided not to cut themselves off from him but to carry on very much as before. Josephine was to retain her title of Empress; she would be allowed to live at Malmaison and would be given two other houses; she would receive an annual income from the national exchequer and the privy purse. Eugène refused Napoleon's offer of a kingdom, lest it be interpreted as a reward for falling in with the Emperor's plans. "Cost us what it might," wrote Hortense, "we resolved to let our thoughts dwell only in the honorable position assured to our mother. Our wishes were subordinated to her interests."

But the worst was not yet over for poor Josephine. Paris was crowded with royalties gathered to celebrate Napoleon's victory at

Wagram and the anniversary of his coronation. Still his Empress, Josephine was obliged to play her part in these splendid public functions. She played it with all her customary grace, but Constant noticed that her expression was one of "gloomy thoughtfulness," and that her pale cheeks were always brightened with rouge. There was a Te Deum in Notre Dame, a State Opening of the Legislative Body, a banquet at the Tuileries, and a reception at the Hôtel de Ville. And then came the most heartbreaking ceremony of all, the signing of the deed of separation.

The arranging of the divorce had presented no problem to Napoleon. His civil courts annulled the civil ceremony of 1796; his ecclesiastical courts annulled the religious ceremony of 1804. It only remained for the deed of separation to be signed. At nine o'clock on the evening of December 15, the Imperial family assembled in Napoleon's study at the Tuileries. Eyes bright with triumph, they took their places to witness the downfall of Josephine. Except for Joseph—desperately defending his crown in Spain—Elisa, who was pregnant, and the independent Lucien, they were all there: the parsimonious Madame Mère; the surly Louis; the skittish Jérôme; the boastful Murat; Joseph's modest wife, Julie; Jérôme's devoted wife, Catherine of Württemberg; the lovely, empty-headed Pauline and the scheming, unscrupulous Caroline. This was the moment towards which they had all been working for years. Eugène Beauharnais stood beside Napoleon; he was trembling so violently that it seemed as if he must fall. Josephine, wearing a perfectly plain white dress with no ornament whatsoever, entered on the arm of the sobbing Hortense. She seated herself in an armchair in the center of the room. She seemed quite calm.

She did not remain calm for long. When Napoleon, himself in a highly emotional state, had read aloud his statement, she had to read hers. She got no further than the first few words, and then fell back, sobbing, into her chair; the speech had to be finished for her. That over, there was the record of the proceedings to be signed. Napoleon's signature came first, then hers, and then the triumphant signatures of all the other Bonapartes. Barely able to walk, Josephine left the room on the arm of Hortense. She was Napoleon's wife no longer.

Later that night, when the Emperor had gone to bed and his valet Constant had not yet left him, the bedroom door was suddenly flung open, and Josephine, red-eyed and disheveled, burst into the room. She tottered towards the Emperor's bed, and sobbing violently, threw her arms about his neck. At this he, too, was reduced to tears. "Come, come, Josephine my love, don't give way like this," he murmured, "come, you must be brave, you must be brave! I shall always be your friend." Choked with tears, Josephine could make no reply, and for a few minutes there was no sound other than their mutual sobbing. Suddenly Napoleon realized that his valet was still there. "Constant, leave the room," he said thickly. The valet obeyed and withdrew to an adjoining room. An hour later he saw the Empress leave the Emperor's apartment and return to her own.

The following day she left the Tuileries for Malmaison. Wearing a heavy veil and leaning on the arm of her daughter, she made her way through the crowd of silent court officials gathered in the hallway of the palace. She held a handkerchief to her eyes. "Everyone present was moved to tears as this adorable woman crossed the short distance to her carriage," says Constant. She stepped into it without so much as a backward glance at the home which she was leaving forever. The coachman slapped the reins and the carriage swung away into the rain-dark afternoon.

"If he is happy," she said to Hortense, "I shall not regret what I have done."

It was ironic that it should be through Josephine, sacrificed in the interests of the dynasty, that the dynasty would, in the end, be continued. Her grandson (Hortense's youngest boy), and not Napoleon's own son, would re-establish the Empire. And it is interesting to trace her characteristics—her seductive charm, her prodigious tact, her genuine kind-heartedness—through successive generations of the dynasty. Hortense, her son Napoleon III, and his son the Prince Imperial, all had something of Josephine's ability to win hearts and inspire loyalty. As her presence had always soothed the rough edges of Napoleon's personality, so did her Beauharnais strain live on to soften and civilize the Bonaparte characteristics of the coming generations.

♔   ♔   ♔

The Bonapartes now sprang into action. Having intrigued for fifteen years to get rid of one "stranger" in the family, they were resolved not to have another. Corsicans first and royalties second, they were determined that Napoleon should marry within the family. Only thus could they be sure that their positions, and more important, their brother's enormous fortune, would remain secure; they did not want him marrying another extravagant woman with a family of her own to elevate and support. Nor did the idea of some match with a foreign princess appeal to them; clannish to the core, only a woman of their own Corsican blood would be good enough. Here was an excellent opportunity for consolidating the family. But who was there for him to marry? Most of his nieces were hardly out of their nurseries; the eldest of them was just fourteen years old—and she was Charlotte, the daughter of the exiled Lucien. But the ever-vigilant Madame Mère now saw in this girl an opportunity of killing two birds with one stone. Napoleon and Lucien would be reconciled at last and France would have a Bonaparte empress.

Three days before Napoleon's divorce was finalized, she wrote to Lucien to tell him the glad news. Always having believed that Lucien's continued exile was Josephine's fault, she now assured him that with Josephine out of the way and Hortense living apart from Louis, Napoleon was much more kindly disposed towards his own family. His sentiments were already "quite different from what they have been hitherto." All that was now needed for a *rapprochement* was for Lucien to divorce his wife, and then, wrote Madame Mère optimistically, "we shall all be contented." There was no reason why he should not start this new relationship by sending his daughter Charlotte, known as Lolotte, to spend some time with her in Paris.

The family were determined to press their candidate on Napoleon as soon as she arrived. "Up to the present," wrote Elisa to Lucien, "nothing gives me any inkling as to who will be the new wife of the Emperor. If any prayers were heard, this choice [Lolotte] would put an end to a division very painful to my heart." But Lucien did not seem to feel nearly as strongly about the proposed match as the rest of his relations. He knew exactly what Napoleon's terms would be, and he was not prepared to comply. Letizia's fervent letters to Lucien, however, led him to believe that Napoleon might be prepared to recognize his wife, Alexandrine, after all, while her equally fervent discussions with Napoleon led him to believe that Lucien was about to yield to his demands. In December 1809 Lucien despatched an envoy named Campi to Paris to discuss with Napoleon the whole question of their relationship. Napoleon and Campi decided that Lolotte would be sent to Paris to stay with her grandmother (the Emperor seems to have known nothing of the marriage scheme as yet), but when it came to the matter of Lucien's own marriage, Napoleon remained firm. "I don't mean to recognize a woman who has been brought into the family in spite of me," said Napoleon. "Lucien has always deceived me. . . . I blame myself for having recognized even his first marriage, and for not having had Madame Jouberthon arrested."

When Campi reported back, Lucien was extremely disappointed at the outcome of the discussions. Campi's news, he claimed, destroyed all his hopes. There would be no question of his ever divorcing his wife. Campi, primed by Napoleon, waited until Lucien was away from home, and then tackled Alexandrine herself about the divorce. Like Lucien, she refused to consider it. She regretted, she said, "that she could not conform to what his Majesty described as political necessities."

If Alexandrine, at the time of her marriage to Lucien, had been a young woman of somewhat uncertain virtue, she was now a matron of irreproachable honor. Ambitious and flamboyant in her youth, she had developed into a true Roman mother—proud, passionate, devoted to her home and family. She shared many of her husband's tastes, and in spite of the fact that Lucien was not always faithful, they were a well-matched couple. Her unswerving loyalty did much towards alleviating the irritations of his continued exile. Although divorce between them was out of the question, they agreed that there was no reason why Lucien's daughter Lolotte should not go to Paris. By the time they finally sent her off, however, Napoleon had already chosen his new empress. Letizia's dream of a Bonaparte empress faded, although she did not give up hope of a reconciliation between her sons. If Lolotte could not share Napoleon's throne, she might at least be a means of drawing her father nearer it.

Lolotte and Campi arrived in Paris in March 1810. "As soon as her clothes are ready, I shall take her to the Emperor," wrote Letizia to Lucien, "and I am sure that she will be kindly received. I will write and tell you about it tomorrow. Heaven grant that, at the same time, I will be able to tell you of the only thing that my happiness lacks—your reconciliation."

But that was not to be. Although Napoleon was quite impressed by his niece (she had the Bonaparte features and all the Bonaparte assurance), she in no way softened his attitude towards her parents. Madame Mère, bitterly disappointed at the failure of her plans, wrote a despairing letter to Alexandrine, begging her to give up her husband. "It is the only way to escape the disgrace which threatens him, as well as your children . . . ," she wrote. "Do not hesitate between a life of sorrow and bitterness which you must expect if you are obstinate, and the prospect of a happy future, in which your children will be recognized by the Emperor and may succeed to crowns. . . ."

But Alexandrine had seen enough of the bickering and backbiting and jockeying for position which characterized those to whom Napoleon had given crowns; all she wanted was to be allowed to "live in peace in some corner" of her brother-in-law's empire.

In the meantime Lolotte, instead of bringing Napoleon and Lucien closer together, was driving them further apart. Intensely loyal to her father and stepmother, she resented some of the things she heard said about them in Madame Mère's household. Her letters home were loaded with complaints about her grandmother's avarice and spiced with gossip about the behavior of her uncles and aunts. As these letters were sent by ordinary mail and not by special courier, they were opened, copied, and resealed. This was all part of the postal system of the Grand Empire. The copies were sent to Napoleon, who, according to one of his secretaries, "amused himself by reading them one Sunday in the presence of his family, assembled after a family dinner in the drawing room of Saint-Cloud." As each member of the family had been "made the target of a more or less well-directed satire," Napoleon's amusement soon turned to anger. Extremely annoyed at his niece's ungrateful behavior, he arranged for her to be sent home the very next day. She, of course, was delighted.

"Ah! my little Papa, you were right about not wanting to go up there," she cried out on reaching home once more. "I am sure that America would be better."

Lucien, in fact, had for some time been considering leaving Europe and starting afresh in America. Now, with the last hope of a reconciliation gone, his mind was made up. Accompanied by his wife, his six children (two by Christine Boyer and four by Alexandrine), his chaplain, his doctor, his brother-in-law, his secretary, his children's tutor, an artist, and twenty-three servants, Lucien embarked on the *Hercules,* an American ship bound for the United States. He was the first of Napoleon's brothers to consider seeking refuge in America; it was soon to become a very popular haven for dethroned Bonapartes.

But he never reached there. The *Hercules* was stopped by a British frigate off the coast of Sardinia, and Lucien surrendered himself as a prisoner of war. He and his family were taken to Malta, where they seem to have been imprisoned in some style, and then, having spent three months amid "very pleasant surroundings," they were shipped off to England. They arrived off Plymouth on December, 12, 1810, and landed the following day.

He stepped ashore a hero. His lifelong opposition to Britain's arch-enemy had made him an immensely popular figure in England; cheering crowds turned out to greet him, and although technically a prisoner of war, he was overwhelmed with messages of welcome and offers of hospitality. The British newspapers had a field day. Such was Bonaparte's tyranny, they said, that even his relations could no longer endure it and were obliged to seek refuge in Britain, "the home of true freedom." Lucien accepted Lord Powis's offer of his country seat near Ludlow, and having spent a few weeks there, bought himself an estate called Thorngrove in Worcestershire. Here he arranged all his treasures—his books, pictures, statues, busts, bronzes, and gems—and resigned himself to the life of an English country gentleman. Both he and Alexandrine devoted themselves to writing, to the education of their children, and to the development of the estate. He lived, says one of his friends, "like a really wise man, without any false pretensions to philosophy. His style of life excited much curiosity in England, but he studiously retired from observation with a calm and natural dignity which inspired general respect."

It must all have seemed a long, long way from the tinseled splendors of his brother's empire; an empire more splendid now that it had as its Empress a princess of the long-established and indubitably royal house of Hapsburg.

CHAPTER SIX

⚜   ⚜   ⚜

IN April 1810 Napoleon married the Archduchess Marie Louise, eldest daughter of the Emperor Francis I of Austria.

It must have been of some slight consolation to the ex-Empress Josephine to know that at the time of her divorce, Napoleon had no idea of whom his next empress would be. He was not, therefore, marrying for love; what he was marrying, he admitted frankly, was a womb. But whose womb was it to be? As early as 1807 a list of marriageable princesses, their ages ranging from twelve to eighteen years, had been drawn up for Napoleon's inspection, and by February 1810 he had definitely decided on the Archduchess Marie Louise. Characteristically, having once made up his mind, he lost no time in getting the business settled. The Emperor Francis, so recently defeated by Napoleon at Wagram, cynically approved the marriage contract, and Marshal Berthier was dispatched to Vienna to claim the Archduchess's hand. They were married by proxy in Vienna on March 11, the Archduke Charles standing in for the Emperor of the French. Two days later the young bride, sobbing her heart out at the prospect of leaving her adored father and, worse still, of uniting herself with his archenemy, left Austria for France. At the Austro-Bavarian border she was met by the sweetly smiling, ostensibly solicitous Caroline, who had been sent by Napoleon to accompany his new wife on her long journey to Compiègne.

As yet Napoleon had no idea what Marie Louise looked like. He would overwhelm with questions any pages or aides-de-camp who had seen her, but none of their polite answers seemed to supply him with a complete picture.

"Tell me frankly," he said to one aide-de-camp recently returned from Vienna. "How did the Archduchess Marie Louise impress you?"

"Most favorably, Sire," he answered correctly.

" 'Most favorably' does not convey any information," said Napoleon tersely. "Come now, how tall is she?"

"Sire, she is a good height," replied the cautious young man; and then, sensing the Emperor's exasperation, added, "about as tall as the Queen [Hortense] of Holland."

"Ah! that is very nice. What color is her hair?"

"Fair, much like that of the Queen of Holland," replied the aide, realizing that he had pleased his master.

"Good," said Napoleon. "And her complexion?"

"Very white, with a very bright color, like the Queen of Holland," came the pat answer.

"Ah!" said the delighted Emperor, "then she is like the Queen of Holland?"

"No, Sire," answered the adroit young man, "and yet I have given an absolutely truthful answer to every question you have asked."

Napoleon dismissed him, and turning to Talleyrand, said, "I cannot get a word out of them! I see that my wife is ugly, for not one of these confounded young fellows has been able to say that she is pretty. Well, as long as she is kind and bears me healthy sons, I will love her as though she is the most beautiful woman on earth."

The trouble was that Marie Louise was neither ugly nor beautiful; "More ugly than pretty, she has a very fine figure," was how Metternich summed up her looks. What might have been a soft, gentle face was marred by the heavy Hapsburg jaw and the somewhat prominent teeth. Her skin, when looked at closely, was slightly scarred from smallpox. Her figure, although good, was graceless; compared with the lithe Josephine, she was like a block of wood. But at eighteen years of age she had youth on her side. She had a big, healthy body; a mane of fair hair; bright, if somewhat vague blue eyes; and firm rosy cheeks. "Everyone thought her very well-looking, very tall, much better than they expected," was one comment on her arrival in France.

And in the same way that her looks were neither good nor bad, so did her character evade definition. Hers was essentially a negative personality; she had always to be seen in relation to others, she appeared to have no mind of her own. There was an elusiveness about her, a quality of indifference; one did not know what to think of her, or what she herself was thinking. She was a simple, modest, innocent, unambitious girl, yet she remained strangely unattractive. One could sympathize with her, but one could never get to like her.

Her upbringing was largely responsible for this lack of character. Reared in the cloistered, formal, old-fashioned court which revolved around her father, the Austrian Emperor, her days had been carefully mapped out; she had never had to make a decision in her life. Sheltered from any contact with the harsh world beyond the palace walls (her pets were all female, even her lesson books were censored), she had developed into an unquestioning, obedient young girl, always conscious of her duty towards her all-powerful father. He was the center of her world, the fountainhead from which she derived all her benefits, the master from whom she took her commands. For Marie Louise had always to have someone to tell her what to do; like a looking glass, she could mirror but never originate an image; like the moon, her light was merely a reflection of the sun's rays.

But even she, docile creature that she was, found it difficult to comply with her father's wish that she marry Napoleon. Brought up to look upon him as nothing less than an ogre, the thought of being married to him appalled her. But her tears and her pleadings made no impression on her indifferent father; he was kind but firm, and in the end she gave way. At no stage did she ever dream of actually refusing to comply with his wishes; and now he was able to announce that his daughter had "surrendered herself to her fate with patience and wisdom."

She surrendered herself, in fact, with trepidation. Like someone enduring a bad dream, she went ahead with the preparations for her marriage. For a week Vienna was *en fête,* and the young Archduchess, manipulated by the wily Metternich, moved like a marionette through the various ceremonies preparatory to her departure. The climax of these fetes was the wedding by proxy; seldom had the old Augustinian Church seen so brilliant an assembly or, it might be added, so passive a bride. On the morning that she left Vienna, her father offered her a final piece of advice. "As soon as you are alone with the Emperor, you must do absolutely everything he tells you. You must agree to everything that he asks you. . . . Understand that, Maria Louisa." She understood it. The one thing which Marie Louise understood perfectly was how to obey.

It was at the frontier town of Braunau that she was met by Caroline Murat, Queen of Naples. Napoleon, now that he was about to mingle his own bourgeois blood with the bluest blood in Europe, was determined to combine the new Napoleonic splendor with the old Bourbon protocol. The last Hapsburg bride to come to France had been Marie Louise's great-aunt, Marie Antoinette; not only were the details of her reception to be closely followed, they were to be improved upon. Where the Bourbons had sent a princess to receive Marie Antoinette, the Bonapartes were to send a queen. The fact that she was very much a parvenu queen and that the throne she occupied belonged by right to Marie Louise's grandmother, the ex-Queen of Naples, was unfortunate, but Caroline hoped, by lavish use of her somewhat synthetic charm, to turn their meeting to good account.

The news that Napoleon had decided to marry Marie Louise had come as a distinct shock to Joachim and Caroline Murat. For years they had worked to get rid of Josephine; they had hoped for some obscure, pliable Empress who could easily come under their sway. Instead, Napoleon, by turning his face towards the foremost royal house in Europe, would probably turn his back on his own family. Who knew, if his royal bride were to gain sufficient influence over him, he might, in his new *ancien régime* mood, give Naples back to its rightful rulers. To combat this possibility, Caroline was determined to be the first to gain the confidence of the new Empress. She would use every trick to win her over.

She failed utterly. From the very first moment of meeting, Marie Louise took an instinctive dislike to Caroline Murat. Chic, vivacious, and self-assertive, Caroline made her greeting so effusive that this inelegant, stolid, timid German girl was put on her guard immediately. In an extraordinarily misspelled and unpunctuated letter to her father, the Emperor, Marie Louise mentioned her reservations with regard to the overfriendly Caroline. "Oh Lord, what a difference between the French and Viennese ladies! The Queen of Naples kissed me and behaved in a very friendly way to me, but I do not trust her; I do not believe that zeal to be of service was the sole motive of her journey. . . ."

It was not, and as the long journey towards France progressed, it became more and more obvious to Marie Louise that Caroline was trying to gain control over her. At Munich, Caroline dismissed the Countess Lazanski, Marie Louise's only Austrian companion, and from then on hardly ever let the young Empress out of her sight. But the more she tried to ingratiate herself, the more stubbornly did Marie Louise resist her advances. To Napoleon, Caroline wrote tactfully: "It is enough to see Marie Louise to fall in love with her"; what she really thought of this shy, suspicious, uncommunicative daughter of the Hapsburgs, she kept to herself.

As it was at the château of Compiègne that Marie Antoinette's bridegroom had awaited her arrival, Napoleon was determined to do no less for his bride. He had the palace redecorated at vast expense, and then filled it with the brilliantly gowned and uniformed members of his brand-new aristocracy. At his sister Pauline's insistence, he got Murat's celebrated tailor to make him some new clothes, and even tried to get Hortense to teach him to dance. With the exception of Joseph, who was still battling in Spain, and of course, Lucien, he assembled his entire family to welcome the new Empress. Queen Julie of Spain was there, King Louis and Queen Hortense of Holland, King Jérôme and Queen Catherine of

Westphalia, King Joachim of Naples, Princess Elisa, Princess Pauline, and Prince Eugène and his wife, Princess Augusta. The ex-Empress Josephine had tactfully retired to her new château of Navarre.

"As for the Emperor," says Hortense, "his mind was entirely taken up by the thought of his young wife." He had at last seen a portrait of her, and was thrilled to recognize the famous Austrian underlip. "Ah!" he exclaimed, "that is indeed the Hapsburg lip." No matter that it was her ugliest feature; it was the hallmark of the noblest family in Europe, and worth half-a-dozen perfectly modeled Bonaparte mouths. He had taken to sending her letters each day, and she, ever conscious of her duty and a little touched by his attentions, had taken to answering them. In fact, after the first few days she found herself looking forward to his little notes; it was almost fun deciphering that terrible handwriting. "By degrees," says Constant, "her answers became longer and more cordial, so that the Emperor read them with evident pleasure." Imperceptibly, with the Austrian night behind her, she turned her gaze towards the rising sun of France.

By now Napoleon was almost beside himself with impatience. Her cortege seemed to be taking such an age to reach Compiègne. When he heard that it would reach Soissons, the stage before Compiègne, on Wednesday evening and Compiègne the following day, he decided to wait no longer. On Wednesday afternoon he and Joachim Murat clambered into a carriage and drove through the blinding rain in search of the slowly approaching procession. When they reached it, the Emperor, bundled up in his old gray redingote, leaped out of his own carriage, dashed through the rain towards the Empress's coach, wrenched open the door, and flung himself inside. As someone had shouted "*Vive l'Empereur*" a second before Napoleon's assault, the startled Marie Louise did at least have the consolation of knowing that this small wet man embracing her so eagerly was indeed her husband. Nor did his eagerness stop there. Finding her very much to his taste, he decided that the cortege would not stop the night at Soissons after all, but continue on to Compiègne. That poor Marie Louise was feeling tired and looking disheveled bothered him not at all. The horses were lashed on through the rain-dark night, and it was almost ten o'clock by the time they reached the château. Here the exhausted Marie Louise had to face the critical stares of Napoleon's assembled court and to submit herself to the embraces of his various relations. Even these courtesies he cut short and hurried her off to their private apartments. Although they were not to be married until some days later (there was to be a civil wedding on April 1 and a religious one the next day), such formalities did not bother Napoleon. He had married Marie Louise with the sole purpose of providing himself with an heir, and he was going to waste no time about it. Lord Liverpool was right in considering Napoleon's conduct that night to be rather "more of a rape than a wooing."

"My friend," said the beaming Emperor to one of his generals the following morning, "you ought to marry a German girl. They are the best women in the world, sweet-tempered, kind, and as fresh as roses."

♧   ♧   ♧

The religious ceremony on April 2 precipitated another family row. It was again a question of the Empress's mantle. One would have imagined that the objections of Napoleon's sisters to carrying Josephine's train in 1804 could not possibly have been raised again on this occasion. Marie Louise was a princess of one of the oldest royal houses in Europe, and the Bonaparte sisters did not, as yet, harbor any personal feelings against her. But still they refused to carry her mantle. The humiliation to which they were now being subjected was even greater, they claimed, than it had been in Josephine's day; then they had been mere courtesy princesses, now they were queens or sovereign princesses. Caroline was particularly adamant about not having to fulfill this "servile function." As she had *accompanied* and not *attended* the Empress on her journey to France, she thought it right that she should continue to play this role at her wedding. The fact that she was able to cite a Bourbon precedent for her attitude won the day, and Napoleon let her have her way. Queen Julie of Spain, Queen Catherine of Westphalia, and the Princesses Elisa and Pauline had no such precedent to fall back on. They presented themselves in a body at the house of Madame Mère in an effort to get her to champion their cause. Letizia, who had by now learned not to bite the hand that fed her, gave them no encouragement. She reminded them that Napoleon was accustomed to being obeyed; he might be in the wrong on this occasion, but "if he persists in his demand, you must do as he bids you." At that very moment the Emperor himself entered, and giving his mother a grateful look, reduced the women to silence with a few harsh words.

It might have been on this occasion, or after another of those numerous family mutinies, that Napoleon gave vent to an exasperated tirade against his relations. His three sisters were in the room at the time. "I don't believe any man in the world is more unfortunate in his family than I am," he exclaimed. "Suppose we sum up. Lucien is an ingrate. Joseph is a Sardanapalus. Louis is a paralytic. Jérôme, a scamp."

"As for you ladies," he said, lowering his eyes and dropping his voice, "*you know what you are.*"

They might or might not have known what they were, but they knew they did not want to be train-bearers to the Empress Marie Louise. But Napoleon remained firm. On the day of the ceremony Queen Caroline; Eugène's wife, Augusta; and Princess Stéphanie of Baden walked ahead of the Empress carrying tapers, while behind, supporting the famous train, walked Julie of Spain, Hortense of Holland, Catherine of Westphalia, and the Princesses Elisa and Pauline. Hortense, who seldom complained about anything other than the churlish behavior of her husband, must have been slightly put out to know that the train she was helping to carry was the very one which her mother had worn at her coronation six years before. Indeed, throughout the magnificent ceremony Hortense noticed the spectators glancing at Eugène and herself in order to note their reactions. "I sincerely believed," says Hortense, "that my mother was happier in her quiet retreat than surrounded with all this pomp. . . ."

As Marie Louise, in a dress weighted with diamonds, a crown heavy with jewels, and a mantle barely supported by a group of surly sisters-in-law, moved like an automaton through a succession of ceremonies, spectators could not help comparing her with her predecessor. On these great public occasions Josephine had always been at her best; Marie Louise was at her worst. The upstart Empress had known how to dress, how to move, how to smile, how to talk; the princess of the oldest royal house in Europe was as inelegant, as stiff, as expressionless, and as tongue-tied as a schoolgirl. "Nothing," said Constant with a wealth of meaning, "could have been more different from the first Empress than the second." Josephine seemed to have had all the qualities of the aristocrat; Marie Louise, those of the bourgeois.

Years later Napoleon himself summed up the differences between his two wives. "The one (Josephine) was all art and grace; the other (Marie Louise) was all innocence and simplicity. At no moment of her life had the ways and habits of the former ever been other than pleasant and seductive. It would have been impossible to find fault with her in this respect. She made the art of pleasing her constant study, obtaining her effect while concealing her method of doing so. Every artifice imaginable was employed by her to heighten her charms, yet so mysteriously that at most one had but the merest suspicion of it. Marie Louise, on the other hand, ignored artifice and anything like dissimilation; all roundabout methods were unknown to her. The former never asked for anything, but was in debt everywhere. The latter, if in want of anything, never hesitated to ask, nor did she ever purchase anything without feeling conscientiously obliged to pay at once. Both had kind, sweet dispositions and were deeply attached to their husband."

Once the wedding festivities were over and the bride and groom had retired to the comparative seclusion of Compiègne, they began to take an increasing delight in each other's company. Napoleon, who had half expected some vain, petulant, decadent princess, was filled with admiration for this unaffected, good-natured, diligent young girl. Only just out of the schoolroom, she had not yet shaken its habits of discipline, and certain hours each day were put aside for her drawing lessons, her embroidery lessons and her reading periods. Compared with Josephine who, according to Madame de Rémusat, was too idle ever to toy with a little handwork, Marie Louise was extremely industrious. And in thrift she could equal any Corsican woman. "It is those qualities by which the Empress is kin to the good housewife class of woman that he [Napoleon] values most in her," reported Metternich to the Emperor Francis.

And she, in her dependent way, adored him. To her father she wrote: "I can only repeat to you how happy and contented I am and, I am convinced, always shall be. You will only understand this when you come to know the Emperor personally. Then you will see how good and lovable he is in private life, and what a noble-hearted man he is. I am persuaded that you would love him too." She had come to France expecting a monster, and had found a dumpy, affectionate, entertaining middle-aged man instead. Marie Louise had a way of not concerning herself with things which did not affect her personally, and to her Napoleon was simply a kind and attentive husband. Not long after her marriage she remarked to Metternich that she felt some of the Viennese imagined her being subjected to "daily torments," whereas, in fact, she was not a bit afraid of Napoleon. "But I am beginning to think," she added, "that he is a little afraid of me."

He was not afraid of her, of course, but he was still a little in awe of her. To him, she was still something of a symbol; she represented his ultimate triumph. Through her he had at last achieved respectability; through her he had related himself to almost every royal house in Europe; through her he would establish the fourth French dynasty, and thus achieve immortality.

And yet, far from feeling inadequate beside her, far from feeling the need to watch himself lest he betray his plebeian origins before this palace-born princess, it was he who had to guide and instruct her in the business of being an empress. Her shyness gave her a cold, withdrawn manner; she had no memory for names and faces; she had not the slightest idea of how to make conversation. Loathing public appearances, receptions were a form of torture to her; someone once swore that as she came up to be presented to the Imperial pair, Napoleon whispered urgently to Marie Louise: *"Pleine de grâce, pleine de grâce."*

But if she was something of a disappointment to him in public, she was everything he could wish for in private. "He has told me twenty times," reported Metternich to the Emperor Francis, "that he has never had a home, although he has often yearned for one, but that since his marriage, his longing has become a reality." Happily, Marie Louise kept very aloof from Napoleon's brothers and sisters; the only member of the family with whom she was at all friendly was Hortense. Before her marriage Metternich had warned her that although Princess Pauline was the most beautiful woman in the world, and Queen Caroline the wittiest, Queen Hortense would be the only one of whom she could make a friend. And it was true. Any slight chance that there might have been of her becoming friendly with Pauline had been ruined by the latter's outrageous behavior. One day Pauline made a rude sign with her fingers behind the Empress's back; unfortunately for the impish princess, Napoleon happened to see her gesture reflected in a looking glass. His reaction can be imagined.

But although Marie Louise avoided the adult members of her husband's family, she and the Emperor would sometimes have his various nieces and nephews to visit them; Napoleon was particularly fond of having breakfast with these children. One morning, when Hortense's two little boys, Napoleon-Louis and Louis-Napoleon, were breakfasting with the Emperor and Empress, Napoleon diverted the youngest boy's attention and then stole his boiled egg. Little Louis-Napoleon promptly took up a knife, and pointed it towards his uncle, said: "Give me back my egg or I will kill you."

"What, you rascal," exclaimed the Emperor in mock horror, "would you kill your uncle?"

"I must have my egg," insisted the boy, "or I will kill you."

The Emperor returned the egg. "You will be a fine fellow," he laughed.

Princess Elisa's daughter Napoléone, at five years old, was already beginning to display those traits of pride and independence which were to characterize her behavior in later life. She could not endure the jokes which the Emperor was always making at her expense. "Let us return to Florence," she once said haughtily to her governess after her uncle had made her the butt of yet another joke. "I am not understood here." Marie Louise was very fond of little Napoléone. The Princess Elisa, she informed the Emperor of Austria, "is very intelligent. She's ugly, but she has a daughter . . . who is the most beautiful child I have ever seen."

By the beginning of the year 1811 Napoleon was beginning to look forward to the birth of a child of his own. His fears that he might have been too old to procreate had proved groundless. "What is the latest age at which one can still become a father?" he had asked Corvisart anxiously. "I'm only forty, but does a man of sixty who marries a young woman have children?"

"Sometimes, Sire."

"And a man of seventy?"

"Invariably," answered the doctor.

His state of jubilation on realizing that he had been successful was difficult to describe. "Look at her figure," he shouted to Hortense, pointing proudly to the *enceinte* Marie Louise. "If it is a girl, it will be a little wife for your son Napoleon, for *she* must not go out of France or marry outside the family." From now on Napoleon was unceasing in his attentions towards his wife; he showered her with gifts; he canceled any engagements which might take him away from Paris; he organized elaborate amusements for her; he personally selected a wet nurse for the unborn child; he had the famous *accoucheur* Dubois moved into the palace. Couriers were sent galloping down the long white roads to carry the news of the imminent birth to every court in Europe.

The pains began during the night of March 19. Pages were sent scurrying all over Paris to round up members of the family and various dignitaries, and from every church in the city the bells started ringing out to announce that the Empress's hour was at hand. Hortense arrived at the palace to find it jammed; even in the Empress's bedroom there was hardly room to move for the press of relations, courtiers, ladies in waiting, and doctors. Hortense, Julie, Pauline, and Eugène remained in an anteroom, and from time to time Napoleon would come in to report on what was happening in the other room. "According to whether the pain was more or less acute, he seemed more or less nervous." The fact that the labor was lasting so long distressed him; he wanted to know whether there was any way of knowing in advance what the sex of the child would be. With his heart set on having a son, he was nevertheless preparing himself for a disappointment. Towards five in the morning the Empress's pains subsided and she fell asleep. Napoleon went off to have a bath; bathing in almost scalding hot water was his favorite method of easing his tensions. On this occasion, however, he had not been in his bath for fifteen minutes when Dubois, the *accoucheur*, came rushing in. He was almost out of his mind. It was going to be an extremely difficult delivery and he did not think that he would be able to save both mother and child. Which life should he spare? Without hesitation Napoleon said that the Empress's life must be saved. "Think only of her," said the Emperor.

Struggling into his dressing gown, Napoleon followed the doctor into Marie Louise's bedroom. He embraced his wife and then stood beside her for a while, holding her hand. "Not being able, however, to master his emotion," says Constant, "he went out into an adjoining room, and there, trembling, and with ear bent to catch the slightest sound, he waited."

The child being in an abnormal position, Dubois was obliged to use forceps. The sight of them terrified poor Marie Louise. "Because I am an Empress, why must I be sacrificed?" she cried out. Finally, towards nine that morning, the child was delivered. It was a boy. For seven minutes it lay, seemingly lifeless, while Napoleon kissed and encouraged his exhausted wife; and then, by touching the baby's lips with brandy, by patting it and wrapping it in warm napkins, it was coaxed into life. Only when it uttered its first cry did Napoleon seem to notice it. Dazed, but with a dawning awareness of the fact that he now had a son, he "went alternately from mother to son, as if unable sufficiently to feast his eyes on both."

As the Emperor hurried off to give the order for the firing of the cannon to announce the birth, he bumped into Hortense.

"It is over," he said, breathing with difficulty, "she is saved."

He looked so pale and miserable that Hortense was almost afraid to ask her next question.

"Is it a boy?"

"Yes," he answered blankly, and when the delighted Hortense tried to embrace him, he pushed her aside.

"Ah!" he cried. "I cannot grasp all that happiness. The poor woman suffered so dreadfully."

It had been announced that a twenty-one-gun salute would be fired for a girl, and a hundred-and-one salute for a boy. As the twenty-second report crashed out, the vast crowd collected outside the palace seemed to go mad with joy. Hats were flung into the air, old soldiers wept unashamedly in the streets, and the spring morning was loud with shouts of "*Vive l'Empereur.*" Constant, watching the frenzied crowd from a window of the Tuileries, noticed Napoleon also peeping out from behind the curtains at his cheering subjects. He seemed to be profoundly touched by the spectacle. His eyes, says Constant, were wet with tears.

The boy was named Napoleon Francis Charles Joseph and given the title of the King of Rome. For centuries the heir to the Holy Roman Empire had been called the King of the Romans; Napoleon, who always thought of himself as the heir to Charlemagne, would be content with no less a title for his son. "I envy him, for glory awaits him, whereas I had to run after it. . . ." said Napoleon. "To take hold of the world, he will have only to stretch out his hands."

Even such a momentous event as this could not remain unsullied by a family feud. On the occasion of Marie Louise's first reception after her confinement, a state couch was prepared for her own use, and near it were placed three armchairs for the use of Madame Mère, Queen Julie of Spain, and Queen Hortense of Holland. Napoleon, coming down to inspect the seating arrangements before the reception, promptly had the three armchairs removed. His mother, he said, was not a queen, therefore she was not entitled to an armchair, and if she could not have one, then neither should Julie and Hortense. He had three stools brought in instead. When the three Imperial ladies arrived and discovered that they were not to have armchairs, "they withdrew at once with an offended air," and refused to attend the reception. "This incident," reports Madame Durand, the Empress's first lady, "increased the coolness which already existed in the private relations of the family."

♚ ♚ ♚

No sooner had Napoleon secured an heir for his Empire than it began falling apart. Of the puppet kings which he had set up to rule over the states bordering France, his brother Louis was the first to revolt. It was the old story: Napoleon wanted his brother to be a French governor and his brother wanted to be a national king. "If I made one [of my brothers] a king," sighed Napoleon on St. Helena, "he imagined that he was king by the grace of God. He was no longer my lieutenant; he was one enemy more for me to watch." Napoleon had been dissatisfied with his brother's handling of Dutch affairs for some time; in spite of all Napoleon's efforts to enforce his Continental blockade against Britain, British goods still seemed to find their way into Holland. In vain did he urge Louis to be more strict; Louis maintained that his first duty was towards his Dutch subjects, particularly the merchants. Exasperated,

Napoleon sent troops into Holland, and in March 1810 Louis was obliged to sign a treaty whereby his kingdom was considerably reduced in size. The French troops, instead of remaining on the left bank of the Meuse as agreed, penetrated ever deeper into Louis's territory. Towards the end of June, as the French were converging on Amsterdam, Louis decided to abdicate. He retired to Haarlem, where he wrote his act of abdication; he passsed the throne of Holland on to his son Napoleon-Louis, and failing him, the boy's brother, Louis-Napoleon. At midnight on July 4 he left Haarlem, and for a while no one seemed to know where he was. Napoleon, on hearing of the abdication, was afraid that Louis might have sailed for America or, like Lucien, to England. It was not until a fortnight later that he heard that Louis was at Töplitz, in Bohemia. As Töplitz was renowned for its baths, Louis would have every opportunity of spending his days in the manner he enjoyed most, caring for his ailing body.

Hortense was at Plombières when she heard the news of her husband's abdication. On the same day she received a letter from Napoleon informing her that he was going to annex Holland. Some months previously he had refused her and Louis an open separation; now he assured her that Louis's abdication had set her free. She could live tranquilly in Paris; he would not force her to live with Louis again.

As her two little sons were safe with the Emperor at Saint-Cloud, Hortense decided to join her mother at Aix-en-Savoie. And it was here that she once more took up the threads of her turbulent friendship with a young general by the name of Charles de Flahaut.

They had first met several years after Hortense's marriage to Louis. The natural son of Talleyrand, the dashing Charles de Flahaut was utterly unlike his subtle-tongued, impassive-faced father. He was two years younger than Hortense, handsome, well built, with a boyish face and an engaging manner. A typical young officer of the Napoleonic era, he had the usual predeliction for light-hearted love-making. During the first few months of their friendship Hortense had convinced herself that she was merely fond of him; it was only when Caroline Murat started to show an interest in him that she realized that she was in love. Whether he was in love with her or whether he merely wished to make use of her, the Empress's daughter, to further his own military career, one does not know, but what does seem certain is that at this stage their friendship was still platonic. When he was away on campaign, they would send each other little gifts; when he was home on leave, she would give him talks on the superiority of friendship over love. They even sang duets together.

That his affair with Caroline, which he seemed to be conducting at the same time, was equally innocent, is extremely doubtful. Just before Caroline left Paris to ascend the throne of Naples, she confessed to Hortense that she was violently in love with Flahaut, and he with her. "I dread the grief that my departure will cause him!" she cried dramatically. Pretending that she suspected nothing of Hortense's feeling for Flahaut, Caroline wanted Hortense to promise that, if he were to try and console himself with her, she would discourage him. "You are the only woman I dread," declared Caroline. "I cannot tell how you do it, but you have the secret of attracting and arousing interest. There are women much handsomer than you—myself, for instance. I know I am the prettier of us two, but you must have a charm of which I know nothing, because everyone is drawn to you. A thousand times I have tried to make Monsieur de Flahaut say he disliked you. He never would do so. . . ."

Caroline's confession that she and Flahaut were lovers made poor bewildered Hortense "more wretched than I can describe." Faced with the certain knowledge that he had deceived her, all her love for him revived. No amount of rationalizing could lessen that love or ease her pain.

Caroline Murat left for Naples, Charles de Flahaut went off to war, and Hortense resumed her quiet life in Paris. He was wounded during the Wagram campaign, and when he returned to Paris some months later, he again "renewed protestations of eternal devotion" to Hortense. But it was not until this visit to Aix-en-Savoie that she and Flahaut were alone together for more than a few hours. "For the first time since I knew that I loved him, I now saw him constantly," she says. And it was probably here that their six-year-long friendship ceased to be platonic. But even this could not secure for her his whole-hearted affection; before very long the devoted Hortense, so awkward and tongue-tied in his presence, so articulate in her letters to him, was again plunged into misery. "I was jealous with the concentrated jealousy that embitters the soul because it does not utter a word of complaint but consumes us the more for its silence." She had no illusions about Flahaut. He had a splendid presence, a good mind, a quick wit, and charming manners, but he was incapable of returning her love. "Completely absorbed by the interest of the moment in charming any woman who seemed attracted to him, he frequently hurt the feelings of another whom he seemed to have forgotten. . . ."

In September 1811, six months after the birth of the King of Rome, Hortense gave birth to Charles de Flahaut's child. The affair was shrouded in secrecy. Flahaut obtained leave from the Army, and in mid-September he met Hortense at the village of Prègny, near Aix. It had been given out that Hortense was to visit her brother Eugène in Italy and, accompanied by Flahaut, she set off on the supposed journey. At the first stop, their child was born. It was a boy.

Within a week Charles was back in Paris, and within a month Hortense was home as well. The secret had been well kept; not even the Empress Josephine knew about it. Charles de Flahaut's mother took charge of the little boy (had not her own son Charles been a love child?) and he was given the name Charles Auguste Joseph Louis Demorny—Demorny being the name of an old pensioner who had posed as the baby's father at the registration of its birth.

Some forty years hence, as the famous Duke de Morny, this child would take his place in history at the right hand of his half brother, the Emperor Napoleon III. One by one the cast of the Second Empire was assembling.

      ♔   ♔   ♔

On May 9, 1812, Napoleon left Paris to take command of the Grande Armée. He was headed, this time, for Russia. All Europe watched as the vast body of men—French, German, Italian, Polish, Austrian, Swiss, and Dutch—inched their way eastward towards the river Nieman. But few watched more closely than the members of Napoleon's family. Sovereigns by the grace of Napoleon, their thrones depended entirely on his victories; defeat for the Emperor could mean dethronement for almost a dozen satellites.

His Empress, Marie Louise, was one of the few who feared for his safety more than she feared for her throne. "Send me news of yourself very often, my dear one," she wrote. "I love you very tenderly. Do not forget her who calls herself till death, your tender and affectionate wife and friend, Louise." Without him she was rudderless. During the two years of their married life she had come to depend on him utterly; she missed his example, his advice, his encouragement in public life, and being a young, highly sexed girl, she missed his affectionate presence in private. Being Napoleon's wife meant almost everything to her; being Empress of the French meant very little. With him out of the country she became lonely, bored, unaccountably restless and vaguely uneasy; her Imperial duties were sadly neglected.

That her maternal duties were likewise neglected (as some have claimed) was not strictly true. Marie Louise had plenty of mother love for her little son; it was just that she had so little opportunity to give it. From the very moment of his birth the King of Rome had been enmeshed in court protocol and provided with everything he could possibly need. He had a chief governess, four lesser governesses, a doctor, a group of first ladies, a wet nurse, several women of the wardrobe, men of the wardrobe, cradle rockers, ushers, valets, and a host of lesser servants. One did not keep such a considerable body of people occupied by allowing the child to remain with its mother all day.

Besides this, Marie Louise was terrified of injuring the little boy. Knowing how much he meant to Napoleon, it was safer for her not to handle him too often or to fondle him too much. No such fears, however, bothered Napoleon. He adored his little son, but he was very rough with him. He would toss him up in the air, he would roll him round on the carpet, he would smear his face with gravy, he would almost suffocate him with great bear hugs. It must sometimes have seemed to Marie Louise that the little King of Rome was getting quite enough love and attention from his father without her having to butt in. Better to leave him to the Emperor; the boy would become hopelessly spoiled if both his parents were to heap him with this almost hysterical affection. In fact, although from all accounts Napoleon's son was a lovable little boy, he was already a very precocious one. "I am the little king!" he would cry out, and his proud, adoring father would clasp him in his arms and cover his face with kisses.

Napoleon was considerably less proud of the other kings he had created. In Spain, Joseph's position was worse than ever. The Spanish insurgents, assisted by Wellington's army, refused to be quelled. Although Joseph himself had no talent for waging war, his task was made even more difficult by the insubordination of the French marshals. Their combined incompetence had, by this time, lost France the center, the south, and the west of the country; it was no wonder that the peace-loving Joseph began to think in terms of abdication once more. "If the Emperor means to disgust me with Spain, I shall have to give it up without delay," he wrote to Julie, who had steadfastly refused to exchange Mortefontaine for Madrid. "In that case all I want is quiet. It is enough for me to have tried two kingdoms, and I do not want a third. For I want either to live peacefully on a property I shall buy far away from Paris, or to be treated properly as a king and a brother."

Strangely enough, it was his brother Lucien, still in exile in England, who now tried to come to Joseph's aid. Unable to keep aloof from public affairs any longer, he attempted to interest Lord Castlereagh, the British Foreign Secretary, in his brother Joseph's plight. There had been rumors of a possible peace between England and France, and Lucien suggested to Lord Castlereagh that in the event of such a peace, Joseph be retained as King of Spain. A Bonaparte king in Spain, provided he were independent of Napoleon, would be a better bet for England than a restored Bourbon, he argued. And when, a few months later, news of the Russian disasters and of a conspiracy to overthrow Napoleon reached England, Lucien again exerted himself on Joseph's behalf. If Napoleon were to be killed or rejected, he said, Joseph should be proclaimed Emperor. The peace-loving, unambitious Joseph would be much more acceptable to all moderate men in France than the Bourbons, and would be no menace to the rest of Europe. Castlereagh, who had very little time for any of the Bonapartes, peace-loving or not, paid scant attention to Lucien's proposals, and his schemes came to nothing.

Whether Lucien himself had harbored any hopes for the success of his plans is doubtful, for at this period he was writing to his brother Louis, the ex-King of Holland, suggesting that they both go and live in America. Louis, still undecided as to whether he should live the life of a hermit or attempt to regain his lost crown, gave an evasive answer. He had left Töplitz by now and was living at Gratz, a hundred miles south of Vienna. Here he spent his days consulting various doctors, and his nights, writing poetry. Although Napoleon had made it clear that he had no objection to his brother's returning to France, Louis refused to move from Gratz. It seems that the presence of Hortense in Paris kept him away; until Napoleon would allow him to divorce her (they were merely separated at present), he intended to remain in exile. He inundated his eldest son Napoleon-Louis with letters, but seemed to have very little interest in his youngest boy, Louis-Napoleon. Caroline's hint that the child might not be his own son had developed into a conviction in his brooding, suspicious mind.

Jérôme, Napoleon's youngest brother, proved no less of a thorn in the Emperor's side than any of the others. Like Louis of Holland, Jérôme of Westphalia resented having to make his country conform to Napoleon's Continental blockade; but unlike Louis, Jérôme valued his crown more than his country. When he complained to the Emperor that the French troops stationed in Westphalia were crippling the country, Napoleon instructed his brother to "put order and economy into the finances of Westphalia, which is the worst-governed state in the Confederation." In spite of the fact that Westphalia was bankrupt, Jérôme ignored his brother's advice and continued to live in the most sumptuous possible style; his palace of Napoleonshöhe was the scene of some of the most brilliant fetes in Europe. No one could play at king better than Jérôme.

In the summer of 1812, in spite of Jérôme's often-proved incompetence, Napoleon decided to put him in command of a wing of the *Grande Armée* during the campaign against Russia. By now Napoleon—this shrewd judge of men, this past master in the art of war—should have known better. Jérôme, delighted at the opportunity of winning for himself a little military glory, set off for the front in a manner worthy of an Oriental potentate. His enormous baggage train carried tents, carpets, tables, chairs, looking glasses, bedding, chests of plate, table linen, china, glass, champagne, silver-lined saucepans, and cases of monogrammed toilet equipment. His wardrobe alone filled seven huge wagons; he brought with him no less than three hundred and eighteen silk handkerchiefs. It is no wonder that his sister Pauline has sometimes been called "Jérôme in petticoats." He seems to have had an idea that after a successful Russian campaign Napoleon would make him King of Poland; in the event of such an elevation he certainly did not mean to be caught unprepared. "He had a quick and apt mind," wrote Countess Potocka, who saw him in Warsaw on his way to the front. "With a touch more of the legitimate sovereign and a touch less of puerile vanity he might have passed for a distinguished prince; but, being a spoiled child of fortune, he used and abused her bounty. . . . It was stated that every morning he took a bath of rum, and every evening a bath of milk. His servants, they said, put up the liquor in bottles, and sold it at a rebate. . . ." The Countess, one may be sure, was exaggerating (although there was a story of his having invented a bath of Bordeaux wine), but his frivolous behavior tended to encourage this sort of story.

His part in the Russian campaign was a complete fiasco. Instead of following up his first very minor victory over the Russians, he frittered away his time in the captured town and let the enemy get away. Napoleon was furious. "It is impossible to make war in this way," he wrote. "You only occupy yourself with trifles, you talk of nothing else, and I am pained at seeing that with you everything is littleness. You are endangering the whole success of the campaign on our right. It is impossible to make war in this way."

Realizing at last that Jérôme could not be trusted, Napoleon gave

the command of the whole right wing, including Jérôme's forces, to
Marshal Davout. On hearing this, Jérôme was wild with disappointment.
"What!" he wrote home to his queen, Catherine. "Am I, the commander
of the right wing, comprised of four army corps, to be under the orders
of a mere marshal, who commands but a single corps . . . ! It is desired that
I shall serve—I, the commander of the right—under the orders of a
marshal. I do not desire this, and I cannot, that is all. I resign. It is quite
simple."

And he did resign. It was given out that his health had failed and that
he had been forced to return to Westphalia. Napoleon never forgave
him for what he considered his desertion, but then Napoleon should
never have entrusted him to a command in the first place. Jérôme
returned to Napoleonshöhe, and while the *Grande Armée*, including his
own Westphalian corps, suffered the terrible hardships of the Russian
campaign, he once more gave himself over to his dissolute life. The
entertainments at the Westphalian court had never been more magnificent, or the scenes on the road from Moscow more grim, than they
were during that winter of 1812.

The behavior of Napoleon's sisters at this period seems to have been
slightly less irritating to Napoleon than that of his brothers.

Elisa, who had added Tuscany to her domains, was now a Grand
Duchess, with the city of Florence as her capital. Here, in the ocher-
colored Palazzo Pitti, she did her best to emulate the Medici by ardently
encouraging the arts. Plain in her youth, she seems to have become even
plainer with the advance of middle age, and unlike the majority of her
brothers and sisters, she cared not a scrap for clothes. She had a
standing order for two dresses and several hats to be sent from Paris
each month; her annual dress bill was usually less than Pauline, or
Jérôme for that matter, would pay for a single creation.

Her duchy, like most countries in Europe, was suffering from
Napoleon's rigid enforcement of his Continental System. The once
prosperous port of Leghorn had been entirely ruined, and at about this
time the first signs of unrest began to manifest themselves. Napoleon,
always quick to sense insurrection, ordered her to take vigorous action
against the agitators, but Elisa, claiming that "violent measures were
alien to her nature," remained sanguine. She assured the Emperor that
Tuscany, under her benevolent rule, would remain loyal to the Empire.
Believing her, Napoleon withdrew a large number of French troops; the
time was fast approaching when he would need every single man he
could lay his hands on.

Pauline, usually so oblivious to anything other than her health and her beauty, seemed, in a way, to sense the coming disasters. This year was a particularly sad one for her. Never very well, she was in real pain during the autumn of 1812; none of her doctors seemed to know what the trouble was. While at Aix-les-Bains, where she spent her days stretched out upon an elegant chaise-longue, she heard that one of her lovers, an officer of whom she had been particularly fond, had been killed at the terrible battle of Borodino. Although she had another lover on hand to divert her, the news came as a distinct shock, and for some days at least, she was desolate. Advised by her doctors to avoid the winter, she journeyed south, and spent the next few months moving from place to place. When Napoleon gave orders for her latest admirer to rejoin his regiment, her health, which had improved slightly in the South of France, took a turn for the worse, and she was again plunged into the deepest melancholy. "We never see a soul," complained one of her ladies. "We spend our entire existence looking on at Her Highness being moved from one bed to another."

Almost instinctively, without fully appreciating the dangers towards which her beloved brother Napoleon was heading, she began to retrench. She dismissed several servants, she reduced the salaries of some of her ladies, she sold a number of horses. She began to spend immense sums of money on jewelry; it seemed a better risk than state securities at present. When, during the following year, she heard that disaster was beginning to overtake Napoleon, she unhesitatingly sold a superb diamond necklace and offered him the proceeds.

No such gesture would ever have occurred to Napoleon's youngest sister, Caroline Murat. Her energies were directed towards preserving her own crown, not his. It was no easy task. Relations between Murat and his wife had gone from bad to worse. He, lending an attentive ear towards those who suggested that he set himself up as an independent king, was intriguing against Napoleon, while she, stripped of all power by the jealous Murat, was in turn intriguing against her husband. And at times it almost seemed as though Napoleon were intriguing against both of them. He had once even threatened that unless Murat enforced the Continental blockade more efficiently, he would dethrone him. Murat had promptly dashed off to Paris to placate the Emperor, while Caroline, convinced that if she joined her husband, Napoleon would take the opportunity of their absence from Naples to annex it, refused to attend the baptism of the King of Rome. Their mutual apprehensions in no way united husband and wife, however, and in June 1811 Murat issued two decrees whereby he hoped to rid Naples of the members of the French party surrounding the Queen. Napoleon quickly forced Murat to annul the decrees, and Murat countered by placing Caroline in a state of semicaptivity. This did not last long, for in order to allay Napoleon's suspicions that he was plotting against him, Murat was obliged to send Caroline to Paris to soothe her brother. Much as she now despised her husband, Caroline loved her crown more, and she set off for Paris. There she was assured that the Emperor had no intention of annexing Naples. Napoleon, about to embark on his Russian campaign, had need of Murat's services; he could not afford to alienate him now by taking away his throne.

In May 1812 Murat left for Russia and Caroline became Regent of Naples. This was probably the happiest period of her life. Responsibility brought out all her capabilities. Until this moment she had made use of her talents to further her own ends; now she used them to govern her country energetically and efficiently. Her shrewdness, her tirelessness, the soundness of her judgments, amazed her ministers; she proved to be an infinitely better statesman than her vain, overexcitable husband. Even her private life, now that she had no need to further her aims by whatever means came to hand, was above reproach.

The news of her growing popularity and influence disturbed Murat. By December 1812 Napoleon, on the disastrous road back from Moscow, had abandoned the wreck of his *Grande Armée* to Murat, and he in turn, anxious about affairs in Naples, handed over the command to Eugène de Beauharnais and hurried home. Convinced that Napoleon would never recover from this terrible campaign, Murat galloped south, determined to save his own kingdom.

Napoleon arrived back in Paris on December 28, 1812. He had left for Russia with 600,000 men; he returned with some 42,000, many of whom were wounded and dying. Only on his return was the magnitude of the disaster fully realized by the French people. They were not invincible after all. True, there had been some reverses in Spain, but never when Napoleon himself was in command. Now, for the first time in his career, his return home was not a triumphant one.

Hortense hurried to the Tuileries to welcome him back. She found him tired and preoccupied. Misfortune seemed to have sobered him. She asked whether the retreat from Moscow had really been as bad as his dispatches had led them to believe.

"I told the whole truth," answered Napoleon.

"But we were not the only ones to suffer," she argued. "Our enemies too must have suffered very heavily."

"No doubt," he said quietly, "but that does not console me."

        ⚜   ⚜   ⚜

The rot had set in. It would not be long before the whole hastily erected fabric of Napoleon's Empire would collapse. The Emperor had lost his *Grande Armée* on the road from Moscow, and while he scratched around to raise another, Joseph lost him Spain.

In spite of repeated instructions from the Emperor to abandon Madrid and retire to the north of Spain, Joseph remained in his capital. By the time he finally decided to leave, it was too late to make an effective stand elsewhere against Wellington's advancing army. All through the spring of 1813 the French troops fell back before the British; it was not until the middle of June that they were able to give battle. It was at the city of Vitoria that the two forces met. Joseph, who had spent the day before the battle amusing his Spanish mistress, is reported to have shown admirable calm and courage on the day of the battle itself.

But a commander needs more qualities than these to ensure success, and by nightfall King Joseph was fleeing north through the rain, leaving his badly defeated army behind him. Within a day or two he was writing to Julie to tell her to expect him back at Mortefontaine, and before the end of June he had crossed the frontier into France. From Saint-Jean-de-Luz he wrote to Napoleon asking for help; Napoleon's answer was to relieve him of his command and hand his army over to Soult. "All the blunders in Spain," stormed Napoleon, "are the result of my own ill-judged consideration for the King, who not only does not know how to command an army, but in addition to this, cannot take an honest view of his own powers and leave the command to a soldier."

Napoleon, who, in spite of all Joseph's weaknesses, was still fond of him, tried to break the news of his supercession as gently as possible, but when Joseph heard that he was to hand over his command, he was furious. No amount of rampaging would change Napoleon's mind, however, and Joseph was obliged to resign himself to the situation with as good a grace as possible. Towards the middle of July he received Napoleon's permission to return to Mortefontaine, and on the last day of the month his carriage came swaying down the avenues of his country estate. The smell of the warm summer woods, the sight of the still, shimmering lakes, the affectionate presence of Julie and his two daughters must have been soothing to the soul of this tired, disappointed man during the months that followed.

Louis had lost the crown of Holland; Joseph had lost the crown of Spain; Jérôme now lost the crown of Westphalia.

By the spring of 1813 it was obvious that there was going to be fighting in central Germany, and as Westphalia lay directly in the path of the advancing enemy, Jérôme began showing signs of agitation. Contrary to the Emperor's wishes (Napoleon wanted to avoid all appearance of panic), Jérôme packed his wife off to France, and her departure was quickly followed by that of the wives and families of all French officials. In vain did Jérôme try to allay fears by keeping up his usual lavish entertainments; it was only when Napoleon won several victories over the Russo-Prussian army in May that confidence was restored. Napoleon and Jérôme met at Dresden, and it was here, at this crucial moment in Napoleon's career (the news of Joseph's defeat at Vitoria was undermining his chance of negotiating a favorable peace), that Jérôme chose to raise a personal matter with his harassed brother.

Jérôme was thinking of taking a third wife. Napoleon had annulled his first marriage to Elizabeth Patterson in 1805. Since then Jérôme had kept up a desultory correspondence with her; he had even, at one stage, suggested that she and their little son come and live in Westphalia. Elizabeth, with a typical show of spirit, had replied to the effect that Westphalia was not large enough to accommodate two queens. In 1812 he had sent her an overwhelmingly affectionate letter, assuring her that "sooner or later everything will be arranged," and that she had no better friend than he. Her answer had been to petition the Maryland legislature for a divorce. It was granted in January 1813, and she promptly wrote to Napoleon suggesting that she return to France and that he grant her a title. She wished to assure her son's future, she said. Napoleon, however, was far too busy to attend to her petition.

At Dresden, Napoleon told Jérôme about Elizabeth's divorce, and Jérôme immediately proposed another. Although he and Catherine had been married for several years, she was still childless. Jérôme suggested that for "reasons of state," he should now divorce her and marry someone capable of giving him an heir. The lady he hoped to marry was his latest mistress, already some months pregnant by him. With his throne in its present precarious state, it really mattered very little whether he had an heir or not, and anyway, Napoleon would not hear of a divorce. He advised his brother to set his mistress up in some castle, and no doubt told him to be grateful for so gentle and devoted a wife as Catherine.

Hardly had the brothers parted at Dresden than hostilities broke out once more. Things went badly for the French, and by September the Cossacks were pouring across the northern border of Westphalia. To his credit, Jérôme refused an invitation to join the enemy and fight against his brother. He fled the capital, and a few days later the Russians marched in. Within a week the French troops had forced them to march out again, and Jérôme, who had had nothing whatsoever to do with their eviction, returned in triumph. It was a very short-lived triumph, however, for on the very day that he re-entered Napoleonshöhe, the Emperor sustained a terrible defeat at Leipzig. This was the famous "Battle of the Nations," one of the great turning points in Napoleon's career. From then on he was on the defensive, and by the end of the year the disorganized French Army was retreating across the Rhine. With it retreated Jérôme, the ex-King of Westphalia.

It was at this moment of defeat, when both Joseph and Jérôme had lost their crowns and Napoleon was in grave danger of losing his, that Louis made an effort to regain his own lost kingdom.

When the Emperor Francis, in spite of the fact that his daughter was Napoleon's wife, joined the anti-French coalition in 1813, Louis felt that he could no longer continue to live in Austria. He moved, instead, to Switzerland. From there he wrote to Napoleon, asserting his claim to the Kingdom of Holland and suggesting that he be restored in order to rally his Dutch subjects to Napoleon's cause. Louis, in common with his brothers Joseph and Jérôme, never for a moment doubted the loyalty of his ex-subjects. Certain that Napoleon could not afford to refuse his request, Louis opened negotiations with certain of his former ministers. The Emperor's reply to what he considered his brother's latest act of folly was very much to the point. He ignored the talk of restoration and said that if Louis were prepared to return to France as a French prince, he would be welcome, but that if he insisted on regarding himself as the King of Holland, he had better stay away. Louis, who had, in fact, re-entered France by now, quickly scuttled back to Switzerland.

By December the advance of the victorious Allies made Switzerland unsafe, and in spite of Napoleon's clearly stated terms, Louis set off for Paris once more. Here he steadfastly refused to give up his claims to the throne of Holland, and dared Napoleon to evict him. As the Emperor had more important things to worry about than the pretensions of his brother, and as he wanted to avoid a family scandal, he allowed

Louis to remain. With the French forces reeling back in retreat on every front, Louis, at least, sustained a personal victory.

It was by their weaknesses that Napoleon's brothers had contributed to his downfall; his sisters Elisa and Caroline were to make their contribution in a much more positive manner.

After the retreat from Moscow, Murat, seeing the writing on the wall, began to cast about for the best way of saving his throne. He opened secret negotiations with Austria, with the British, and with the Italian patriots. It seems that at first Caroline knew nothing of her husband's intrigues, but when she found out about them, she gave him her full support. From this point on her conduct was almost worthy of a Borgia. While writing honeyed letters to her brother, assuring him of her undying loyalty, she made use of any means, fair or foul, to further her cause. In the summer of 1813, while Murat was fighting side by side with Napoleon, his wife was in constant touch with the enemy. After the defeat at Leipzig, Murat, realizing that the end was near, hurried back to Naples. He had heard that Austria and Britain were prepared to guarantee his throne in exchange for his neutrality. Stopping at Milan on the way home, he was hailed by the anxious population as the "savior of Italy" and this unexpected reception put another idea into his already swollen head. The mere preservation of the Neapolitan throne seemed a small thing beside it. He suggested to Napoleon that if he, Murat, were made king of an independent and unified Italy, Napoleon would be able to count on the support of every Italian in the struggle against Austria. It was a shrewd move, because once in control of all the forces in Italy, Murat would be in a much better position to treat with the Allies. Although Napoleon did not actually agree to the proposal, he intimated that he might consider it. At this point, however, the Allies issued Murat an ultimatum. Either he join the coalition against France, in which case his throne would be assured, or else Austria would feel free to attack him. Although loath to abandon his dreams of becoming King of Italy, Murat, urged on by Caroline, consented.

On January 11, 1814, Napoleon's sister Caroline and her husband betrayed him and threw in their lot with his enemies.

A day or two later Madame Récamier, who was then living in Naples, was visiting Queen Caroline. Suddenly a door of Caroline's drawing room burst open, and Murat, wild-eyed and disheveled, stumbled into the room. Seizing the visitor's hands, he poured out an almost incoherent account of his predicament and asked her what he should do. Madame Récamier, not realizing that he had already betrayed Napoleon, advised him to remain faithful to France. "Then I am a traitor," shouted Murat, and flinging open the window, pointed to the British ships already entering the bay. He then buried his face in his hands and burst into tears. At this Caroline rushed up, and giving him a little orange-flower water to drink, managed to calm him and send him out of the room. No sooner had he left than she threw herself into her visitor's arms and likewise burst into tears. Between sobs she begged Madame Récamier to pity her at this difficult time. She babbled on about her husband's lack of courage, her affection for her children, her "hourly" thoughts for Napoleon. "If you could search my heart," she cried dramatically, "you would understand what torture I am doomed to bear."

Whether or not this was all a clever piece of play-acting in order to impress Madame Récamier, and through her, her scores of influential friends, one does not know. When Napoleon heard of their treachery, he was speechless with rage. "The conduct of the King of Naples is infamous," he wrote to Fouché, "and for that of the Queen there is no name."

Elisa's behavior, if slightly less dramatic, was no less treacherous. Working hand in glove with the wily Fouché, she came to an agreement with her brother-in-law Murat. His army came marching towards Florence, and after a show of resistance, she allowed them to enter unmolested. The Florentines went wild with joy. Her slight show of resistance, however, had been taken quite seriously by her subjects, and they now gathered outside the Palazzo Pitti, screaming for her removal. She left Florence the following day, her carriage having to force its way through an insulting filth-hurling mob. She made for Lucca, and from here, having ordered the evacuation of all French troops, she announced that she had broken with her brother's Empire. The reward for her treachery was to have been the guarantee of her domains, and while waiting for Murat to make good his promise, she surreptitiously annexed a few neighboring districts. She was soon disillusioned. In March a combined Anglo-Sicilian force landed at Leghorn and marched on Lucca. When she sent an envoy to protest, the British commander replied that unless "that woman" were sent away immediately, he would have her arrested. There was nothing for it but to flee, and stopping just long enough at Genoa to pick up her somewhat bemused husband, Bacciochi, she headed for France.

If the onset of misfortune revealed all the worst qualities in Napoleon's brothers and sisters, they revealed everything that was admirable in the character of his mother. Adversity always brought out the best in Letizia. Although she had conducted herself with dignity, and on occasion with majesty, during the Empire, her shortcomings—her avarice, her clannishness, her vindictiveness—tended to make her look ridiculous in the midst of so much prosperity and power. But unlike her sons and daughters, she had remained uncorrupted. And now that it seemed as though the crash, which she had so long predicted and saved against, was about to come, her qualities of greatness were revealed once more. Always the champion of the son who needed her most, she now gave Napoleon her wholehearted support. Her calm, her clear-sightedness, her energy, her devotion, her tenacity, even her meanness, was to stand him and her family in very good stead in the lean years ahead.

♛ ♛ ♛

On January 23, 1814, Napoleon, about to rejoin the Army, took leave of the officers of his newly formed National Guard of Paris. Always a shrewd propagandist, he now staged a highly emotional farewell for their benefit. When the officers had assembled in the Salon des Maréchaux at the Tuileries, Napoleon, Marie Louise, and the three-year-old King of Rome entered. With his son in his arms, his Empress by his side, and such of his family as were still loyal to him standing behind, Napoleon addressed the men. In a voice trembling with calculated emotion, he told them that he was entrusting to their care the city of Paris, his wife, and his child. Heartfelt shouts of *"Vive l'Empereur"* drowned the end of his speech, and Hortense reports seeing many eyes filled with tears. A few days later, she said, some of these same men were heaping Napoleon's name with abuse.

The Emperor had appointed Marie Louise Regent (a post which she was singularly ill suited to fill) and his brother Joseph Lieutenant-General of the Empire. It was only with the utmost difficulty that Napoleon had got Joseph to renounce his rights as King of Spain. Although it was over six months since he had fled from Spain, Joseph had refused to abdicate; it needed a firm letter from Napoleon and the promise that he could still call himself King Joseph to make him change his mind. Louis (still insisting that he was the King of Holland) came limping into the Tuileries to wish his brother good luck, but Jérôme, who had now transferred his court to Compiègne, was told that he would not be welcome. His extravagance, his giddiness, his refusal to renounce his title of King of Westphalia had infuriated even the long-suffering Napoleon beyond endurance. Elisa and Caroline were knee-deep in treachery in Italy while

Pauline, who had given her entourage strict instructions that she was not to be told any bad news, was keeping warm in the South of France.

It was Josephine's daughter, Hortense, and not one of Napoleon's blood relations, who spent the last evening with him and Marie Louise at the Tuileries. And it would be Josephine's son, Eugène, who in spite of an offer from the Allies, would be the only member of the family to remain loyal to him in Italy. Marie Louise spent most of that last evening in tears, and every now and then Napoleon would take her in his arms and say; "Don't be sad. Trust me; do you think that I have forgotten my profession entirely?"

He had not. In many ways this campaign of 1814 was one of his most brilliant, but he was fighting against hopeless odds. After the first few French victories he rejected the idea that France be reduced to her pre-Revolutionary size, and fought on to secure at least her "natural" frontiers. The Allies now wisely decided to ignore his insistent attacks in their rear and to stake everything on a speedy advance on undefended Paris. Their gamble paid off; by the end of March they were in sight of the capital.

On the twenty-eighth of the month the anxious Joseph assembled the Council of Regency at the Tuileries. It was decided that Marie Louise and the King of Rome were to leave Paris the following day. Certain members of the Council, Talleyrand amongst them, had argued that the flight of the Empress would have a bad effect on morale in Paris, but Joseph claimed that the Emperor had given him strict instructions that his wife and son were not to fall into enemy hands. "I would rather my son were dead than brought up in Vienna as an Austrian prince," the Emperor had said. When Hortense, who had been waiting outside the Council chamber, heard that the Empress was about to leave Paris, she was appalled. When she warned the bewildered Marie Louise that her flight would lose her her crown, the Empress answered, "Perhaps you are right, but that's what's been decided, and if the Emperor has to reproach anyone, it won't be me."

By dawn the following morning the courtyards of the Tuileries were crammed with carriages. It took hours for the jostling, gesticulating, near-panicky crowd of fugitives to get themselves and their luggage accommodated in the assortment of vehicles which had been commandeered for the flight. Madame Mère and Queen Catherine of Westphalia were to accompany the Empress; Louis was to follow later. Joseph and Jérôme remained behind to organize the defense of Paris; they might have saved themselves the trouble. Towards ten o'clock the docile Marie Louise took her seat, but when the moment came for the King of Rome to follow his mother, there was an extraordinary scene. The little boy, sensing that something was amiss, refused to leave the palace. He kicked, he screamed, he threw himself onto the ground; nothing, he shouted again and again, would induce him to leave. It was almost as if he realized that he was never to see the Tuileries, or Paris, again. His years of glory—the hundred-and-one gun salute at his birth, the host of fawning royalties at his baptism, the near hysterical acclamations each time he made an appearance—were over. The long anticlimax of his life was about to begin. They had to carry him forcibly into the coach. That accomplished, the long line of carriages jolted forward and moved slowly up the still leafless Champs-Elysées, headed for Rambouillet.

Joseph, Julie, Jèrôme, Louis, and Hortense remained in Paris. The following morning the two ex-kings, Joseph and Jérôme, rode up to the heights of Montmartre to command the defense of the city. They were surrounded by a brilliantly uniformed staff, made up not only of Frenchmen, but of the Spanish and Westphalian officers whom the two brothers had refused to dismiss. Amongst the Spaniards was a certain Colonel de Montijo; some forty years hence his as yet unborn daughter would be the next Empress of the French. And some sixty years hence she, too, like her predecessor, Marie Louise, would be fleeing from Paris.

At ten that morning Joseph, realizing that Paris could never be held, sent a message to Julie telling her and her daughters to leave at once; she followed the Empress to Rambouillet. Hortense, who had at first looked upon the flight of the Imperial family as nothing less than a betrayal, was also finally prevailed upon to leave. Louis had threatened that unless she joined the Empress, he would take their two sons away with him. She set off on the night of March 29, and the following evening arrived at Rambouillet. Marie Louise and her party had already moved on towards Blois, but Joseph, Julie, and Jérôme were there. They told her that Paris had fallen. The following morning Hortense took her leave and set off to join her mother, the ex-Empress Josephine, at Navarre. The others drove off to Blois to join the Empress.

At Blois were now assembled the tattered remains of Napoleon's once magnificent court. Of the members of the family there were the Empress and the King of Rome, Madame Mère, Joseph, Julie and their two daughters, Louis, Jérôme and his wife, Catherine. The Emperor himself was at Fontainebleau; defeated, exhausted, deserted, he was negotiating with the victorious Allies. The result of these negotiations reached the family on the morning of April 7. Napoleon had abdicated. He was to be banished to the island of Elba.

The news threw poor Marie Louise into a quandary. On first hearing, a week before, that Napoleon had arrived at Fontainebleau, her one desire had been to join him. He, however, thinking that she might be useful to him as a go-between with her father, the Emperor Francis, had kept her at arm's length; his evasive answers had perplexed and unsettled her. Having always to depend on someone else for guidance, and being unable to make contact with her husband, she now turned towards her father. Surely he, who loved her so much, and who knew how much she, in turn, loved Napoleon, would help her. On the day before she heard of her husband's abdication, one of the Czar's aides-de-camp rode into Blois to explain that her Regency had now come to an end and that she must proceed to Orléans. At Orléans she was told that her father was waiting to see her at Rambouillet. When the moment came for Marie Louise to take leave of Madame Mère and go to her father, she said, a little anxiously, "I hope you will always retain benevolent feelings towards me."

"That," answered Napoleon's mother in her honest, unsmiling way, "will depend on you and your future conduct."

They parted company, and Marie Louise hurried on to Rambouillet. And here, at Rambouillet, this irresolute, ingenuous girl was assured that she had nothing to worry about, that she and her child would be cared for, that there was really no hurry about joining her husband on Elba, that she should go to some spa to regain her health and calm her nerves before coming to any decisions. Grateful to have her mind made up for her, Marie Louise agreed to return home to Schönbrunn for a few weeks and then to go on to some spa. Once she had recuperated fully, they said, she could see about joining Napoleon on Elba, if she wished. . . .

Napoleon, in the meantime, was on his way to Elba. Arriving in the South of France, he called on his sister Pauline at her villa near Orgon. In order to avoid the hostile demonstrations of his erstwhile subjects (they had gone as far as to hang a blood-smeared effigy of him from a gibbet in one town), he had been forced to disguise himself. It was thus in a bulky greatcoat and a huge fur cap that he presented himself to his sister. Pauline, who had not the slightest idea that he had abdicated, was amazed at the sight of her brother in this bizarre costume.

"Oh, Napoleon," she cried out in her charmingly naïve way, "what *have* you done?"

He had, he explained to his scatterbrained sister, just lost his empire.

CHAPTER SEVEN

※　※　※

LIKE leaves before the wind, the Bonapartes were now scattered across the face of Europe. The Allies had allowed Napoleon and Marie Louise to retain their titles of Emperor and Empress, and his mother, brothers, sisters, and their children, the titles of prince and princess. Napoleon himself was at Elba where, with characteristic energy and that extraordinary attention to detail, he set about organizing his little domain. He overhauled its haphazard finances, he improved its happy-go-lucky defense system, he made plans to rebuild its long-neglected roads. And having lost none of his passion for palaces, he had his Mulini palace enlarged and refurnished, he bought a country house at San Martino, he acquired a summer residence at La Madonna del Monte. He had to be prepared, he said, for the arrival of Marie Louise and the King of Rome from Austria. Having dominated a continent for ten years, he had now to content himself with managing the affairs of a small island; it was extremely unlikely that he would remain content for long.

In August 1814 Madame Mère arrived at Elba. She had been in Italy since the *débâcle*, and ever since then had been trying to get permission to join her son. Her arrival delighted Napoleon, and she had hardly landed before he was whisking her round the island to point out various places of interest. As the Mulini palace was still being enlarged, she was accommodated in one of the houses nearby. She had not been there for more than a few weeks, however, before he took her to stay in a little hilltop village. While they were there, a rumor swept the island that the Empress Marie Louise and the King of Rome had arrived at last.

The woman and child who had landed were not, in fact, the Empress and her son, but Marie Walewska and her four-year-old boy, Alexandre. This gentle, devoted woman, who had been living unobtrusively in Paris all these years, had come to spend a few days with her protector. Napoleon entertained her at La Madonna del Monte and they appear to have discussed the little boy's future. Napoleon's illegitimate son by Marie Walewska was to inherit far more of his father's drive and ability than would his legitimate son by Marie Louise. Mother and child left the island a few days later.

His next visitor was a much less shadowy personality. It was his second sister, Pauline. In May, on her way to visit her sister Caroline, still clinging to her throne in Naples, her ship had called at Elba. She had spent only a day with her brother on this occasion, but at the end of October she returned and arranged to pass the winter on the island. She was housed in a suite of six rooms on the first floor of Napoleon's palace. This circumstance added strength to the rumor, already prevalent for some years, that Napoleon and Pauline enjoyed an incestuous relationship. In his memoirs Baron Mounier claimed that he had been told that one of Pauline's letters from Elba had been intercepted by the police; in it she was said to have complained that since being there, she had "had only this rotten old man"—her brother Napoleon. This was typical of the sort of story which the secret police (working now for the restored Bourbons) were so anxious to spread about the recently discredited Bonaparte family. There seems to be no truth in the accusation whatsoever. If Pauline had indeed been looking for a lover, there were dozens of handsome young officers surrounding Napoleon on Elba, just as there were dozens of pretty young women on the island if Napoleon had wanted a mistress. Pauline had never had the slightest difficulty in seducing anyone she wanted, and the indications are that by now Napoleon was much less active sexually than in former years.

No, Napoleon was grateful for Pauline's presence for quite different reasons. With her matchless beauty, her expensive clothes, and her light-hearted manner, she imparted an aura of sophistication, of importance, almost, to Napoleon's small provincial court. Madame Mère, who felt much more at home on Elba than ever she had amongst the splendors of the Tuileries, could not provide the *élan* which Napoleon's household so badly needed. Now there were countless balls, dinners, receptions, and amateur theatricals, at all of which Pauline presided with her customary somewhat insouciant grace. Her ill health seems to have been temporarily forgotten, although there were still days when she refused to walk a step, and had to be carried around the island in a sedan chair.

Living so close to Napoleon was not easy, even for this carefree young woman. He would scold her for her extravagance, he would criticize her clothes, he would insist on her treating him like a reigning sovereign. But she seems to have taken it all quite well, and most of the time he was grateful for her presence. Her gaiety, coupled with his mother's devotion (not to mention the large sums of money she was advancing him,) did much towards softening the edges of his exile. "She and Pauline would reconcile me to life here for a long time, if I were in need of consolation," was the slightly backhanded way he expressed his appreciation.

Madame Mère and Pauline were the only members of his family to visit him in exile; the rest seem to have been far too busy salvaging what they could from the wreck of his Empire. His eldest brother, Joseph, having allowed both Paris and the Empress to fall into the hands of the enemy, had fled, first to Lausanne and then to Geneva. As the Bourbons had decreed that the Bonapartes must sell all their property in France within six months, Joseph had got rid of his beloved Mortefontaine and bought himself a house on the shores of Lake Geneva. Expecting this to be his home for many years, he set about rearranging his magnificent art collections. His wife, Julie, who had never, at any stage of their married life, displayed much enthusiasm for living with him, did not change now. She obtained permission for herself and her daughters to remain quietly in Paris; she intended to join Joseph, but somehow never seemed to do so. It is unlikely that Joseph ever pressed the point; he usually managed to get along very well without his wife. Although he was quite fond of her, he never hesitated to seek amusements away from home; he had, as a man of pleasure, "a somewhat checkered life." But being kind-hearted as well as licentious, he tried to keep the knowledge of his love affairs from his wife; in a society seething with gossip, it is unlikely that he succeeded very often. "He loved her," says Madame Junot, "as a friend, and as the mother of his daughters."

The setting of Napoleon's star meant the ascent of his brother Lucien's. As soon as the preliminaries of peace were signed in April 1814, Lucien quitted England and returned to Rome. Thorngrove was left behind, and he was able to take possession of his principality of Canino and his Roman palazzo once more. In the full flush of triumph, he wrote Napoleon a magnanimous letter, announcing that he was willing to forgive and forget and that he would always be at his brother's disposal. These were no empty sentiments, and Napoleon was to take him at his word sooner than he expected. In the meantime Lucien resumed his archaeological and literary hobbies; in May he published his epic poem *Charlemagne*, dedicating it to Pope Pius VII. The statuesque Alexandrine, more at home among the terra-cotta-colored *palazzi* of Rome than ever she had been among the cold country houses of England, now bore him a fourth son. It is ironic that the branch of the family not eligible for the succession was the one to produce the most sons. This fourth boy, christened Pierre, was to be the wildest young Bonaparte in a generation of exceptionally wild young Bonapartes.

Louis, having fled first to Switzerland, now came to stay with his brother Lucien in Rome. From here he wrote to Hortense, asking that his eldest son, Napoleon-Louis, be sent to him. Hortense refused. His irritation at her refusal was increased when he heard that the new King of France, Louis XVIII, had conferred upon her the title of the Duchess of St.-Leu. Louis published a formal protest against this creation of an independent duchy for his wife, and appealed to the Paris courts to compel Hortense to give him custody of their eldest son.

Hortense, in fact, had emerged from the *débâcle* almost intact. This was largely due to Josephine's friendship with Czar Alexander. As soon as the Russian Emperor had arrived in Paris, he had asked to meet the ex-Empress Josephine, then living at Navarre. Although loath to negotiate with Napoleon's enemy, Josephine's concern for the future of her children, Eugène and Hortense, overcame her pride, and she returned to Malmaison to meet the Czar. To meet Josephine was to be enchanted by her, and Alexander soon fell under her spell. Although she was now over fifty years of age and a little plump, her elegance was still exceptional, and her charm, unsurpassed. Arm in arm with the strange, sensitive, seductively mannered Czar of all the Russias ("If he were a woman, I should fall in love with him," Napoleon had once written to Josephine), she would stroll through her celebrated rose garden, radiating happiness as she walked. Not forgetting the object of these meetings, she lost no time in summoning Hortense and Eugène to Malmaison.

Hortense, distant at first, finally succumbed to Alexander's charm. It was difficult, in fact, to repel anyone so eager to help. He made a fuss over her little sons, he expressed his admiration for Napoleon and his contempt for the restored Bourbons, and most important of all, he pressed for the creation of the Duchy of St.-Leu for her.

Alexander's visits to Malmaison were followed by calls from most of the foreign royalties then in Paris. Hortense's two sons found this host of new kings and princes extremely confusing. Which of these unfamiliar royalties, they wanted to know, should they call uncle; Louis-Napoleon, the youngest, had assumed that all kings were his uncles.

With the future of Hortense and her sons assured, Josephine turned the Czar's attention to Eugène. Twice during the last months of the Empire, Eugène's father-in-law, the King of Bavaria, who had himself joined the Austrians, had incited Eugène to desert Napoleon. Eugène, in marked contrast to the other Bonapartes in Italy, had refused. He had held firm in the face of the advancing Austrians, but had finally been forced to surrender. After the fall of the Empire he had placed his wife, Augusta, and their children in the care of her father, the King of Bavaria, and had come to meet the Czar at Malmaison. One of the clauses in the treaty drawn up at the time of Napoleon's abdication had specified that Eugène be given a "suitable domain" somewhere, and Eugène was naturally anxious to find out what domain it would be. Alexander could tell him nothing further; Eugène would have to wait until it was discussed at the coming congress in Vienna. Within a few weeks, however, Eugène had something even more pressing to occupy him.

On May 24, 1814, Josephine, who was suffering from a cold, gave a dinner party at Malmaison. After dinner she and the Czar escaped from the heat of the house and strolled about in the cooler air of the garden. As Josephine was wearing one of her light gauzy dresses, her cold got worse, and by the following morning she was seriously ill. Three days later she was dead. Her last coherent words, they said, had been: "Bonaparte . . . the island of Elba . . . the King of Rome." For three days she lay in state in the vestibule at Malmaison while over twenty thousand people filed by to pay her homage. She was buried in the little parish church of Rueil. The only Bonapartes present at the funeral were her two little grandsons, the ten-year-old Napoleon-Louis and the six-year-old Louis-Napoleon. Hortense and Eugène had retired to St.-Leu.

In a family remembered chiefly for its vices, Josephine was destined to be remembered chiefly for her virtues.

♔   ♔   ♔

Elisa had by now joined the growing colony of Bonapartes in Italy. Through Metternich's intervention, she and Bacciochi were allowed to live undisturbed in a villa near Bologna. The zest with which she flung herself into social life does not seem to have allayed the suspicions of the Austrian police; confident that the former Duchess of Tuscany must be plotting with the French party in her old domains, they opened every letter she received and noted every visitor. They discovered nothing. In July 1814 she gave birth to a son whom she named Frédéric; it was unfortunate that when she did finally produce an heir, there was practically nothing left for him to inherit.

The following month another of the Bonapartes produced a son; after seven years of marriage the faithless Jérôme and the faithful Catherine were blessed with a child. It was given the name of Jérôme

Napoleon; it was the same name that had been given to his half brother, Elizabeth Patterson's son, nearly ten years before.

Whereas not long ago Jérôme had been only too eager to divorce his wife, he now hung on to her for dear life: her father, the King of Württemberg, was one of the victorious Allies. Napoleon had hardly abdicated before Jérôme had bundled Catherine off to Paris to get permission for the two of them to live in Württemberg. She was told that she would always be welcome, provided she divorced Jérôme first. This she considered "a most revolting proposal," and wrote to her father to tell him what a kind and affectionate husband Jérôme was. The King was not convinced.

Rebuffed by her father, Catherine was befriended by her cousin, the Czar. Much more kindly disposed towards the Bonapartes than the other victorious sovereigns, he promised to use his influence to do something for Jérôme, and in the meantime granted Catherine a pension. On this she and Jérôme set up house, first in Bern, then in Gratz, and finally in Trieste. Whenever Catherine wrote to her father suggesting that she and her husband come to Württemberg, he wrote back insisting that she divorce Jérôme and come alone. She would never even consider it. The selfish, feckless, philandering Jérôme had a far better wife than he deserved.

Joachim Murat, on the other hand, had exactly the sort of wife he deserved. He and Caroline, alone amongst the Bonapartes, were still managing to hang on to their throne. It was no simple matter, as Ferdinand, King of the Two Sicilies, was agitating for the restoration of his dominions. Ferdinand's claims were raised by Talleyrand (now serving the restored Bourbon King) at the Congress of Vienna, and opposed by Metternich. It seemed that Metternich's interest in the affair went deeper than was generally supposed; in her scramble to power, Caroline had once needed Metternich's helping hand, and she had secured it in the most effective way she knew. Metternich, according to Talleyrand, was by now passionately in love with Queen Caroline, and even Louis XVIII spoke darkly in terms of a modern Antony and Cleopatra.

With Austria thus championing his cause, Murat should have been satisfied. But his was not the temperament to lie low when there was uncertainty in the air. The intrigues at Vienna unsettled him; surrounded by newly restored rulers, he became ever more apprehensive for his own throne. "You know Murat's temper," said Metternich sagely, for he, like Talleyrand, always played a double game. "Sooner or later, he will make a slip, by which we shall profit."

Metternich was right. Murat made his slip in the spring of 1815, on the receipt of a momentous piece of news.

⚜ ⚜ ⚜

On March 5, 1815, as Hortense was returning home from a drive, a friend galloped up to her carriage and thrust his head into the window. "Have you heard the great news, Madame?" he cried. "The Emperor Napoleon has landed at Cannes." Napoleon, with a handful of men, had escaped from Elba and was making for Paris

Once the first shock had worn off, Hortense's thoughts were for the safety of her sons. She hurried home and packed them off to the country. The next few days passed in a blur of uncertainty, with dozens of conflicting rumors flooding Paris and a host of anxious Bonapartists crowding her salon. By the tenth of the month, when the news of Napoleon's amazing advance towards Paris had been confirmed, Hortense herself was obliged to go into hiding to escape arrest. For the following nine days, while more and more Frenchmen rallied to Napoleon's standard— until the few hundred men with whom he had landed had swollen to an enormous force—Hortense remained hidden in an attic. It was only when she noticed the ultraroyalist painter living in the house opposite busily dusting a full-length portrait of one of the ex-Emperor's ministers that she realized that her period of hiding was almost over. That evening she was told that Louis XVIII had fled Paris the night before, and the following day she was able to return home in safety. On her way back, she noticed the Parisian shopkeepers frantically obliterating the Bourbon lilies on their signs and replacing them with the bees and eagles of the Empire.

The Emperor, his bloodless march from the south to his capital accomplished, was due to arrive in Paris that evening. Hortense changed into a court dress and hurried to the Tuileries. So enthusiastically was she cheered on her arrival that for a moment she imagined Napoleon to have arrived at the same time; her sentimentality being blended with cynicism, she could not help smiling at the almost hysterical reception from those who a few days before had not even bothered to greet her. Inside the palace there was no less enthusiasm. Queen Julie arrived (she was in Paris trying to regain possession of Mortefontaine) and together the two Bonaparte queens made their smiling way through the crush of courtiers waiting for the Emperor's arrival. It was noticed that the Napoleonic bees which had once decorated the carpet in the throne room had been covered with Bourbon lilies, and that by tugging at these superimposed cyphers they came away, revealing the original design under-neath. Immediately the entire company were crawling about on their knees, wrenching off the offending lilies and shrieking with laughter as they worked. Within half an hour the throne room carpet was once more swarming with golden bees.

Napoleon arrived at nine o'clock. His appearance was greeted with an ear-splitting shout of *"Vive l'Empereur."* He was wearing his old gray overcoat, and so great was the press of cheering, waving, weeping admirers that he was unable to move a step. "For heaven's sake, get in front of him, so that he can move," shouted someone, and Lavallette, one of his devoted officers, placed himself in front of his hero and walked slowly backwards while Napoleon advanced. Lavallette, in a highly emotional state, could only see the Emperor through a smudge of tears, and in his delirium he kept repeating: "What! It's you! It's you! It's you at last!"

Napoleon, like a man in a dream, his eyes closed and his hands stretched out in front of him, moved slowly up the staircase, his plump face catlike with smiling. Hortense and Julie, who from fear of suffoca-tion had had to fight their way out of the intoxicated throng, now saw him being "caught up by a thousand arms and carried in triumph to his own apartments." Determined to greet him, they once more plunged into the melee and managed to force a passage to his drawing room. Eagerly they stepped forward to embrace him. Napoleon, until a minute ago so ecstatic, eyed his two advancing sisters-in-law coldly.

"What chance," he asked icily, "has brought you here?"

The following day Hortense had the opportunity of explaining what Napoleon considered to be her fraternization with the enemy. The presence of her two little boys and her protestations that it was for their benefit that she had accepted the Duchy of St.-Leu softened Napoleon's heart, and by the end of the interview he and Hortense were back on their old familiar footing. He spoke of Josephine, and when, a few days later, he and Hortense walked through Josephine's lovely gardens at Malmaison, he appeared to be deeply moved. "How all these places remind me of her!" He sighed. "I cannot believe she is no longer here!"

Napoleon wanted Hortense to do him a favor; she was to write to the Empress Marie Louise, telling her something of Napoleon's enthusiastic reception by the French, and assuring her that the Emperor was looking forward to her arrival. Napoleon, knowing that Marie Louise had always been fond of Hortense, imagined that a letter from her might encourage his Empress to come back; none of his own letters had met with any success. Hardly had he landed in France before he had written to Marie Louise, asking her to join him, but neither this first appeal, nor any subsequent one, had been answered. Her presence was very necessary to lend respectability to his latest venture; with the daughter of the Emperor of Austria once more on the throne of France, and his grandson, the little King of Rome, its heir, Napoleon's regime would regain a solidity sadly lacking at present.

But Marie Louise did not come. Nor, with the exception of an occasional moment of uncertainty when urged by the French members of her suite, did she ever have any intention of coming. Her sojourn at Aix, where she had gone to recuperate after the collapse of the Empire, had been more pleasant than she had anticipated. The Emperor Francis, knowing his daughter and knowing how necessary it was for her to have someone on hand to guide her, had issued orders that some Austrian officer attend her on her journey. The officer chosen for this task, a certain Count von Neipperg, was instructed to try, by any means he considered effective, to dissuade her from joining Napoleon on Elba. As the thirty-nine-year-old Neipperg was handsome, well built, virile, worldly, smooth-tongued, charmingly mannered, and anxious to carry out his instructions, he used the means which came most readily to hand.

The simple Marie Louise, separated from the two men to whom she had always turned for support—her father and Napoleon—now turned to the nearest man available, and he met her more than halfway. Bewildered by world-shaking events for which she was no match, agonized at the thought of having to make any decisions on her own, disturbed by stories she had recently heard of Napoleon's infidelities, Marie Louise tried to shift her troubles onto Neipperg. She was relieved to find that his broad shoulders could bear them without difficulty. He became her adviser, her friend, her confidant, and finally—as she was an affectionate, highly sexed girl of twenty-two—her lover. The accusation that Marie Louise did not join Napoleon on Elba because she was in love with Neipperg is not strictly true; Napoleon had become associated in her mind with trouble, and trouble was the one thing she tried all her life to avoid. The chances are that had it not been Neipperg who finally dissuaded her from joining Napoleon, it would have been someone else— her father, or Metternich, or some other man of their choosing.

The news of Napoleon's escape from Elba threw Marie Louise into a fresh quandary. Having returned from Aix and settled quietly at Schönbrunn to await the decision of the Congress on her future status, Napoleon's return brought a resurgence of her own confusion. Clinging, as always, to what was familiar and to hand, she allowed Neipperg to convince her that she must publicly repudiate Napoleon. How much better it would be for her to accept the diminutive Duchy of Parma offered her by the Congress, and so secure a peaceful future for herself and her son, than to expose herself to the dangers of Napoleon's latest escapade. Thankful for advice which required no effort from herself, she broke once and for all with her husband. She left his torrent of letters unanswered and agreed to the dismissal of certain Frenchmen in her service. She hoped, she intimated to Napoleon, that he would appreciate how grateful she was to him, that he would understand her unhappy situation, and that he would bear her no resentment. The one concrete fact to emerge from this blur of well-meaning sentiments was that she would not under any circumstances be returning to France. That episode of her life was over. When the Allies, forgetting for a few weeks the dissensions which had plagued the negotiations at the Congress, united to crush Napoleon, they marched towards France with the blessing of Marie Louise, ex-Empress of the French.

♛   ♛   ♛

Napoleon's wife stayed away, but his brothers—with the exception of the disgruntled Louis—returned in full force.

Joseph, moving swiftly to avoid arrest by the Swiss government, arrived in Paris a few days after Napoleon. Here he took up residence in the Palais Royal. Lucien, deciding at long last to throw in his lot with his brother, and in no fear of arrest, moved more leisurely, and arrived from Rome towards the middle of April. Jérôme, also threatened with capture, escaped from Trieste in a Neapolitan ship, and after a stay in Naples, landed in the South of France. He immediately assumed the airs of a king, and by the time he reached Lyons, the erstwhile refugee was surrounded by a considerable court, including ladies in waiting, although his Queen, Catherine, was still in Trieste. With the escape of Jérôme, the Austrians had forced her and her little son to retire to Gratz, in Austria, and from here she was moved to Göppingen, in her father's Kingdom of Württemberg. During the Hundred Days, and for some months afterwards, she was a virtual prisoner at Göppingen.

Louis, who always had an inflated idea of his importance to Napoleon, promised to return on condition that he could divorce Hortense and get control of his sons. Napoleon would not hear of divorce, and Louis, much to Hortense's relief, remained in Italy. A few days before the Emperor's arrival from Elba she had heard that the legal proceedings which Louis had started in order to get custody of Napoleon-Louis had been successful. The order to hand over her eldest son within three months, which would have been so heartbreaking at any other time, had been quite forgotten (and of course, discounted) in the confusion of Napoleon's arrival. The Emperor wanted as many Bonapartes about him as possible now, and for the present Hortense's two sons were safe.

The faithful Madame Mère arrived in Paris at the beginning of June. She was delighted to find Napoleon and Lucien reunited, and if only Louis had been there, her happiness would have been complete, and her sense of family satisfied. Someone who saw her at the Opening of the Chambers a few days after her arrival claimed that she was still one of the handsomest women who had ever lived. "Her beautiful black eyes, shaded by long lashes and surmounted by delicate arched eyebrows, might have challenged comparison with those of many young women in brightness and expression." Although she was sixty-five years old at the time, she had a better figure than most women half her age, and she moved with all the dignity of a born princess.

Her three daughters did not follow her to France. Elisa, not nimble enough to make her escape from Bologna, was arrested by the Austrians and taken to the castle of Brünn, in Moravia. She remained here under close, if kindly, guard for the duration of the Hundred Days. Pauline, who had set out from Elba with every intention of going to France, was waylaid on the coast of Italy when her ship was obliged to take shelter. Her foolish broadcasting of the news that Napoleon had escaped from Elba led to her arrest, and she was imprisoned in the castle of Compignano. In vain did the lovely Pauline protest that her arrival in Italy was by merest chance and had nothing to do with politics; with Italy once more in a restless state, the Austrians were taking no chances, and Napoleon's sister was kept firmly under lock and key. It was the first time in her life that she was suspected of being an incitement to anything other than sin.

Murat, convinced that the Allies would never safeguard his throne, now decided to join Napoleon once more. Napoleon, desperately in need of all the men he could find, accepted Murat's offer, advising him to prepare for war. The hot-headed Murat, however, imagining that his dreams of becoming King of Italy were about to be realized, did not wait for further instructions, but marched against the Papal States at the head of forty thousand men. He issued a proclamation calling upon the Italians to rise up against their Austrian oppressors; but the Italians ignored the invitation, and Murat's force was completely routed by the Austrians at Tolentino. He fled to Naples, and from there escaped to France, where he offered his sword to the Emperor. Napoleon, infuriated at Murat's rash adventure, declined the offer.

Caroline, who had been acting as Regent in his absence, had been obliged, first to surrender the little Neapolitan fleet to the British, and then, in the face of an insurrection against her in the city, to seek refuge on one of the British ships. At night, from the deck of the *Tremendous*, she was able to see the glow of the illuminations and hear the thunder of cannon as her late subjects celebrated the restoration of King Ferdinand. By day she underwent the more intimate humiliation of having abuse shouted at her from the dozens of little boats collected around the *Tremendous*. Her plea to be allowed to join her husband in France was not granted, and she and her children were shipped off to Trieste. There is a story that as Caroline, in the *Tremendous*, was sailing away from Naples, she crossed the vessel carrying the restored Ferdinand back to his kingdom. As the captain of the *Tremendous* was obliged to fire a salute in honor of the new monarch, he warned Caroline not to be alarmed at the sound of the guns.

"*Monsieur*," replied the ex-Queen of Naples proudly, "the sound of cannon is neither new nor unpleasant to the ear of a Bonaparte."

As a sop to public opinion more than anything else, Napoleon now decided to grant France a more liberal constitution. (In this he had his brother Lucien's enthusiastic support. Lucien had always claimed to abhor Napoleon's absolutism and under his guidance a new constitution was drawn up.) The new democratic regime was inaugurated on June 1, 1815, at a solemn ceremony in the Champ de Mars. Dressed in his Imperial robes and flanked by his brothers, resplendent in white velvet tunics, plumed hats, and mantles embroidered with golden bees, Napoleon swore fidelity to the new constitution. Then he turned his attention to a task much more to his taste: the distribution of the eagles to the assembled regiments. The first ceremony had been a gesture to popular sentiment, the second, a slap in the face for the Allied Powers.

Watching this grandiose ceremony from a special gallery set aside for the court were Hortense and her two sons. Whether or not these brilliant scenes made a lasting impression on the mind of the seven-year-old Louis-Napoleon, one does not know; but the restoration of a liberal empire such as this became for him an *idée fixe* in later life. As the superbly uniformed troops passed by in review, Hortense herself was filled with foreboding. Fouché, noticing her expression, asked her why she looked so sad.

"Ah!" replied Hortense, "after this comes war, and that is a dreadful thought."

"What can one do?" said Fouché, with a shrug. "The Emperor has just missed a great opportunity. I advised him to abdicate today. Had he done so, his son would have succeeded to the throne and war would have been avoided."

Napoleon had disregarded Fouché's advice. He would never have been able to stand aside while Fouché and Talleyrand ruled France in the name of his son, and he realized, moreover, that the Allies were determined to eradicate the Bonapartes, root and branch. Only by winning a resounding victory over them could he hope to secure the throne for himself and his son, and this he was determined to do. The first days of June were devoted to preparations for the coming struggle.

On Sunday, June 11, the Emperor gave a farewell dinner for his family at the Elysée palace. Jérôme had already left Paris to take command of a division in the 2nd *corps d'armée* (Napoleon was not going to entrust him with anything bigger this time), but the rest were there: his mother, Joseph, Lucien, Julie, and Hortense. Napoleon seemed to be in good spirits, although Hortense considered his gaiety a little forced. After dinner Joseph's daughters, Zenaïde and Charlotte, and Hortense's sons, Napoleon-Louis and Louis-Napoleon, joined the party, and Napoleon, always at his best with children, entertained them charmingly. After this the family adjourned to the large salon of the palace, where Napoleon took informal leave of his court.

There is a legend that at some stage during the evening little Louis-Napoleon, running up to his uncle, cried out, "Sire, I don't want you to go to the war; those wicked Allies will kill you!"

Napoleon is reputed to have turned to Marshal Soult and said, "Embrace the child, Marshal; he has a good heart. Perhaps one day he will be the hope of my race."

Before leaving Paris at four the next morning, Napoleon light-heartedly assured his companions that he planned to spend the following Sunday in Brussels. He spent it, in fact, at Waterloo.

♛   ♛   ♛

On the afternoon of June 20, 1815, Hortense and her circle were gathered in her salon to hear Benjamin Constant give a reading of his latest novel. At the very moment when the author had reduced the entire gathering, including himself, to tears, there was a knock at the door. Hortense was told that the Duke de Rovigo wished to speak to her. He told her that there were rumors that the Emperor had sustained a terrible defeat near the Belgian village of Waterloo. That evening the news was confirmed. Joseph had received the dispatches; the disaster was complete. The Emperor was due back at the Elysée that night.

He arrived, disheveled and exhausted, at eight the following morning. He threw himself into a hot bath and sent for Joseph and Lucien. Hortense arrived, but was told that she would not be able to see him until after his meeting with the Council of Ministers. She returned again in the late afternoon, and found him walking alone under the trees in the Elysée garden.

"Well, what have people been saying to you?" he asked her as she advanced towards him along the path.

"That you have been unfortunate, Sire," she answered simply.

He said nothing for a few minutes, and then, walking away, motioned her to follow. His listlessness, his aimlessness, his overwhelming depression, appalled her. He sat down at his desk and shuffled through a pile of letters without seeing them; he seemed unconscious of the fact that she was there. When dinner was announced, he remembered her and invited her to keep him company at table. He hardly spoke during the meal. After dinner his mother, Joseph, and Lucien arrived. Hortense, never really at ease in their company, withdrew. Lucien had spent most of the day trying to rally the hostile members of the Assembly to Napoleon's cause, but he had had no success. The Emperor, they had claimed, was standing in the way of peace, and only when he had disappeared would France be saved. Unless he abdicated, they would vote for his deposition. The fiery Lucien, flinging aside his long professed republicanism, was all for Napoleon dissolving the Assembly—by force if necessary—and assuming dictatorial powers, but by now Napoleon had lost heart. He seemed incapable of making up his mind.

The following day, after further stormy scenes in the Council chamber, Napoleon decided to abdicate. With the crowd still shouting "Vive l'Empereur" outside the windows of the Elysée, the Emperor dictated his abdication message to Lucien. "My political life is over," he dictated to his disapproving brother, "and I proclaim my son, under the title of Napoleon II, Emperor of the French."

Thus, on June 22, 1815, a four-year-old boy, living hundreds of miles away in Schönbrunn Palace in Vienna, became Emperor of the French. His reign was to last a few days only.

Having abdicated, Napoleon did not seem to know what to do next. He was constantly discussing future plans with his brothers; Jérôme had arrived back from Waterloo by now, and both he and Lucien were confident that, with the King of Rome having been proclaimed Emperor, all was not yet over. Napoleon and Joseph were less sanguine. Hortense and Madame Mère, displaying more common sense than any of the men, realized that this irresolution was madness; unless Napoleon got away as quickly as possible, his life would be in danger. Encouraged by Madame Mère, Hortense begged Napoleon to come to some decision. If he was planning to go to America (and this seemed to be his latest intention), then he should get to a port while there was still time. If he favored Austria, then he should throw himself at the mercy of his father-in-law, the Emperor Francis. She herself advised him to appeal to the Czar Alexander; he was loyal and generous and could be trusted. Why did Napoleon not write to him?

To all this frantic outpouring of advice, says Hortense, Napoleon answered not one word. When he did speak, it was to ask her what she intended doing. Exasperated at his state of immobility, she cried out, "Ah! Sire, I don't care what becomes of me, I can only think of you. The worst of my suggestions is better than this inaction."

A day or two later Napoleon asked Hortense whether he might spend a few days with her at Malmaison before setting sail for America. In spite of the shocked protests of her friends, who were still thinking, at a time like this, of propriety, Hortense agreed, and went ahead to prepare for his arrival. Once he was there, all his thoughts seemed to be of Josephine. Hortense found him walking in Josephine's rose garden one morning, and when she joined him, he sighed, and said, "My poor Josephine! I can't get used to being in this place without her! I seem to keep on seeing her coming along one of the paths and picking these flowers that she loved so much! Poor Josephine." Then, seeing Hortense's blue eyes swimming with tears, he added, "But still, she would have been very unhappy now. We only ever quarreled about one subject—her debts, and about them I scolded her a great deal. I have never seen anyone so full of grace as she was. She was a woman in the fullest sense of the word, variable, lively, and with the best of hearts. . . . "

Later that day their party at Malmaison was joined by Madame Mère, Joseph, Lucien, and Jérôme. And a day or two later Hortense was introduced to a member of the Emperor's family whom she had never met before. Napoleon sent for her at midday, and she found him in the garden talking to a boy of nine or ten. Drawing her aside, he said, "Hortense, look at this child; whom is he like?"

Without hesitation she answered, "Your son, Sire; he is the image of the King of Rome."

"You think so?" asked the Emperor. "Then it must be so. The sight of him has moved me—I who did not think I had a tender heart! You seem to know about his birth. How did you find out?"

"Sire, people have talked about it a great deal, and this likeness proves they were not mistaken."

"I admit I doubted for a long time if he was my son. All the same, I had him brought up at a school in Paris. . . . I wished to see him, and like you, I was struck by his resemblance to my son."

The boy was Napoleon's son by Eléonore Dénuelle, the woman whom Caroline had introduced to the Emperor in the early days of the Empire. It was his birth, in 1806, which had finally proved Napoleon's sexual potency. Hortense asked the Emperor what he planned to do with the boy; Napoleon said that when he reached America, he would send for him. While the Emperor went off to speak to the boy's guardian, Hortense addressed the child. He was, she says, "as beautiful as an angel." She asked him if he was happy at school and what games he played. He told her that lately he and his friends played at making war on each other. There were two sides, he explained seriously, the one called Bonapartists, the other Bourbonists. Hortense wanted to know to which party he belonged.

"I am one of the King's men," answered the boy.

When Hortense asked him why, he answered that it was because he liked the King and did not like the Emperor. On being asked his reasons for not liking the Emperor, he said, "I have no reason, except that I belong to the King's party."

Clearly the child had not the slightest idea of the identity of the plump, kindly man speaking so earnestly to his guardian.

During luncheon, Napoleon could speak of nothing but the boy. "The sight of that child moved me," he said; "he resembles my son. I did not think that I was capable of such emotion as he has aroused. . . ." He saw another of his sons the following morning. Marie Walewska and her boy came to say good-by to the Emperor. The farewell upset poor Marie so much that Hortense was obliged to lunch alone with her, lest the rest of the company see the terrible state she was in. Throughout these final days Napoleon never once mentioned the absence of his legitimate son. A few weeks before, Méneval, Napoleon's ex-secretary, who had since been in the service of Marie Louise, had returned to France from Vienna. Before leaving, he had asked the little King of Rome whether he had any messages for his father. Drawing Méneval away from the others in the room, the boy had whispered, "Monsieur Méneval, you will tell him that I always love him very much."

With the Prussians drawing nearer to Malmaison every day, Hortense was in an agony of apprehension. There were two frigates waiting at the port of La Rochelle to convey Napoleon to America, but every day's delay lessened his chances of getting away safely. Either he would be taken prisoner by the advancing Prussians or else his ship would be captured by the waiting English. With Napoleon ignoring her persistent appeals for him to hurry and get away, Hortense applied to Joseph. But he seemed every bit as irresolute as his brother. It was only on June 29 that Napoleon finally managed to get started. One by one he took leave of his tearful followers and relations. He left Madame Mère to the end. The celebrated actor Talma, himself just having taken leave of Napoleon, was witness to the final farewell between mother and son. Napoleon seemed quite calm, and except for two tears which trickled down Letizia's cheeks, she was calm also.

"Farewell, my son!" she said.

"Farewell, Mama," he answered.

Wrapped in a long gray overcoat and followed by a handful of officers, Napoleon left Malmaison and walked swiftly to the gate where a coach was waiting. As he was about to clamber inside, he looked back for a moment, then flung himself into the carriage. The coachman slapped the reins and the coach started down the road. It was the beginning of a journey which was to end, five thousand miles away, at St. Helena.

As the shadows shifted across the lawns at Malmaison and the Empress Josephine's roses glowed gold in the late afternoon sun, Napoleon's companions trailed back into the darkening house. The sun was about to set on the First Empire. "So it's the end of all this, then. . . ." mused Talleyrand. "What a downfall for history to record. To give one's name merely to an adventure instead of to one's century!"

But for once, Talleyrand was wrong. This was not by any means the end of the name Napoleon.

PART THREE

The Years Between

1815–1852

CHAPTER EIGHT

⊕ ⊕ ⊕

"But what shall we do in that forlorn place?" asked Napoleon of one of his companions when he heard that he was to be exiled to the island of St. Helena.

"Sire," replied his admiring chamberlain, the Count de Las Cases, "we will live in the past. Do we not read the lives of Caesar and Alexander? We will have a still better: we will reread *your* life, Sire!"

"Of course," answered the Emperor, brightening. "We will write our memoirs. . . . After all, one must fulfil one's destiny—that is my great principle! Let mine be accomplished!"

And during the five and a half years he spent on St. Helena, he devoted himself to this accomplishing of his destiny, writing the story of his past with an eye fixed firmly on the future. If there were any chance of his son's regaining the Imperial throne, it would have to be against a background of liberalism. Napoleon II would have to offer democracy to the French and encourage nationalism in the people of Europe; therefore Napoleon I must present himself as a democrat, a champion of national aspirations, and a friend of peace. It was no easy task, but the martyred Emperor and his devoted disciples set to it with a will. By the masterly playing down of his more highhanded moments and the spotlighting of his rare bursts of liberalism—particularly the short-lived constitution of 1815—he hoped to pave the way for the restoration of his dynasty. The Napoleonic legend was beginning to take shape; St. Helena, which was to see the death of Bonaparte, was about to witness the birth of Bonapartism.

It was for this birth of the Napoleonic legend (which would, in time, contribute towards the restoration of his empire) that Napoleon's exile on St. Helena is chiefly significant. Napoleon, for all his crying out against the inadequate accommodation, the humiliating restrictions, the lack of due respect to his person, was astute enough to appreciate the dramatic possibilities of his exile. What better place to inaugurate a creed than on this lonely wave-lashed, wind-swept rock? "It is better for my son that I should be here," he once declared frankly. "If he lives, my martyrdom will win him a crown. . . . If I die on the cross—and he is still alive—he will come to the throne."

Propagating the doubtful virtues of Bonapartism suited him admirably. Always a great talker, he could now talk to his heart's content, while his companions—Count Bertrand, Count de Las Cases, Count de Montholon, and Baron Gourgaud—tried to keep pace with the torrent that came tumbling from their master's lips. Up and down the small, hot, ill-furnished rooms of Longwood House he would strut, his followers setting down his words frantically, always, notes one of them, "one or two or even three sentences behind." He would think nothing of sending for one of his officers at four in the morning and subjecting the sleep-bemused man to a whirlwind of dictated reminiscences lasting well into the day. And at night, when all the house, when all the island— except for the ever-vigilant sentries—was asleep, there would come the ceaseless churning of that voice and the *scratch, scratch, scratch* of some swiftly moving pen.

Although the need to secure the future of his dynasty colored much of his reminiscing, it by no means colored it all. When he was not dictating, he would talk on every topic under the sun; no subject was too insignificant—or too significant—for that extraordinary mind. The journals kept by his companions contain Napoleon's views on such diverse subjects as religion and women's clothes, politics and gardening, medicine and love affairs, military history and food. And time and again, in characteristically frank, and often indelicate, manner, he would discuss the various members of his family. He was seldom complimentary.

His mother alone escaped his caustic tongue. Imprisoned on this lonely Atlantic island, his thoughts often turned to the island of his birth, and to the woman who had raised him. It was, he claimed, to her firm and kindly handling during his boyhood that he owed his subsequent rise to power. She was a Roman; a woman of the old school. "My mother," he said one day to Gourgaud, "was a superb woman, with great intelligence."

Intelligence, however, was a quality sadly lacking in the majority of her children. Distance and misfortune seemed to have afforded Napoleon a somewhat clearer view of their shortcomings. He realized that he should never have entrusted them with crowns. "People have often vaunted my strength of character," he said one day to Las Cases. "Well, I was nothing but a wet hen, especially for my own people—and they knew it. Once they had swallowed the first rebuff, they kept at it, and their stubbornness and persistence always won the day—I got tired of haggling. They did with me what they pleased."

Joseph, he said, was a fool. He fancied himself as a soldier and a ruler, whereas he was incapable of carrying out even the simplest project. He should never have been made king, either of Naples or Spain. The Neapolitans had preferred Murat, with his aggressively military air, and in Madrid Joseph had thought of nothing but skirts. He was happiest in the company of women, not only for sexual pleasure, but because he enjoyed their society.

Lucien had merely posed as a Republican. The Republicans themselves had had no time for him; when Napoleon had accepted his services during the drawing up of the new constitution in 1815, not one Republican had rallied to his cause. Lucien had stolen a great deal when he was a minister during the Consulate; when Napoleon had refused to allow him to marry the Queen of Etruria (this was a typically Napoleonic distortion of the truth), Lucien had gone off and married a whore.

He had done more for Louis than for any of the others. Napoleon was fond of recalling those early days at Auxonne, when he and Louis had shared a room and had subsisted on the elder brother's meager pay. Louis had been very promising in those days, very handsome. The women had all been attracted to him. Now he was simply a dunce! When Napoleon came across a booklet written by Louis in which he defended his conduct in Holland and accused his brother of despotism, the Emperor sighed. "Ah! Louis, you too!"

Another book concerning one of his family—lent to him by the Governor of St. Helena, Sir Hudson Lowe—was a scandalous account of the court of Westphalia during the reign of his brother, ex-King Jérôme. It is doubtful whether its revelations either shocked or surprised Napoleon. Jérôme's philanderings were not news to him; neither was his conceit. "My family has never upheld me," he remarked one day. "My brothers have as many pretensions as if they could say: 'The King, our father.' "

He rated the capabilities of his sisters Elisa and Caroline somewhat higher. Elisa, he said to Montholon, had "noble qualities and a respectable intelligence." There had never been much intimacy between them—their temperaments had been too different. Caroline, although every bit as able as Elisa, he never forgave for her treachery. Pauline alone retained his affection. She was, he claimed, the most beautiful woman in Europe.

But his thoughts seemed to revert most frequently to Josephine. In these sunset years of his career memories of this woman whom he had loved in the days of his dawning greatness came coursing back. Perhaps there was something in the quality of the seductively warm, starlit evenings that reminded him of her; perhaps, surrounded by a bitter, bickering, dowdy, dissatisfied household, he had come to appreciate anew her kindness, her calm, her chic, her sympathy. "She was really an amiable woman—elegant, charming and affable . . . ," he said to his doctor. "She was the goddess of fashion; all the styles originated from her; everything she put on appeared elegant; and she was so kind, so humane—she was the best woman in France." He assured Count Bertrand that he had really loved her. He had never respected her—she was far too great a liar to command respect—but she had something, he did not know what, that attracted him. She was all woman; her backside, he mused, was the sweetest in the world.

He would go on to compare her qualities with those of his second Empress, Marie Louise. Marie Louise was indifference personified, innocence personified—the very antithesis of Josephine. She had never lied. She had been devoted to him. She was, he told Gourgaud, "a charming child." He never tired of telling them about his first meeting —that day that he had scampered through the rain and flung himself into her coach; or about her *accouchement*—sparing none of the intimate details and playing up his own role in the drama. About her more recent exploits he was less loquacious. If questioned about the unbroken silence from Vienna, he forced himself to make excuses for her. "I believe that Marie Louise is just as much a state prisoner as I am myself . . . ," he would say. I have always had occasion to praise the conduct of my good Louise, and I believe that it is totally out of her power to assist me; moreover, she is young and timorous." But he knew about her lover Count von Neipperg, and in his heart he must have known that he would never see her again.

The person who preoccupied him most, the one about whom all his dreams for the future revolved, was the one whom he hardly ever mentioned—his infant son. And yet one had only to enter his two little rooms at Longwood to realize how important a place the boy held in Napoleon's affections. "Over the fireplace hangs a very small glass, together with several pictures," reports Las Cases. "On the right is a portrait of the King of Rome, sitting on a sheep, by Aimée Thiebault; and on the left hangs, as a *pendant* to it, another portrait of the young prince, sitting on a cushion and putting on a slipper; . . . lower down is a small marble bust of the King of Rome, . . . at the foot of the couch, and directly in view of the Emperor when he reposes on it, which he does the greater part of the day, hangs Isabey's portrait of Maria Louisa, holding her son in her arms."

One of Napoleon's valets mentions still other paintings of the little king; one of him on his knees praying to God for France; another, "very young and naked with his head in a helmet," lying on a bed of laurel within the gaudy shade of the massed flags of France. Later Napoleon received yet another portrait, one in which the boy was depicted in rather less bizarre fashion, sporting a white satin coat.

This wealth of portraiture, comforting as it must have been to the adoring father, could not reconcile him to his son's absence. He longed for more tangible proof of the boy's existence. With pathetic eagerness he snatched at any little thread which might bind him closer to the absent prince. Such threads were rare indeed. One was provided by a young botanist who had come to St. Helena with the Austrian commissioner (each of the victorious Allies had sent a commissioner to the island to report on Napoleon's captivity), and who had previously been employed in the gardens at Schönbrunn Palace. Before leaving Vienna, a package containing a curl of blond hair cut from the head of the King of Rome had been thrust into his hands; it had been entrusted to him by the French nurse who had accompanied the young king into exile. This French nurse happened to be the mother of Napoleon's valet on St. Helena. Arriving on the island, the young botanist had sent for the valet, handed him the package, and given him news of the Imperial heir, whom he had often seen at play in the park at Schönbrunn. The valet had hurried back to Longwood and given the lock of hair to his delighted master. The Emperor had fondled it, bemoaning the fact that it should be from his servants, and not from his Empress, that he had received this news of his son.

Actually, he had had high hopes on the arrival of the Austrian commissioner, believing that he would be the bearer of some official news from the Hapsburg court. As the weeks went by and none was forthcoming, Napoleon had to fall back on a less direct method of communicating with the representative of the Emperor of Austria. Madame Montholon, the wife of one of his officers, was instructed to attend the races and to ask the wife of the Austrian commissioner for news of Napoleon's son. Her mission appears to have been fruitless, but it seems that the commissioner's lady was not slow in acquainting others with details of the Imperial child. One finds the Governor, Sir Hudson Lowe, writing "of the King of Rome, of whose beauty, intelligence, and dignity of whose infantile manner, the Baroness . . . seems quite full."

It was the Governor himself who afforded the father some pleasure by informing him, through an aide, that there was a picture of his son on the island. The print was actually an engraving of the King of Rome in a newspaper, and Lowe arranged for it to be sent up to Longwood immediately. The Emperor was "excessively pleased," and had it shown, not only to his own suite, but to some of the English officers guarding him as well. He informed them—for so did the island society seethe with gossip—that he had known about the engraving's being on the island for three months past.

Another thread was from a less reliable source. In May 1817 news arrived at Longwood that a marble bust of the King of Rome had been brought to the island by a gunner aboard the *Baring*, who had instructions to sell it to the Emperor for a hundred louis. It was a poor piece of work, a conventional likeness executed by a stonecutter in London and tricked out with the Legion of Honor in order to convince the all-too-gullible Emperor that it had been modeled from life. Napoleon was overjoyed on seeing it, and promptly ordered Count Bertrand to pay the gunner three hundred guineas for it. When Lowe hinted that the wretched work was not worth even the hundred louis first demanded, the Emperor exclaimed that to him it was worth a million! Eagerly, in a foam of excitement, he set it on the mantel and proudly commended it to his companions. Did Gourgaud think that it was the Empress, or the sculptor, who had chosen the eagle of the Legion of Honor? How proud he must be, sighed one of the women, to be the father of such a beautiful child! That sweet face would melt the heart of the most ferocious wild beast, claimed the Emperor. "He gazed on the bust," reports his doctor, "for several minutes, with great satisfaction and delight; his face covered in smiles and strongly expressive of paternal love and pride. . . . No person who had witnessed this scene could deny that Napoleon was animated by the tender affection of a father."

Nor could one deny that his enthusiasm for this amateur piece was the enthusiasm of a man who has found some relief from an embarrassing situation. Here was tangible proof that Marie Louise had not forgotten him; he was somehow able to convince himself that she had commissioned it, that his son had actually sat for it; he could even wonder whether it was the Empress who had chosen the decoration for the little chest. With this present from his Empress on display for all to see, he could prattle on about the neck being too deep-sunken or the child looking like its mother, for he was experiencing a little happiness on a subject which usually left him profoundly unhappy. In the ordinary way, the situation was too poignant to bear talking about. On the few occasions that he did mention his son, it was always with sadness and concern. "They have taken my son away from me, just as they used to take the children of the vanquished to adorn the trophy of the victors," he once sighed. "Nothing more barbarous has been perpetrated in modern times."

He knew by now that the boy was being reared as an Austrian archduke. To the ex-Emperor of the French this was a source of acute anxiety. What education would they give him? What sort of principles would they engraft on his youthful mind? What if he should be weak in intellect? Or if they should inspire him with hatred of his father? He realized that communication between them was impossible; there was no "faithful tradition" to bind them more closely together. At best he could hope that his memoirs, that the journals of his companions, that his carefully nurtured "legend" would reach the growing boy and guide him towards his destiny.

"But to overcome false precepts learned in early life, to counteract the errors of a bad education, requires a certain capacity, a certain strength of mind and decision of judgment which fall not to the share of everyone. . . ."

Did he suspect, prophetically, that his son lacked this "strength of mind," this "decision of judgment"? Did he fear that this painstaking building of a legend might be in vain? For as day followed dreary day, and the threads which bound their two exiled lives together frayed and fell apart, Napoleon seemed, at times, almost overwhelmed with the utter hopelessness of the situation. When on the morning of his forty-eighth birthday Gourgaud presented him with a little bouquet "on behalf of the King of Rome," Napoleon sighed, and said, "Bah! The King of Rome thinks no more of me than of . . ."

"Put that by," he said sharply to his valet one day, thrusting a snuff-box into his hand, "it is always meeting my eye, and it hurts me." It was, surmised the ever-vigilant Las Cases, the snuffbox bearing the portrait of the King of Rome.

♔   ♔   ♔

That Napoleon was thinking constantly of his son there is no doubt; that the little boy was giving his father much thought was less certain. He was, on the contrary, being given every encouragement to forget him.

Once Napoleon had been defeated at Waterloo, the dearest wish of the victors was that the events of the last twenty-five years be erased from memory and that Europe be restored to its pre-Revolutionary and pre-Napoleonic normality. Napoleon himself was imprisioned on St. Helena, and the deposed Bourbons were brought out of exile and lovingly reinstated. The movements of the remaining Bonapartes were severely restricted, although Europe knew the characters of Napoleon's brothers far too well to worry about their aspirations. In all cases the ambition of the remaining adult Bonapartes was to be allowed to live in peace and—what was more important—comfort.

There remained Napoleon's son. Never had so small a child been so great an embarrassment. All the glories, all the menace of Napoleon's Empire were now concentrated in this little boy; while he lived, Napoleon had an heir, and the system against which Europe had fought so desperately for the last fifteen years had a figurehead. What was to be done with him? Several centuries earlier he would probably have been poisoned; in these more enlightened times one had to devise more subtle means of minimizing his importance. Luckily, he was still young enough to be molded into whatever form was thought advisable, and to this end his grandfather, the Emperor of Austria, spurred on by the shrewd Metternich, directed his energies.

All traces of the boy's French Imperial past were to be eradicated, and he was to be turned into a German princeling. One by one his French attendants—those adoring women who had accompanied him from France —were stripped away and replaced by an Austrian household. A trio of tutors, headed by the upright but unimaginative Count Dietrichstein, were appointed to supervise his education and teach him German. His infant titles—King of Rome, Napoleon II, Prince of Parma—all following in rapid and scarcely comprehended succession, were scrapped and replaced by the thoroughly Germanic name of Duke of Reichstadt. His father's name Napoleon was exchanged for his grandfather's name Francis; he was henceforth known as Franz. He was encouraged to look upon the Emperor of Austria as the center of his little world, and to consider himself a member of the Hapsburg family. In fact, with his head of blond curls, his fair skin, and his milky-blue eyes, he already looked like a Hapsburg. His origins—the identity of his father and his years as the King of Rome—were shrouded in mystery; when he questioned his tutors about his dimly remembered past, he was given oblique, evasive answers.

And yet there were indications that he knew more than he was prepared to divulge. "Knows a great deal about the past," noted one of his tutors, "but in this connection maintains a silence which is quite extraordinary in a child." Finding that direct questions never drew direct replies, he, too, became more subtle in his quest for information. He would want to know why he no longer had pages, he would ask the name of the present King of France, he would wonder why he had once been called the King of Rome. "Oh, if only I were in Paris!" he was heard to sigh one day.

He knew, by the interest which his presence always aroused in company and by the crowds that came flocking to Schönbrunn, that there was something special about him. One day, when walking with one of his tutors in the park behind the palace, a group of boys shouted out the name "Napoleon"; the sound of it threw him into so deep a state of abstraction that the tutor could not get a word out of him. "I know something," he would say, "but I don't say it because it's a secret." It was not denied that he was Napoleon's son; but his father's history and whereabouts were mentioned as little as possible, and then only in such a way as to impart the minimum amount of information. This cocoon of uncertainty, of secrecy, in which he was always enveloped started to affect his personality; he began to change from the affectionate, exuberant little boy who had scampered so joyously amongst the bowing and curtsying groups at the Tuileries into a shuttered, introspective youngster— charming on the surface, enigmatic below.

The one person who might have answered his questions—Marie Louise, his mother—was no longer in Vienna. After endless hagglings at the Congress of Vienna, she had been made Duchess of Parma, Piacenza, and (Pauline Bonaparte's old principality) Guastalla. In April 1816 she took up residence in her new domain. On hand, to attend to her every need, was the virile Count von Neipperg. By now Marie Louise was head over heels in love with him. Beside this new passion, her four-year association with Napoleon was as nothing. Napoleon, always conscious that she was the daughter of the Emperor of Austria, the symbol of the crowning point of his career, had treated her as a precious plaything; Neipperg treated her as a woman. What she had imagined to be love for Napoleon had been little more than a schoolgirl crush; it was Neipperg who brought her womanhood into full bloom. Marie Louise has been accused of having no heart, of being shallow in her affections; nothing could be further from the truth. She loved Neipperg with every fiber of her being until the day he died. There is no doubt that had he been exiled to some lonely island, she would have followed without a second's hesitation.

Life in the Duchy of Parma suited her. She was never cut out to be an empress. She cheerfully left the business of government to Neipperg and gave herself over to a life of provincial domesticity. Her hobbies, which had seemed so bourgeois at the Tuileries, were perfectly suited to the palace of Parma. She could eat enormous meals and not care about losing her figure. She could wear comfortable clothes and not mind about looking unfashionable. She could lie in bed half the morning and not bother with public appearances. In May 1817 she gave birth to a daughter, and two years later she had a son. Neipperg, in Chateaubriand's superb phrase, was busily laying his eggs in the Eagle's nest. These illegitimate children were created Countess and Count of Montenuovo (an Italianized form of Neipperg) by the Emperor Francis. It was not until after the death of Napoleon that Marie Louise married Neipperg. A divorce could possibly have been arranged earlier (there was some doubt as to the validity of her marriage to Napoleon anyway), but she never suggested it. Perhaps she wanted to save his pride; perhaps she did not want to draw unnecessary attention to herself.

Marie Louise had accepted the Duchy of Parma on the understanding that it would be passed on to Napoleon's son after her death. It was, in fact, for his sake alone that she insisted on being given possession of these three little provinces. With her strong distaste for public life, or, indeed, for any responsibility, nothing would have suited her better than to have settled down with Neipperg and her son on some obscure country estate in Austria. But anxious to provide for the future of the little boy, she had resigned herself to the wearing of a crown once more, at least until the boy was old enough to succeed her. However the Allied Powers had no intention that a Bonaparte ever wear a crown again, even one so trifling as that of Parma. Hardly had Marie Louise been informed that her son would inherit her domains than the Powers decided that her son was to become a private citizen in her father's empire. It was only in 1818, after repeated naggings on her part, that his future position was finally fixed. It was then, at the age of seven, that he was created Duke of Reichstadt. Reichstadt was the name of the chief property of the Bavarian Palatinate, which the Emperor Francis had decreed should pass to Napoleon's son on the death of Marie Louise. The boy was to be addressed as Serene Highness (and not Imperial Highness), and the archdukes of

Austria were to take precedence over him. The reading of the patent which created him Duke of Reichstadt took place in the presence of a mere handful of people in a private room of one of the Hapsburg summer residences. It was all a far, far cry from the hundred-and-one-gun salute that had boomed over Paris to announce to the French Empire the birth of the King of Rome.

♔ ♔ ♔

The King of Rome was in Vienna; it was the rest of the Bonapartes who were in Rome.

Banished from France, the bulk of the Bonaparte family sought refuge either in Rome or in some other Italian city. The Pope, despite the cavalier treatment he had suffered at the hands of Napoleon, made them feel welcome, and besides, they had always considered themselves almost as much an Italian family as a French one. The coming years of exile were to strengthen this tendency.

The colony of exiles was headed by Madame Mère. Older, sadder, but not one whit less noble, she bought herself a magnificent *palazzo* in the heart of the city and crammed it with souvenirs of her son's empire. Not that she needed any reminding of his days of power; her thoughts, these days, were entirely taken up with him; her overweening desire was to see him restored to freedom. On first hearing that he had been banished to St. Helena, she had written to the Allied Powers, begging permission to join him. Her letter had gone unanswered. From then on she hungered for any scrap of news from the island, and made several appeals to his captors, either for news of him or for some alleviation of his imprisonment. This very understandable concern for her son's plight roused the suspicions of the oversensitive Bourbons, and it was soon being rumored that she was supplying Corsican agents with millions to start an insurrection in favor of Napoleon. When the Cardinal Secretary of State, at the insistence of the French ambassador, called on her in connection with these rumors, she replied somewhat sharply to the effect that if she did indeed possess millions, she would use them to arm a fleet to rescue the Emperor, and not to gain adherents for his cause. He had, she assured the Cardinal Secretary of State, enough of those already.

Although sick with anxiety for her son's welfare, her pride in his achievements was undiminished. When she drove out, she continued to use her carriages with the Imperial arms emblazoned on the doors. Europe had "bowed to the dust" before her son's arms for ten years, she claimed; why should she be ashamed of them now?

The year 1818 presented her with the opportunity of showing her appreciation in a more practical manner. Count Bertrand had written from St. Helena asking the family to send out a priest, a maître d'hôtel, and a cook. The British promptly suggested that they choose a doctor to go out as well. After an interminable delay, Madame Mère allowed five of the most unsuitable men imaginable to be dispatched to St. Helena. The priest was a doddering, ill-bred old man of almost seventy; his assistant was younger and more loutish; the doctor was an inexperienced, bumptious young man with a talent for self-advertisement; the maître d'hôtel was one of Madame Mère's footmen; and the cook was a mere youngster in very poor health. The arrival on St. Helena of this unprepossessing bunch appalled the exiles. What could have made Madame Mère consent to the choice of this unlikely collection?

The truth was that Madame Mère was under the influence of a German clairvoyant, who may or may not have been a spy for Metternich. Claiming to be receiving her information direct from the Virgin, the clairvoyant is supposed to have assured Madame Mère that Napoleon had escaped from St. Helena. Cushioned in the arms of angels, he had been carried off to some other country, from which the seer was receiving news of him. He was well and happy and would soon be returning. Believing every word of this extraordinary story, Madame Mère decided that the letters which she was receiving from St. Helena were forgeries. Her son had escaped and the British were trying to pretend that they still held him captive. In October 1818 she told her daughter-in-law, Jérôme's wife, Catherine, that Napoleon was on his way to Malta. And on another occasion Las Cases (who had by now returned from St. Helena) was likewise assured that Madame had proof that Napoleon was no longer a prisoner.

This, then, was the reason why Letizia had not bothered unduly about the quality of the men who had been sent to St. Helena. Her son was no longer there. Why waste money on acquiring the services of well-qualified people when there was no one left to serve? She was quite sure that when the little party arrived at St. Helena, they would find Napoleon gone. It was only when, some two years later, one of the party returned with news of him, that her eyes were finally opened. She then learned the bitter truth that not only was her son still very much a prisoner, but that he was dying.

Throughout this trying period, Pauline had done her best to make her mother see reason. Her repeated allegations that the clairvoyant was a fraud had led to a distinct coolness between mother and daughter. In the ordinary way, they were very close. Whatever her children's failings, Madame could not blame them for long, and she had come to appreciate the warmth of Pauline's nature during their stay with Napoleon on Elba. If she had any complaint against Pauline's behavior now, it was that she seemed to be seeing far too much of her son's captors—the English. With Napoleon safe on St. Helena, the English were displaying an extraordinary interest in his relations; no visit to Rome was complete these days without an invitation to, or at least a glimpse of, one of the Bonapartes. Although Madame Mère granted audiences to very few, Pauline seemed to be keeping open house. In the charming Villa Paolina, with its lavishly furnished rooms and its beautifully tended gardens, she held court to scores of admiring Englishmen and to an occasional appreciative Englishwoman. Far from having forgotten Napoleon by consorting with his enemies, as many suggested, she lost no opportunity of pleading for some lightening of his punishment. Napoleon himself appreciated this. "Pauline is in Rome," he said one day to Gourgaud, "where she sees many English people. All the better, so many of my enemies are gained over by her."

Now in her late thirties, Pauline was beginning to lose her celebrated looks; visitors began to talk in terms of "traces of her former beauty." Conscious of the change, she withdrew the famous seminude statue by Canova from public view—the contrast between statue and model was becoming a little too pronounced. The care and adornment of her body still remained her overriding passion in life, and if her guests were lucky, they might be treated to the sight of a page devoting a couple of hours to the washing, creaming, perfuming, and manicuring of her lovely feet. She and Prince Borghese, from whom she had lived apart for many years, were finally legally separated at this time.

Lucien was back in Rome. By throwing in his lot with Napoleon during the Hundred Days, he had forfeited the good will gained by his long years of exile during the Empire, and he was now mistrusted by the Allied Powers. But the Pope remained a good friend, and Lucien was soon back at Canino, writing long-winded poems, burrowing for antiquities, and giving his wife Alexandrine a child every year or eighteen months. His two eldest children, the daughters of his first wife Christine Boyer, were married in 1815 and 1818 respectively. Charlotte became Princess

Gabrielli, and Christine, the Countess de Posse. When one remembers that their mother had been an impoverished and illiterate innkeeper's daughter at the time of her marriage to the equally impoverished Lucien, their marriages were indicative of the considerable change in the family fortunes.

At one stage Lucien planned to join Napoleon on St. Helena, but this *grande geste* came to nothing. He remained in Rome, living opulently and well beyond his means.

Also in Rome, but living a very different sort of life, was the surly Louis. Having been in Italy throughout the Hundred Days, and in Austria for some years before that, the collapse of Napoleon's Empire did not affect him unduly. His chief preoccupation was still his failing health. Before long, however, he acquired another interest in life. After years of unsuccessful demands, he finally managed to get control of his eldest son, Napoleon-Louis. A lawyer informed Hortense that the boy was to join his father, and in late 1815 the eleven-year-old Napoleon-Louis arrived in Rome. Now Louis had every opportunity to play the martinet. Nothing that Hortense had done for the boy had been right. He was idle, irreligious, ill disciplined, ill educated. Louis set about rectifying these faults with a will. The poor child was subjected to a strict daily routine; every aspect of his life, from religious instruction to the cleaning of his nails, was supervised by his father. Tutors—all pronounced unsatisfactory by the demanding Louis—came and went in a steady stream. When, after several years of this regimented life, Napoleon-Louis returned to his mother on holiday, she hardly knew him. He seemed to be getting as frail and as sulky as his father. His appearance strengthened her resolve never to part with her youngest son, Louis-Napoleon.

The rest of the family—with the exception of Joseph—were in Trieste. At the fall of the Empire, Jérôme, ex-King of Westphalia, had rejoined his wife in her father's kingdom of Württemberg. They remained for two years, more or less prisoners, while Catherine's father repeatedly begged her to divorce the worthless Jérôme. She refused. Unable to break her resolution, the King of Württemberg finally gave way. Jérôme and Catherine were allowed to leave Württemberg, and were given the title of the Count and Countess de Montfort. They moved, in 1817, to Trieste.

The annual allowance which had been awarded them by Catherine's father proved hopelessly inadequate for the extravagant Jérôme. Within a matter of months he was seriously in debt. He appealed to Madame Mère for help. In answer to his first request, she sent him money; in answer to his second, she sent advice. "Imitate me," she commanded. "Retrench!" If only, she wrote, she could impart some of her character to him; surely Catherine was strong-minded enough to save. But Jérôme insisted on living in a semiregal state, and his wife was too devoted to complain. In 1820 she gave birth to a daughter whom they called Mathilde. This little girl very nearly became the next Empress of the French.

While Jérôme and Catherine had been living under a cloud of disapproval in Württemberg, his first wife, Elizabeth Patterson, had been basking in the sunshine of social success in France. Her return to Europe had coincided with the fall of her brother-in-law's empire, and to her slight surprise but intense gratification, she found herself the center of a great deal of flattering attention. Talleyrand praised her wit, Madame de Staël extolled her beauty, the Duke of Wellington admired her spirit. She counted Chateaubriand, Humboldt, and Canova amongst her friends. Europe, she suddenly discovered, suited her admirably. She was, she assured her father, the wealthy but homespun William Patterson, out of her element in America, whereas here in Europe "beauty commands homage, talents secure admiration, misfortune meets with respect." Elizabeth Patterson was never handicapped by false modesty.

The climax of her stay in Paris was when King Louis XVIII expressed a wish to meet her. She declined the invitation. Her admiration for Napoleon, in spite of his ruthless treatment of her, prevented her from bending the knee to his successor. As she had received a pension from the ex-Emperor, she said, she felt that she could not now consort with his enemies. Ingratitude, she claimed stanchly, was not one of her vices.

Despite her enthusiasm for France ("I am in the first society in Europe . . ."), she returned to America in 1816. Her only son, Jérôme, whom she called Bo, was there, and the only thing more important to Elizabeth Patterson than her own position was his. No son could have had a more ambitious mother. She had left him behind at school in Maryland, but did not want to deprive him of her beneficial influence for too long. Certain that "the talent with which nature has so lavishly endowed him might lead him to the highest eminence in Europe," she wanted to be on hand to guide these talents. What he did with his "splendid intellectual endowments" depended, she said, on how she directed them. He was, at this time, ten years old.

Caroline, ex-Queen of Naples, now known as the Comtesse de Lipona (an anagram of Napoli), was another member of the family living in Trieste. With her were her four children, Achille, Letizia, Lucien, and Louise; Murat was dead. Having been ignored by Napoleon during the Hundred Days, after the fall of the Empire he had decided to stage his own return from Elba—setting off from Corsica to recapture his old Kingdom of Naples. The adventure was a complete fiasco. Dressed in one of his superb uniforms and followed by several dozen men, he landed in Italy one Sunday morning in 1815. His appearance raised not the slightest enthusiasm, and by nightfall he was in prison. He was tried, found guilty, and sentenced to death. On October 13, having written a flowery but strangely moving letter to his wife Caroline, he faced the firing squad. The last words of this brave, showy, conceited warrior were very characteristic.

"Soldiers," he cried calmly, "aim at my heart, but spare the face."

The news of his violent end came as a shock to Caroline, but it did not break her heart. On hand to comfort her was General Macdonald, a fine-looking Corsican (despite his name) who had been Minister for War at Naples. "Fate," wrote one of her friends, "in depriving her of all the favors with which Fortune had overwhelmed her, had been powerless to rob her of the most precious of all. A faithful friend remained to her. The qualities of this man, like his attachment, were superior. . . ." It was rumored that the General had become her second husband, and that Caroline, once Queen of Naples, had become Madame Macdonald. When the news of her intended marriage reached Napoleon on St. Helena, he considered it a terrible disgrace. At thirty-four she was far too old to be bothering about "the little business" any more, he reckoned. The "human species," he sighed, was very strange.

Elisa, too, was living in Trieste. Her days of greatness over, she devoted herself to the welfare of her two children, Napoléone and Frédéric, and to the nursing of her considerable fortune. Although her political life was over, she still retained her somewhat self-conscious interest in the arts, and her home, the Villa Vicentina, was usually filled with a court of aspiring artists and musicians. Her husband, Bacciochi, seems to have played no more active a part in these sunset years than he had during her high noon in Tuscany. In August 1820, at the age of forty-three, she died. The official cause of her death was "putrescent and bilious fever," but as there was no autopsy, the actual cause is uncertain.

When the news of her death reached St. Helena, it seemed to depress Napoleon immeasurably; for hours he sat motionless in an armchair.

"Elisa has just shown us the way!" he said at length to his doctor. "Death seemed to have overlooked my family. Now it is beginning to strike. My turn cannot be far off."

     ♛   ♛   ♛

Joseph, ex-King of Spain, was in America. After Waterloo he had made his escape from France in an American brig, and getting safely through a British squadron, had landed in New York some five weeks later. Here he was welcomed with open arms. The arrival of a wealthy and cultivated ex-monarch, particularly the brother of the most famous man of the time, was no everyday occurrence in the United States, and Joseph was soon the center of an admiring circle. Assuming the title of Count de Survilliers, he took up residence in a large house on the banks of the Hudson River.

Never one to live in anything but complete comfort, and having decided to remain in the States, Joseph started looking round for a permanent home. He decided on an estate called Point Breeze, near Bordentown, New Jersey. The property consisted of several hundred acres of lushly wooded countryside, through which wound the Delaware River. Joseph spent large sums improving the existing old house, and then filled it with the books and pictures which he had had shipped out from France. As the years went by, Point Breeze, like Mortefontaine before it, became renowned for its elegance and its hospitality. "I can scarcely tell . . . ," enthused one of Joseph's guests, "of all the wonders and treasures accumulated in this exile home where the Count loved to live, surrounded by all the souvenirs and luxuries of his early life." It is to Joseph's credit that twice, in 1817 and 1819, he wrote Napoleon, offering to exchange the luxuries of Point Breeze for the hardships of St. Helena; but Napoleon declined both offers. Other visits which Joseph planned were of a distinctly more conspiratorial nature; several plots to rescue the Emperor were conceived at Point Breeze, but they all came to nothing. The final one, which might have had some chance of success, was forestalled by the news of Napoleon's death.

Joseph's wife, Julie, who had never shown the slightest interest in following her husband on his foreign sojourns, remained behind in Europe. Her health, she vowed, would never stand the journey. Husband and wife had gone their own ways for so many years now that neither of them felt the separation. With Julie in Europe were her daughters Zénaïde and Charlotte, both in their teens and both approaching marriageable age. Dutiful daughters, they divided their time between their parents, spending long periods with their father in America.

Not that he needed the company. He had bought himself a second property in Jefferson County, in the State of New York. A vast tract of uncultivated country, he called it his Wilderness. Here he would take friends on shooting expeditions, and here, too, he would pursue a sport somewhat more to his taste, having installed a young mistress, Annette Savage, the daughter of a Quaker family living in Philadelphia. Joseph divided his time between the cultured pastimes of Point Breeze and the illicit delights of the Wilderness.

After a year or two Annette Savage presented her aging lover with a daughter, for whom the delighted Joseph made ample provision. This illegitimate daughter married a certain Mr. Benton, and years later, during the Second Empire, husband and wife visited Paris. The long-suffering Napoleon III received them at the Tuileries and granted a pension to his illegitimate cousin. At the fall of the Second Empire Mrs. Benton's pension ceased, and for the following twenty years the daughter of the ex-King of Spain supported herself by teaching music. She died, in poverty, at Richfield Springs in 1891.

Another of Joseph's woman friends, but undoubtedly a platonic one, was his brother Jérôme's first wife, Elizabeth Patterson. Fresh from her triumphs in Europe, she returned to Baltimore in 1816. Never one to neglect an opportunity of furthering her ambitions, she lost no time in looking up her brother-in-law Joseph. He received her kindly, and was very impressed by the good looks and the lively intelligence of her son, Bo. She no doubt poured out her usual stream of complaints about the provincialism and crudeness of life in America, and convinced him that living in Europe suited her much better. Joseph assured her that when next she crossed the Atlantic, she would be warmly received by the Bonaparte family. His bland assurances took root.

Within the next few years it began to look as though a bond much closer than friendship was about to unite the families of Joseph Bonaparte and Elizabeth Patterson.

♛   ♛   ♛

Hortense, driven from pillar to post by the suspicious Allies after the fall of the Empire, had come to rest, temporarily, in Augsburg, Bavaria. That she was allowed to set up house there was due to the efforts of her brother, Eugène. Eugène's devoted wife, Augusta, was the daughter of the King of Bavaria, and the King, whose affection for Eugène had withstood the collapse of Napoleon's power, agreed to help the desperate Hortense. Grateful for this place of refuge, Hortense gathered together such possessions as she had been able to save and settled down to the quiet life she loved so well.

There was a time when she had imagined that she and her lover, Charles de Flahaut, might live happily together, but he was no less promiscuous now than in his younger days. Life with such a man would be impossible for the sensitive, highly romantic Hortense. Towards the end of the year 1815 he wrote from England, telling her that he had met and been attracted to Miss Margaret Elphinstone, the daughter of Lord Keith. Suffused with melancholy, Hortense wrote back, wishing him well and advising him to marry her. Gratefully, he accepted her advice, and he and Margaret Elphinstone were married the following summer.

Hortense's sense of aloneness throughout these years was somewhat relieved by the presence of her brother, Eugène, and his family. Of all Napoleon's relations, Eugène had weathered the recent storm best. Although never granted the principality promised him at Napoleon's first abdication, the Czar had championed his cause and he was able to retain all his property in France and Italy. Sheltered under the wing of his father-in-law, the King of Bavaria, and adored by his wife and children, Eugène was far more content now than ever he had been in his days as viceroy to Napoleon. Mild-mannered, self-effacing, and kindly, he was much better suited to life in a small German court than to the hurly-burly of Napoleon's Empire. To Hortense, he was always the *beau ideal* of a gentleman.

Her enthusiasm for her brother was not shared by all Bonapartists. The ease with which Eugène had adapted himself to the new situation, the eagerness with which he had accepted a new German title—the Duke of Leuchtenberg—the doggedness with which he clung to his considerable fortune, smacked of ingratitude, even treachery, to some. When certain members of the Bonaparte family appealed to the Allied sovereigns to end Napoleon's captivity, Eugène felt obliged to add his voice, and addressed what has been considered a very weak letter to his patron, the Czar. In it, he referred to Napoleon as his "mother's husband" and the guide in his (Eugène's) military and diplomatic career. His cautious appeal did neither better nor worse than Madame Mère's more resounding one. Napoleon remained where he was.

Hortense's chief comfort during these years, however, was her small son, Louis-Napoleon. With her eldest boy in the care of his father in Rome, Hortense found herself turning more and more towards this youngest child. He was well worthy of the affection she lavished on him. Dreamy, kindly, sensitive, sentimental, full of loving gestures and disarming observations, he was a true Beauharnais. When his older brother said he wanted to be a soldier, Louis-Napoleon said that he wanted to be a flower-seller. When, on a cold day, he met a begger boy in the street, he stripped off his coat, shoes, and stockings and gave them to him. His mother's ladies called him "Princess Louis." But in addition to the Beauharnais charm, he had inherited the Beauharnais tendency to drift with the tide; he was lazy, inattentive, and self-indulgent. And growing up in his mother's almost exclusively feminine household, he was thoroughly spoiled.

In these boyhood days the Bonaparte in him was still dormant. The Empire which had so recently collapsed was something dimly remembered; the family portraits and Imperial souvenirs which crowded his mother's home were more real than his own fading memories of more triumphant days. But his mother's anecdotes of life in the palaces of France and his uncle Eugène's tales of valiant deeds on the battlefield began to fire his fertile imagination. Behind those pale-blue heavy-lidded eyes, an obsession was beginning to take root.

When Louis-Napoleon was twelve, Hortense dismissed his tutor Abbé Bertrand and employed another by the name of La Bas. In the hands of this ardent, scholarly, disciplined young man, Louis-Napoleon's somewhat limp personality began to take shape. Hortense had been far too soft with him; the atmosphere of sentimentalism, of melancholy, of mild hypochondria in which she always moved had affected the boy; it needed all La Bas's rigidly imposed discipline to counteract her influence. But he succeeded, and within six months not only Hortense, but La Bas himself, was amazed at the progress the boy had made. There was obviously more to Louis-Napoleon than a melting charm of manner. Who knew, wrote the boy's old tutor Abbé Bertrand to La Bas, there might be a great future in store for the boy yet.

♚　♚　♚

While the new emperor was growing up in Augsburg, the old one was dying on St. Helena. The six-year exile was drawing to a close. The floorboards of that ramshackle little house no longer creaked beneath the Emperor's strutting footsteps, the haphazardly furnished rooms no longer re-echoed to the sound of his animated voice. Towards the end of the year 1820 Napoleon started complaining of a pain in his side; it was, he said, like the "gentle thrust from a sharp blade." As the thrusts became progressively less gentle, the Emperor became progressively weaker. The slightest exertion exhausted him. With his declining vigor, his appetite declined, and soon he could stomach nothing but bouillon. He vomited frequently. In March 1821 his illness seemed to take a sudden turn for the worse. His attacks of pain, coupled with violent nausea, increased, but he stubbornly refused to take either the advice or remedies of his own doctor or to receive the physician offered him by Sir Hudson Lowe. When he was finally prevailed upon to see the British doctor (who, primed by the Governor, was skeptical of Napoleon's condition), he persistently scorned his cures. He had never had much faith in doctors, and in fact, none of those who attended him on St. Helena seemed able to diagnose his illness accurately. Before long the Emperor was unable to stand without assistance, and his vomiting increased. It was at last realized at Longwood that he was a dying man.

If his physical powers were failing him, his mental prowess was not. That fresh, formidable mind was as alert as ever, and now, marshaling his deserting energies, he set it to accomplishing the final task of his life: the drawing up of his testament. Each afternoon as the island sun shifted the shadow of the little house towards the east, Montholon would sit beside his bed, writing steadily to the sound of that failing voice. With an extraordinary, almost bourgeois, attention to detail, and with an eye to a much wider audience than his beneficiaries, he began to dispose of his legacy. Publicly he bequeathed to his family a wealth of intimate souvenirs; privately, a wealth of imperious advice. He told them where they should live (Rome or Switzerland), whom they should let their children marry (noble Roman families, or in the case of Joseph's daughters, the Washington and Jefferson families), and to whom they should give their allegiance (they could, he said, kiss the Pope's backside, because that was tantamount to kissing no one's backside; they were not, however, to kiss the backsides of the kings of England, Naples, or Sweden). He left considerable sums of money to his two illegitimate sons, Charles Léon and Alexandre Walewski. He recommended both these boys to the care of Count Bertrand. Marie Louise, he announced, had always been a source of pride to him; he would think tenderly of her to the end. Were these still his genuine sentiments, or were they pronounced with a view to easing his son's pathway to the throne?

His instructions for the burial of his body had a similar historic ring.

"I desire that my ashes repose on the banks of the Seine, in the midst of the French people whom I have loved so dearly."

To Bertrand he gave less heroic instructions. He would like his body to be laid to rest in the cemetery of Père-Lachaise; they could bury him between two of his marshals and erect a little column in his honor. Otherwise, if the Bourbons would permit it, he would like to be buried in Saint-Denis, amongst the kings of France. If, on the other hand, they refused to allow the return of his corpse to Paris, he would like to lie on an island at the swirling embrace of the Rhone and Saône rivers; and if the mainland of France were refused to him entirely, they were to take him back to his birthplace, Corsica, and bury him in the cathedral at Ajaccio. And lastly, in the unlikely event of his body having to remain on St. Helena, he would like to be buried in the shade of the willows near a spring from which the water for the house was fetched each day. The place was known as Geranium Valley.

But his chief thoughts were directed towards his son.

"I urge my son never to forget that he was born a French prince and never to lend himself to being an instrument in the hands of the triumvirs who are oppressing the peoples of Europe. He must never fight against France nor harm her in any other manner. He must adopt my motto: 'All for the French people.' "

Added to these triumphant sentiments were various more tangible but no less momentous legacies. The inanimate objects associated with the father's most glorious days were to be passed on to the son. The cloak of Marengo, the sword of Austerlitz, the alarm clock of Frederick II, the uniforms, boots, linen, camp beds, weapons, saddles, orders, decorations, seals, watches, books . . . these were all to be handed to the young Napoleon on his sixteenth birthday.

"I desire that this slender legacy may be dear to him, as retracing for him the memory of a father of whom the whole world will speak to him."

This mass of souvenirs was backed up with pages of advice. The boy must not think of avenging his father's death; rather must he take advantage of it. He should not try to imitate his father; he must be a man of his own times. He must not make war with the same determination as his father; such things are not done twice in one age. Napoleon had saved the dying Revolution; he had cleansed it of its crimes, he had revealed it to the world as a splendid thing. His son must not allow the new ideas which the father had planted in Europe to die. If he could bring all these seeds to fruition, he would be a great ruler. Napoleon predicted that the

Bourbons would not last. As soon as he himself was dead, the world would realize how great had been his contribution to mankind. That would be his son's opportunity to regain the throne. . . .

On and on that eager voice would run, becoming fainter and fainter until, towards sunset, it died down altogether. Then his companion would quietly bow himself out of the room and the exhausted Emperor would drift into a restless sleep. Within an hour or two he would wake, drenched in sweat and dizzy with nausea. His devoted valets would change his linen or mop up his vomit. They even, on occasion, coaxed him into taking a little medicine. But each day he became weaker; the end could not be far.

Towards the end of April they moved him out of his stifling bedroom into the airier drawing room. Having settled into it, he turned to his doctor. He had long suspected that he would die of cancer, as had his father before him, he said, and fearing that the disease was hereditary, he wished to safeguard his son. The doctor was to examine his stomach very carefully after death and deliver a detailed and accurate report to his son. The doctor promised.

His dying thoughts, then, were still all for the boy in Vienna. A full-length portrait of his son hung above his head, and when the bed curtains were lifted, he could, by raising his eyes, look at the golden-haired likeness of the young king. Imagining that the sight of this picture saddened him, his companions took it down, but on noticing its absence, he gazed all round the room in search of it. Too ill to speak, he looked at each of the people gathered round his bed in turn, as if to say, "Where is my son? What have you done with my son?"

On the day before he died, he turned to one of his valets. "What is the name of my son?" he asked faintly.

"Napoleon," answered the young man.

The Emperor died at eleven minutes to six on the evening of May 5, 1821. He was fifty-two years of age. All day his companions in exile had been gathered around the narrow canopied bed set in the center of the drawing room. The Emperor lay on his back, his thighs spread and his feet together; his hands, those soft white hands of which he was so proud, lying limply at his sides. Other than a slight spasmodic jerking, caused by hiccups, he lay quite still. Now and then his doctor would lean forward to wet his lips with a sponge, or to feel his weakening pulse. The barely perceptible sound of his breathing grew fainter and slower until it was lost to the listening room.

With a sudden flash of sunlit silver, two doves fluttered down onto the window sill and sat cooing happily through the long afternoon, regardless of repeated attempts to drive them away. They remained until evening.

The sun sank suddenly into the sea. The evening gun thudded, buffeting through the unbearable stillness. The room was swiftly drained of form and color and the tropic night pressed in through the open windows. The doctor leaned forward. When he straightened up again, he did not lift his head. Napoleon was dead.

The autopsy took place the following afternoon. It was performed by Napoleon's own doctor, Antommarchi, assisted by five British doctors. The British drew up and signed a report on their observations; Antommarchi refused to add his signature. The body, they said, was found to be covered in an extraordinarily thick layer of fat. The bladder was small, which accounted for the Emperor's frequent urinations. One of the British doctors present noted that there was scarcely any hair on the body and that its appearance was soft, almost feminine. The genitals, he said, were exceptionally small. Antommarchi claimed that the liver was enlarged; the British doctors denied this. A diseased liver might have been caused by the climate of St. Helena; the British, it has been suggested, were not going to admit to this. But all the doctors present agreed that Napoleon had died of cancer of the stomach. A theory has since been propounded that Napoleon had been poisoned. His symptoms very much resemble those of arsenic poisoning, and his body showed none of the wasting away typical of cancer patients. His assassin, it is suggested, was a member of his suite in the pay of the Bourbons. The theory might well be correct.

The post-mortem over, the body was prepared for the lying in state. The Emperor was dressed in his uniform of the *chasseurs à cheval* of the Imperial Guard. For want of more suitable containers, his heart and stomach—which had both been removed during the autopsy—were housed in a sponge cup and a silver pepper box and placed beside the body. Napoleon had wanted to have his heart taken to Marie Louise, but the British would not allow it to be separated from the body. They had orders that the Emperor was to be buried on St. Helena, and there he would stay, sponge cup, pepper box, and all. On May 7 the body was encased in four coffins—one tin, one mahogany, one lead, and the last, mahogany again—and on the following morning it was buried. Eight stalwart grenadiers, staggering beneath the weight, carried the Emperor's remains down the steep pathway to Geranium Valley. A grave had been dug beneath the willow trees, and into it, with the help of a specially

Fig. I. One of two tapestries, after a cartoon by David, ordered by Napoleon I for his own reception room. The originals were lost and only recently were the cartoons discovered in the attic of the Louvre. The replicas, done on the famous Gobelin looms, show the Imperial Bee as an important feature of the background.

FIG. II. The birthplace of Napoleon I, Ajaccio, Corsica. After a drawing by Eric Pape.

FIG. III. Young Napoleon Bonaparte at school in Brienne. Engraving from a painting by Realier-Dumas.

Fig. IV. Madame Mère, Letizia Ramolino Bonaparte.

Fɪɢ. V. Napoleon I, from a painting by Isabey.

Fᴵɢ. VI. Napoleon with a group of nieces and nephews (from left: Letizia Murat, Napoleon-Louis, Napoleon I, Louis-Napoleon [Napoleon III], Louise Murat, Achille Murat, Lucien Murat); from a painting by Ducis.

FIG. VII. Joseph Bonaparte, King of Spain.

Fig. VIII. Elisa Bonaparte, Princess Bacciochi.

Fig. IX. Lucien Bonaparte, Prince of Canino. From a drawing by Belliard.

FIG. X. Hortense de Beau-
harnais, Queen of Holland.

FIG. XI. Louis Bonaparte,
King of Holland. From a
drawing by Belliard.

Fɪɢ. XII and XIII. Detail (right) of the famous Canova sculpture of Pauline Bonaparte, Princess Borghese; full-length below.

Fig. XIV. Caroline Bonaparte Murat, Queen of Naples.

Fig. XV. Joachim Murat, King of Naples. From a painting by Gérard.

Fig. XVI. Jerome Bonaparte, King of Westphalia. From a painting by Gros.

Fig. XVII. Mme. Elizabeth Patterson Bonaparte, from a portrait by Gilbert Stuart.

FIG. XVIII. Sketch from the David portrait of Empress Josephine painted for the coronation of Napoleon I.

FIG. XIX. Detail from the Gérard portrait of Empress Josephine.

Fig. XX. Eugène de Beauharnais.

Fig. XXI. Detail from the Gérard portrait of Empress Marie Louise.

Fig. XXII. The marriage at the Louvre of Napoleon and Marie Louise. From the painting by Rouget.

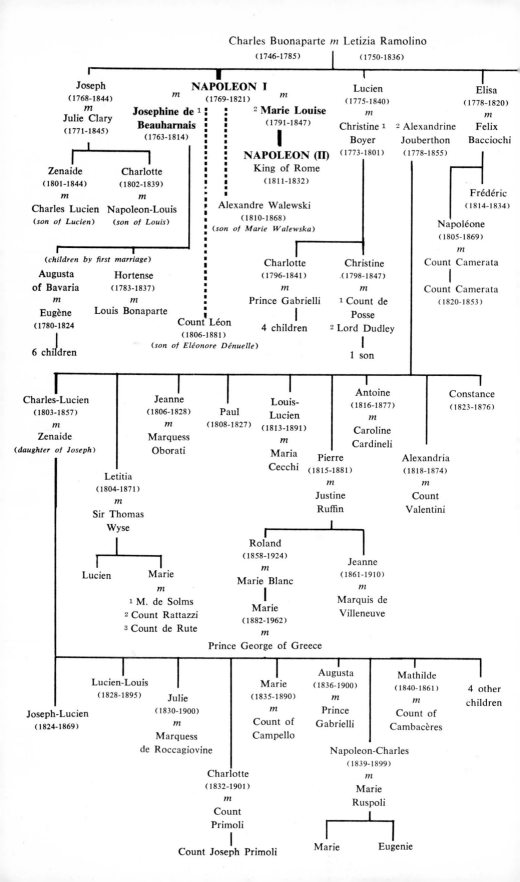

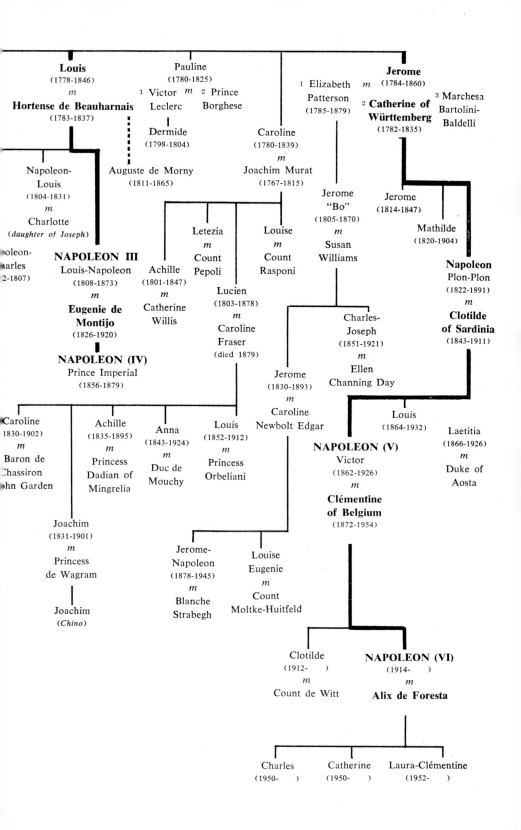

FIG. XXIV. The Duke of Reichstadt, son of Napoleon I and Empress Marie Louise.

Fig. XXV. Count Léon, son of Napoleon I and Eleonore Denuelle.

Fig. XXVI. Count Walewski, son of Napoleon I and Maria Walewska.

FIG. XXVII. Prince Louis-Napoleon, son of Louis Bonaparte and Hortense de Beauharnais, later Napoleon III.

FIG. XXVIII. Emperor Napoleon III.

Fig. XXIX. Empress Eugenie.

FIG. XXX. Eugenie, shortly after her marriage to Napoleon III.

FIG. XXXI. Princess Mathilde Bonaparte.

Fig. XXXII. Prince Napoleon ("Plon-plon") with his wife, Princess Clotilde of Sardinia.

Fig. XXXIII. Jerome Patterson Bonaparte.

Fig. XXXIV. Prince Lucien Murat.

Fig. XXXV. The Imperial Family of the Second Empire.

Fig. XXXVI. "The Four Napoleons," from a Second Empire print.

Fig. XXXVII. Napoleon III and Bismarck after the Battle of Sedan. From a painting by Camphausen.

Fig. XXXVIII. The Duke de Morny, son of Hortense de Beauharnais and Charles de Flahaut.

FIG. XXXIX. The Prince Imperial.

FIG. XL. Prince Victor Bonaparte.

FIG. XLI. The Empress Eugenie in exile.

erected crane, the coffin was lowered. It was covered with a huge flagstone, which was then sealed and coated with cement. The Governor, always on the alert lest Napoleon escape, was taking no more chances with the dead Emperor than he had with the live. The ceremony over, the little band of exiles each picked a willow frond, and made their way back to Longwood, pausing now and then to look back into the small green valley where their master lay buried.

The passing of one and a half centuries has not changed Geranium Valley much. One still makes one's way down the steep track until one reaches a little gate. Beside it is a wooden sentry box; above it flips a tricolor, beyond it is the clearing in which Napoleon was buried. It is a beautiful setting. Behind, on three sides, the wooded slopes rise steeply, and on the fourth they fall away to a view of the shimmering sea. In the center, sheltered by dark cedar trees, lies the grave. Tall black railings surround a flat whitewashed stone. The grave is unmarked. This had been the Governor's ultimate insult—and ultimate compliment. Napoleon's companions had asked for the following inscription, in French:

NAPOLEON
Born at Ajaccio, August 15, 1769
Died at St. Helena, May 5, 1821

But Sir Hudson Lowe had insisted that they add *Bonaparte* as well, and rather than agree to this demeaning of their Emperor, the French had decided to leave the stone bare. It was as well. The world was not going to forget Napoleon because no name was written on his grave. His name was to be written across a century.

In one respect Geranium Valley has changed since those days: the grave in which they buried Napoleon is now empty.

CHAPTER NINE

❦ ❦ ❦

NAPOLEON'S son, the Duke of Reichstadt, was ten years old when he heard the news of his father's death. One of his tutors, sensing, perhaps, that the boy was more attached to the memory of the Emperor than most people realized, chose the moment for breaking the news very carefully. It was not until evening that he drew the boy aside and told him that his father had died on St. Helena. Prepared though the tutor had been for some show of emotion from his pupil, he was amazed at the violence of the boy's reaction. For a child who had not seen nor heard from his father since he was three years old, Reichstadt's flood of tears came as a great surprise. The following day, when another of his tutors commiserated with him on Napoleon's death, the child again broke into bitter choking sobs. All these years, while the Hapsburg court had been doing its best to blur the memory of his father, Napoleon had become an ever more clearly defined figure in the son's imagination. With his mother in Parma, his grandfather, the Emperor Francis, not always accessible, and his tutors representing the less agreeable facets of his life, Napoleon had become a sort of focal point in the boy's mind. Now this focal point was gone.

A few days later Reichstadt received a letter from his mother, Marie Louise. She had heard how deeply affected he had been by the news, and she wrote to comfort him. It would be ungrateful of him, she lectured quite unnecessarily, to forget all Napoleon's goodness to him in his years of infancy. She felt sure that he would try to emulate his father's virtues while avoiding "the rocks upon which he had wrecked his life."

To a friend she was more frank. "I confess I was extremely affected by it; although I never had a very intense feeling of any kind for him, still I cannot forget that he was the father of my son, and that far from ill-treating me, as all the world supposes, he was always full of consideration for me—which is all that can be expected from a marriage of policy. Therefore I am greatly grieved; and although one may be glad that he ended his unhappy existence in a Christian way, I could have still wished him many years of life and prosperity—provided he had kept apart from me."

Marie Louise donned mourning for three months (her period of mourning happily coincided with the last weeks of her latest pregnancy), and attended a memorial service in honor of "the Most Serene Consort of our august Princess." But if she imagined that by observing these formalities she would have had done with Napoleon once and for all, she was very much mistaken. The autumn brought the Emperor's companions in exile back from St. Helena, and they were soon swarming across Europe with news, messages, and souvenirs for Napoleon's various relations. It was his doctor, Antommarchi, who presented himself at Parma. Napoleon had instructed Antommarchi to tell Marie Louise all about his last days and to claim an annual pension from her. The agitated Marie Louise left Neipperg to deal with Antommarchi; he was told, firmly but kindly, that an interview with the ex-Empress was impossible, and that the business of the pension would have to be referred to Vienna. Antommarchi withdrew, but not before he had told Neipperg about Napoleon's wish that his heart be given to Marie Louise for burial in Parma. The suggestion threw poor Marie Louise into a state of alarm, and she dashed off a letter to her father, begging him to see that Napoleon's heart remained where it was.

"Apart from the fact that the burial of his heart in Parma would be a fresh shock to me," she wrote, "it would also be a pretext for all ill-disposed people to make a pilgrimage here, and that would be exceedingly unpleasant for me in my position, for I desire nothing more in this world but peace and quiet; I rely, dearest Papa, upon your gracious cooperation to put a stop to this affair."

Marie Louise need not have fussed; England had no intention of allowing Napoleon's heart to be buried anywhere other than where it was.

Antommarchi did, however, manage to leave Napoleon's death mask with Marie Louise. Some weeks later a doctor in the household noticed some children dragging a plaster object along the floor by a piece of string, as though it were a toy carriage; when he picked it up, he saw that it was the Emperor Napoleon's death mask.

None of Napoleon's companions was allowed to come anywhere near his son. As the death of Napoleon was already beginning to give birth to a renewed interest in the Napoleonic story, it was more imperative than ever that his son be kept in obscurity. As early as 1817 it was claimed that Joseph Bonaparte, the boy's uncle, was planning to restore him to the Imperial throne, and from then on, throughout Reichstadt's boyhood, Europe was seething with stories of various plots to overthrow the Bourbons and proclaim the boy Emperor. Of all these rumors Reichstadt was kept in complete ignorance. But he could not be kept in ignorance about his father much longer. With his passionate interest in things military—in this he was very much Napoleon's son—he would have heard his father's name mentioned time and again during military discussions at court. His tutors noticed how avidly he snatched at any crumb of information about the Napoleonic Wars, and dreaded the time when they would have to deal with the immediate past. They still talked of Napoleon as a talented but misguided and overambitious man whose love of conquest had brought about his own downfall. The description was accurate, but it was becoming increasingly obvious that it was falling on deaf ears.

Within a few years Reichstadt was allowed to read the memoirs published by Napoleon's companions on St. Helena. That they were biased and often inaccurate, he could not suspect; that this was a true picture of his illustrious father, he never doubted. This detailed bringing to life of someone so long shadowed and played down by his tutors must have been an extraordinary experience for him. To see Napoleon now, aureoled in the kindly light of his biographers, to read of his frequent references to himself, to discover that love for himself which shines so undeniably through all the St. Helena memoirs, must have been poignant in the extreme. And how avidly he must have read and reread his father's final advice to his son and heir. "I urge my son never to forget that he was born a French prince. . . ."

Reichstadt, with all the ardor and idealism of youth, proclaimed that it would be his rule of conduct for life. In a passionate letter to Marie Louise he told her that he was planning to follow in the footsteps of his illustrious father; there could, he wrote earnestly, be no more admirable model.

When Reichstadt turned sixteen, Napoleon's companions in exile, eager to carry out the Emperor's dying wishes, made ready to hand over to his son the Imperial relics with which they had been entrusted. They applied for leave to go to Vienna. It was refused, but Metternich assured them that they could leave what he called "the objects" at the Austrian embassy in Paris. They would, he promised, be given a signed receipt. Very wisely, they declined the offer.

"The Prince," explained one of Reichstadt's tutors at about this time, "is not a prisoner, *but* . . . he is in a very special position."

⚜ ⚜ ⚜

Like a ship under full canvas, her adolescent son bobbing like a cork in her wake, Elizabeth Patterson now sailed once more into Bonaparte waters. Unable to bear what she considered the provincialism of America a moment longer, and determined that her son, Bo, should acquire the gloss that only an education abroad could give, she returned once more to Europe. Being as practical as she was ambitious, she settled in Geneva. Here Bo could be educated as well, and at less expense, than in some larger city, and from here they were within easy reach of the other members of the Bonaparte family living in Italy. Although Betsey herself lived very modestly (every penny had to be saved for Bo), she lost no time in cultivating wealthy and influential friends, and before long her foresight had paid off. When John Jacob Astor, whom she had charmed in Geneva, went on to Rome, he mentioned Betsey to Pauline Borghese. Pauline, always on the alert for some diversion, immediately interested herself in the affairs of her sister-in-law, and Mr. Astor wrote to Betsey to tell her that Princess Borghese was eager to meet her. What interested Betsey even more than the invitation was Pauline's offer to make some provision for Bo. "I am rich and have no child," said Pauline, "and find myself in every disposition to do everything for him."

The news delighted Betsey, but having been led up the garden path by the Bonapartes once before, she did not immediately avail herself of Pauline's invitation. She made careful inquiries about the family first. What she found out was not reassuring. "I believe some of them are amiable," she reported to her father in Baltimore, "but when there is a question of parting with money, good will is generally exposed to a great trial. . . ." Pauline, her friends reported, was rich but unreliable; Madame Mère was a "great economist"; Betsey's ex-husband Jérôme spent everything he could; Joseph, in America, was by far the richest. Their promises were not to be taken too seriously. "The Bonapartes are all alike, very affectionate in words, but without the least intention of parting with a farthing."

For all her well-founded distrust of their intentions, Betsey could not bring herself to decline the invitation to Rome. The opportunity of moving into that *beau monde* surrounding the Bonaparte family was too good to miss. It was true that it would mean interrupting Bo's education and meeting the expense of the journey herself, but with the possibility of Pauline's doing something for the boy, it was a chance worth taking.

Bo, as always, fell in with his mother's plans. It is unlikely that she ever consulted him on the matter. Although he had not turned out to be quite the intellectual giant she once thought him, he had grown into a good-looking boy with agreeable manners. The Bonapartes, she felt, would be very impressed. It was to his grandfather in Baltimore that Bo revealed his true views on all this social junketing. "Since I have been in Europe," wrote the homesick boy, "I have dined with princes and princesses and all the great people of Europe, but I have not found a dish as much to my taste as the roast beef and beefsteaks I ate in South Street." Such sentiments would have shocked his ambitious mother.

Betsey Patterson and Bo arrived in Rome towards the end of the year 1821. The Bonapartes were delighted with them. They had had no idea that Betsey was so good-looking, so charming, so amusing, or that Bo was such a gentleman. Pauline lavished gifts on mother and son, and even Madame Mère was induced to part with forty guineas so that Bo might buy a horse. They met Lucien Bonaparte and his large family and Louis Bonaparte and his eldest son Napoleon-Louis. All agreed that the Baltimore Bonapartes were relations to be proud of, and that Bo compared very favorably with his cousins. "I am amazed at him," wrote Madame Mère to Joseph. "It is hardly possible to find so much aplomb and good sense in one of his age. . . ."

So taken were they with the sixteen-year-old Bo that they decided that he must be kept in the family. It was agreed that he would marry Charlotte, Joseph's second daughter. Betsey's reaction to the proposal can be imagined; this was the realization of all her dreams. Charlotte would be immensely rich one day, and Bo's position in European society would be assured. She had sometimes feared that he might develop silly ideas about marrying for love, as so many young people in America did; this European way of arranging a match was much more to Betsey's taste. She was a very fond parent, she assured her father, but no foolish affection for her son would ever make her sanction an improper match for him. And Bo? He seems, as usual, to have raised no objections. "Bo feels the propriety of doing what *I* please on the subject of marriage, and has no foolish ideas of disposing of himself in the way young people do in America."

In fact, the reason why Bo was so eager to comply with his mother's wishes was that he saw in this proposed match an opportunity of getting back to his beloved Baltimore. "My grandmother and my aunt and uncle talk of marrying me to my uncle the Count of Survilliers' daughter," wrote the docile Bo to his Patterson grandfather. "I hope it may take place, for then I would return immediately to America to pass the rest of my life among my relations and friends."

To his delight, it was decided to send him back to America at once in order to see his uncle Joseph and his intended bride Charlotte. He arrived in New York in the spring of 1822, and made straight for Point

Breeze. Betsey remained in Rome, torn between her desire to direct Bo's matrimonial affairs in person and her inclination to prolong her stay amongst the Bonapartes. She would, in fact, have done better to have accompanied Bo to America. Before long she had quarreled with her sister-in-law Pauline. It was inevitable that these two vain, beautiful women should fall out sooner or later; Pauline found Betsey's wit a little too sharp for her taste, and Betsey found Pauline to be "capricious beyond all possibility of expression." The settlement which Pauline had promised Bo never materialized. "She chooses," reported Betsey, "a new heir every week." Things were further complicated by the news that Betsey's ex-husband Jérôme and Catherine were due to arrive in Rome. Betsey declared that she had not the slightest desire to see the ex-King of Westphalia, and that she imagined he would be far too ashamed of himself to wish to see her. She made up her mind to return to Geneva, there to await the outcome of Bo's talks with his uncle Joseph.

On her way north she broke her journey in Florence for a few days. One morning, while strolling through the picture galleries of the Pitti Palace, she came face to face with Jérôme and his second wife. They had not seen each other for seventeen years. That had been in Lisbon in 1805, when he had taken leave of her, declaring his undying love and promising to return within a few days.

Now, for the space of a few seconds, they stood rooted to the floor, staring at each other. It was, of course, Jérôme who broke first. "That is my American wife," he whispered hoarsely to Catherine, and darted downstairs. Catherine followed, and Betsey was left alone amongst the pictures to calm her fluttering, but slightly triumphant, emotions.

Far from resenting the presence of Jérôme's first wife in Italy, the generous Catherine did all she could to further her interests. She wrote to Joseph, urging him to allow Charlotte to marry Bo and saying how happy this union would make her. She and Jérôme had heard so many good reports of his son from his relations that they now decided to contribute something towards his upkeep. But Betsey knew her ex-husband far too well to be taken in by these promises; he could not live on his own allowance, let alone make a contribution to someone else's. No, all hopes were pinned on the match between Bo and Charlotte.

In this she was to be disappointed. A few weeks later Bo wrote to tell her that the marriage was off. For some reason which she was never to understand, Joseph decided against the match; it was possible that in alienating Pauline, Betsey had ruined Bo's chances. Pauline, Joseph assured his wife, Julie, had not retained her "kindly sentiments" towards Bo.

Once the keen edge of Betsey's disappointment had worn off, she took refuge in abuse. "There is nothing can, or ever will, surprise me in that family," she declared, and was highly gratified to hear from a tactful friend in America that Charlotte was "in size a dwarf, and excessively ugly." As, according to Betsey, there was no one in the world who combined "greater intelligence with more remarkable personal beauty" than Bo, he was probably well rid of the hideous little Charlotte.

"The only thing left for us to do," wrote Betsey to her father, "is to try and give him ambition, to prevent him making a foolish match. . . . I wish Bo's education to be particularly attended to—in that no money is to be spared; every other kind of saving is a gain, and no one can be more disposed to save than I am, but a good education is never too highly paid."

Betsey Patterson was nothing if not resilient, and conquering her disappointment, she once more devoted herself to mapping out a brilliant future for Bo. In 1822 he entered Harvard, where he seems to have been a diligent enough pupil, and where he was inundated with letters from his mother—half of them on the subject of economy and the other half on the necessity of making a good marriage. "Love in a cottage," she lectured, "is even out of fashion in novels." She would consider an amiable, prolific daughter-in-law a very poor compensation for all her years of sacrifice on his behalf.

On graduation he was once more brought to Europe where, without his mother, he made a round of visits to his various Bonaparte relations. It was now that he met his father, his father's wife, Catherine, and their three children, Prince Jérôme-Napoleon, Princess Mathilde, and Prince Napoleon—always known as Plon-Plon. The family took to Bo immediately, and Jérôme was eager for him to make his home with them. Nothing would have suited Bo less. Fond though he was of them all, he was appalled at their extravagance and their idleness. They breakfasted, he told his grandfather, between twelve and one, they dined between six and seven, they had tea at midnight. They never got to bed before half past one in the morning. Their days were devoted to killing time and spending money. "I am glad I came to Rome to see my family," he wrote earnestly to his grandfather, "but their mode of living and thinking is so entirely different from my habits of living and thinking, that I do not enjoy my residence in Rome." He had always considered America, he said, the only country for him, and this visit to Rome had convinced him of it. When he returned to the States in the late summer of 1827, he knew, without the slightest doubt, that he was returning home.

♔　♔　♔

The first generation of exiled Bonapartes had settled in Italy; the second tended to be settling in America. In 1822 Caroline Murat's eldest son, Achille, now twenty-one, came to stay with his uncle Joseph at Point Breeze. Unlike either his swashbuckling father or his grasping mother, Achille was a steady young man who took an immediate liking to life in the States. Its wholesomeness and its lack of formality were much more to his taste than the social merry-go-round of life in the great houses of Europe. Determined to settle in America, he bought an estate in Tallahassee, Florida. To such an extent did he turn his back on the glories of Napoleon's Empire that in a year or two he joined the postal department, eventually becoming postmaster of Tallahassee. For a boy who had once been His Royal Highness, the Crown Prince of Naples, it was very much another way of life.

He married, not a Bonaparte cousin (his mother had wanted him to marry Joseph's much-sought-after daughter Charlotte), but a certain Miss Catherine Byrd Willis. In this, at least, he unintentionally complied with the wishes of the late Napoleon. Catherine Willis was the great-niece of George Washington, and Napoleon had once instructed his nephews in America to marry into the Washington and Jefferson families. Like so many of the Bonapartes, the worthy Achille could not long keep out of print, and within the next few years he published several political tracts; they all sang the praises of his adopted country.

His brother Lucien was quite different. As dissolute as his brother Achille was dedicated, Lucien Murat's presence at Point Breeze was a trial even to the easygoing Joseph. He drank; he gambled; he ran up enormous debts. Time after time Joseph was obliged to pay off his nephew's clamorous creditors. With true Murat ingratitude, the raffish Lucien would promptly fling himself into a fresh orgy of spending.

As neither Bo nor Achille had married Joseph's daughter Charlotte, Lucien's mother had hoped that he might be successful. Either the "hideous little dwarf and regular vixen" (as the disillusioned Betsey now referred to Charlotte) did not appeal to the devil-may-care Lucien, or else Joseph did not fancy him as a son-in-law. When Lucien did get married a few years later, his bride was a Miss Caroline Fraser whose parents were friends of Joseph's, and frequent guests at Point Breeze. Besides being pretty, high-spirited and charming, Caroline Fraser was very rich—a combination irresistible to the headstrong and impoverished young Lucien. When Caroline's father, who certainly did not relish the idea of Lucien as a son-in-law, discovered that his daughter was in love, he ordered her to break with Lucien immediately. She refused, and when Fraser insisted, the pair eloped.

Joseph was furious. He claimed that Lucien had violated his hospitality, and refused to have anything more to do with him. The Frasers likewise washed their hands of their daughter, and the young couple were obliged to start their married life in a modest house in nearby Bordentown. Caroline's fortune was quickly squandered by her happy-go-lucky husband, and she was forced to open a school in the village. She bore Lucien five children. Of these, her fourth child, Anna Murat, was to take her place in history as the great friend and confidante of the next Empress of the French.

Joseph's eldest daughter, Zénaïde, was married to his brother Lucien's eldest son Charles. This boy, who had been born the day before Lucien's marriage to Alexandrine Jouberthon, had cost his father all his rights as a member of Napoleon's family. It was because of this child's illegitimate birth and Lucien's subsequent marriage to the boy's mother that Lucien had forfeited his claim to the Imperial succession. Had Napoleon ever recognized the marriage, Charles would now have stood next in line after Napoleon's own son, the Duke of Reichstadt. It was as well that he did not, for Charles Lucien was completely without Imperial ambitions. Every bit as hotheaded as his father, the one talent he did possess was not likely to count for much in the hurly-burly of the political world: Charles was an ardent ornithologist. At Point Breeze he was never happier than when rambling through the woods, studying the abundant bird life. The discovery of many hitherto uncatalogued birds led to his publication of several books on ornithology in North America. He and Zénaïde had twelve children; the Lucien Bonapartes, in marked contrast to the rest of the family, had always been prolific.

Joseph's second daughter, Charlotte, having either refused or been refused by Betsey's son Bo and by Achille and Lucien Murat, now married her cousin Napoleon-Louis, the eldest son of Louis and Hortense. Napoleon-Louis seemed to have shaken off his father's inhibiting influence as he grew to manhood, and Hortense was gratified to see him developing into a frank, friendly, and handsome young man. The vivacity of his manner, the air with which he wore his clothes, and the gold rings which gleamed in his ears gave him the look of an amiable gypsy, but Napoleon-Louis was no fool. Unlike so many members of the second generation of Bonapartes, he had a very deep interest in the political movements of the day, and when little more than a boy, he had associated himself with various revolutionary organizations. His father, anxious to protect him from becoming too deeply involved in these underground movements, moved from Rome to Florence, where he hoped the young man would keep out of mischief.

Napoleon-Louis's marriage to Charlotte disappointed the sentimental Hortense somewhat. Although Charlotte was by no means as deformed or ugly as Betsey Patterson liked to believe, she was small and very slightly misshapen. On the credit side, however, she was rich, talented, and intelligent. Napoleon-Louis seemed to be very fond of her, and the marriage, considering that it was an arranged one, was very happy.

In 1829 Betsey's son, Bo, married Susan May Williams, an honest, uncomplicated, thoroughly American girl with whom he was very much in love. As Susan Williams represented almost everything Betsey abhorred (except that she was rich), Bo could not bring himself to tell his mother about the engagement. He confided in his grandfather Patterson, who had always disapproved of Betsey's gallivantings around Europe, and in his uncle Joseph, who had remained his friend even though he had not become his father-in-law. They both complimented Bo on his choice and encouraged him to go ahead and marry Miss Williams. Mr. Patterson took it upon himself to break the news to Betsey. Having for years been subjected to her taunts against the way of life, the city, and the country which he loved, he was probably not sorry for this opportunity to bring her down a peg or two. He kept the news until a couple of days before Bo's wedding.

Her reaction was extreme. She could hardly believe it. Was it for this that she had scrimped and saved to give Bo a good education? Was it for this that she had fought her way into the best society in Europe, that she had gone out of her way to cultivate friends in high places, that she had schemed to find him a bride amongst his Bonaparte cousins? Was this her reward for those years of sacrifices, of plans, of dreams? How *could* Bo, who knew how much store she set by his making a brilliant match, who with his looks and his intelligence could have married into one of the first families in Europe, tie himself down to a little American nonentity? It was inconceivable! How *could* he settle down in Baltimore after having sampled the elegance, the sophistication, the excitement of life in Europe? How *could* he, after all she had done for him, "disgrace himself" in this way?

"I have endeavored to instill into him, from the hour of his birth," she wrote with bitter emphasis to her father, "the opinion that he was much too high in birth and connection ever to marry an American woman." The Americans themselves, she claimed, had had enough sense and good taste to realize that she had risen above them, and had always treated her with the "respect and deference due to a superior."

If Betsey was heartbroken, the rest of the Bonaparte family was delighted. Congratulatory letters poured in. Bo's grandmother, Madame Mère, his uncles Joseph, Louis, and Lucien, his aunt Julie, his stepmother, Catherine, his cousins Napoleon-Louis and Charlotte, all wrote to wish him happiness. His father wrote a particularly affectionate letter. Bo's marriage to an unknown but wealthy American girl suited Jérôme very well; it simplified his own position vis-à-vis his son considerably. A match between Bo and one of his Bonaparte cousins might have raised the whole question of his legitimacy again; this way the boy would be more than ever content to lead a life of obscurity across the Atlantic. He would make no demands—either for family rights or for family money.

There was nothing that the savagely disappointed Betsey could do. She had not been able, she told her father sourly, to make a silk purse out of a sow's ear any more than he, her father, had been able to make a sow's ear out of a silk purse. If Bo was going to be satisfied with life in Baltimore, that was his business. "I," she wrote proudly to her long-suffering father, "would rather *die* than marry anyone in Baltimore."

♛   ♛   ♛

Less than three years after the death of his stepfather, Napoleon, the forty-three-year-old Eugène de Beauharnais died. He had suffered a stroke in the summer and during the following winter his life ended.

His marriage, despite the fact that he had been dragooned into it by Napoleon, was a happy one, and through his children there passed into many of the world's reigning houses his qualities of tact, loyalty, and amiability. Perhaps the most perceptive summing up of Eugène's character came from Napoleon himself. Eugène, said the Emperor, was less brilliant and had less prestige on the field of battle than Joachim Murat; he was not "an Ajax, the type of warrior in action." And although he was, in truth, a mediocrity, there was "more proportion, completeness, and harmony about him." He was, said Napoleon, a man, and a *whole* man.

His death was a sad blow to his sister Hortense. With him gone, there was no longer any inducement to remain in Augsburg. She sold her house and moved into the little castle of Arenenberg, perched high above Lake Constance in Switzerland. This castle (it was hardly more than a villa), set amongst picture-postcard scenery and furnished with Hortense's already outdated Empire pieces, was to provide the venue for much Bonaparte intrigue in the years ahead. Here her youngest son, Louis-Napoleon, was to dream his dreams of a Second Empire, and here, in turn, his son would dream *his* dreams of a third.

The next one to die was Pauline. Her health, always fragile, had worsened since the death of Napoleon in 1821. In the autumn of the year 1824 she discovered that her latest, and last, lover, a beautiful young musician named Pacini, was deceiving her. The knowledge of his infidelity must have come as a cruel shock to this woman, who until now had always commanded unswerving devotion. To save face, she broke with him, but the break did not save her from the realization that she was losing her whole *raison d'être*—her ability to inspire admiration. Having no interest in life other than the cult of her beauty, she now abandoned herself to the life of an invalid. She was reconciled with her husband, Prince Borghese, in the spring of the following year, but the reunion brought little satisfaction to either. She found him dull; he found her capricious. In June she drew up her will. Her brothers Louis and Jérôme and her sister Caroline were her chief heirs. Joseph she considered rich enough. To Louis's handsome son Napoleon-Louis, who had rather taken her fancy during the last few years, she left the Villa Paolina; to Napoleon's son, the Duke of Reichstadt, she left San Martino, Napoleon's house on Elba. She left orders that on her death she was to be embalmed and buried in the Borghese vault in the Church of Santa Marie Maggiore in Rome.

She died on June 9, 1825, at the age of forty-four. The story that she faced death wearing a ball gown and clutching a looking glass in her shrunken hands is not true, but the fact that it was widely believed gives some clue to the sort of reputation she enjoyed. If, in a life remarkable only for its gossamer-like quality, she did possess one solid virtue, it was her fidelity to Napoleon. Seldom has a family shown less loyalty to its benefactor; Pauline's was always unquestioned.

♔   ♔   ♔

The year 1830 was a time of revolution. The revolt in France against Bourbon rule, which Napoleon had predicted on St. Helena, broke out in July. Up went the barricades, out came the tricolor, into exile trundled the reactionary King Charles X, and Louis Philippe, the Duc d'Orlèans, was proclaimed King of the French. It was claimed that had Napoleon's son, the Duke of Reichstadt, shown himself to the French people during these feverish July days, he would undoubtedly have been hailed as the Emperor Napoleon II. But Metternich saw to it that he did not, and instead of Napoleon's handsome nineteen-year-old son, the French got a dowdy middle-aged monarch of decidedly bourgeois tastes.

The overthrow of the Bourbons and the enthroning of Louis Philippe had led the Bonapartes to hope that if they themselves could not reign in France, they could at least live in it. They were to be disillusioned. One of Louis Philippe's first moves was to reaffirm the law of 1816, whereby members of the Bonaparte family were banished from the country. So recently elated by the news from France, the Bonapartes were now bitterly disappointed. It was not so difficult for the older generation to resign themselves to a further period of exile; it was the younger ones who felt the continued banishment most keenly. They were itching to identify themselves with their country and to play their part in these new liberal movements.

But the days when a revolution could be restricted to one country were over. The July Revolution in France was echoed by uprisings in half-a-dozen other European countries. Italy, which had been smoldering for years, now burst into flame as well. And where the flames were hottest were to be found the two sons of Louis and Hortense.

Hortense and her youngest son, Louis-Napoleon, had arrived on one of their periodic visits to Rome in the autumn of 1830. On their way south from Arenenberg they had stopped off at Florence to spend a few days with Napoleon-Louis and his wife, Charlotte. During the July Revolution the handsome Napoleon-Louis had been called upon to lead a movement in France to restore his cousin, the Duke of Reichstadt. Very wisely, he had refused; such a movement would almost certainly have led to civil war. Much to the gratification of both Hortense and Charlotte, Napoleon-Louis had remained firmly at home.

Their short stay in Florence over, Hortense and Louis-Napoleon continued on to Rome. They had not been there for a month before Louis-Napoleon was expelled from the city. Not only had the young man been seen riding round Rome sporting a tricolor saddle-cloth, but the Papal authorities claimed to have proof that he was planning to overthrow the government and proclaim himself regent for his cousin, the Duke of Reichstadt. He had intended, they said, to make his cousin's old title, King of Rome, a reality. With the Papal Guard threatening to escort him across the border, Louis-Napoleon fled Rome and joined his brother in Florence.

By the New Year all Italy seemed to be in a state of revolt. Late in January the two brothers left Florence to join one of the rebel armies fighting against their Austrian masters. When Hortense, hot on their trail, arrived in Florence, she found a letter from them informing her that as Bonapartes they had felt compelled to help the cause of the downtrodden. Torn between pride in their high principles and anxiety for their safety, Hortense set off to find them. Traveling through dangerous country on a false passport, she spent an agonized week looking for them. Her search ended at Pesaro on March 19. Here she was reunited with her youngest son, who told her that his brother, Napoleon-Louis, had died two days before. He had died, somewhat unromantically, of measles, and had been buried in the cathedral at Forlì.

There was no time for mourning. Hortense's remaining son was in great danger. They hurried on to Ancona; a few days later the town surrendered to the victorious Austrians. Before mother and son could escape, Louis-Napoleon also came down with measles. Despite the fact that the house in which they were living was commandeered by the Austrians and filled with soldiers, Hortense concealed Louis-Napoleon until he was better. With an Austrian general in the next room, the young man did not dare cough, let alone speak. When he had recovered, she disguised him as a footman and drove hell-for-leather across Italy. She was doing the one thing which no one would have dreamed of her doing: in spite of the fact that she had been banished from France, she was making for Paris. She had decided to throw herself on the mercy of King Louis Philippe.

Mother and son entered France a week after leaving Ancona, and were in Paris by April 23, 1831. It was sixteen years since they had been forced to flee their country: to Louis-Napoleon it was like returning to the Promised Land. He had been eight when he had last seen Paris; now he was twenty-three. Three days after their arrival Hortense had a secret interview with the King. She assured the somewhat apprehensive Louis Philippe that she was en route to London, but that she would appreciate his protection when she returned to Switzerland. Although he was kind to her, he was obviously eager to see her move on, particularly as the news of her presence in Paris was beginning to leak out. Having only just settled into office, Louis Philippe's government was terrified of a Bonapartist uprising. The rooms of Hortense's hotel overlooked the Place Vendôme; was it by pure chance that there was a popular demonstration in favor of Napoleon II at the foot of the Vendôme column on May 5—the tenth anniversary of Napoleon's death? It was suggested that she and her son leave Paris as soon as possible. They set out for England the following day.

In London they met several Bonaparte relations. Christine, Lucien's daughter by his first wife, Christine Boyer, had divorced Count de Posse and had married Lord Dudley Stuart. She now lived in London, and lost no time in calling on her aunt Hortense. News of the July Revolution had made even the phlegmatic Prince Achille Murat forsake Tallahassee and hurry over to Europe, and he too came to confer with his cousin Louis-Napoleon. They learned that Napoleon's two illegitimate sons, Count Léon and Count Walewski, were also in England. When Louis-Napoleon heard that young Walewski was in London, he asked rather sharply why he was not in Poland, supporting the revolutionaries. His reproof was unfair. No less a Bonaparte than his legitimate cousins, Alexandre Walewski had played his part in the Polish uprising against Russia; he was now in England to raise funds for the insurgents. Unknown to each other now, Louis-Napoleon and Walewski were to be closely associated in the years ahead.

Towards the end of July the passports for which Hortense had been waiting arrived, and on August 7 mother and son crossed the channel to Boulogne. Avoiding Paris, they visited Josephine's tomb at Rueil, and then journeyed on home to Arenenberg. Within a few months Louis-Napoleon was to hear momentous news which would help give direction to his as yet amorphous ambitions.

♔   ♔   ♔

The July Revolution had riveted the attention of all members of the Bonaparte family on Vienna. Here Napoleon's son, whom none of them had been allowed to see for sixteen years, was living out his days in his gilded prison. Sensing that if any move was to be made to have him proclaimed Emperor, they, and not he, would have to be the ones to make it, Napoleon's brothers set about trying to contact him. Joseph had already written from America to the French Chambers, upbraiding them for choosing Louis Philippe instead of the Duke of Reichstadt as their sovereign; now he wrote to the Emperor Francis, Marie Louise, and Metternich, putting forward Reichstadt's claims. "I will answer for the success of the undertaking," he declared airily; "only invested with the tricolor scarf, shall Napoleon II be proclaimed!" The letters were ignored.

The next one to stir himself was Lucien. Emerging from his comfortable exile in Rome, Lucien demanded to be given a passport enabling him to travel to Vienna. His brother Joseph's protest to the French Chambers had done more harm than good to his nephew's cause, he claimed; he himself would explain to Metternich exactly why it was so important that Napoleon II be restored. France, under Louis Philippe, was heading for disaster; only Napoleon's son would be able to avert the imminent danger. "Will you tell Prince Metternich," said Lucien grandly to the Austrian ambassador in Florence, "that he may count on me when the opportunity arises." Metternich's reply to this generous offer was to refuse him the passport.

It was now Jérôme's turn. In November 1831 he asked for permission to send a secret agent to Vienna. This agent was to get from the Austrian Cabinet approval for the restoration of Napoleon II. Permission to send his secret agent was refused.

Napoleon's brothers had failed dismally in their efforts to get in touch with Reichstadt; it was one of his nieces who succeeded.

Elisa Bacciochi's daughter Napoléone was twenty-four years old in 1830. Five years previously she had married an Italian count by the name of Camerata, by whom she had had one son and from whom she had since been separated. She now lived in Rome. Amongst all the second generation of Bonapartes, no one was more a Bonaparte than she. So strong, in fact, was her family pride, that she once boasted (in Camerata's presence) that she would never have allowed anyone other than a Bonaparte to father her son; the child's father was assumed to have been either Napoléone's uncle Jérôme or her cousin Louis-Napoleon. Whether or not the boast was true, one does not know, but it was very typical of Napoléone. Often dressed as a man, usually sporting a tricolor ribbon, always to be seen on horseback, frequently signing herself "Napoleon," Countess Camerata was an outspoken, strong-minded, highly adventurous young woman. Napoleon was her God.

The July Revolution set her blood afire. "Who," she declaimed melodramatically to a somewhat startled visitor one day, "can foresee the end of all this?" As far as she was concerned, there could only be one end to it—the restoration of Napoleon II—and she unhesitatingly set out to play her part. Somehow or other she wangled a passport to Vienna, and within a few days she was on her way. Stopping only for a day or two with her aunt Caroline, the ex-Queen of Naples, at Trieste, she pushed on towards Vienna. It was at Baden that she first caught a glimpse of the Duke of Reichstadt. Instead of being overawed by the sight of Napoleon's son (so handsome in his well-tailored white uniform), she leaned out of her carriage and shouted aggressively, "Aren't you ashamed to be wearing the Austrian uniform?"

When next their paths crossed, her attitude was rather more deferential. One evening, when Reichstadt was on his way to pay a visit to one of his tutors, Napoléone cornered him on the doorstep. Clutching one of his hands, she raised it to her lips, and kissing it passionately, exclaimed, "Who can prevent me kissing my sovereign's hand?"

Her sovereign was much too startled to do anything of the kind, but once the door had been shut on her, he was all agog to know who she was. No one could tell him. It was only on receiving several letters from her, couched in the most heroic terms, that he learned that she was his cousin. By then, of course, Metternich knew who she was, too. He also knew what she was doing in Vienna; she had, he reported to the Austrian ambassador in Rome, "undertaken nothing less than to persuade the Duke of Reichstadt to escape and place himself at the head of the adherents of the house of Bonaparte." The police lost no time in moving her on. She went first to Prague, hoping that Reichstadt might visit it and be more accessible there than in Vienna; but when he did not, she returned to Italy. "One day," wrote the disillusioned young woman, "he may recover from his temporary abasement and prove himself worthy of his lofty origins. . . ." Napoléone's brief hour of glory was over; when the Empire was restored, over twenty years later, it would not be due to her efforts. Her only son, the young Count Camerata (who might well, as she claimed, have been all Bonaparte), was also to have his hour of glory, but the outcome was to be infinitely more tragic.

And Reichstadt himself? What was his reaction to the July Revolution? What steps was he taking to regain his father's throne? Had sixteen years of Metternich's supervision achieved their object? Was Napoleon's son now a dyed-in-the-wool Hapsburg?

He looked the perfect Hapsburg. Tall, slender, straight-backed, with a tumble of corn-colored hair and the typical family lip, his Teutonic good looks were further enhanced by his white uniform with the order of Saint Stephen shimmering on his chest. He was, in appearance, very much the son of Marie Louise; only his eyes, those darting, discerning blue eyes, betrayed him as Napoleon's son. "He has his father's glance in which he most resembles him," noted someone who had known Napoleon. "His eyes, which are not so large as Napoleon's, are deeper set, and have the same expression, the same fire and energy." All the tender prettiness inherited from his mother could not quite mask the spirit of the Corsican; by a glance, by an attitude, by an expression, the Napoleonic characteristics were always breaking through.

His preoccupation with dress was not Napoleonic; Napoleon had never given his clothes much thought. His son, on the other hand, was always dressed in the height of fashion. This sartorial flamboyance, coupled with his penchant for bizarre walking sticks, caused his tutors to whisper to each other about his vulgarity. But Reichstadt did not dress in order to shock his tutors; he dressed to create a good impression. To this same end he cultivated a suave, seductive manner, rendered all the more fascinating by virtue of his legendary position. He had only to enter a drawing room for every eye to be on him. "His figure full of grace," enthused one of his tutors, "the beauty of his features, his liveliness, the ease with which he expressed himself, the elegance of his manners and of his clothes, and above all, his destiny, attracted all hearts to him." This adulation left him by no means unmoved. His gilded charm, his gloss of manner, his showiness (Metternich considered him a first-rate actor), which so delighted the Austrian *haute monde* as he bowed and nodded his way through the Viennese salons, curtained a strong egotism. Here he was his father's equal; his personality was extremely self-centered. "Because it pleases or does not please me, and that is enough," he once flung out, and on that dictum he tended to live his life. "If God gave me permission to address Him a petition which He could fulfil," he once cried, "I should ask Him to descend from His throne and let me occupy it." Permission for this petition was presumably never granted.

He was prepared, though, to accept a humbler throne than that; indeed, he would have been glad of any throne had the astute Metternich ever allowed him to occupy one. He never ceased to keep an ear cocked for news of a vacant kingship; his anxiety to wear a crown left him always fretful and discontented. The Sardinian ambassador in Vienna was right when he wrote home reporting that Reichstadt was "hotheaded, vehement, possessed by quenchless thirst for action and an extraordinary ambition."

Ambition was the key to his character. It was the hub about which the spinning wheel of his young life revolved. Born the son of a man who had distinguished himself to an extent scarcely credible to the Europe of the nineteenth century, Reichstadt longed to prove himself worthy of the Great Napoleon. It was his ardent desire to imitate him in all things. Napoleon had been a great soldier; therefore he must be a great soldier. He had inherited his father's passion for military science; devoting himself to a military career was thus an agreeable enough task, and his ambition to distinguish himself in the army overruled all other passions. It overruled, too, any more moral considerations. For, as his father had done before him, he tended to shift the blame for his own mistakes onto the shoulders of others. When he read a history of the campaign of 1796 by the Archduke Charles, he professed himself astonished that the author should admit his errors of generalship so honestly. He would never be guilty of such damaging frankness. "Leading spirits" should not be measured by ordinary standards, he claimed self-importantly. There is no doubt that he considered himself a leading spirit.

He applied himself mercilessly to his career. At night he would push through book after book on politics, history, economics, and military strategy; by day he would drill his battalion—he had been promoted to a colonel in the Vasa Regiment—firmly and professionally. He allowed nothing to check his all-pervading ambition to establish himself as a leader of men. He was preparing himself for a great destiny. If France called him, he once confided to a friend, he would not hesitate to answer her call. If Europe tried to keep him from his father's throne, he would "draw his sword against the whole of Europe."

But when the call did come, he faltered. The July Revolution threw him into a quagmire of uncertainty. The Hapsburg warred with the Bonaparte. He was torn between the familiar everyday world and the world of his dreams; between his genuine love for the Emperor of Austria and his longing to become the Emperor of the French; between the timidity which he had inherited from Marie Louise and the pretensions which had come to him from his father; between his inability to make decisions and his longing for action. Having all Napoleon's egotism and none of his genius, he was like a bird with clipped wings: the will to fly was there, the ability to do so was not. They called him *l'Aiglon*, and an eaglet he remained all his life; it is doubtful that he would ever have grown into an eagle.

At no time were his divided loyalties more apparent than during the Italian insurrections in which his cousins, Hortense's sons, were playing such an active part. When the revolutionary movement reached Parma, Marie Louise was forced to flee her palace and Austrian troops were sent to support her. Reichstadt begged to accompany the men, but, as usual, permission was refused. Had he been allowed to go, he would, in fact, have been fighting against his own supporters. His companions had never seen him in so agitated a state before; he seemed to be "in the grip of a perpetual fever." Denied the opportunity of seeing service in Parma, he longed for the revolution to spread to Austria. He assured his mother that the army would know how to deal with "the people of Vienna." Was this the boy who had been instructed by his father never to "lend himself to being an instrument in the hands of the triumvirs who are oppressing the peoples of Europe"?

These bursts of enthusiasm were always followed by long periods of despair. He felt that he lacked experience, that he did not have enough knowledge, that his judgment was immature. At times it seemed as though he would never have confidence enough to break his bonds. The July Revolution came and went, and Napoleon's son remained in Vienna. . . .

There was another reason for his agonized irresolution. He was very ill. He had grown up fast; in fact, he was still growing, and his chest was narrow. Living a life of such feverish activity (he was on the parade ground all day and in all weathers, and humped over his books at night), he neglected himself. He would gallop through the afternoon and then attend the opera without changing his clothes; he would dash out in the driving rain without the protection of a coat; he would often forego his meals, and he never got enough sleep; he would shout himself hoarse as he marched his men to and fro. It is small wonder that his voice would fail as he gave commands, and that his fine skin would turn pale and transparent. Often his doctor would find him stretched out on a hard cot in a state of utter exhaustion.

Like his father, he had little faith in doctors. In spite of their warnings, he forced his frail body further and further in his quest for military glory. Besides, such remedies as his doctors did suggest would have been of little value; they were treating him for an ailing liver when he was suffering from consumption. Despite his prolonged spasms of coughing, his frequent spitting out of blood, and his bouts of fever, the doctors seemed blissfully unaware of the real trouble. Nor did Reichstadt's headstrong behavior help. One day in the spring of 1832, after galloping for several miles and returning home exhausted, he set out for a carriage drive in a knife-edged April wind. When the wheel of his carriage broke, he leaped to the ground to save himself, and lay there on the damp earth, too weak to get up. He reached home in a fainting condition. Congestion of the lungs set in the next day. Only now did his doctor organize a hurried consultation with his colleagues and prescribe a long holiday in the sunshine as the only solution for the Duke's condition. It was decided that he should go to Italy. Until such time as he was strong enough to travel, he was to quit Vienna and take up residence at Schönbrunn Palace.

He was quartered in the very rooms that his father had occupied twenty-five years before. In this sumptuous suite Napoleon and Marie Walewska had spent their nights, and here Napoleon had finally decided to divorce Josephine. It was in order to secure an heir that Napoleon had divorced his wife; now, a quarter of a century later this heir lay dying, his destiny unfulfilled.

A few weeks previously he had received a letter from Marchand, who had been Napoleon's chief valet on St. Helena. Marchand wrote to inform Reichstadt that he had been endeavoring to pass on some Napoleonic souvenirs to him for years. Anxious to hand over these precious relics, Marchand asked if he might give them to the young Duke personally. The letter had been censored by Metternich. In it he had enclosed a note instructing Reichstadt that no attention was to be paid to the valet's request. Reichstadt, sick, sad, and limp with lethargy, raised no cry of protest, and Marchand's humane mission remained unfulfilled.

Where was Marie Louise while her son lay dying? Why had she not hurried home from Parma to be by his side? Her absence at this critical time is often quoted as proof positive of her indifference. But the situation was more complicated than that. Time and again she was reassured by her son's doctors that there was nothing to fear; as late as May one finds her writing to a friend to tell her that she had heard that Reichstadt was improving daily. Reports from her father, the Emperor, and from her son's tutors were equally encouraging. It was only when Metternich, who, in spite of his loathing for Reichstadt, had some regard for appearances, insisted that she come to Vienna, that she set out. But she dawdled on the way, and did not reach Schönbrunn until late in June.

Her initial alarm at seeing her son's fever-bright eyes and cadaverous cheeks seems to have been dispersed as the summer days succeeded one another, for she was able to write and tell her father about the patient's gradual recovery. She would move about Reichstadt's room, her sweetly empty face all kindness, all concern, for in her way she loved the boy dearly. Perhaps the sight of him lying there served as some sort of reproach; she had always been content to leave him in the care of others, to trust his education, his upbringing, his health to those whom she always, in her self-effacing way, assumed knew better. Was some chord in her conscience now struck when she saw to what a piteous state Napoleon's son had been reduced while she had been spending all those years with the children of her lover, Neipperg? Could that be the reason why she sometimes came to bend over his wasted frame the last thing at night before he drifted off into uneasy sleep? "I desire nothing more in this world but peace and quiet," she had once written; here was yet another unasked-for event crowding upon a personality which was no match for it.

Although Reichstadt was still quite fond of his mother, he by now saw her for what she was. He knew about her children by Neipperg, and the knowledge had shocked him very deeply. "If Josephine had been my mother," he once said, "my father would not be buried at St. Helena and I would not be languishing here in Vienna. Oh, she [Marie Louise] is kindhearted but weak; she was not the wife my father deserved."

Napoleon II died, at the age of twenty-one, a few minutes after five o'clock on the morning of July 22, 1832. At four that morning one of his companions, realizing that the end was near, scurried through the vast slumbering palace, whispering his alarming tidings to the members of the court. A handful of relations, doctors, officers, and servants assembled, Marie Louise trembling so violently that she could scarcely stand. A young chaplain hurried into the room to administer extreme unction. Reichstadt watched his approach calmly. As the priest moved about, now kneeling, now standing, now bending forward, now laying his hands on his forehead, Reichstadt's eyes never left him; he seemed to follow every move of the sad ceremony. A scuffling sound broke throught the humming of the prayers as Marie Louise, almost fainting, was helped onto a chair. In a little while she knelt down. The room was breathless.

Was there anything in this scene to remind one of Napoleon's death on St. Helena? Not at first glance, certainly. There seems little parallel between this palatial apartment, graying in the light of the slow dawn, and that unpretentious little room, lit by the tropical sunset. Nor do these stolid, aristocratic Austrian countenances bear much resemblance to the sharply edged parvenu French faces surrounding Napoleon. And this young man, drifting out of his sad, short, unremarkable life, differs so vastly from his mature parent, dying, with destiny accomplished, after a career of incredible achievement. But there were similarities. They both died in exile, and they both, these two men whose overriding passion had been war, died in bed.

A little after five Reichstadt moved his head from side to side. After that he died.

The autopsy was held the following day. It proved conclusively that Reichstadt had died of tuberculosis. That he had died, as many claimed, of sexual overindulgence, there was no sign. This inevitable story was spread around and only too readily believed by those who were unable to understand how a young man, a duke, virile, handsome, sought after, could one season be in the very best condition, and the next, look so old and dissipated. He must, it was argued, have been leading an aging and dissipating life; his early death must have been brought on by his indiscriminate love affairs. The symptoms of tuberculosis and syphilis were, to the medically simpler minds of the early nineteenth century not unalike, and the Duke's typically tubercular vivacity gave rise to the theory that his restlessness had led him to indulge in all sorts of amorous indiscretions. In French circles it was believed that this sexual activity had been encouraged by Metternich, who was eager to rid himself of his diplomatically embarrassing charge. He is supposed to have planted these seeds of decay by introducing Reichstadt to various Viennese ballerinas, including the celebrated Fanny Essler. There is a story that sometime after the Duke's death, when Fanny Essler had satisfied the appetite of a certain wealthy young Englishman, he had adjusted his eyeglass and said, "Thank you, now I have seen the grave of the Duke of Reichstadt."

These rumors of sexual depravity were quite untrue. The Duke was far too obsessed with making a name for himself to fritter away his time and energies on indiscriminate love-making. His great friend Prokesch admits that the boy did experience "natural instincts." Reichstadt often spoke to Prokesch about these feelings, "but in a tone of perfect innocence. This he would never have done had he known closer intercourse with women. The shame of misdoing would have betrayed him. He was strictly moral. He had impulses, but nothing more." Prokesch's protestations might be a little naïve, but Reichstadt does seem to have been considerably less licentious than the average young nobleman of the day.

A more recent theory accuses Metternich of being much less obliquely responsible for Reichstadt's death than by merely encouraging his liaisons with a few voluptuous ballerinas. It has been claimed that the Duke died of arsenic poisoning and that it was Metternich who killed him. As with the similar theory about Napoleon's death, the claim might well be true.

Reichstadt's body, taken to Vienna at dead of night, lay in state in the chapel of the Hofburg palace the following day. He was buried late that afternoon in the Imperial crypt of the Kapuzinerkirche. No less a Hapsburg in death than in life, his remains were deposited in one of the anonymous copper coffins reserved for all the archdukes of Austria. Only the Latin inscription gave it its distinction. "To the eternal memory of Joseph Charles François Duke of Reichstadt, son of Napoleon, Emperor of the French, and of Marie Louise, Archduchess of Austria, born in Paris, March 20, 1811, honored in his cradle by the title of King of Rome. . . ."

They condescended, in the end, to give him back his legitimacy and his title. Safely dead, the Austrians allowed him to become once more the King of Rome, son of Napoleon, Emperor of the French.

Visiting the Imperial crypt in the Kapuzinerkirche is a strange experience. It is like some macabre dormitory. From wall to wall, in ordered rows, hardly discernible in the gloom, lie the coffins. Here, in one hundred and thirty-eight dusty leaden caskets, the members of the Imperial family sleep their last sleep. Some lie in sad, simple little boxes, others in high-plinthed sarcophagi, aflower with statuary. Within all the cold grayness of that vault there is a single splash of color. On the coffin of Marie Louise lies a posy of artificial violets, tied with a yellow and blue ribbon. The purple of the Imperial flower of France, caught with the bold colors of lower Austria, seems almost irreverent amongst the somber Hapsburg caskets. It is a pretty reminder that once, in fear and humility, they allied their ancient house with that of the upstart Bonapartes. It was Marie Louise who planted the Napoleonic violet in Hapsburg soil. It has a right to flower in that venerable vault.

The place where Reichstadt's coffin used to stand is empty. It is marked by a dark patch on the paved floor. Beside it is a notice on which is lettered, in German, these words: "On this spot stood, from 1832–1940, the coffin of the Duke of Reichstadt, son of Napoleon."

The coffin was taken away under the most extraordinary circumstances.

CHAPTER TEN

⚜ ⚜ ⚜

THE death of the Duke of Reichstadt, following so soon that of Hortense's eldest son, Napoleon-Louis, changed the whole pattern of the Imperial succession.

For the first time in something like thirty years Joseph once more became the titular head of the family. Next in line came his brother Louis. But as Joseph was now in his sixties and even less ambitious than he had been in younger days, and as Louis was a permanent invalid with no imperial aspirations whatsoever, it was Louis's son, Louis-Napoleon, who now became the actual pretender to the throne. He, in turn, was followed by his uncle Jérôme, and Jérôme by his two sons, Prince Jérôme-Napoléon and Prince Napoleon, known as Plon-Plon. Lucien and his pack of sons were, of course, excluded from the succession.

Taking his role as head of the family very seriously, Joseph, after sixteen years, left America and returned to settle in Europe. He arrived in London in August 1832, and immediately wrote to his brothers Lucien and Jérôme and to his nephew Prince Louis-Napoleon (Louis was ill), inviting them to attend a family conference. Achille Murat from Tallahassee was still in London, and so was Charlotte, Joseph's daughter and widow of Napoleon-Louis.

The family discussions on the hopes of an Imperial restoration were marked by caution on the part of Napoleon's brothers and impatience on the part of his twenty-four-year-old nephew, young Louis-Napoleon. The tutelage of La Bas and his baptism of fire during the uprisings in Italy in 1831 had changed him from a dreamy well-mannered boy into an ambitious, if no less charming, young man. Reichstadt's death had made him very conscious of the fact that he was now the Imperial pretender; not only did he emphasize his normally distant, if friendly, manner, but he began making contact with various undergound Bonapartist organizations. A born conspirator, Louis-Napoleon was never happier than when in secret consultation with his supporters. It was a taste which he was never to outgrow. All this political activity alarmed his aging uncles, who, unlike their vigorous nephew, were content to await events rather than precipitate them. Their somewhat inconclusive family council over, Lucien, Jérôme, and Louis-Napoleon returned to the Continent, leaving

Joseph in England. "All the Bonapartes," sighed the exasperated young Louis-Napoleon, "are dead."

Home again at Arenenberg, Louis-Napoleon dedicated himself to the Bonapartist cause. He published several political pamphlets, he built up a hard core of loyal adherents, he watched French political trends like a hawk. It was obvious that France was becoming dissatisfied with its compromise king, Louis Philippe, but that it would be any more satisfied with a Bonaparte emperor was uncertain. What, in fact, did France know of him other than that he bore his uncle's name? "I know that my name is everything," he wrote to a friend, "but that my personality still counts for nothing." Sometimes the immensity of the task he had undertaken seemed overwhelming, but he remained resolute. "It is because I know all the difficulties I would encounter . . . that I have laid down the principle of following only the inspirations of my heart, of my reason, of my conscience; of not allowing myself to be stopped by any consideration of secondary interest . . . in short, of walking in a straight line, whatever difficulties I may meet on the road, and of raising myself to such a height that the dying rays of the sun of St. Helena may still illumine me."

These years of planning for a Bonaparte restoration saw the death of three women closely associated with the First Empire. Jérôme's wife, Catherine of Württemberg, died in 1835; Madame Mère, in 1836; and Caroline Murat, in 1839.

Catherine had been unwell for some years, and in the summer of 1835 her condition became worse. Always plump, she suddenly became enormous. The doctors in Florence, where Jérôme and his family were now living, thinking that it might be dropsy and not knowing what to do about it, advised her to consult another doctor in Lausanne. Accompanied by her husband and her three children—Jérôme-Napoléon, Mathilde, and Plon-Plon—Catherine spent the autumn in Lausanne. By November it was clear that she was dying. "I see that death is drawing near, but I'm not afraid," she whispered to the people gathered round her bed. Then, turning to her faithless husband, she added, "I have loved you more than anyone in the world. Jérôme. I am ready to go, but I wish that I could have bade you farewell on French soil."

She died on November 25, 1835. One hopes that at least for a few days after her death Jérôme remembered the years of her unstinting love, but even this is doubtful. It is far more likely that he was worrying about the pension from Württemberg, which had ceased with her death. Hopelessly in debt in spite of her allowance, how was he to manage without it?

Two months later Madame Mère died. Not many years short of ninety, she had outlived even members of the third generation of Bonapartes. One of Lucien's sons had been killed in the Greek War of Independence in 1827, Louis's son Napoleon-Louis had died in 1831, Napoleon's son the Duke of Reichstadt had died in 1832, Elisa's only boy, Frédéric, had been thrown from his horse and killed in 1834. "There is some evil influence hovering over the third generation of Bonapartes," she said. "They all die violent deaths."

Almost blind, almost paralyzed, she lived in her somber palace, surrounded by busts and portraits of her famous family. Her children and her grandchildren, in fact, filled her thoughts. When it was suggested that the law exiling the Bonapartes from France be repealed in her case, her reply was characteristically sharp. Those who talked of making an exception of her, she said, simply did not understand her principles or her character. All her life she had chosen to share the misfortunes of her children; why should she cease to do so now? She wanted, she claimed, to be left alone in her sufferings, to carry her integrity to the grave. "I will never separate my lot from that of my children."

On January 27 she caught a cold, and six days later she died. Lucien and Jérôme were the only two of her children to be beside her at the end. Joseph and Caroline had been refused permission to come to Rome, and Louis was too ill to undertake the journey. She lay in state in one of the great rooms of the Palazzo Bonaparte, and she was buried in the church of the Sisters of the Passion in Tarquinia, near Civitavecchia. Fifteen years later, when her grandson Louis-Napoleon became ruler of France, he had her body taken back to Ajaccio in Corsica. Over the entrance to the vault in which it lies buried is a black marble slab; on it, in Latin, is inscribed her name, and below it, the simple title, "Mother of Kings."

Caroline Murat had left Trieste, and had been living in Florence since 1831. All Florence, according to her, flocked to pay their respects, while the foreigners came in "crowds." In spite of this, and in spite of the devotion of General Macdonald, she was bored. Her sons, Achille and Lucien, had gone to America, and her daughters, Letizia and Louise, had both married Italian nobleman. Much of her still formidable tenacity of purpose was now directed towards wangling herself a pension from the French government; it says something for her powers of persuasion that she succeeded. It is also notable that on the death of General Macdonald, although she was in her late fifties, she lost no time in replacing him. The name of her latest lover was Clavel, and he seems to have been somewhat less her slave than the good general. They appear, in fact, to have been an evenly matched pair. There is a story that as Caroline lay dying on May 18, 1839, Clavel, wanting to be paid for his services, tried to force her to sign a will in his favor. Only the timely arrival of her children saved them from losing their inheritance. Clavel did not quit her home without some compensation, however. It was rumored that he sold to her heirs, for a considerable sum of money, the letters she had written him.

♣ ♣ ♣

The spring of the year 1836 found Jérôme Bonaparte (now a widower), with his three children, visiting Hortense at Arenenberg. The thirteen-year-old Plon-Plon had already been there for some months, as Hortense had invited him to live at Arenenberg for a while after his mother's death. Louis-Napoleon had undertaken to tutor him in history and mathematics and to teach him how to skate. Even at this age young Plon-Plon, squat, dark-haired, and sallow-complexioned, bore a distinct resemblance to the Great Napoleon; the liveliness of his mind and the surliness of his temper were Napoleonic as well. At present so happy in each other's company, the cousins were to be at loggerheads for the rest of their lives; in many ways the future relationship between Louis-Napoleon and his cousin Plon-Plon was to echo the association between Napoleon and his fiery brother Lucien.

When the rest of the family arrived in April, it was the sixteen-year-old Mathilde who took the center of the stage. No less Napoleonic in her looks than her brother Plon-Plon, and just as precocious, she was a delightful creature—warm-blooded, high-spirited, romantic. Even Hortense, who had very little time for any of the Bonapartes other than her own son, was captivated by the girl's rosy charm. As for Louis-Napoleon, he fell in love with her on sight.

Love was, for him, no new sensation. During the last dozen or so years of his life he had fallen in and out of love countless times. He had only to see a pretty face to fall in love with it. There were combined in his nature two sensual strains—the sentimental, seductive strain of the Beauharnais and the more virile, promiscuous characteristics of the Bonapartes. Although not especially handsome, he did have physical qualities which women found attractive. His shortness of stature was compensated for by a flattering warmth of manner, his lugubriousness of feature, by a gentleness of expression. The beaklike nose, the olive complexion, and the too-large head were usually forgotten after one glance from those veiled, heavy-lidded gray eyes. "I have heard," noted General Ricard, "that many women were thrilled by this look; for whatever is mysterious and unintelligible always attracts women." But if Louis-Napoleon fell in love with every pretty woman he met, at least half their number returned his love. By 1836 his name had already been linked with dozens of women, ranging from princesses to chambermaids.

It was no wonder, then, that he fell in love with the fresh-faced, quick-witted Mathilde, or that she returned his love. Arenenberg, with its views over the lake, its leafy park, its air of bittersweet nostalgia, was an ideal setting for the dawning romance, and the sentimental Hortense gave the young lovers every encouragement. On one occasion she dressed Mathilde in one of her old high-waisted, filmy Empire dresses, and the result caused much admiration; on another she accompanied them on a moonlit outing on the lake with a group of singers following in another boat. She was even prepared to trade the last of her jewelry in order to make a substantial constrition towards her son's marriage. For by now it had been arranged, between Hortense and Jérôme, that Mathilde should marry Louis-Napoleon.

Louis, the boy's father, was not nearly so starry-eyed about the proposed match. He knew Jérôme, and he knew that Jérôme had no money. When the two brothers met in Florence to discuss the marriage, Jérôme admitted that Mathilde would have no dowry. Hortense, too, now that the family had left Arenenberg, was having second thoughts about the arrangement; for all Jérôme's assurances that the Württemberg family would make some provision for Mathilde, she was uneasy. Negotiations dragged on all through the autumn. Louis would give no definite sanction; Jérôme would promise no definite dowry; Hortense would give no definite support. It was Louis-Napoleon who, in October 1836, settled the matter once and for all.

At dawn on the morning of October 30 he made his first attempt to re-establish the Empire. Supported by a handful of loyal Bonapartists, and riding at the head of one of the regiments sympathetic to his cause, he attempted to induce the garrison at Strasbourg to march behind him to Paris. The adventure was a fiasco. Within two hours Prince Louis-Napoleon was under arrest. He was sent to Paris, from where, without trial, he was shipped off into exile in North America. King Louis Philippe, having no desire to give the young Bonaparte pretender any publicity, had very wisely decided that the less fuss made about the conspiracy, the better. He was put aboard the *Andromède* and sent by the slowest possible route across the Atlantic.

So incensed was Jérôme by what he considered his nephew's fool-hardiness, and so hurt was Mathilde at not being taken into her betrothed's confidence, that the engagement was broken immediately. It is unlikely that either party suffered any real heartbreak. Louis-Napoleon wrote telling Hortense that he had had a premonition that he would never marry Mathilde. While walking across the park at Arenenberg on day, he had come across a tree which had been shattered by lightning. He had realized then, he told his mother, that his marriage, too, would be "broken by fate." Mathilde's comment on their engagement, made years later when she knew Louis-Napoleon much better, was considerably more matter-of-fact. "Had I married him," she said robustly, "I think that I might have broken open his head just to see what was in it."

   ♛   ♛   ♛

Prince Louis-Napoleon landed at Norfolk, Virginia, on March 30, 1837. He landed with vague intentions of settling down in America; he remained there, in fact, for less than three months. It might have been the brevity of his visit, or it might have been what the family considered his impetuosity at Strasbourg, that prevented him from making contact with his relations in America. Whichever it was, there seems to be no evidence of his having met any of them. Before leaving France, he had written to his uncle Joseph in England, asking for letters of introduction; his request had remained unanswered. Joseph considered that his nephew had done the Bonapartist cause untold harm by his Strasbourg adventure; he had behaved, claimed Joseph, as though his father and uncles no longer existed. Achille Murat and his family were at Tallahassee; Lucien Murat and his family, at Bordentown; Bo and his wife, Susan, were in Baltimore. Louis-Napoleon saw none of them.

The Baltimore Bonapartes, Bo and Susan, had had a son in 1830; like his father and his grandfather, he was called Jerome. His birth had brought no joy to Bo's mother, Betsey; one does not know that she even congratulated the couple on his birth. Yet when she returned to America four years later and held her grandson in her arms, her hard heart softened somewhat. Perhaps this latest Jerome Bonaparte would prove himself more worthy of her. By now Betsey was becoming decidedly eccentric. Although only in her fifties and still very handsome, she was beginning to live in the past. The enormous trunks which she had brought back from Europe were crammed with souvenirs of her brilliant youth: her wispy wedding dress, the ballgown which the late Pauline

Borghese had given her, the dress she had worn at her presentation at the court of Tuscany. Even Jérôme's wedding finery had been carefully preserved.

Her more recent clothes, on the other hand, were sadly neglected; always careful with money, the years had turned her into a miser. She was to be seen in the streets of Baltimore, always wearing the same black bonnet with its orange feather and carrying the same red umbrella. Another carefully cherished relic of her past was her disdain for Baltimore and the United States. "A residence of a few months in the *Etats Unis*," she wrote dryly to a friend, "would cure the most ferocious republican of the mania for republics."

Another of Louis-Napoleon's relations in America at the time was Pierre Bonaparte, the fourth son of Napoleon's brother Lucien and Alexandrine Jouberthon. If some of Lucien's sons were surprisingly well behaved, Pierre was dissolute enough to make up for them all. No Bonaparte sheep was blacker than he. There is a story that in his early youth, when he and his brother Louis-Lucien had gone shooting moufflons in Corsica, they had both fallen in love with a beautiful peasant girl named Maria Cecchi. Whereas in earlier times the brothers, who were by now quarreling violently over the girl, would have settled their difference by a duel, they decided to gamble for her. The two princes signed an agreement whereby whoever won the card game would marry the girl. They played, and Pierre lost. Louis-Lucien, faithful to his word, married the girl, but his passion soon spent itself and they were separated. Pierre, the loser, not yet eighteen, sailed for America, where he set about forgetting his disappointment with such gusto that there was no tavern in New York too sordid for his name to be known in it. From this point on his recklessness, his extravagance, his uncontrollable temper would be a constant embarrassment to his family, and to his cousin Louis-Napoleon, in particular.

If Prince Pierre Bonaparte left an unspeakably bad reputation behind him in America, Louis-Napoleon left a surprisingly good one. Although he was every bit as capable of flinging himself into the pleasures of life as his cousin, he seems to have been particularly discreet during his stay in America. Perhaps it was because he had very little money; perhaps it was because he felt that as pretender to the French throne, he should behave with suitable dignity. Whichever it was, New York society was very impressed by this grave, temperate, well-mannered young prince who spoke so affectionately of his mother and so convincingly of his claims to the crown of France.

It was this affection for his mother, Queen Hortense, that caused him to leave America. In June he had a letter from her, telling him that she had been ill; unbeknown to her, one of her household had added an anguished message, "*Revenez, revenez.*" Louis-Napoleon immediately booked a passage back to Europe, and by July 10 he was in London. Here he directed all his energies towards procuring a passport that could get him to Arenenberg. Although his uncle Joseph remained aloof, his cousin Christine, Lady Dudley Stuart, hurried to offer her services. Her intervention with the Austrian ambassador proved fruitless; nor would the Prussian ambassador do anything for him. It was finally with an American passport, made out in the name of Robinson and signed by the Swiss minister, that he got away.

Louis-Napoleon reached Arenenberg early in August. Hortense was dying of cancer. Her son's arrival revived her a little, but it was clear to her devoted companions that she did not have long to live. During those last days, with the pale autumn sunshine flooding the house and brightening its old-fashioned Empire décor, Hortense spoke often of Paris, of the Emperor, and of her mother, Josephine. It was a pity that she, always such an admirer of Napoleon and always such a believer in the abilities of her son, could not live to see him revive Napoleon's Empire. She died, after much suffering, on October 5, 1837. She was fifty-four years old. They buried her near Josephine in the little church at Rueil. Louis-Napoleon was not allowed to attend the ceremony, but amongst the mourners were Hortense's old lover, Charles de Flahaut, and their son, Auguste de Morny. Many years later, Hortense's simple grave would be surmounted by an ornate monument bearing the triumphant Imperial inscription: "To Queen Hortense, from her son Napoleon III."

An altercation between the French and Swiss governments concerning Louis-Napoleon's presence so near to France caused him to leave Arenenberg and make for England. Once established there, he played his role of Imperial pretender for all it was worth. He set up house, first in Carlton House Terrace and then in Carlton Gardens; he drove around London in a carriage emblazoned with the Imperial eagle; he became a leading member of Lady Blessington's circle. Realizing that it would need rather more than this show of elegance to make the public take his Imperial claims seriously, he published an ambitious manifesto on Bonapartism, *Les Idées Napoléoniennes*, and a somewhat more homely piece entitled *Lettres de Londres*. The first was a rehash of Napoleon I's St. Helena brand of Bonapartism to suit the aspiring Napoleon III; the second was a highly flattering study of the pretender himself.

The publication of *Les Idées Napoléoniennes*, plus Louis-Napoleon's not only settled but positively aristocratic way of life, had reconciled his uncle Joseph to him once more. Joseph had returned to England from a visit to America in 1839, and early the next year Jérôme followed. Uncles and nephew seemed to be on the friendliest of terms, and were frequently to be found dining at each other's well-appointed houses. These polite family scenes were soon violently disrupted by the arrival of a fourth Bonaparte: this was Count Léon, Napoleon's illegitimate son by Eléonore Denuelle.

Since that day in 1815 when the young Count Léon had been brought to say good-by to Napoleon at Malmaison and Hortense had marveled at his likeness to the King of Rome, he had led an extraordinarily profligate life. Having changed from a well-mannered, good-looking youngster into a raffish, irresponsible, ill-tempered braggart, he had a limitless capacity for getting into trouble. That his mother Eléonore, having married three times herself, ever bothered to check his growing depravity, is doubtful. He gambled away the vast sums of money granted him by Napoleon; he quarreled with his old friends and was swindled by his new; he involved himself in duels and was caught up in a squalid litigation; he even accused his mother, whom he detested, of fraud. This latest action, which, like most others in his life, he lost, ended with his being thrown into the debtors' prison at Clichy. When he emerged, he was, of course, penniless, and not even the customary playing up of his romantic origins and his Napoleonic resemblance seemed to help.

Yet when he arrived in England in 1840, he appeared to be living in considerable luxury. He had put up at Fenton's Hotel and was entertaining lavishly. His claim to be a commercial traveler in patent lamps semed highly unlikely; what seemed more probable was that he was in the pay of Louis Philippe's government. There was a theory that he had been sent to England by the French government in order to provoke a duel with Prince Louis-Napoleon. The affair was meant to end with Louis-Napoleon's being either killed or banished.

The Bonapartes had been warned of Count Léon's arrival. He called on Joseph; he called on Jérôme; he called on Louis-Napoleon. None would receive him. After his fourth attempt to see the Imperial pretender, Count Léon wrote him an insolent letter. Addressing him as his "little cousin." he tried by open insults and veiled threats to provoke Louis-

Napoleon into some imprudent response. The Prince merely sent him a message to say that he had no intention of answering his letter. Count Léon promptly wrote another, more insulting still. He accused Louis-Napoleon of not having a drop of French blood in his veins. This time his letter was more successful; the Prince accepted his cousin's challenge, and a duel was arranged for the following morning.

The adversaries met on Wimbledon Common. Napoleon's nephew, kindly, mild-mannered, laconic, faced Napoleon's son, loutish, excitable, bombastic. Léon would not agree to Louis-Napoleon's choice of weapons, and before the argument could be resolved, the police arrived on the scene. Duelists and seconds were bundled off to Bow Street police station, where they were discharged with a warning and the threat of a heavy fine.

Count Léon, having failed at his mission, returned to France and into temporary obscurity. During the Second Empire he would persistently petition his erstwhile adversary for more money. Louis-Napoleon always granted his requests, but he steadfastly refused to receive him. "I cannot forget that London affair," he would say.

While the French government was trying its best to get rid of Napoleon's successor, it was doing its utmost to pay homage to the Napoleonic legend. In an effort to bring a little glitter to his own lack-luster regime, King Louis Philippe attempted to identify himself with the glories of the First Empire. Napoleon's statue was once more hoisted atop the Vendôme column, his Arc de Triomphe was completed, the imperial battle pictures were given a home in the palace of Versailles. And, as a crowning gesture, it was decided to bring Napoleon's body back from St. Helena. No less a person than one of the King's sons, the Prince de Joinville, was chosen to carry out this sacred, if melo-dramatic, errand. The French ambassador asked the British for permission to remove the precious remains, such of Napoleon's companions in exile as were still alive were rounded up to accompany the expedition, and in July 1840 the *Belle Poule* set sail from France for St. Helena.

This gave Louis-Napoleon the opportunity he had been waiting for. Now, when the minds of Frenchmen were filled with thoughts of the Emperor, would be the time to re-establish the Empire. Who, if not a Bonaparte, should welcome Bonaparte back? Louis-Napoleon's first scheme was to attack the returning *Belle Poule* in mid-ocean, to board it, pirate-fashion, and to bring the Emperor's remains back to France himself. It would have been a magnificent gesture. This plan, however, was abandoned for a less theatrical but equally hazardous one. On August 4

Prince Louis-Napoleon and a party of supporters sailed from England in a hired steamer, headed for Boulogne. Here, as at Strasbourg four years before, Louis-Napoleon attempted to rally the garrison to his cause. This expedition was no less disastrous than the other; by eight o'clock on August 6, Louis-Napoleon and his followers were under arrest. This time Louis Philippe's government was taking no chances. Prince Louis-Napoleon was sentenced to perpetual imprisonment in the fortress of Ham.

"How long," remarked Louis-Napoleon dryly, on hearing his sentence, "does perpetuity last in France?" For him, it lasted six years.

On the very day that Louis-Napoleon was locked up in the fortress of Ham, the *Belle Poule* arrived off St. Helena to release the Great Napoleon from his prison.

It took all night, working by lantern light in a steady drizzle, to exhume the Emperor's coffin. When, in the gray of early morning, the four coffins were opened, Napoleon's body was found to be practically intact. His companions, grown old in the twenty years since they had buried him in Geranium Valley, were amazed to see the unchanged face of their Emperor. It was nothing short of a miracle! More cynical minds have considered the extraordinarily well-preserved state of the body to be the result of arsenic poisoning. Having feasted their eyes on those cameolike features once more, the coffins were closed and placed in an elegant ebony casket brought out from France. Over it was draped a violet velvet pall embroidered with golden bees, and it was then carried to the quayside. The coffin, weighing over a ton and a half, was lowered into a longboat and rowed out to the *Belle Poule*. As it neared the waiting ship, the sun, for the first time that day, burst suddenly through the clouds; in this blaze of light did Napoleon leave his island prison.

He reached Paris on December 15. At dawn that day, in the presence of a vast concourse of people, his coffin passed under the Arc de Triomphe and down the Champs Elysées to the Hôtel des Invalides. Nothing that could be achieved by paper, paint, and plaster had been spared to make him welcome. In an age of vulgar taste, Napoleon's funeral was the acme of vulgarity. An immense hearse, needing every one of those sixteen richly caparisoned horses to drag it, lumbered between rows of mock-marble figures, eagle-crowned columns, vast funeral urns and outsize calico tricolors. It reached the Hôtel des Invalides late in the afternoon, and after a long and tedious ceremony, during which the fashionable congregation chatted amiably and the crew of the *Belle Poule* chewed tobacco, Napoleon's remains were laid to rest in a flamboyant catafalque. To accommodate this catafalque, the altar had been removed; "And why not?" mused the watching Thackeray wryly. "Who is God here but Napoleon?"

The ceremony finally over, King Louis Philippe, highly satisfied with the day's work, hurried home through the winter darkness. Did he suspect, one wonders, as he drove in the direction of the Tuileries, that this much-publicized return of Napoleon's coffin would prove to be a nail in his own?

♔　　♔　　♔

Once the engagement between Louis-Napoleon and Jérôme's daughter Mathilde had been broken, father and daughter lost no time in looking for another husband. For Jérôme it was imperative that his daughter marry someone with money; for Mathilde, that she marry someone and get away from home. The passing years had taught Jérôme nothing; still as dissolute at fifty as ever he had been at twenty-five, his shameless cadging and his blatant amours were causing Mathilde acute embarrassment, and Florence much amusement. Still, it was not easy to find a suitable husband. Mathilde was a princess, it was true, but she was a parvenu, and poor; an impoverished but legitimate princess, or one both *noveau riche* and *noveau royale*, would have been much easier to place. To add to her disadvantages, Mathilde had a very exalted idea of her own position. To her a Bonaparte princess was equal to any princess in the world, and she considered herself well worthy of a son of the King of France or the Czar of Russia. Luckily, she was young, attractive, vivacious, and far more intelligent than the average princess; she would not, one felt sure, remain unmarried for long.

Her aunt Julie (ex-Queen of Spain) and Julie's daughter Charlotte (widow of Napoleon-Louis), who both lived in Florence, were her confidantes. Julie was now almost seventy, a small, shriveled, kind-hearted old lady who always defended Mathilde against her often unreasonable father. Charlotte, widowed for six years, was in her mid-thirties; like her mother, she was a sensitive, self-effacing, warm-hearted woman. She was also a Bonaparte, and her widowhood had not, therefore, been a lonely one. Her lover was a certain Count Potocki, and the two seem to have loved each other very passionately. As he was married, Charlotte had to be content with a secret liaison. Her cousin Mathilde was one of the few people who knew about it.

In the spring of 1838 Charlotte left Florence for Rome. She would give no explanation for her departure. Her family begged her to remain in Florence, but she, usually so meek, insisted on going. After a stay of a few months in Rome, she wrote home to say that she was moving to Genoa; on the way there she died. It was given out that she had died of a ruptured aneurysm; actually she had died in childbirth. Always looked upon as a model of virtuous widowhood, poor Charlotte had been terrified lest her own name, and that of Count Potocki, be sullied. She had planned to go to Genoa for her confinement, but had been forced to stop at a small seaside village. The birth had proved complicated, and Charlotte, never strong, had died of hemorrhage. Her death almost broke her lover's heart.

It was soon after Charlotte's death that her cousin Mathilde met the man she was going to marry. He was a Russian named Anatole Demidov. The fact that he had a house in Paris appealed to Mathilde enormously; the fact that he was rich beyond belief was enough for Jérôme. Anatole Demidov was young, handsome, popular and, with his barely concealed streak of brutality, very attractive to women. But he was a parvenu. His father and grandfather, having made their money in trade, had never been accepted by the Russian nobility. He now saw in the graceful and cultured Mathilde an opportunity of bettering himself socially; she was, after all, the daughter of a king. For her part, though by no means in love with him, she found him attractive and distinguished. His immense wealth would give her a setting worthy of her intellectual and social gifts. As yet she knew nothing of his vulgarity or his bad temper, and he, nothing of her independent spirit.

The wily Jérôme, before sanctioning the marriage, got Demidov to pay most of his debts, and then sold him, for a vast sum, his wife Catherine's pearl necklace, which should have gone to Mathilde anyway. He even tried to keep the dowry for Mathilde which he had wangled out of his brother Joseph. The bargaining finally concluded, Mathilde and Demidov were married on November 1, 1840. Their wedding luncheon was presided over by the aging Queen Julie.

Within a matter of weeks the newly married pair had run into trouble. Demidov, revealing a coarseness unsuspected by his wife, fell out with the Russian ambassador in Rome. When news of their quarrel reached Russia, Czar Nicholas ordered Demidov home. Mathilde had hoped to spend her honeymoon in Paris; instead, she had to endure a six-week drive to St. Petersburg. Demidov, apprehensive of his reception by the Czar, proved a surly and inconsiderate traveling companion. Once established in the magnificent Demidov mansion in St. Petersburg,

Mathilde was overwhelmed with kindness by the Imperial family. To her husband they were less kind; the Czar, in fact, treated Demidov distinctly coldly. This did nothing towards improving the swiftly deteriorating relationship between husband and wife. Demidov, instead of being grateful for the fact that Mathilde's tact and intelligence were lessening the Czar's anger, resented her success. Yet it was due to her efforts that her husband was not subjected to anything more than coldness on the part of Nicholas, and that they were finally allowed to leave Russia. Mathilde was not sorry to say good-by to this country of dazzling wealth and appalling poverty.

They reached Paris for a short stay in August 1841. It was Mathilde's first experience of the city which had once been the capital of Napoleon's Empire, and stanch Bonapartist that she was, the sight thrilled her. She herself was an immediate success. Her very real interest in the arts brought painters, poets, writers, and musicians flocking to her salon, and her unaffected charm earned her the friendship of King Louis Philippe's unassuming family. When she and Demidov, after another short visit to Russia, returned to Florence in 1843, she was no less popular there. Housed in the sumptuous Demidov palace, she was known as the "great lady of Florence."

Hand in hand with her increasing social stature went the rapid erosion of her marriage. Demidov, always difficult, was becoming impossible. He bullied her, he insulted her, he humiliated her, he deceived her. He had never kept a mistress for more than three years he told her, so why should she expect him to keep her for longer? At one of her parties, after Mathilde had said something cutting to his latest mistress, Demidov lunged towards her and slapped her twice, resoundingly, across the face. This was not the sort of treatment that the proud Mathilde found easy to forgive. It was obvious that they could not stay together much longer.

In the meantime her father, Jérôme, had married again. For his third wife he had chosen the Marchesa Bartolini-Baldelli. She was fifteen years younger than he, handsome, sweet-natured, easygoing, and very rich. Jérôme, glad enough to get his debts paid yet again, was too conscious of his kingly, or at least princely, status to consider anything but a morganatic marriage. The gentle Marchesa agreed, hoping no doubt that time, and her money, would soften her husband's pride and that she would one day be entitled to call herself a princess. But for the remainder of their life together Jérôme insisted on referring to her as "Madame la Marquise." This kind-hearted woman was to suffer even more cruelly at the hands of her dissolute husband than had his first two wives, Betsey Patterson and Catherine of Württemberg. For the present, however, Jérôme was happy enough to be spending her money. This did not, of course, prevent him from trying to borrow yet more from Demidov. One day he called on Mathilde and asked her to approach her husband for a loan. Mathilde, far too proud to put herself in Demidov's debt, refused, but when Jérôme implored, she gave way. Steeling herself, she went to her husband to ask for the loan. When he, no less proud, refused, she flung herself at his feet and begged him for it. With a deft movement he yanked the bell cord, and before Mathilde had time to scramble to her feet, the footman had come hurrying in.

"You see," shouted the triumphant Demidov, "Napoleon's niece has thrown herself at my feet to get me to give money to her father."

The unhappiness of Mathilde's married life was somewhat compensated for by her meeting with a sculptor named Nieuwerkerque. Count de Nieuwerkerque was Mathilde's *beau ideal* of a man. Massively built, luxuriantly bearded, unaffectedly mannered, he looked, it has been said, like a lion at rest. For all the vigor of his appearance, however, he was a kindly, subtle, intelligent man, and a very successful artist. Mathilde met him while he was on a cultural tour of Italy with the Count de Chambord, and was drawn to him immediately. Beside him, Anatole Demidov was a boor. Before the end of his Italian sojourn, Mathilde was passionately in love with the handsome sculptor, and more determined than ever to break with Demidov. Her opportunity came in 1846. The Czar, who had been so kind to her during her visit to St. Petersburg, passed through Florence that year; hearing of her troubles with Demidov, he promised to do something for her. In July he summoned Demidov to Russia. With her husband away, Mathilde sped to Paris, where, throwing discretion to the winds, she lived openly with her lover. At the end of the year the Czar gave her her freedom. She was granted a separation from Demidov and an extraordinarily generous allowance. Her ex-husband was forbidden ever to return to Paris, and Mathilde, free, rich, and overwhelmingly in love, settled down to life with Nieuwerkerque.

She never saw Demidov again.

    👑   👑   👑

During the six years that Louis-Napoleon—still dreaming of a second empire—was imprisoned in Ham, most of the Bonapartes associated with the First Empire died.

Lucien, in youth the *enfant terrible* of the family, and in maturity the highly esteemed Prince of Canino, died in 1840. By far the ablest of Napoleon's brothers, the history of the Empire might have been very different had Lucien been at the Emperor's side during the years of victory. When, in 1815, Napoleon did accept his services, it was too late. The indiscretions of his youth—his outspokenness, his impetuosity, his dishonesty—were more than atoned for by his devotion to his second wife Alexandrine. For her sake, and for the sake of their children, he had steadfastly refused Napoleon's offer of a crown. He was sixty-five when he died; his eldest son Charles, the ornithologist and husband of Joseph's daughter Zenaïde, succeeded to the title of Prince of Canino. Charles and his family had by now returned from America and were living in Rome.

Joseph died in 1844, at the age of seventy-six. He had left England three years previously, and had been reunited with his wife Julie in Florence. A man of moderate abilities, he had been too small for Napoleon's grandiose schemes. Had he been allowed to remain at Mortefontaine, playing a social rather than a political role in the Empire, he would have been a happier and a more successful man. Of all his brothers, and in spite of his weaknesses, Napoleon had loved him best. Joseph's wife Julie did not long survive him. Always delicate, she had spent most of her last years stretched out upon a sofa. She was, remembered her niece Princess Mathilde in later years, shriveled with age, her scraggy neck always encircled with black neck bands. She died in 1845 at the age of seventy-four.

The irascible Louis died the following year. An invalid for the greater part of his life, Louis had been almost paralyzed for the last few years. He left his couch only to be wheeled around the garden of his Florentine villa or beside the sea at Leghorn. The passing years had reconciled him to his only surviving son, Louis-Napoleon, and the young man's continued imprisonment upset him very much. Towards the end of 1845 he wrote to the French government, asking for an amnesty for his son, or if this were impossible, at least a temporary release so that Louis-Napoleon might visit him. His request was refused. When Louis-Napoleon himself asked the King for leave to visit his dying father, his petition was likewise refused. Father and son never saw each other again, for Louis died aged sixty-eight in July 1846. In youth the most promising and attractive of Napoleon's brothers, for most of his life he had been a bitter, selfish, and maladjusted hypochondriac.

Jérôme, the last of the brothers, was still very much alive. In 1847, however, his eldest son by Catherine, Prince Jérôme, died at the age of thirty-three. This made his youngest son, Plon-Plon, his successor. That same year Jérôme was given permission to return to France, and accompanied by his new wife, the gentle Marchesa, and by the fiery Plon-Plon, he came back to Paris. He had been away for thirty-two years.

The ex-Empress Marie Louise died in 1847. Having outlived her first husband, Napoleon, and her second husband, Neipperg, she had married a third time. Her latest husband, like Neipperg, was her chamberlain, but unlike Neipperg, he was a man of somewhat austere habits. His name was Count Bombelles.

"Count Bombelles, whom I dreaded at first, enchants me . . . ," wrote Marie Louise soon after he had entered her service. "He combines all the qualities that one can desire—firmness of character with gentleness of manner. He is such a virtuous man; he is a real find."

So virtuous, in fact, was Bombelles, that Marie Louise had to propose marriage to him before he was able to serve his mistress as thoroughly as Neipperg had done. Although their union lacked the magnificence of her marriage with Napoleon and the ardor of her marriage with Neipperg, it was a happy one; Bombelles proved himself a gentlemanly and attentive consort, and to Marie Louise, any husband was better than none. Was there, none the less, just a hint of disappointment in her avowal that her latest husband was a "real saint"?

On December 9, 1847, her rheumatism, with which she had been troubled for many years, seemed suddenly to get worse. She was forced to go to bed, and her doctors diagnosed rheumatic pleurisy. Just over a week later, five days after her fifty-sixth birthday, she died. Almost thirty-five years before, as a timid, bewildered girl, she had fled France at the collapse of Napoleon's Empire; had she lived a few more months, she would have seen another Napoleon busy establishing himself as master of France.

These years, which had seen the death of so many of the older generation, saw the birth of at least two of a new. They were not, however, legitimate Bonapartes.

Prince Louis-Napoleon was never one to waste time. Despite the fact that he was a prisoner at Ham, he made excellent use of his enforced leisure. Rising early, he would devote his days to studying or writing; the range of his interests was extraordinarily wide. He wrote a pamphlet on percussion caps for the French artillery; he wrote a piece comparing England in 1688 to France in 1830; he started work on a *Life of Charlemagne;* he wrote a book on his favorite subject, the artillery; he wrote a pamphlet on the beet-sugar industry; he contributed articles to the local press; he published an essay entitled *L'Extinction de Pauperisme;* he conceived a plan for cutting a canal across Nicaragua, uniting the Atlantic and Pacific oceans. And he wrote hundreds of letters to friends and relations.

His days were occupied; it was the nights—those dank, misty nights —that he found so long. To shorten them, he took a mistress. Her name was Alexandrine Vergeot, and she was employed as an ironing woman in the fortress. She was twenty years of age, well built, good-looking, with a cloud of chestnut hair and a pair of bright blue eyes. A simple, healthy girl, she soon succumbed to the prince's practiced charm. She remained his mistress for the duration of his captivity. She bore him two sons, Eugène in February 1843 and Louis in March 1845. Louis-Napoleon provided generously for their future, and during the Second Empire, took a very real interest in their affairs. Eugène, after some years in the diplomatic service, was created Count d'Orx; Louis, a more turbulent personality, spent much of his life in Mexico, and was created Count de Labenne just before the fall of the Empire. Alexandrine herself, having married, lived out the rest of her life in retired comfort, a stone's throw from the Tuileries.

At six o'clock on the morning of May 25, 1846, Louis-Napoleon shaved off his beard, rouged his cheeks, dressed himself in a workman's blouse, and putting a plank across his shoulder, walked out of his prison. Repairs had been going on in the castle for some time; one more workman passing out of the gate was not noticed by the sentries. The Prince had just passed the last guard when his pipe fell from his mouth and was shattered on the paving. With admirable presence of mind, he stooped down and picked up the pieces. Then he made for a neighboring grave-yard, where, as planned, there was a carriage waiting to pick him up. Twenty-four hours later he was in London.

Ten years of misfortune—the disasters of Strasbourg and Boulogne, the exile in England and America, the imprisonment in Ham—had not weakened his faith in his future. But they had blunted his impetuosity. He was still determined to be Emperor of the French one day, but he would choose that day more carefully now. When his cousin, the Marchioness of Douglas (daughter of Josephine's niece Stéphanie of Baden), asked him whether he planned to give up his ambitions, his answer left her in no doubt.

"I do not belong to myself," he answered with unself-conscious gravity. "I belong to my name and to my country. It is because my fortune has twice betrayed me that my destiny is nearer its accomplishment. I bide my time."

His cousin Plon-Plon now joined him in England. At twenty-four Jérôme's youngest son looked more like the Great Napoleon than ever, though in personality he was more like his uncle Lucien at the same age. Like the young Lucien, Plon-Plon was an avowed Republican, and was violently opposed to Louis-Napoleon's ambitions for re-establishing the Empire. The Bonaparte family should serve France, he declared, not rule it. His radical views naturally clashed with Louis-Napoleon's more moderate ones; whereas, beyond the establishment of the Empire, Louis-Napoleon's political creed was somewhat vague, Plon-Plon was uncompromisingly a man of the Left. During their frequent discussions on the future of France (a subject which obsessed them both) Plon-Plon would air his liberal views in his usually excitable and dogmatic fashion while his cousin calmly countered them. Although Plon-Plon's beliefs were in many ways admirable, and although he had a good brain, he had a very unfortunate manner. He was overemotional, hypercritical, bad tempered; he was incapable of inspiring trust or commanding sympathy. Like his uncle Lucien, he could have been the new Emperor's right-hand man; he remained, throughout and beyond the Second Empire, a mere thorn in his side. His ardent antimonarchical views did not prevent him from accepting from his uncle the King of Württemberg, a very generous annual allowance. When, in 1848, France once more became a Republic, and Plon-Plon, in the full flush of his republican enthusiasm, wrote to his royal uncle signing himself Citizen Bonaparte, the King immediately stopped his allowance. So sincere and dedicated a republican would feel pained, thought his uncle, at receiving money from a king.

Towards the end of the year 1847, when Plon-Plon joined Jérôme in France, Louis-Napoleon must have wondered how much longer he himself would be compelled to remain in exile.

It was not long. Early in 1848 revolution broke out again in Paris. Louis Philippe's resistance to the growing demand for electoral reform led to the erection of barricades, and for three days Paris was up in arms. The King was bundled into a cab and driven away, and France became a Republic once more. The news threw Louis-Napoleon into a froth of excitement. "The Republic is proclaimed," he cried to his cousin, the Marchioness of Douglas, "it is for me to be its master." She told him to stop dreaming. He hurried across the channel to offer his services to the Provisional Government, and they sent him hurrying right back. Never one to lose the opportunity for a little propaganda, he issued a public

228

protest in which he claimed that his compliance with the wishes of the Provisional Government was proof of "the purity of his intentions" and of his patriotism.

Actually, his latest withdrawal from France proved that he had learned the virtue of patience. Ten years ago he might have attempted to take the throne by force; now he wanted to have it offered to him. When his supporters urged him to put himself forward as a candidate for the elections to the Constituent Assembly, he wisely declined. The time, he judged, was not quite ripe; France was still too inflamed. His cousins did not show the same restraint; three of them stood as candidates, and it was significant that all three were returned. These new deputies were the ill-natured Plon-Plon, the raffish Lucien Murat (who had come hurrying over from the States), and the notorious Pierre Bonaparte. A trio less likely to add luster to the name of Bonaparte could not be imagined.

In a series of supplementary elections, held a few weeks later, Louis-Napoleon did allow his name to be put forward; as a result he was returned in four departments. This was the signal for a carefully organized outburst of Bonapartism: party newspapers were founded, adulatory biographies and no less adulatory portraits were sold in the streets, processions formed and marched along the boulevards, chanting his name. Cries of "*Vive Napoleon*," and, more significantly, "*Vive l'Empereur*," were heard once more throughout the cities of France. In June the law exiling the Bonapartes from France (to all practical purposes already abrogated by the presence of three Bonapartes in the Assembly) was repealed, and Louis-Napoleon was free to take his seat as a member of the government.

And still he bided his time in London. In June another bloody insurrection broke out in Paris, and was suppressed with difficulty. Louis-Napoleon, very shrewdly, had kept his hands clean during these four days of bloodshed. In September, when things had simmered down, there were further supplementary elections. His name was again put forward, and he was elected in five constituencies. Deciding that this would be the opportune time to return to Paris, he and his latest mistress left England and settled in a suite of rooms at the Hôtel du Rhin in the Place Vendôme. His windows looked out on the Vendôme column, now crowned by the statue of the Great Napoleon.

The new Republican constitution became law in October 1848. From Louis-Napoleon's point of view its most significant feature was that the President of the Republic would be elected by universal suffrage. He never had any doubt that in spite of the worthiness of some of the other candidates, he would be elected: the name he bore assured him of success. The legend created by Napoleon on St. Helena, and kept alive by King Louis Philippe, had done its work; the name Napoleon had become a household word in France. "In country places the Emperor is venerated without reserve," wrote the German poet Heine. "There is a portrait of *the Man* hanging in every cottage. . . ." Some peasants even believed that the Great Napoleon himself had come back; when, some years hence, the future Empress was to journey through some country districts, she would be somewhat startled to hear herself greeted with heartfelt cries of *"Vive Marie Louise!"* What did surprise Louis-Napoleon when the results of the plebiscite were announced, however, was the size of his majority. His nearest rival had obtained less than 1,500,000 votes; he had polled over 5,500,000. On December 20 Louis-Napoleon was proclaimed President of the new republic.

That day he took up residence in the Elysée Palace. It was here that Napoleon I had signed his abdication over thirty years before, and where, before setting out for Waterloo, he had gathered the little Louis-Napoleon in his arms and claimed that he would one day be the hope of his race. When the general in command of the troops escorting the new President to his official residence smilingly suggested to Count Molé that he take Louis-Napoleon to the Tuileries instead of the Elysée, the Count answered wryly that the new Bonaparte would get there soon enough, of his own accord.

♛   ♛   ♛

Louis-Napoleon, being accused on one occasion of having nothing of the Great Napoleon about him, replied, with as much exasperation as wit, that he did, on the contrary, have his relations.

Like bees to the honey pot, the Bonapartes now came swarming back to Paris. They came, like the first Napoleon's relations, to get as much as they could and to give as little as possible in return. Still not sure that Louis-Napoleon's luck would hold, they were careful not to associate themselves with him too closely; they would accept any favors, but be ready to cut all connection with him at a moment's notice. And he, one of the most generous and kind-hearted of men, paid up uncomplainingly.

Jérôme, with his children Mathilde and Plon-Plon, was already in Paris. Having been appointed governor of the Hôtel des Invalides, Jerome lived in great style, squandering his wife's money and appearing at official functions with the order of the crown of Westphalia on his chest. The presence of this sixty-five-year-old roué at receptions and reviews was a source of continual embarrassment to Louis-Napoleon; it was a pity that this dissolute old man should represent the one surviving link between Napoleon's Empire and the Empire which the new President was planning to inaugurate. His son, Plon-Plon, was no less embarrassing. Louis-Napoleon had sent him as ambassador to Madrid, and on the way to Spain, Plon-Plon had publicly announced that the new President was being dominated by a reactionary group and that in order to right this situation, the electors should return opponents of the Government rather than moderates. The extremists were delighted, and promptly proposed to nominate Plon-Plon for twenty departments. Instead of recalling his impetuous cousin, the long-suffering Louis-Napoleon wrote to him, explaining that his aim was to bring stability to France, and that he would appreciate his cousin's help rather than his opposition. Once in Spain, Plon-Plon cultivated the enemies of the regime and made no secret of his views that the Bourbon dynasty should be kicked off the thrones of Europe. It is no wonder that Queen Isabella asked for his recall. When Louis-Napoleon heard of his cousin's very undiplomatic behavior, he referred to him, in that soft-voiced cynical way, as a monster.

Princess Mathilde was the only member of the family to be of any real use to the new President. As Louis-Napoleon was still unmarried, Mathilde acted as hostess at the Elysée. It was a role for which she was eminently suited. With her Junoesque appearance, her cultivated mind, and above all, her ardent championship of the Bonaparte cause, she made an ideal first lady. There were rumors that the cousins, who had been engaged in their youth, would now marry each other, but it is unlikely that either contemplated it very seriously. Louis-Napoleon was very devoted to his latest mistress and Mathilde was still passionately in love with Nieuwerkerque.

The Lucien Murats had arrived in force from America. With the death of Achille Murat, the postmaster of Tallahassee, in 1847, the raffish Lucien had become head of the family. Much to the amusement of his friends, and even his relations, Lucien regarded himself as the pretender to the throne of Naples. When, soon after their arrival, the family came to stay with Mathilde at her country place at Breteuil, she was shocked at their behavior. Prince Lucien was fat, bombastic, and stupid, and his wife, the former Caroline Fraser, a timid creature with no control over her husband or children. They had four children at the time, Caroline, Joachim, Achille, and Anna; all were undisciplined and uneducated, and the best that Mathilde could find to say was that Anna, the youngest, seemed to become more beautiful by the day.

Lucien Bonaparte's sons, Charles, the ornithologist, and Louis-Lucien and Pierre, who had gambled for the hand of the Corsican peasant girl; Napoléone Camerata and her only son; Count Bacciochi, one of Elisa Bonaparte's relations; Stéphanie of Baden's daughter, the Duchess of Hamilton; Napoleon's illegitimate sons, Count Léon and Alexandre Walewski; Hortense's illegitimate son, Auguste de Morny; these were some of the members of the family who now came crowding into Paris. The more circumspect were to come when the Empire was an established fact rather than an uncertain prospect.

"All my dreams of happiness were surely realized!" gushed one of Lucien Murat's daughters. "Visions of crowns and thrones, grandeur and state, crowded on my dizzy brain, not seen in the dim past but now spread before me in a wide horizon, picturing the future arising in golden splendor from the cloud that so long obscured our destiny."

This was all very well, but they were all content to leave the actual achieving of this "golden splendor" to Louis-Napoleon. Except for Mathilde, who encouraged him, and his half brother, Morny, who actively supported him, there was not one of his relations upon whom Louis-Napoleon could rely during this critical period. The less this unprepossessing batch of Bonapartes was in evidence, in fact, the better his chances for restoring the Bonaparte dynasty.

He set about it very carefully. It was not until he had been President of France for three years, during which time his popularity had increased enormously, that he felt ready to make the next move. His term of office as President would be up the following year; when, in July 1851, the Chamber rejected the proposal to make him eligible for re-election, he decided to strike. On December 2—the anniversary of Austerlitz and of Napoleon's coronation—he staged his *coup d'état*. Leading political and military rivals were arrested in their beds, troops were massed in the streets, proclamations were pasted up announcing the dissolution of the Assembly. The change was received calmly; when Louis-Napoleon rode out into the streets that morning, his reception was restrained but not hostile. Behind him rode ex-King Jérôme. He and his son Plon-Plon had had a hurried consultation that morning; it was decided that the father would go to the Elysée to associate himself with Louis-Napoleon, while the son would keep in touch with the Republicans. Whichever way the cat jumped, their position would be secure. It seemed, for the moment, that the father was on the winning side.

Two days later it was not quite so certain. Fighting broke out in the streets, and it was only after considerable bloodshed that the insurrection was put down. Louis-Napoleon was never to forget this slaughter. Later that month a nation-wide plebiscite authorized a presidential term of ten years by a huge majority. Louis-Napoleon was now undoubted master of France; the proclamation of the Empire was simply a matter of time.

It came a year later. Yet another plebiscite authorized the "re-establishment of the Imperial dignity in the person of Louis-Napoleon Bonaparte." His majority this time was 7,500,000 votes. In recognition of the boy who had died in the palace of Schönbrunn, he styled himself Napoleon III. On the morning of December 2, 1852—again, on the anniversary of Austerlitz and the coronation—the Emperor Napoleon III passed under the Arc de Triomphe and cantered down the misty Champs Elysées towards the Tuileries. France was an Empire once more, and Paris woke that morning to a dimly remembered world of crowned *N's*, Imperial eagles, and golden bees.

PART FOUR
The Second Empire
1852–1870

CHAPTER ELEVEN

♦ ♦ ♦

THERE was, as Plon-Plon had said, nothing of the Great Napoleon about this new Emperor of the French. Victor Hugo called him *Napoleon le Petit*, and when set against the first Emperor of the French, he seemed little indeed.

Napoleon III, in 1852, was forty-four years of age and not much to look at. He was squat and stumpy, with rather short legs and a too-large head which lolled to the left when he walked. "Everybody," commented the diarist Charles Greville, "is struck with his mean and diminutive figure and vulgar appearance." Greville could be cruel, but the description was not far off the mark. To make the best of his unfortunate figure, Napoleon III affected a self-consciously military air (he was almost never out of uniform and almost always on horseback), but his fiercely waxed mustache tended to droop after an hour or two, and his sallow complexion was certainly not that of a man of action. Nor was his expression particularly soldierly. His gray, lackluster eyes, always half hidden under heavy lids, gave his face a veiled, inscrutable look—distinctly more conspiratorial than martial. For those who, because of his accession to power by means of a bloody *coup d'état*, believed him to be an astute and unfeeling tyrant, he certainly looked the part.

Yet, for all these physical shortcomings, there was a certain majesty in his bearing; even Greville had to admit that his manners were good, and "not undignified." And it was claimed that to speak to him was to be fascinated by him. His calm, his sincerity, his kindliness, his occasional flashes of humor, were guaranteed to captivate any companion. To the melancholy, meditative manner of his father, Louis, he brought all the charm of his mother, Hortense. He would sit, more often the listener than the talker, twirling the ends of his mustache or stroking his little pointed imperial, and the visitor would come away enchanted. "It was impossible not to be struck with his simplicity," noted one of his guests, "his being so naturally and totally without any air of assumption of greatness, though not undignified, but perfectly *comme il faut*, with excellent manners and easy, pleasant, fluent conversation."

Napoleon I had once given his stepson Eugène de Beauharnais a very sound piece of advice. This was soon after he had made him Viceroy of Italy. Unless a ruler knew more about his subject than any other man in the room, it was better for him to keep silent. It was on this maxim that Eugène's nephew, Napoleon III, based his dealings with his fellow men. The immobility of his features, the enigmatic look of his eyes, his air of grave attention, seemed to indicate a depth of intellect and a strength of character. Yet was the Emperor as deep and strong as he appeared? No one seemed to know. It was so difficult to find out. He so seldom voiced his opinions and so rarely reacted visibly that it was almost impossible to know what was going on behind that masklike face. One of his ministers claimed that the words one spoke to him were like stones flung down a well: one heard their sound, but one never knew what happened to them. He was the sort of person who invited confidences, but never gave any in return. "To fathom his thoughts or divine his intentions would try the powers of the most clear-sighted," reported the British ambassador. "No one's advice seems to affect him. He seems a strange mixture of good and evil. . . ."

If he was indeed a mixture of good and evil, then the good pre-dominated. It was in this, more than in his appearance, or his manner, or his conversation, that Napoleon III differed most from Napoleon I. The Duke of Wellington once complained that the Great Napoleon was no gentleman; he would never have leveled this accusation against Napoleon III. Where the first Napoleon had been selfish, conceited, hard-hearted, militant, and contemptuous of his fellow men, the third was generous, modest, gentle to the point of femininity, and with a very real concern for the welfare of others. His virtues, in fact, were to be his undoing. Kind-heartedness is not the most essential quality in a sovereign; it too often degenerates into weakness. When, in his quiet way, he once said to one of his ministers, "What a pity you are so angry!" the minister, with admirable insight, replied, "With a pity you are not!"

One could never for a moment imagine this interchange between Napoleon I and one of his counselors.

There was, however, one parallel between the two Emperors; neither of them, at the inauguration of their Empires, had a direct heir. Napoleon I's heirs in 1804 had been his brothers' sons; Napoleon III's heirs were his uncle Jérôme and his cousin Plon-Plon. It was a sobering thought. The continuation of the dynasty was therefore as important to this Napoleon as ever it had been to the first. Fortunately, the new Emperor was not tied to an infertile bride; he was free to choose whomever he liked. Thus far his attempts to find himself an empress from amongst the princesses of Europe had been singularly unsuccessful; even the most threadbare royalties showed a marked disinclination to ally themselves to this Bonaparte adventurer. So few queens of France seemed to die peacefully on the throne, no one was prepared to take the risk. Queen Victoria experienced a nasty moment when a hint was dropped into the ear of the British Foreign Secretary that Napoleon III favored a marriage with her niece Princess Adelaide of Hohenlohe. The problem was neatly sidestepped by Victoria's suggesting unofficially that the matter be decided by the Princess and her parents, adding that, as they were Protestants, she did not think their acceptance very likely. Face was thus saved all round.

Lord Palmerston, in his bluff way, declared that as the Emperor had not the slightest hope of making a match illustrious enough to "counterbalance the annoyance of an ugly or epileptic wife," he would do better to follow the promptings of his heart rather than his head. And this is exactly what the Emperor did. In fact, when he trotted down the Champs Elysées to the Tuileries on that misty morning in 1852, his choice had been all but made. Within a month, the Empire had an Empress.

And here was another parallel between the two Emperors. When Napoleon III got married, his family, some of whom were hardly on speaking terms with each other, instantly united in opposition to the woman who now became their Empress. But she was not, they were to discover, another Josephine.

♛　　♛　　♛

Eugenie de Montijo had been born in Granada in 1826. Her father, the Count de Montijo, was a grandee of Spain. He had sat his horse beside Joseph Bonaparte during the unsuccessful defense of Paris in 1814, and had fought with the French in the Peninsular War, with the result that Eugenie had been brought up in a decidedly Bonapartist atmosphere. Her mother's background was rather less impressive. The Countess de Montijo was the daughter of William Kirkpatrick, a Scots wine merchant who had once been Consul for the United States at Malaga. If the Kirkpatricks had been illustrious once, they were less so now. What the countess lacked in social distinction, however, she more than made up for in drive; with her passion for politics and her appetite for amusement, she kept herself very much in the public eye. If the retiring Count was his daughter Eugenie's favorite parent, it was to the bustling, vivacious Countess that she owed her subsequent position in the world. In addition to Eugenie, the Montijos had another daughter, Paca, a year or so older than Eugenie; she was as grave and withdrawn as her sister Eugenie was talkative and high-spirited. As the Montijos were not rich, the two girls were brought up in Spartan fashion, but this did not prevent the Countess from indulging her taste for travel. In 1834, leaving her ailing husband in Madrid, she took her daughters to Paris, and from then until five years later when the Count de Montijo died, the three Montijo ladies were constantly on the move. The succession of second-rate hotel rooms and overnight coach journeys toughened Eugenie; in later years she was never to care a fig for her own comfort. But if physical refinements were lacking, so, unfortunately, were mental; although Eugenie de Montijo was sent to school in Spain, France, and England, she received the scantiest of educations. Life, her exuberant mother used to declare, was the true school.

It was in 1836, at the age of ten, that Eugenie got her glimpse of her future husband, at the Préfecture de Police in Paris. She was spending the day there with the children of the prefect; Louis-Napoleon was waiting to be shipped into exile after his Strasbourg fiasco. Already a highly romantic little girl and steeped in the Napoleonic legend, the sight of the Imperial pretender stirred her childish imagination.

With the death of the Count de Montijo, mother and daughters returned to Madrid. The girls were growing up, and their mother was beginning to seek suitable husbands. Paca was a lovely girl, dark-haired, dark-eyed, with a warm smile and a gentle manner. Eugenie was superb. Tall, beautifully made, with a skin like marble and a mass of chestnut hair, she drew every eye. Possessing a wonderfully natural grace, her every movement was a delight. Every tilt of that russet head, every turn of that slender neck, every flutter of those tiny hands, was an enchantment. Yet even more remarkable than her luminous beauty or her effortless grace was her vivacity—an exceptional sparkling, quicksilver quality. But for all her radiance, she was not as popular as she might have been. Possessing all the pride, the fire, the vibrancy of the women of Spain, she lacked their femininity and their formality. Her boisterousness, her virility, her very naturalness could be embarrassing; she seemed, for Spanish taste, a shade too assertive, a touch too overconfident; her free-and-easy cosmopolitanism sometimes made her seem to be nothing more than a quick-tongued adventuress.

In 1844 her sister, Paca, married the Duke of Alba. Even the ambitious Countess de Montijo was satisfied. Of all the grandees of Spain, none was so illustrious or so rich as the Duke of Alba; the Countess had every reason to be pleased. Next, she turned her attention to Eugenie. Who knew, with this infinitely more lovely daughter, she might be able to do better still.

In 1849 Louis-Napoleon, now President of France, sent his cousin

Plon-Plon as ambassador to Madrid. The Countess, ardent Bonapartist that she was, welcomed him to her home, and he, a no less ardent Bonaparte, needed only one glimpse of her daughter to take advantage of her hospitality. The surly, impetuous Plon-Plon began to pay court to the animated if no less impetuous Eugenie. In view of their bitter enmity in later life, this romantic dawn of their relationship is interesting. Plon-Plon was rather disconcerted to find that the lovely Spaniard preferred talking politics to making love. But as politics was a subject which Plon-Plon could not avoid for very long either, the two were soon arguing away for all they were worth. Plon-Plon, of course, was an avowed Republican; Eugenie was a Legitimist. If the Bourbons were not to be restored in France, she said, then she was all for Louis-Napoleon re-establishing the Empire. Whether Eugenie ever considered marrying the disgruntled Plon-Plon, or, for that matter, he, her, is extremely doubtful. Within a few months they had both returned to Paris, where Eugenie met his much more amiable cousin—the Prince President of France.

They met at a party given by Princess Mathilde. Mathilde had known Eugenie for some years. A forthright, unconventional personality herself, Mathilde had rather liked this high-spirited Spanish girl, and knowing her cousin's taste in women, imagined that as a casual mistress, Eugenie would suit him very well. In part, she was right. Louis-Napoleon was captivated by this blue-eyed auburn-haired beauty who spoke so interestingly of her travels; Eugenie, in turn, was impressed by this attentive and well-mannered prince. But as for becoming his mistress, that was quite another matter. Although they met frequently during the following months, and although the Prince found himself more and more drawn to her, it was becoming clear that she was not quite as free and easy as she seemed. For all her beauty and her vivacity, sexually Eugenie was as cold as ice; it was a quality which her shrewd mother would have done everything to encourage during these early stages. And the more Eugenie—from inclination rather than design—held herself aloof, the more besotted did poor Louis-Napoleon become. If she had given the impression of being an adventuress, she was certainly not behaving like one. One summer evening, when the Montijo ladies were alone in the company of the Prince and a chamberlain, he proposed a walk and offered his arm to Eugenie. "*Monseigneur,*" she answered, blushing violently (and no one blushed more prettily), "my mother is with us. . . ." There was nothing for it but for him to give his arm to the Countess and to make the stroll as short as he decently could.

After the *coup d'état* (towards the achieving of which Eugenie impulsively offered the Prince all the money she had) Louis-Napoleon invited the Montijos to a great hunt at Fontainebleau. The sight of Eugenie in her tricorn hat and her riding habit was almost too much for him to bear; he declared his love, but he did not, as yet, propose marriage. In December 1852 mother and daughter were invited to Compiègne; Louis-Napoleon was now Emperor, and for the first time his marked attentions towards Eugenie began to alarm the Bonapartes. Mathilde was particularly put out. Her position as first lady had been very agreeable; if she had to relinquish it, let it be to some foreign princess and not to this flashy *femme du monde*. "One may make love to Mademoiselle de Montijo," said Plon-Plon to his cousin, "but one does not marry her." One of Lucien Murat's daughters reported (and reported it disapprovingly) that Eugenie had said that the "only way to her bedroom was through a well-lit church." And old Jérôme, a past master in the arts of love, claimed that he had always maintained that Louis-Napoleon would marry "the first woman who will turn his head and who will refuse him her favors." The Emperor, almost beside himself with desire, paid no attention to their carpings, and on January 12, 1853, during a reception at the Tuileries, he asked Eugenie to marry him. Primed by her mother, she got him to put the proposal down in writing; the Countess de Montijo was not long in giving her consent.

Ten days later the Emperor made the official announcement of his intended marriage to the senators, deputies, and councilors of state. Realizing that his choice was not a popular one, his statement was somewhat defensive. The alliance which he was forming was "not in accordance with the traditions of ancient policy," he said, but surely its romantic nature could not fail to appeal to the French people. Had not Napoleon I's love match with Josephine been more successful than his political alliance with Marie Louise? He did not doubt that Eugenie, gracious and good, would "revive the virtues of the Empress Josephine." As she was Spanish (although at heart a Frenchwoman), there would not be hordes of relations on whom "honors and dignities would have to be showered"; this shaft, one felt sure, was directed at the clamorous Bonapartes, Murats, and Bacciochis. His speech over, the Emperor was politely applauded by the assembled dignitaries, and flanked by his uncle Jérôme and his cousin Plon-Plon, left the throne room. From this point on Jérôme, a connoisseur of women himself and far too astute to bite the hand that fed him, kept his mouth shut about his nephew's marriage; Plon-Plon, who for all his professed Republicanism, considered himself the Imperial heir, made no attempt to conceal his bitterness.

That night, in a somewhat self-consciously heroic letter to her beloved sister, Paca, Eugenie (now installed with her mother at the Elysée) wrote of the terror she felt at the prospect of becoming Empress. It was not the knife of the assassin she feared so much as the thought of not making her mark. They had cried *"Vive l'Impératrice"* for the first time that day, she told her sister; God grant that this would always be their cry. If it were not, however, then the bad times would find her even firmer and more courageous than the good. It was a strangely prophetic letter.

Napoleon and Eugenie were married a week later. The civil ceremony took place on the evening of January 29, 1853. Dressed in pink satin, Eugenie was received by the gallantly smiling Mathilde and the stony-faced Plon-Plon. They led her to where Napoleon, surrounded by all available members of his family, was waiting to take her into the Salle des Maréchaux. Here, where Napoleon I had commended Marie Louise and the King of Rome to the care of the National Guard before setting off on the disastrous campaign of 1814, Napoleon III took the first step towards securing the future of the restored dynasty. The register in which the marriage was to be inscribed was the one which had been used during the First Empire. Its first entry was the act of adoption by Napoleon of Josephine's son Eugène; its last was the birth certificate of the King of Rome. To it were now added the names of the Emperor Napoleon III and the Empress Eugenie.

The ceremony over, the company moved forward, two by two, to greet the newly married couple. The Austrian ambassador escorted the Emperor's cousin, the Duchess of Hamilton. The Duchess, who, as the daughter of Stéphanie of Baden, was hardly in a position to throw stones, was furious at her cousin's choice of bride. Trembling with indignation, she assured her escort that she intended making a scene when they reached the Imperial couple. Was she determined to do so? asked the ambassador. On hearing that she was, he withdrew his arm. "I beg the Duchess to walk on alone," he said politely. "I shall not follow her." This exchange brought the irate duchess to her senses, and she had to content herself with making the iciest obeisance possible.

The religious ceremony took place the following day. Eugenie, a dedicated rather than a devout Catholic, had longed to be married by the Pope, but Pius IX, remembering Napoleon I's treatment of Pius VII, was taking no chances. When, although he was still young and active, he excused himself on the grounds of his "great age and infirmities," Napoleon III very wisely did not press the point.

With Josephine's diadem on her red-gold hair, and Marie Louise's sapphire belt around her tiny waist, Eugenie drove beside the Emperor from the Tuileries to Notre Dame. In imitation of similar state occasions during the First Empire, they drove in the very coach Napoleon and Josephine had used for their coronation, and in which Napoleon and Marie Louise had driven to their wedding. On the occasion of Napoleon's second marriage, the gilt crown surmounting the coach had tumbled down and rolled in the dust; on the occasion of Napoleon III's marriage to Eugenie, the same thing happened. It was an ominous sign.

For all the garish decorations within the cathedral, for all the brilliant uniforms and glittering dresses (Mathilde in gold-embroidered green velvet), for all the scarlet of the clergy and the blaze of fifteen thousand wax candles, Eugenie more than held her own. Like Josephine, she knew how to dress. But where both the prevailing fashion and her own taste had tended to make Josephine look seductively elegant, Eugenie always looked assertively smart. In the years ahead her chic was to earn her the title of *La Reine Crinoline*. For her wedding she wore a white velvet dress, all asparkle with brilliants and a trailing veil of English *point* lace. "Her beautifully chiseled features and marble complexion," enthused one English spectator, "her nobly set-on head, her exquisitely proportioned figure and graceful carriage were most striking, and the whole was like a Poet's Vision!" Mathilde was less enthusiastic. All that white, she thought, gave her a sickly look.

But Napoleon was more than satisfied with his bride's appearance; when the ceremony was over and she appeared in her going-away clothes (red velvet trimmed with fur), he was even more satisfied. Flushed with excitement, she embraced the group of stiffly smiling Bonapartes, and then drove off with Napoleon towards Saint-Cloud. They were to spend their honeymoon at the little château of Villeneuve l'Etang in the park of Saint-Cloud. One hopes that in spite of the well-known frigidity of the bride, the prize was worth waiting for.

If Maxime du Camp is to be believed, Mathilde's comments on the new Empress, made at dinner that evening, were almost unprintable. From now on she always referred to Eugenie as *Elle*.

♛   ♛   ♛

Unable to rely on the legitimate Bonapartes for support, Napoleon III was coming to depend more and more on the illegitimate ones. Napoleon I's son Count Walewski, and Hortense's son Auguste de Morny, were both invaluable to the new Emperor during these years.

When Hortense's lover, Charles de Flahaut, had married Margaret Elphinstone and gone to live in England, young Auguste had remained in

France with his grandmother. The July Revolution of 1830 and the overthrow of the Bourbons had enabled Charles de Flahaut and his family to return to France, and once they were established in Paris, Auguste went to live with them. In that age of easy morals he was warmly welcomed by Margaret de Flahaut and her five daughters and under the patronage of his father young Auguste was soon making his mark in Parisian society. Calling himself Count de Morny, a title to which he had not the slightest claim, this elegantly dressed, charmingly mannered and hard-headed young man was received everywhere. Nowhere, however, was he more warmly received than at the home of Madame Le Hon, wife of the Belgian ambassador. They had met at the Chantilly races; Madame Le Hon, slightly older than he, had been attracted by his suave manner; he, by her golden-haired beauty. This mutual attraction had quickly matured into love, and as Madame Le Hon's husband, a patriotic Belgian, always put country before self, their liaison was allowed to flourish undisturbed. The daughter of a rich Belgian banker, Madame Le Hon was able to meet Morny's financial as well as his physical needs, and as he was as good a businessman as a lover, he took advantage of her generosity. The return of the ambassador to Belgium was followed by a legal separation between husband and wife, with the result that Morny and his mistress could now conduct an even more open affair. He took a house beside hers, which the wits called "Faithful's kennel," and the two gave themselves over to a life of unrivaled brilliance. With his stylish clothes, his string of race horses, and his collections of paintings, Morny was the envy of every *viveur* in Paris, while her salon was reported to be second to none. When, through her influence, he was elected to the Chamber in 1842, their already considerable circle was enlarged by some of the biggest political and financial names of the day. Morny always knew how to cultivate the right people. To a social manner worthy of his maternal grandmother, Josephine, he added an opportunism worthy of his paternal grandfather, Talleyrand.

When the revolution of 1848 brought Morny's half brother, Louis-Napoleon, back to France, he lost no time in contacting him. Except for a physical resemblance (they both had a slightly veiled look) and their insatiable sexual appetites, Hortense's two sons had little in common. Where Napoleon III was a kindly dreamer, Morny was a hard-hearted realist; where the former had an almost complete disregard for money for its own sake, the latter was a corrupt and successful financier; where the Emperor—once he had restored the Empire—was weak and vacillating, his half brother was strong and clear-sighted. This antipathy between them was apparent from the start, but circumstances forced them to work together. Louis-Napoleon needed a cool-headed man whom he could trust, and Morny, in his own phrase, felt it necessary to place himself "on the side of the broom handle."

With his subtle mind and his wide knowledge of the political and financial affairs of France, Morny very quickly became an accepted member of the inner circle around Louis-Napoleon. The *coup d'état* of December 2, which established Louis-Napoleon as the master of France, was very largely Morny's doing. His calm, his perception, his iron determination, were exactly the qualities neded for this delicate operation. While Louis-Napoleon was claiming that Hortense's ring, with the word *Espére* engraved on it, would asure them of success, Morny was concentrating on the more practical aspects of the job. "Moral considerations apart," Eugenie once said, "December 2, which was mainly his work, was a masterpiece. . . . How far superior to Brumaire, when lack of foresight was only equaled by clumsiness, and Bonaparte himself lost his head!" When, as Morny had predicted, fighting broke out on the third day after the *coup d'état,* he lost no sleep over the resulting bloodshed. Once calm had been restored and Louis-Napoleon's dictatorial regime inaugurated, Morny, as Minister of the Interior, became the most important man in France after Louis-Napoleon himself.

His hour of glory was brief. Once the Prince had secured his position by foul means, he began, as his uncle Napoleon had done, to retain it by fair. The new regime, born in shame, was to be clothed in respectability. If Louis-Napoleon wanted to found a legitimate and respectable dynasty (and this was his dearest wish), then he would have to be careful of the company he kept. As the illegitimate son of his mother, Morny would have to be dropped. Morny, by parading his close relationship with Louis-Napoleon, had rather invited this rejection, but was nevertheless incensed when he realized what was happening. Both he and his mistress, Madame Le Hon, had a great deal to say about the Prince's ingratitude. The final break came when the new dictator confiscated the estates of King Louis Philippe's family. Although the money raised from the sale of the property was used by Louis-Napoleon for the most praiseworthy purposes (amenities for the poor), his autocratic action alienated many of his supporters. Morny, who had been very well treated by Louis Philippe's family, was particularly incensed. Whether he, who had so often been involved in shady financial transactions himself, was genuinely outraged at the confiscation of the property, or whether he saw it as a political blunder with which he did not want to be associated, one does not know. Whichever it was, he immediately resigned as Minister of the Interior. Louis-Napoleon did nothing to stop him.

For the next few years Morny devoted himself to both making money and spending it. Few men in Paris could do it more successfully than he. In many ways Auguste de Morny came to epitomize the *nouveau riche* society of the Second Empire; in an age of unprincipled, cynical, pleasure-loving dandies, none was more so than he. With his cat's-whisker mustache and his pointed imperial, his superbly tailored clothes and his long cigars, the Count de Morny was to be seen everywhere. On the doors of his carriages were emblazoned his escutcheon, bearing, unashamedly, a hydrangea (hortensia) barred.

The Second Empire was too lacking in men of talent, however, for the Emperor to do without Morny's services for long. In 1854 he was appointed President of the Legislative Chamber (in this autocratic regime it was a position which allowed him plenty of time for more amusing pursuits), and in 1856 he was sent as ambassador to Russia. The most brilliant years of the Count de Morny's already brilliant life were only just beginning.

♛　♛　♛

Apart from his looks, Count Alexandre Walewski seemed to have inherited very little from his father Napoleon I. Gentlemanly, loyal, honest, and even-tempered to the point of dullness, he was very much his mother's son.

Marie Walewska had not long survived the fall of Napoleon's Empire, and on her death young Alexandre had been taken back to Poland. Here he had grown up in the care of an uncle. No less a patriot than his mother (it was said that he dreamed of becoming King of Poland one day), he had joined in the Polish revolt against Russia in 1831, and it was in the cause of this rebellion that he had gone to England later that same year. His stay in England turned him into an enthusiastic Anglophile; whether it was admiration for English institutions or English womanhood is not certain, but before long he had married Caroline Montagu, a daughter of the Earl of Sandwich. Her early death and his remarriage to an Italian woman in no way weakened his regard for England; his knowledge of the English way of life was to stand him and his cousin Louis-Napoleon in very good stead in the years to come.

Almost the most notable feature of Walewski's career in the years prior to the Revolution of 1848 was his liaison with the celebrated tragedienne Rachel. Famous no less for her amours than for her acting, it was said that she loved the solemn Walewski more than any other man. In 1844 she bore him a son whom he formally recognized as his own, and who was christened Antoine Walewski. As he had, in addition, four legitimate children by his two marriages, there were five Walewski grandchildren of Napoleon I living during the Second Empire. His affair with Rachel ended when, on paying her an unexpected call one evening, he bumped into the Duke de Grammont, just leaving. Determined to be done with her, he hurried off to Italy.

Here he met and married Marie-Anne de Ricci, a member of the illustrious Poniatowski family. He was now in his late thirties; she, fifteen years younger. They were an attractive couple—he with his smooth Napoleonic features and quiet manner, she with her delicate good looks and youthful vivacity. "This young woman is charming," King Louis Philippe's sister had written on meeting her. "She is more than pretty, because she has the ornament of natural simplicity. She will be a great success in Parisian society."

The Princess was right, but it was not to be during her brother King Louis Philippe's reign that Countess Walewska would achieve this success. Although Walewski had never worked for Louis-Napoleon's cause, the year 1848 brought a change in his fortunes as well. He was promoted from Florence (where he was minister to Tuscany), first to Naples, and then, as ambassador, to London. It was a very important post, and Walewski was eminently suited to fill it. Louis-Napoleon had long ago decided that by cultivating an alliance with England, he would avoid the rock on which the Great Napoleon's Empire had floundered. In choosing an Anglophile like Walewski as ambassador, he hoped to win and retain England's support in the years ahead.

The ambassador's capabilities were put to the test at the *coup d'état* of 1851. So successfully did Walewski explain it away to Palmerston that the Foreign Secretary approved it almost without a murmur. Queen Victoria and the Prime Minister were far less ready to sanction it, and the impetuous Palmerston was dismissed. Once the Foreign Secretary had been got rid of (and it was her *bête-noir* Palmerston far more than the *coup d'état* itself that Victoria minded), relations between the two countries resumed their friendly course.

A feather in Walewski's cap was the presence of the old Duke of Wellington at a dinner in the French Embassy, when the victor of Waterloo proposed a toast to the new Napoleon. And when Wellington died some months later, Walewski—whom everyone knew to be Napoleon's son—followed his coffin to St. Paul's.

"I beg you to count at all times on my sincere friendship," wrote Napoleon III in gratitude for all the stalwart Walewski was doing, "and to believe that I consider myself happy to possess in you so able and loyal a representative."

These were the palmy days of the Anglo-French *entente*. When Louis-Napoleon proclaimed himself Emperor, Victoria lost no time in accrediting an ambassador to him and in addressing him as "my good Brother, the Emperor of the French." The Crimean War, during which England and France were allies against Russia, further strengthened the alliance. Victoria and Albert attended a costume ball at the French Embassy, the French ambassador and his wife were entertained at Windsor, Napoleon III and Eugenie paid a state visit to England, the Queen and Prince Albert went to Paris. Throughout these years Walewski, honest, urbane, and dependable, fulfilled a duty very much to his taste. As a reward for his achievements, the Emperor recalled him and appointed him Foreign Minister. One of his first tasks was to preside over the Peace Congress at the successful conclusion of the Crimean War. He did it with a very real distinction.

Housed in one of the most luxurious mansions in Europe, married to a beautiful woman of exceptional social gifts, working in complete accord with his cousin the Emperor, Count Walewski was at the zenith of his career. But he was too simple and incorrupt a man for the Second Empire. The rot was about to set in.

♔   ♔   ♔

One morning in the year of 1853, young Count Camerata, the only son of the eccentric Napoléone Camerata (daughter of Napoleon I's sister Elisa Bacciochi), was found dead in his room. He lay on his bed, a pistol by his side and his right eye blown out of his head. A few days later a beautiful young actress, Elisa Letessier, known professionally as Mlle. Marthe, took her own life by means, it was reported, of a pan of charcoal. A week or so afterwards a member of the French secret police, Zembo by name, was found under Hungerford Bridge in London with a dagger through his heart. These three deaths set Second Empire Paris seething with rumors.

The most generally accepted story was that young Camerata, finding himself hopelessly in debt, had committed suicide, and that Elisa Letessier, heartbroken at his death, had done the same. The announcement of the marriage of the Emperor to Eugenie de Montijo had led to something very like panic on the Bourse, and it was said that Count Camerata had lost a great deal of money on that occasion. Having appealed in vain to his rich mother, Napoléone Camerata (who had now reverted to her title of Princess Bacciochi) and to Jérôme, who, it was claimed, owed him money at the time, he took his own life.

Caroline Murat, the daughter of the fat, bombastic Lucien Murat and granddaughter of the ex-Queen of Naples, tells another story. As hatred for the Empress Eugenie is the *leitmotiv* throughout Caroline's reminiscences, the story must be taken with reservations. Count Camerata, having lost a great deal of money on the Bourse and having been told that he had to find a certain sum by the morning, had gone to the Tuileries and thrown himself at the Empress's mercy. She received him coldly, reminded him of the countless times the Emperor had come to his aid before, and refused him any assistance. "Half mad" with worry, he had "flung himself out of her private boudoir," crying, "If I do not find two hundred thousand francs this evening, I shall blow my brains out!"

The Empress, says Caroline Murat, was not in the least affected by this anguished outcry. Camerata was not, she says meaningfully, a Spaniard; he was "only a relation of the Emperor's."

He went home, he went to bed, he woke early; and while his valet was out getting the newspaper, he shot himself. Eugénie saw to it that he was buried "like a dog."

Having given this version, Caroline proceeds to give another. She mentions no name on this occasion, but it is abundantly clear that Eugenie is again the villain. One evening, at a reception in the Tuileries, while the Count Camerata was standing with the Empress on his arm, he whispered, "I love you" to her in Italian. The endearment was overheard by one of the ladies in waiting, who immediately reported it to the Emperor. On the following day the secret police raided the Count's apartments in search of compromising evidence. Led by the "zealous Zembo," they demanded that Camerata hand over the letters he had received from the Empress. Camerata, "ready to defend the lady's honor with his life," refused. Zembo persisted. In the ensuing struggle, Zembo, losing control, shot the young Count through the head. Next day, while all Paris talked of suicide, "we who knew him," says Caroline, "were well aware that he would never have done such a thing." After the fall of the Empire, when the new government was going through the documents left in the Tuileries, they came across a photograph of a handsome young man whom they believed to be Count Camerata. On the back of it was written, in Spanish, "One must know how to love in secret."

"Had this any connection with the circumstances of his death?" muses Caroline innocently. "I wonder."

The sequel, according to Caroline, was that Zembo disappeared from Paris immediately after the shooting. He crossed the channel, but was hunted down and stabbed in the heart. His assassin was a certain Griscelli, also a member of the secret police, who had been instructed, presumably by Eugenie, to avenge her lover Camerata's death.

The theory that the actress, Elisa Letessier, had killed herself for love of Camerata is not good enough for Caroline Murat either. The secret police had visited her rooms as well. Camerata had entrusted "certain documents" to her (presumably Eugenie's love letters for safe keeping), and as she, no less eager to protect the lady's honor then the young Count, had also resisted the police, she had likewise been shot. Her suicide note, saying that she could not go on living without her lover, was not, claims Caroline, *in her own handwriting*.

The stories are preposterous. In later life Eugenie might well have refused money to one of her husband's wayward relations; in these early days of the reign (she had been Empress for a matter of weeks only) she knew nothing of the Emperor's financial dealings with his cousins. She would probably have referred Camerata to the Emperor, and the Emperor, as always, would have helped him. The other theory, that of her love affair with Camerata, could only have been invented by those unable to appreciate how little Eugenie cared about the opposite sex. Even if it had been suspected that she and Camerata were lovers, it would not, in this licentious Second Empire, have been so shameful a revelation as to end in this melodramatic series of murders.

It is much more likely that Count Camerata, the highly strung son of an eccentric mother, unable to face his creditors, had taken his own life. Viel Castel, that tireless recorder of Second Empire gossip, claims that Camerata, in a suicide note, accused Jérôme of owing him 400,000 francs and of refusing to pay it. "This last brother of the first Emperor is an infamous rascal," says Viel Castel, "and the Camerata affair was not wanted to prove it." On hearing of her lover's death, the actress Elisa Letessier, in best Second Empire theatrical tradition, had done the right thing by him and likewise committed suicide. And poor zealous Zembo under Hungerford Bridge with a dagger through his heart? It could have been coincidence.

♛ ♛ ♛

Few greeted the advent of the Second Empire more enthusiastically than Betsey Patterson Bonaparte. Now sixty-eight years of age and living, much against her will, in Baltimore, this first wife of Jérôme Bonaparte had followed events leading up to the re-establishment of the Empire very avidly. "I never could endure universal suffrage until it elected the nephew of an Emperor for the chief of the republic," she wrote triumphantly to a friend, "and I shall be *charmed* with universal suffrage once more if it insists upon the President of France becoming a Monarch."

When it did insist, and a Napoleon was seated firmly on the Imperial throne once more, the Baltimore Bonapartes, displaying only a slightly less indecent haste than the rest of the family, crossed the Atlantic to warm their hands by the new Imperial fire. "I hope," wrote Betsey to her friend, "that about the middle of July next I shall begin to put the Atlantic between the advantages and honors of democracy and myself." The Baltimore Bonapartes now consisted of Betsey herself, her son, Bo, and his wife, Susan, and their two sons, Jerome, who was twenty-three years of age at the time of the restoration of the Empire, and Charles, who was only two. Leaving Susan and the baby Charles at home, Betsey, Bo, and his son, young Jerome, made for France.

Luckily, their arrival coincided with Plon-Plon's absence from Paris. As old Jérôme's only legitimate son, and therefore the heir—after his father—to the Empire (Eugenie had borne no child as yet), Plon-Plon was naturally not very kindly disposed towards Bo, his father's eldest illegitimate son. But the Crimean War had taken Plon-Plon to the Near East (he was commanding the Third Division), and old Jérôme, free of his son's ill-tempered and restricting presence, was able to give his American son and grandson a cordial welcome. Betsey, of course, held herself aloof. While Bo and young Jerome were with old Jérôme, she was contacting the Murats, lately returned from America, and shuffling around Paris in her old clothes and red umbrella. Displaying a miserliness worthy of her late mother-in-law, Madame Mère, she would pinch all the spare lumps of sugar off the hotel tea and coffee trays and keep them in her room. Once, on leaving Paris for a while, she sent to her grandson, young Jerome, a hatbox crammed with sugar lumps. She had collected them especially for him, she said.

Young Jerome, in fact, was beginning to prove himself more worthy of her than Bo had ever been. Eager for active service, he had been granted a commission in the Imperial Dragoons by Napoleon III, and had been sent out to the Crimea as an aide-de-camp to one of the generals. Except for Plon-Plon, whose record in the Crimea was to be singularly unspectacular, young Jerome was the only Bonaparte prince to see service during the campaign. "Young Murat," grumbles Viel Castel, "who is a soldier by profession, does not volunteer for the Crimea, and the other

Bonapartes are satisfied to draw their senatorial salaries in obscurity. Madame Patterson's grandson bears the honors singly." In the course of that muddled, inglorious campaign, young Jerome somehow managed to distinguish himself. His enthusiasm and courage quickly earned him promotion to full lieutenant, and he returned to Paris at the end of the war sporting several decorations.

Old Jérôme's effusive treatment of his son Bo had cooled after the first few months. The offers of accommodation at the Palais Royal, the open invitation to dine, the carriage always in attendance, had ceased when Jérôme realized that Bo was being rather too well received at court. With his good looks and his pleasant, relaxed manners, Bo was proving a very welcome change from his surly half brother Plon-Plon; informal and unpretentious themselves, Napoleon and Eugenie were delighted with him. So taken, in fact, was the Emperor with his American cousin, that he decided to recognize him as the legitimate son of his parents Jérôme Bonaparte and Elizabeth Patterson. And a clause was unearthed in the Civil Code which would allow Bo to become a French citizen. This was too much for old Jérôme. Primed all the way from the Crimea, where Plon-Plon had heard that the *"bâtards Americans"* were basking in the imperial sunshine, old Jérôme wrote an anguished letter to Napoleon III.

The Emperor's intended decrees, he complained, introduced into his family people who had never been part of it. They cast doubt on the legitimacy of his children Plon-Plon and Mathilde. They paved the way for a lawsuit to be brought against his children regarding his property after his death. "They are an attack upon my honor, and on that of my brother the Emperor, for they annul the solemn engagements we entered into with the King of Württemberg and the Emperor of Russia as a condition to my marriage with Queen Catherine."

It was soon after this that Plon-Plon arrived back in Paris. Unlike young Jerome, he had not distinguished himself in the Crimea. The rumor that it was cowardice that had sent Plon-Plon scurrying to Paris was not true; it was dysentery. Fresh from one campaign, he now flung himself into another—the fight against the Patterson Bonapartes. He was determined to see this particular battle through to the bitter end. Very typically, Napoleon III suggested a compromise solution. He offered Bo a title. This would assure him a position of his own in European society while leaving Plon-Plon as his father's sole heir. Bo refused. The name Bonaparte suited him very well, he said. Plon-Plon now appealed to his late mother's relations, the Württembergs. Bo's insistence on calling himself Bonaparte cast doubt on the legitimacy of Catherine of Württemberg's children, he argued. As Catherine had been related to the Czar of Russia, the business suddenly became an important international issue. There was only one way to solve the whole wretched question; Plon-Plon applied to the Imperial Family Council for an injunction to restrain Bo and young Jerome from using the name Bonaparte. The result of the case was that Betsey's descendants were entitled to continue calling themselves Bonaparte, but that they would not be considered members of the family. Bo was highly indignant when he heard the verdict, and addressed a sharp letter to the Emperor. "Being the victim of calumnies, intrigues and lies," he wrote, "it only remains for me, Sire . . . to go with my son into exile and await the justice which I am convinced Heaven will render me sooner or later."

This was worthy of Betsey at her best. As going "into exile" meant returning to the America that he loved, it was no hardship for Bo to quit France. He rejoined his wife and his son Charles in Baltimore. Young Jerome, his eldest son, remained behind. Unaffected by these family squabbles, he dedicated himself to his military career. He transferred from the Imperial Dragoons to the *Chasseurs d'Afrique*, and was sent to Algiers. Here, in his comic-opera uniform, his waxed mustache, and his pointed imperial, he was indistinguishable from the scores of other young French officers serving in North Africa. Like his father, Bo, he refused the title offered him by the Emperor; the surname Bonaparte was good enough for him. He did, however, accept an annual allowance from Napoleon III. By now, of course, this debonair young soldier was the apple of his grandmother's eye; Betsey was able to begin dreaming her dreams all over again. Here, in the person of her grandson, was a worthy descendant of the Great Napoleon! Napoleon III still had no direct heir, Jérôme was an old man, Plon-Plon was childless and very unpopular in France; one never knew, perhaps young Jerome, or at least one of his sons, might one day wear the Imperial crown. The thing would be to marry him to one of the princesses of the Imperial family. . . .

As a matter of fact, young Jerome was to come quite near to being offered a crown, but the ambitious Betsey would never know about it. The possibility would have driven her almost out of her mind with excitement.

* * *

With so many Bonapartes, Murats, and Bacciochis, legitimate and illegitimate, crowding the court of the Second Empire, Napoleon III decided to divide the family into two sections—the *famille Impériale* and the *famille civile.* The Imperial family consisted of Napoleon and Eugenie, old Jérôme, Plon-Plon, and Mathilde. The civil family was made up of some of the descendants of Napoleon I's brother Lucien, Elisa Bonaparte's daughter, Princess Napoléone Bacciochi, and some of the descendants of Caroline and Joachim Murat.

Old Jérôme, Plon-Plon, and Mathilde were ranked as Imperial highnesses; the rest of the family were simply princes, princesses and highnesses, without the word *imperial*. On their marriage, princesses were obliged to take their husband's names and titles. These stipulations led, of course, to endless squabbles, and Napoleon III usually turned a deaf ear when some third-generation countess still insisted on calling herself a princess. But while the emperor might deny his family what they considered their rightful titles, he never dared deny their allowances. In a typical year, out of his civil list, Napoleon III supported, besides old Jérôme, Plon-Plon, and Mathilde, twenty-one members of the Lucien branch, ten members of the Murat branch, Princess Bacciochi, and young Jerome Patterson Bonaparte. From his own pocket came money for the Countess de Montijo, his two illegitimate sons, Napoleon I's son, the profligate Count Léon . . . the list seemed never-ending. As very few of them ever managed to live within their extraordinarily generous allowances, the Emperor was constantly being obliged to settle their debts. Count Léon's vast debts were settled no less than six times during the reign; Prince Achille Murat got extra allowances, Princess Anna Murat got special grants, almost every month the dissolute Prince Pierre Bonaparte had his pension all but doubled. There were relations whom Napoleon did not see from one year's end to the next and who never had a good word to say for him, living in great style on his generosity. They might hate the sight of the Emperor, but nothing would make them risk an open break with the source from which they drew their wealth and honors.

An exception to this was Marie Bonaparte-Wyse de Solms. A granddaughter of Lucien Bonaparte, she seems to have inherited all his instability of temperament and much of his independence of spirit. Having been struck across the face during a quarrel with her mother about a ball dress, she had stormed out of the house and married the first man to ask her. That he was old, jaded and of doubtful birth and title mattered not one scrap when set against the opportunity he gave her of getting away from home, and the vivacious young Marie became the Countess de Solms. Once married, a somewhat superficial interest in the arts led her to set herself up as a second Madame de Staël; a second Elisa Bonaparte would have been a more accurate description—at best, the people who gathered so avidly around the Emperor's lovely young cousin were second-raters.

Had Marie confined her abundant energies to the arts, she would have been allowed to live her life undisturbed; it was when she turned her meager talents to politics that the trouble started. Like her grandfather Lucien, she seemed to delight in welcoming well-known enemies of the regime, and the anti-Imperialist tone of her salon began to irritate the Emperor. When she published a book libeling the President of the Legislative Chamber, Napoleon decided that he had had enough. She was struck off his list of annuitants and ordered to leave France. When she appealed against the banishment order, Napoleon insisted; when she refused to leave her bed, he sent police to rout her out. She was escorted across the border and deposited at Aix-les-Bains. Here, with typical resilience, she built up another salon; it was every bit as animated and no less antagonistic towards the Empire than her first. Her *"Matinées d'Aix-les-Bains"* became famous. Whenever one of those simple Second Empire parlor games—the filling in of questionnaires—was played, Marie would unhesitatingly give "Victor Hugo" (likewise banished by Napoleon for his opposition to the regime) as her favorite poet, and "The Republic" as her favorite form of government. . . .

Of considerably more value to the Emperor than most members of his family was Count Marius Bacciochi, a connection of Elisa Bonaparte's husband. Born in Corsica in 1803, Count Bacciochi held the post of First Chamberlain. He was, in fact, the Emperor's general factotum, not the least important of his duties being that of *procureur*. A vain, easygoing butterfly of a man with an eye for a pretty woman, he was admirably suited to his task. "All the pretty women at court flattered Bacciochi to reach the Emperor," someone once said, and it was common knowledge that they did not flatter in vain. For his efficiently run *service des femmes*, Count Bacciochi was handsomely rewarded, not only by Napoleon III, but by dozens of visiting male royalties. "A cab and Bacciochi," the earthy King Victor Emmanuel used to bellow on arriving in Paris. "I want nothing else." It was said that within the space of three years Baccochi was decorated no less than fourteen times. His already elaborate uniform was adazzle with orders. As he grew older, he grew more and more bloated, and being afflicted, according to one chronicler, with a "disorder which kept him perpetually on the move," life was somewhat difficult. As Bacciochi was on such intimate terms with his Imperial master for so long a period, his opinion of Napoleon III is valuable: "He is as faithful in friendship," he once said, "as he is faithless in love."

Each Monday evening, when the court was at the Tuileries, there would be a family dinner, followed by a ball. These occasions were known as the "Empress's little Mondays." The guests were usually old Jérôme, Plon-Plon, Mathilde, Napoléone Bacciochi, the fat Lucien Murat and his timid wife, their children Caroline, Joachim, Achille, and Anna Murat, and three of Lucien Bonaparte's granddaughters, who called themselves, in spite of the fact that they were all married and had therefore forfeited their right to the title, Princess Julie, Princess Charlotte, and Princess Augusta.

As the only member of the family at all kindly disposed towards the Empress was the young and lovely Anna Murat, these "little Mondays" could not have been much fun. "Oh! the boredom of these gatherings," wrote Caroline Murat, "which lacked gaiety and life, which were absolutely void of witty conversation, and in which there was no thought save as to who should have precedence—a struggle which was renewed every Monday during the fifty-two weeks of the year! How tired I grew of all the jealousy, of the empty life, the formality, of those court intrigues and of those petty vexations." The cause of all these "petty vexations," implies Caroline, was the Empress herself.

But unlike the Empress Josephine in a parallel situation, Eugenie did not let the hostility of her husband's family bother her unduly. Where Josephine's only weapon against the taunts of Napoleon I's family had been tears, Eugenie gave back as good as she got. The one member of the family of whom she had been slightly in awe was Princess Mathilde; she knew that Mathilde considered her shallow, ill bred, and uncultured, and during the first few months of her reign she had made a real effort to win her friendship. When Mathilde had not responded, Eugenie, no less proud herself, had given up trying. After all, as Empress, she had the whip hand; a breach between them would be Mathilde's loss, not hers. These two, in fact, were very ill suited. Mathilde was an intellectual; Eugenie, for all her quickness of mind, was never that. Mathilde's liberalism was not only political but religious and moral as well; her language, said Eugenie, half admiringly, was sometimes reminiscent of a servant in a Molière play. Eugenie, on the other hand, was conservative through and through; she might have been frivolous, but she was a diehard traditionalist, an unquestioning Catholic, and an extremely virtuous wife. "I was not interested in her," said Mathilde in later life, "she froze me, and had the power to make me unjust."

The result of this coolness between the two women was that, except for the "Little Mondays," Mathilde was seen less and less at court. Still living with the handsome Nieuwerkerque, she devoted herself to building her salon. She was to the Second Empire what Elisa Bonaparte had tried so hard to be to the First—a patroness of the arts. *Notre Dame des Arts* someone once nicknamed her, and to her house flocked all the members of the literary and artistic world. As neither Napoleon nor Eugénie had the slightest interest in, or knowledge of, the arts (once, on being entertained by an American singer of considerable international reputation, Eugenie begged for "Swanee River"), Mathilde had the field to herself. Into a regime that tended to be renowned more for its levity than for anything else, Mathilde did introduce a few more worth-while qualities.

One thing made Eugenie feel self-conscious when confronted by the assembled Bonapartes; she had not yet produced an heir. Several pregnancies had ended in miscarriages. When, in 1855, she accompanied the Emperor on a state visit to England, Queen Victoria drew her aside and gave her a little advice. It was on a subject on which Victoria, with a nursery full of children, was eminently qualified to speak. When, some months later, Victoria returned the visit, she discovered that her advice had borne fruit indeed. Very few of the magnificent fetes organized by Napoleon for the Queen were attended by Eugenie. "The dear Empress . . . ," noted Victoria, "for *really* and *certainly very good* reasons must take great care of herself." Eugenie, in other words, was *enceinte*.

Always a shrewd observer, Victoria's comments on the Imperial couple were very telling. Napoleon III, with his seductive charm, and Eugenie with her youthful sparkle, had bowled her over completely. It needed a rush of adjectives and a wealth of underlinings from the royal pen to do justice to their many qualities. "That he is a very *extraordinary* man, with great qualities, there can be no doubt—I might say a mysterious man. He is evidently possessed of *indomitable courage, unflinching firmness of purpose, self-reliance, perseverance,* and great secrecy; to this should be added, a great reliance on what he calls his *Star,* and a belief in omens and incidents as connected with his future destiny, which is almost romantic—and at the same time he is endowed with wonderful *self-control,* great *calmness,* even *gentleness,* and with a power of *fascination,* the effect of which upon all those who become more intimately acquainted with him is *most sensibly* felt. . . ."

Eugenie she found "full of spirit and courage, yet so gentle, with such innocence and *enjouement,* that it makes the most charming *ensemble.* With all her liveliness, she has the prettiest and most modest manner."

Plon-Plon, the alleged Republican, and Mathilde, the ardent Bonapartist, strongly disapproved of the Emperor's friendship with the Queen of England. They were both compelled, nevertheless, to play their part during this royal visit to Paris. As it was common knowledge that Mathilde was living with Nieuwerkerque, there had been some speculation as to whether Victoria—well known for her propriety—would embrace Mathilde on her arrival. She had kissed her warmly and unhesitatingly. To Plon-Plon, however, the Queen had taken an instant dislike. "Prince Napoléon not very gracious," she noted tersely in her journal, adding that his manner was "rude and disagreeable in the highest degree." When seated beside her at luncheon, he insisted on bringing up the subject of *"les ouvriers"* as often as possible, a subject which sent chills down the spines of even this group of rather liberal royalties. "He seems to take pleasure in saying something disagreeable and biting, particularly to the Emperor, and with a smile which is quite satanic," complained the Queen.

Old Jérôme, as Napoleon I's brother, simply could not bring himself to join in this feting of England's Queen. As Governor of the Invalides (and as such, the custodian of the Great Napoleon's tomb) he knew that he would have to play host to Victoria on her visit there. This was too much to expect. Pleading ill health, he made for Le Havre, and remained there for most of her stay. So it was Napoleon III himself who conducted Victoria to the tomb of Napoleon I. The coffin had been moved from the flamboyant catafalque on which it had been laid on its return from St. Helena, and now lay in one of the side chapels beneath the dome. Napoleon III was having a special crypt constructed for the illustrious remains, but as this had not yet been completed, it was in its temporary resting place that Victoria saw the sarcophagus. Around the chapel stood veterans of the First Empire, holding flaming torches, and in their glancing light Victoria could see the coffin covered with a violet velvet pall which glittered all over with golden bees. "There I stood," she afterwards wrote, "at the arm of Napoleon III, his nephew, before the coffin of England's bitterest foe; I, the granddaughter of that King who hated him most, and who most vigorously opposed him, and this very nephew, who bears his name, being my nearest and dearest ally!" It was, as she said, "strange and wonderful indeed."

On the day before the Queen returned home, old Jérôme was finally induced to come back to Paris to greet her. It was said that it cost him a great deal of heartburning; "I believe . . . ," says Viel Castel, "that the cost must have fallen on the Emperor's purse, for the old wretch does nothing without a money bribe. Like a cabman, he must be paid according to the distance. . . ."

On March 16, 1856, the Empress Eugenie presented her husband with an heir. "How did this happen," asked Lucien Murat's daughter Caroline, in malicious surprise, "when it had been affirmed that this hope was little likely to be fulfilled? In any case, by the grace of God, the skill of Sir Charles Locock, a visit to Eaux Bonnes, and by what other means I know not, the fact was certain."

It was like the birth of the King of Rome all over again. Twenty-four hours before the birth the crowds had started collecting outside the Tuileries. Messengers went scurrying through Paris to summon the members of the family and the great dignitaries of the Empire. The sumptuous rooms started filling up with anxious people; the Countess de Montijo, Plon-Plon, Prince Lucien Murat, and Prince Charles Bonaparte stood about in Eugénie's room; Mathilde lay sleeping fitfully in an adjacent dressing room. It was said that the anger of the Emperor's relations at the Empress's condition was "curious to witness." Eugenie, like her predecessor Marie Louise, was having a difficult time; the child was badly placed and the doses of laudanum which the doctors had been giving her to delay the birth until the twentieth (the anniversary of the birthday of the King of Rome) had not helped. Napoleon III, like Napoleon I, was in a terrible state. Nor were matters improved by the behavior of Plon-Plon. Realizing that the birth of a boy would mean the end of his days as heir presumptive, he was in a state of acute anxiety. In fact, one of the last things that Eugenie, in the most extraordinary pain, noticed before giving birth, was the sight of Plon-Plon's "furious monocle."

The boy was born a little after three in the morning. A doctor dashed into the blue drawing room to tell the anguished Emperor the news. Napoleon, like his uncle, merely glanced at the child and hurried to his wife's side. She was terribly weak.

"Is it a girl?" she asked faintly.

"No," answered the Emperor.

"It's a boy!" she exclaimed.

Afraid of exciting her, he again shook his head.

"Then what it it?" asked the puzzled Eugénie.

When she heard that she had indeed given him a son, she fell into an exhausted sleep.

Beside himself with joy, Napoleon rushed through the rooms, kissing everyone in sight, regardless of their sex. When he realized what he was doing, he apologized, but only for the fact that he could not kiss them all. Quite different was Plon-Plon's reaction. He was speechless with fury.

When he was asked to sign the birth certificate, he refused. One after another they begged him to put his name to the document, but he was adamant. Then Mathilde, rising sleepily and massively from her chair, held out the pen towards him. She had been there, she said threateningly, for twenty-seven hours. She did not intend to stay any longer. What exactly did this whim of his mean? The boy had been born, the evidence was there. Plon-Plon's ill temper was not going to alter the facts. . . .

Snatching the pen, Plon-Plon signed his name. He signed it so aggressively that a huge blot was left on the page. At that moment the hundred-and-one-gun salute, announcing the birth of a prince, started thudding out over Paris, and the crowd in the Tuileries garden went wild with joy.

The christening took place on June 14, 1856. The arrangements led, of course, to a family row. Old Jérôme refused to go, as he had been assigned to the same carriage as Prince Oscar of Sweden and the Dowager Grand Duchess Stéphanie of Baden. Mathilde was upset at being put in the second carriage with the Duchess of Hamilton; *she* was a member of the Imperial Family, she claimed, the Duchess of Hamilton was *not*. "The whole family," sighed Viel Castel, "which ought to be united and homogeneous, disregarding the necessities of their position, do nothing but work for their individual interests and speak ill-naturedly of each other. . . ."

The child was named Napoléon Eugène Louis Jean Joseph, Prince Imperial of France. Many years later, when the Empress Eugenie was a very old lady, someone once asked her what she considered to have been the "most radiant and inspiring" moments of her reign. Without the slightest hesitation she gave this answer:

"First and foremost, the christening of the Prince Imperial on June 14, 1856. During the drive from the Tuileries to Notre Dame, I was alone with the Emperor in our state wedding coach. The Prince Imperial, his attendants and nurses, were in the preceding carriage. It was about six o'clock in the evening. Marshals were riding in procession beside our doors. We were frantically cheered. The sun was just beginning to sink and the Rue de Rivoli was glowing purple; we filed along in this dazzling light. Beside me the Emperor remained silent, doing nothing but return the salutes. I myself was equally silent, for my heart was uplifted by an inexpressible joy, and I kept inwardly repeating to myself: 'It is through this child, through *my son*, that the dynasty of the Napoleons will take final root in the soil of France, just as eight centuries ago the House of Capet was there implanted; it is *he* who will put the final seal on the work of the father. . . .' "

CHAPTER TWELVE

THE worldly Count de Morny, half brother to the Emperor, now moved into the limelight once more. The conclusion of the Crimean War and the death of the Czar Nicholas gave Napoleon III the opportunity to make a fresh start with Russia. He decided to send Morny as ambassador extraordinary to attend the coronation of Czar Alexander II. It was an excellent choice; Auguste de Morny, with his polished manners and his immense wealth, was bound to make a good impression at the formal, sumptuously rich Russian court. Leaving behind his long-established mistress, Madame Le Hon, and stuffing his baggage with duty-free lace and jewelry for resale in Russia, he set off for St. Petersburg. The talented forty-five-year-old roué was an immediate success. So much so, in fact, that when he proposed marriage to the young and lovely Princess Sophie Troubetskoi, she accepted. A lady in waiting to the Czarina, Sophie Troubetskoi was a velvety-eyed blonde with gentle manners. As she was not rich, the Czar, delighted to have supplied a bride for the French ambassador, gave her a sizable dowry, and Morny returned home well pleased with the results of his diplomatic mission. He had reckoned, however, without Madame Le Hon.

His letter to her, announcing his forthcoming marriage, had been distinctly off-hand in tone. "I am about to be married. . ." he had written. "The Emperor wishes it and France desires it. . . . I hope my wife will have no better friend than you and that you will continue to find your way to our home." Madame Le Hon, who had been finding her way to Morny's home for almost two decades, was furious. She went hurrying round to the Tuileries to get the Emperor to call off the marriage. Napoleon explained that this was impossible, but promised to rebuke his half brother.

Thwarted, Madame Le Hon threatened to bring an action against her lover in order to retrieve the vast sums of money she had lent him. The Emperor, afraid of the scandal that such a case would precipitate, decided to have the matter looked into privately. He appointed Rouher, one of his leading ministers, to examine the lady's claim. Rumor has it that the secret police, led by the same Griscelli who was supposed to have murdered poor Zembo under Hungerford Bridge, forced their way into Madame Le Hon's private apartments and confiscated her papers. The result of Rouher's examination was that Morny was compelled to pay her 3,500,00 francs. "They give me three million," complained the Countess, "when they owe me six."

Napoleon, as usual, paid the money out of privy purse, and she consoled herself, it was said, by taking up with Rouher. She never forgave Morny. "I found him a sublieutenant and left him an ambassador," she snorted. Even Napoleon III, who so seldom said anything unpleasant about anyone, called his half brother a *faquin*.

His new wife, Princess Troubetskoi, once away from the overwhelming splendors of the Russian court, revealed herself to be far less mild mannered than Morny had supposed. In fact, she was decidedly eccentric. Henry Greville found her *"très bizarre,* not very gracious in her manner, nor as refined as she looks." She had, says another of her contemporaries, the "tempers, whims, and caprices" of a child of six. Although she was very pretty, the delicacy of her features, the fairness of her complexion, and the light, almost silver color of her hair (all in marked contrast to her black eyes) earned her the nickname of "the White Mouse." Once, at a costume ball at the Tuileries, when the Duke de Dino, dressed as the stump of a tree, refused to move out of her way when she asked him to, she "uttered a fierce growl," and with blue and white gauze streamers flying, flung herself on him. It was hardly the sort of behavior one expected at a court ball. On another occasion, when her husband was giving a large official dinner party, she decided, at the very last moment, not to appear. "He was. . . ." says one of the guests, "quite equal to the occasion . . . playing his part of host with his usual charming grace and apparently unruffled equanimity."

♛   ♛   ♛

On the evening of January 14, 1858, as Napoleon and Eugenie were driving in state to the opera, three bombs were flung at their carriage. Although they were unhurt and were able to show themselves—bloodspattered but smiling—to the wildly cheering audience within the opera house, eight people had been killed and a hundred and fifty injured. The incident, serious enough in itself, was to spark off a train of even more serious events.

When the arrests were made, it was discovered that the bomb throwers had been led by an Italian patriot by the name of Orsini. Although his attempted assassination of the Emperor had failed, his action forced the whole Italian question into the open.

For many years Italy had been controlled by two reactionary powers —the Papacy in the south and Austria in the north. And for several years nationally minded young Italians had worked for the liberation of their country. Notable amongst these fiery young men had been Hortense's two sons, Napoleon-Louis and Louis-Napoleon. Napoleon-Louis had died while fighting for the cause of liberation; Louis-Napoleon had lived on to continue the fight. The liberation of Italy, in fact, was something which had never ceased to concern him personally. As a Bonaparte, or more specifically, as the heir to Napoleon I, he felt almost honor bound to do something for Italy. It was in Italy, of course, that Napoleon I had won his first laurels during the "liberation" campaign of 1796; it was here that Eugène de Beauharnais had acted as Napoleon's viceroy, where first Joseph Bonaparte and then Caroline and Joachim Murat had reigned at Naples, where Elisa had queened it at Lucca and Tuscany. Italy was therefore very much tied up with the Napoleonic legend. Once, when someone had asked Napoleon III what he intended to do for the Italians, he had answered that as his name was Bonaparte, he was fully conscious of the responsibilities that the name carried. Italy, he said, was almost as dear to him as France; he had to watch for an "opportunity."

When Orsini, the romantic Italian patriot, threw his bombs at the Emperor's carriage on that January evening, the opportunity arrived. Napoleon was sharply reminded of his duty towards Italy. Although Orsini was sentenced to suffer death, Napoleon was committed to liberate Italy. In the summer of that year he arranged a meeting with Cavour, chief minister of King Victor Emmanuel II of Sardinia. These two conspirators, Napoleon and Cavour, planned to provoke Austria into a war in northern Italy. But in order to cement the new alliance between Sardinia and France, some gesture involving the two ruling houses was needed. What better than a royal marriage?

King Victor Emmanuel II was a widower, but Napoleon III had no bride to offer him. The King also had a daughter, a sixteen-year-old girl who, by the standards of the day, was more than ready for marriage. Whereas Napoleon I had always had a spare prince or two up his sleeve at times like this, the Second Empire was a little thin on princes of the blood Imperial. The only available one was Plon-Plon, so Plon-Plon it had to be. That he was thirty-seven years old, plump, dissolute, bad-tempered, and an agnostic, and as such, a totally unsuitable bridegroom for this excessively pious young princess, made no difference. Napoleon and Cavour had agreed on the marriage, and Plon-Plon was despatched to Turin to claim her. A dutiful daughter, Princess Clotilde married him without a murmur. Plon-Plon himself was delighted with the match, but for political rather than sentimental reasons. This marriage to the daughter of the King of Sardinia put him, he assured his friends, in a very strong position. "I am ready to act," he exclaimed, "and if any misfortune happened to the Emperor, it would certainly not be that simpleton of an Empress or that little brat of a Prince Imperial that they would fetch." Nor, in fact, would it ever be Plon-Plon.

Princess Mathilde once aptly referred to the union of her brother Plon-Plon and Princess Clotilde as "the devil in a holy water bowl." One of the first things Clotilde did on taking up residence in the Palais Royal was to sprinkle her rooms with holy water; whether by this she hoped to exorcise the traces of her husband's past life, one does not know, but certainly his marriage reformed him not at all. His mistresses—the most notable of whom were Count Walewski's old flame Rachel and the notorious Cora Pearl—continued to visit him at the Palais Royal and to accompany him to the theater. The gentle Clotilde never uttered a word of reproach. She seems, in fact, to have been devoted to her decadent, fractious husband. A simple-minded girl herself, she admired him for his spirited conversation and his strongly held opinions. If he was one of the most unpopular members of the Emperor's family, she was to become one of the most esteemed. Her piety, her charity, and her modesty were a welcome change from the profligacy, the greed, and the vanity of the majority of Napoleon III's relations; even when, at the end of the Empire, the Bonapartes were once more hounded out of France, Clotilde was treated with the utmost respect.

To the Parisians she was almost a saint; to those who knew her better, she was sometimes a little too good to be true. Her shyness could quickly degenerate into surliness. Her ladies in waiting complained that when annoyed with them, she would lower her eyes, purse her lips, and refuse to speak. "She would maintain this obstinate silence for hours," reports one of them, "and leaning back in a corner of her carriage, behind the slow-trotting horses, would vouchsafe neither look nor word to the lady beside her." Only a faint clinking as the Princess counted the beads of her rosary ("more for the sake of holding her companion aloof than with the intention of saying her prayers") would disturb the icy atmosphere. "It was enough to discourage virtue!" exclaimed one of Eugenie's more spirited companions.

Except for an occasional flurry of excitement when Plon-Plon's rudeness resulted in some lady handing in her resignation, life in the Palais Royal was deadly dull. There was nothing to relieve the boredom of waiting on this pious princess. By day her companions would have to trail after her from one church to another, by night they would sit around a table, doing endless needlework. If one of the ladies dared to introduce some general topic, to wonder, for instance, what the outcome of affairs in Italy would be, Clotilde would silence her by saying, "Matters are in God's hands, and what is His will must happen." She might have been right, but it did not make for amusing conversation.

Clotilde's reproving manner extended to the Empress as well. When this small, reserved, plainly dressed little creature first arrived in France, Eugenie, growing smarter and more assured by the day, had presumed to give her a few hints on her dress and deportment. "You seem to forget, Madame," said Clotilde quietly, "that I was born at a court."

Eugenie never forgave her for that.

⚜ ⚜ ⚜

On the question of the Italian war of liberation, Napoleon III and his cousin Plon-Plon were, for once in their lives, in complete agreement. It was Napoleon I's illegitimate son, the honest Walewski, who was opposed to the venture.

In spite of the fact that Walewski was Foreign Minister, the Emperor, realizing that, as a friend of Austria, Walewski would disapprove of the campaign in Italy, kept him in ignorance of the projected meeting with Cavour. This was very much Napoleon III's way. Where Walewski was always frank, open, and clear-sighted, Napoleon III moved secretly and by circuitous routes, imagining himself a more profound politician because of it. It was said that France had two distinct diplomacies during this period: that of Walewski's office—the Quai d'Orsay—and that of the Emperor's study. Discord between so upright a minister and so conspiratorial a sovereign was inevitable. When Walewski realized what Napoleon was up to behind his back, he felt that he could remain at his post no longer. Several times he handed in his resignation, and each time the Emperor, a past master at smoothing out such difficulties, persuaded him to withdraw his offer. The threatened resignations in no way lessened Napoleon's duplicity; the Emperor, still keeping all negotiations in his own hands, continued to make preparations for an Italian campaign. Finally, towards the end of 1859, Walewski, unable to endure his master's policies or methods a moment longer, resigned as Foreign Minister once and for all. This time Napoleon let him go, but not without rewarding him handsomely for his services. Like his uncle Napoleon I, Napoleon III knew the sure way of softening up a disgruntled servant.

There might have been another reason for his generosity towards Walewski. It was rumored that Walewski's wife had become the Emperor's mistress. The former Marie-Anne de Ricci, with her Italianate beauty and her warm, unaffected manner, was a great favorite at court. It was unlikely that such a vibrant young woman should escape the Emperor's roving eye for long. Viel Castel claims that by September 1857 Countess Walewska had "inscribed her name in capital letters on the list of the Emperor's sultanas," and the British ambassador reported that "the way she threw herself at the Emperor was the theme of everybody's conversation. She had neither eyes nor ears for anyone else. . . ." It was noticed that when Queen Victoria visited Napoleon III at Cherbourg the following year she made a point of not kissing Madame Walewska. The magnificent pearl necklace which Napoleon presented to her on her husband's resignation as Foreign Minister surprised no one; the Countess had, it was whispered, more than earned it.

If she was indeed the Emperor's mistress, then she must have played a very careful hand, for she seems to have been as great a favorite with the Empress as she was with Napoleon. Eugenie, who had a penchant for surrounding herself with pretty women, adored her. "The Empress and Madame Walewska are inseparable," wrote one observer, "they wear the same dresses and bonnets, have the same opinions, and concert together, the one in her position of legitimate, the other in that of illegitimate wife, to oppose the Emperor in his Roman policy." Eugénie was always giving her friend little missions. At this period prior to the Italian campaign, the Empress imagined that the Countess, being Italian, could keep her informed on Italian affairs. "My dear Marie," she wrote on one occasion, "I have just seen the Papal Nuncio. I am very anxious to know what effect my words had on him. Try to find out for me."

Besides its confidential tone, this little note illustrates Eugénie's growing awareness of the political possibilities of her position. Still content, during the first years of the reign, to be *La Reine Crinoline* and little else, her period as Regent during the coming Italian campaign would give her an exalted idea of her talent for politics. It was to be, in many ways, a regrettable discovery.

Not all Countess Walewska's adroit handling of both Emperor and Empress could prevent gossip of her alleged affair reaching Eugenie's ears. When it did, the Empress was furious, but Walewski's prominent position prevented her from making too much of a fuss. Her attitude towards the Countess cooled, but there was no open breach. The Countess Walewska remained at court, and the Empress very soon had far more certain and dangerous rivals to contend with. With the opening of the Italian campaign and her own appointment as Regent, she also had far more important things to occupy her mind.

In the spring of the year 1859 Naploeon III marched his armies into northern Italy. There, considerably more by luck than by judgment, he defeated the Austrians in two somewhat indecisive battles. Suspecting that he might not win a third, and appalled at the bloodshed (he did not have his uncle's insensitive stomach), he cast about for some excuse to finish the war. It was provided by Eugénie. She had had warning of a concentration of Prussian troops on the Rhine. Anxious to forestall a possible Prussian invasion while he was still in Italy, Napoleon III concluded a hasty peace with the Emperor of Austria and hurried home. In spite of the fact that he had not, as he had promised, liberated Italy "up to the Adriatic," and that his Sardinian allies had lost faith in him, he returned to Paris a hero. There, on August 14—the official birthday of Napoleon I—he reviewed the troops lately returned from Italy. With the three-year-old Prince Imperial on his saddle-bow before him, and the statue of his illustrious uncle crowning the Vendôme column behind, Napoleon III watched line after line of his superbly uniformed soldiers swing by. Flowers rained from the surrounding windows, and the summer day was loud with shouts of *"Vive l'Empereur!"*

The ceremony marked, in many ways, the high noon of the Second Empire.

♛   ♛   ♛

In the year 1860, when the Second Empire was at its zenith, old Jérôme, the last surviving link with the First Empire, died at the age of seventy-five. It was unfortunate that it should have been he, the most disreputable of Napoleon I's brothers, who had lived on into an Empire which had long since become respectable. It was true that at those military reviews in which the Second Empire excelled, old Jérôme, in his general's uniform (looking for all the world as Napoleon I might have looked in old age), was an ornamental figure; and that at receptions his old world, excessively courteous manners were a refreshing change from the lackadaisical behavior of the *nouveau riche* society of the Second Empire. But that is all. Away from the parade ground or the palace his behavior was appalling. His language was coarse; his manners were vulgar; his morals were atrocious. His favorite entertainment, other than making love, was to go to third-rate theaters where the performers were sometimes dogs or monkeys; there he could sit in the front row, following every move like a delighted child. Once, at a popular play dealing with Napoleon I, when the Emperor was shown scolding his young brother Jérôme, the attention of the audience was distracted by the sight of the real King Jérôme sitting in his box, convulsed with laughter. An incurable spendthrift, he had long since squandered the fortune of his third wife, the mild-mannered Marchesa Bartolini-Baldelli, and as the allowance granted him by his nephew Napoleon III was never enough, he was always borrowing, either from his daughter Mathilde or from the Emperor himself.

When almost seventy, Jérôme acquired a new mistress—a tall red-haired virago—and began to think about getting rid of his gentle wife. Plon-Plon, who hated his stepmother, was more than ready to oblige his father in this matter, and worked out a scheme whereby the Marchesa could be discredited. Like so many of Plon-Plon's ideas, it was clever and diabolical. Jérôme had had an illegitimate son by Madame David, the daughter-in-law of Jacques Louis David, the famous First Empire painter. This boy was known as Jérôme David. The story was put about that Jérôme David was having an affair with his father's wife, and Plon-Plon claimed to have discovered them in a compromising situation. In vain did the poor Marchesa protest her innocence. Old Jérôme either believed, or pretended to believe, the accusations against her, and she was packed off to Florence. Like his second wife, Catherine, the Marchesa had been devoted to the dissolute Jérôme, and his cruel treatment almost broke her heart. To soften the blow, Napoleon III insisted on Jérôme's paying back the money he owed her, and after Jérôme's death, the Emperor granted her a pension. Even Plon-Plon, regretting his shameless behavior, went so far as to pay the rent of her house in Florence.

One of the last glimpses one gets of Jérôme is at the age of seventy-four, when he gave a fete at the Palais Royal in honor of the Empress. Eugénie, dressed in an enormous crinoline of white tulle, and with a wreath of Parma violets on her red-gold hair, was led round the salons by the gallant old roué. Leading her, not by the arm as was then customary, but by his upraised hand, as was the fashion of his youth, he shepherded her among the bowing and curtsying guests. He treated her, said one of her ladies, "with a gracefulness somewhat old-fashioned, but *tout-à-fait chevaleresque.*"

This was the occasion of the famous encounter between the Emperor and his current mistress, the beautiful, disdainful Countess de Castiglione.

At one o'clock in the morning, as the Emperor and Empress were leaving the ball, they met the Countess on the stairs, just arriving. For a minute the three of them—the sensual Emperor, the elegant Empress, and the supercilious Countess—surveyed one another in silence. Then Napoleon spoke.

"You are arriving very late, Madame Countess," he remarked quietly.

"It is you, Sire," answered the cold-eyed Castiglione, "who are leaving too early."

Old Jérôme died on June 24, 1860. His two legitimate children, Plon-Plon and Mathilde, were with him when he died, and his daughter-in-law, Plon-Plon's saintly wife, Clotilde, saw to it that he received the last rights of the Church. While extreme unction was being administered, reports Viel Castel, Plon-Plon "thought it more appropriate to be smoking a cigarette in an adjoining room."

Dead, Jérôme was of much more use to the Second Empire than alive: his funeral gave Napoleon III the opportunity to stage one of those magnificent ceremonies which were such a feature of his regime. Jérôme had been a marshal of France, a prince of the First and Second Empires, a king, and the last of the brothers of the Great Napoleon; as such he was to be laid to rest with all possible pomp. Every available Bonaparte prince was rounded up, and led by Plon-Plon, in a long black cloak, they followed the coffin through lines of troops to the Invalides. Cannon boomed from the Champ de Mars, veterans of the First Empire paraded at the Invalides, and the cortege, escorted by magnificently uniformed cuirassiers, seemed never-ending. Paris had not been treated to so impressive a *fête funèbre* for years.

Notable by his absence amongst the slowly pacing group of princes was young Jerome Patterson Bonaparte, old Jérôme's grandson; Plon-Plon had seen to it that he had been relegated to a place among the princesses in the church. "I felt dreadfully sorry for him," wrote Caroline Murat, with a rare burst of compassion, but added that "I confess I admired his courage in obeying the order, all the more that I knew, had *I* been in his place, wild horses would not have dragged me there. Of course, I reasoned as a woman. . . ."

It seemed, at times, as though the original Caroline Murat had come alive again in the person of her granddaughter.

The bishop who preached the funeral oration was a little hard pressed for something complimentary to say, but by concentrating on Jérôme's faithfulness "to the flag of France" and his exploits at Waterloo (such as they were), he managed to deliver a suitably heroic address. The ceremony over, the Imperial family returned home, well satisfied that they had done their best by their great ancestor's brother. Only one mourner remained. Huddled near the coffin, her gentle face ravaged with tears and her body shaken with sobs, was the Marchesa Bartolini-Baldelli, his last wife.

His first wife, Betsey Patterson, wasted no time on tears. Jérôme was hardly cold before she laid claim to a share of his estate. She maintained that she was the lawful wife of Jérôme Bonaparte and that her son, Bo, was his legitimate heir. The situation had become too complicated for an Imperial Family Council, and Betsey's claim was heard before the Civil Tribunal. The plaintiffs were described as M. Jerome Napoleon Bonaparte (Bo), landowner of Baltimore U.S.A., and Madame Elizabeth Patterson, likewise a landowner of Baltimore. The defendant was His Imperial Highness Monseigneur the Prince Jérôme Napoleon (Plon-Plon), residing in Paris at the Palais Royal. Although Betsey had a very good case, the verdict was a foregone conclusion. To establish Bo as Jérôme's eldest legitimate son and heir would be to bring him into the line of succession. If anything were to happen to the little Prince Imperial, then Bo Patterson Bonaparte from Baltimore would become Emperor of the French, and the succession would pass through him to his son, young Jerome. Although there was much sympathy for the shabbily treated Betsey, the court had no choice. It gave its decision against the validity of the American marriage, denied the legitimacy of Bo, and declared that neither he nor Betsey had any claim to Jérôme's inheritance. The Baltimore Bonapartes lost whatever concessions they had gained a few years earlier at the Imperial Family Council, and were obliged, moreover, to pay heavy legal costs.

Her dreams shattered once and for all, Betsey returned to America. It was almost sixty years since she and Jérôme had been married; during all that time she had worked for the day when she and her descendants could take their rightful place amongst the members of the Imperial family. Now that day had passed forever. Bo returned to his wife and his youngest son, Charles, without regrets; the three of them considered themselves an American family. Their eldest son, young Jerome, now a captain in Napoleon III's army, remained in France. A great favorite at the Tuileries, he was still called, much to Plon-Plon's chagrin, Prince Jérôme.

The American Civil War broke out in 1861. The Emperor, backed by Eugenie, favored the South. Having just proved his liberalism by the campaign in Italy, he hoped to appease French conservatives by doing something for the Confederacy. There was talk of the South's turning into a kingdom and offering a crown to some European prince; of all the monarchs, Napoleon III seemed the most likely one to approach. A Catholic kingdom in North America, closely allied to France, would do wonders for his prestige and secure for him the support of all French Catholics. It was a proposition worth considering. Just how far the negotiations went is not certain, but it was rumored that the Southern crown was offered to none other than the Emperor's cousin, young Jerome. He is reported to have refused the offer. It might have been that the young man was approached too early; Napoleon III, as always, was playing a waiting game, and if things had looked more promising for the South, he might well have helped set young Jerome upon the throne. But it was not to be, and Betsey Patterson again missed the chance of seeing a dream come true.

If Napoleon III's sympathies were with the South, Plon-Plon's, of course, were all with the North. He visited the States for two months that year, and although his journey had no political significance, he expressed great faith in the Northern cause and felt confident that it would eventually triumph. He was received by President Lincoln, he exchanged views with generals of the opposing armies, and he made an extensive tour of the country. Like his cousin Louis-Napoleon twenty-five years before (and unlike the majority of his male relations), he seems to have behaved himself. And again like Louis-Napoleon— although for very different reasons—he did not make contact with his American relations, the Baltimore Bonapartes. It was particularly galling for Betsey, with the verdict of the French court still fresh in her mind, to see this son of Jérôme's traipsing about America in almost regal state. She must have been relieved to hear that he had sailed back to France at the end of September.

♔   ♔   ♔

Unlike her predecessors, the Empresses Josephine and Marie Louise, the Empress Eugenie was very much a personality in her own right. Where the two previous women had been mere shadows of Napoleon I, Eugenie ranks as one of the most important figures of nineteenth-century France. In an era of fascinating woman, few were more fascinating than she.

In the first place, there was her marvelous beauty. Even her bitterest enemies had to concede this. "I cannot say wherein Mademoiselle de

Montijo's beauty lay," admitted one of her most venomous critics, "but she was beautiful indeed." It is very difficult, at this distance, to appreciate Eugenie's rather special looks. The conventionally regal paintings, the stiffly posed photographs, tell so little. For hers was essentially a beauty of coloring and mobility, and these are the very qualities most difficult to record. Her skin, they say, was like marble, yet of such extraordinary translucency as to give her features a delicate glow, a subtle radiance. Her large down-slanting eyes, now blue, now gray, now green, and never without their boldly penciled outline, had a peculiar heavy-lidded attractiveness; there was about them a touch of sadness, which seemed to be echoed by the downward tilt of her finely drawn eyebrows. Her hair, like burnished copper, was so variable in its luster as to seem at times quite dark, at others, quite fair. Her profile had the aquiline perfection of an antique cameo, and with her flawless teeth, her smile could be the most enchanting in the world.

Anna Bicknell, a young woman who was governess to some children living in the Tuileries, tells of her first sight of the Empress. She and one of her pupils were crossing the main courtyard one day when the girl suddenly whispered, "*L'Impératrice!*" and swept to the ground in a deep curtsy. "There was the Empress standing before us," writes Anna, "at a large window on the ground floor, an ideal vision robed in pale-blue silk; the sun, forming a sort of halo around her, rested on her hair, which seemed all molten gold. I was absolutely startled, and my impression was that I had never seen such a beautiful creature. . . ."

Her figure was faultless, and her carriage, superb. Unusually supple, she was a joy to watch; she seemed incapable of making an inelegant movement. Yet she seemed almost unconscious of this fluidity of motion; there was a simplicity, an artlessness, a genuine lack of affectation in her demeanor—she was usually too preoccupied with what she was doing to be aware that she was doing it with extreme elegance. Her choice of clothes revealed this same unaffected grace. Although no woman in Europe was better dressed than she, simplicity came more naturally to her than ostentation. Her reputation for extravagance was wildly exaggerated. She was constantly being accused of wasting money, but, in fact, few women in her position could have been more careful with money than she. It is true that what excessive spending she did was always on dress, but then she was, after all, Empress of the French— those same French who had complained so bitterly about the shabbiness of the previous regime and who had been so bored by the dowdiness of Louis Philippe's queen. Eugenie's own taste in dress was modest. In private she preferred wearing a plain black skirt and a red "Garibaldi" blouse; it was only on state occasions, when appearance demanded it, that she emerged in those breathtakingly lovely clothes. Her interest in dress was often more a matter of policy than of preference; "*toilettes politiques,*" she used to call those dresses which she was obliged to wear in order to stimulate the demand for certain French fabrics and laces. And there is no doubt that her elegance, together with her patronage of Worth, finally re-established the reputation of Paris as the first city of fashion.

Of only one real extravagance could she have been accused, and that was in the matter of shoes. Her feet were marvelously small, and she shod them, in the evenings, in the softest of satin pumps, which she would wear once only and then send to some Parisian orphanage. When one thinks of some of the excesses of past French sovereigns, Eugenie's pile of satin slippers seems a modest extravagance indeed.

But lovely as she was to look at, it was her animation which brought her beauty to life. She had a vivacity, a feverishness, of manner, which kept her constantly on the move; her vitality was exceptional. Being an Empress, she had the usual stock gifts of royalty—even parvenu royalties must have those. She could be dignified and gracious; she had the ability to put people at their ease and the mind trained to remember faces, places and things. But she was no carbon-copy sovereign. She was too natural and impetuous ever to present to the world the smooth mask of royalty. A dozen years of being the Empress had never quite suppressed the *femme du monde*—the eagerness, the effervescence, the unconventionality, was always breaking through.

She tended, at times, to be a little too natural. That the court of the Second Empire got its reputation for frivolity was as much her fault as that of the giddiest member of her entourage. It seemed to be at play from morning to night. The court lived in a whirl of masked balls, amateur theatricals, and games of blind-man's-buff. Now the Empress and her ladies are being painted in a charmingly affected group by Winterhalter; now they are racing, hands clasped, down a steep grassy bank at Fontainebleau, shrilling with laughter as they go. At Biarritz, the Imperial holiday home close to Eugenie's native Spain, a *dame d'honneur* comes shrieking into the room to report that there is a strange man in her bed; the courtiers responsible for the dummy under the lady's sheets are convulsed with laughter, and the evening breaks up in hilarious confusion. . . .

That so vigorous and uninhibited a personality as Eugenie should wish to play a part in the running of her husband's Empire was inevitable. Far from being the Emperor's shadow, it was she, as the years went by, who overshadowed him. In some ways he had encouraged her. Although by no means as clannish as the first Napoleon, Napoleon III would undoubtedly have been glad of some more active support from the members of his family. The only two with any talent—Plon-Plon and Mathilde—held themselves aloof from the Tuileries; he because of his professed Republicanism, she because she disliked the frivolous court. Of his illegitimate relations, Walewski's gifts were more diplomatic than political, and Morny was too corrupt and indulgent ever to make a first-rate politician. Thus, when Eugenie started to show an interest in affairs of state, Napoleon did nothing to discourage her. Her first regency had given her a taste, if not a talent, for politics, and when she found that her opinions were usually listened to with flattering attention by Napoleon's ministers, she began to give them more frequently. Conservative, almost reactionary, in her views, and never afraid to speak her mind, she soon found support amongst the more traditionally minded elements in the Council Chamber. The Emperor, in his hazy way, favored aspiring nationalists and had ideas of liberalizing his own regime; Eugenie, in her dogmatic fashion, championed the Pope, the Hapsburgs, and was all for Napoleon keeping power firmly in his own hands.

Domestic issues never interested her particularly; her forte, she imagined, was foreign policy. Thus, in 1861, when the idea of establishing a Catholic Empire in Mexico was first mooted, she took it up enthusiastically. Here was an opportunity for the sort of *grande geste* she adored; by installing Maximilian, brother of the Emperor of Austria, as Emperor of Mexico, the prestige of Imperial France would be greatly enhanced. Dazzled by the prospect of doing something for Catholicism, the Hapsburgs, and the Imperial regime, and allowing herself to be misled as to the amount of resistance the scheme was likely to encounter in Mexico itself, she flung herself wholeheartedly into the venture. What was meant to be "the great thought of the reign" turned out, in time, to be one of its greatest disasters.

Another reason for the Emperor's letting Eugenie have her way was that it kept her mind off his infidelities. The more absorbed she was in affairs of state, the less likely she was to concern herself with his affairs of the heart. So chaste herself, she could never understand or forgive what he called his "*petites distractions.*" Fearing another pregnancy (which she had been warned might be fatal), she had little taste for the sexual side of married life. But not even his most ardent apologist could claim this as the cause of his tireless philandering; it was his most persistent weakness, and he never made the slightest effort to cure it. Nor did he get much encouragement to do so. "As a rule the man makes the attack," he once sighed to Princess Bacciochi, "but I defend myself and sometimes I surrender." In fact, he *always* surrendered. And each time Eugenie found out about a fresh surrender, she made a scene. As the Empress angry was not a pretty sight, Napoleon came to dread these attacks. It was her pride, far more than her heart, which suffered from her husband's frequent liaisons, and being virtuous herself, she never could adopt the happy-go-lucky attitude towards infidelity so common amongst married couples at court.

The first of his serious affairs was with the beautiful, if callous, Countess de Castiglione. Sent to Paris by Cavour to help win the Emperor over to the cause of Italian liberation, Castiglione seems to have fulfilled her mission admirably. The fact that in her will she left instructions to be buried in the nightdress she had worn at Compiègne during the season of 1857 seems to indicate that this was the occasion on which the Emperor first succumbed to her charms. There is a story that she bore him a son who was known, in later life, as Dr. Hugenschmidt, and who died in 1929. Vain, in fact narcissistic, the Countess de Castiglione delighted in those costume balls which were such a feature of the Second Empire. Her most famous appearance was when she turned up at a reception given by the Countess Walewska as "The Queen of Hearts." One glance at her skintight black gauze dress revealed that she had dispensed with any undergarments, relying on cut-out hearts to cover her more vulnerable spots. When Castiglione greeted the Empress, Eugenie, well aware of her husband's liaison with the reputedly heartless Countess, had given her suggestive costume a coolly appraising look. "Your heart," she said with a wealth of meaning, "seems a little low down."

Twice, during the early 1860's, Eugenie's discovery of some new affair led to something rather more than a few tart remarks. The first occasion had been soon after the death of her only sister, Paca. The Empress, broken with grief—for she had loved Paca very deeply—made her way unexpectedly one day into Napoleon's apartments, and is said to have surprised him there with some pretty young girl. The usual violent scene was followed by her announcement that she was going away. It seems that not only his infidelities, but their never-ending disagreements on the question of the future of the Pope (Napoleon wanted to trim his powers, Eugenie, to safeguard them), had led to her decision. Although it was November, she went to Scotland. "Eugenie's expedition is most astonishing," wrote King Leopold of the Belgians to his niece Queen Victoria. Then he added maliciously, "She also coughs much, and I have never heard Scotland recommended for winter excursions." But in Scotland, by tramping around the misty rain-swept hillsides, Eugenie (not for the last time in her life) regained her composure and settled her nerves. She took advantage of her stay in Britain to consult the eminent gynecologist Locock. He assured her that she was in perfect health, and advised her, with a fine British superiority, to avoid having anything to do with French doctors. When she same south and visited Victoria at Windsor, the Queen noticed that Eugenie never once mentioned the Emperor. The Empress returned home a few days later to a somewhat chastened Napoleon. He did not remain so for long.

The next time things came to a head was during his liaison with Marguerite Bélanger. A pert low-born, pug-faced courtesan, Marguerite Bélanger had captivated the Emperor completely. He had installed her in a house not far from the Tuileries, and hardly a day went by that he did not spend an hour or two there. One evening, when the court was at Saint-Cloud, Napoleon arrived back at the palace in a state of collapse. The Empress was told that he had taken ill while visiting Mademoiselle Bèlanger. This, decided Eugenie, was going too far. In a white-hot fury she summoned her carriage and hurried over to Marguerite's country villa nearby. Pushing her way into the drawing room, she confronted the startled girl.

"*Mademoiselle*," she said violently, "you are killing the Emperor." Warning her to be out of the house by the following day, Eugenie turned on her heel and drove home.

Marguerite did not leave the following day. Napoleon, exasperated by his wife's high-handed behavior (the story had got around Paris in a flash), ordered his mistress to stay where she was. Infuriated at this check, Eugenie announced that if Mademoiselle Bélanger did not go, she would. And she did. Traveling in the luxuriously fitted Imperial train, she went to Schwalbach, in Nassau, and there spent several weeks visiting various royalties. In vain did the Emperor beg her to come home; she was determined to punish him, and besides, she was enjoying herself. This free-and-easy spa life suited her; it reminded her of the days before her marriage. When she did eventually return to Napoleon, it was to be on a new footing. Henceforth she would be his Empress only, not his wife. As he was obviously incapable of curbing his lusts, she intended putting an end to all conjugal relations between them. Napoleon accepted her terms. Anything for a quiet life. Time, he reckoned, would weaken her resolution.

Another reason for Eugenie's ascendancy during these years was Napoleon's worsening health. Never really strong, he had been suffering increasingly from pains in the bladder during the last few years. Although his doctors had once diagnosed a stone, no treatment had been carried out, and the discomfort experienced by the Emperor during subsequent ministrations had made him even more loath to be examined. As at result, the pain had become worse. This, in turn, sapped his energy, clouded his brain, and weakened his resolve. His tendency to evade, to procrastinate, to drift with the tide, became more pronounced as the years went by. By the mid-1860's his habitual air of knowing calm fooled no one; it was generally recognized that the Emperor was weak and irresolute.

Eugenie, on the other hand, was blessed with perfect health. Her energy was a source of amazement to the members of her entourage. At forty she could walk any girl off her feet, and being untiring herself, she would subject her less robust guests to an exhausting round of country rambles. With back erect and head held high, she would move with that quick, effortless grace along the misty autumn paths in the forest at Compiègne, the ladies scurrying to keep up with her, the gentlemen muttering in their beards. Never having known a day's ill health, she had very little patience with the Emperor's sufferings. She put all his ailments down to one cause, and as she had no sympathy with that, she had no sympathy for his illness. And just as his poor health made him unsure and indecisive, so did her boundless energy give her confidence. This difference between them was very well illustrated during the Sadowa crisis in 1866.

Bismarck, as part of his scheme for the unification of Germany, went to war against Austria in the spring of 1866. Expecting Austria to win the war, Napoleon neglected to demand compensations on the Rhine as a reward for his neutrality; when Bismarck, after a lightning campaign, defeated the Austrians at Sadowa, it was almost too late to demand them. But not quite. At a hurriedly arranged Council meeting on the morning after Sadowa, Eugenie enthusiastically supported the idea of massing troops on the Rhine while there was still time to gain some territorial compensation. Napoleon, racked with pain, hesitated to take so bold a step. But Eugenie's strong and impassioned arguments carried the day, and the Council decided in favor of mobilization. The decision was to be published in the official *Moniteur* the next day.

It never was. During the night, away from Eugenie's insistent presence, the Emperor weakened and countermanded the Council's decision. He could not face the risk of a war. As a result, Bismarck's military victory at Sadowa became a crushing diplomatic defeat for Imperial France.

The more Eugenie pushed herself forward, the less she endeared herself to the Bonapartes. Plon-Plon, who had always hated her, could hardly bear the sight of her by now. Their views were utterly opposed. A liberal and an agnostic, he could not tolerate her conservatism or what he considered her clericalism. He blamed all the more restrictive measures of the regime on her. Once, at a public dinner at Compiègne, when the Emperor turned to ask him to propose the health of the Empress, he refused. Eugenie never forgot that insult. Forty years later she recalled that dinner with extraordinary vividness. "He loathed me," remembered Eugenie, "because I brought the Prince Imperial into the world, and so barred his road to the throne. . . . At times he was positively carried away by fury; he raved, he foamed, he became demoniac!"

Although Mathilde behaved with more tact than her brother, she disliked Eugenie almost as much. Once Eugenie's original overtures towards Mathilde had been rebuffed, the Empress very quickly relegated her to the status of the lesser members of the family—the Lucien Bonapartes, the Murats, and the Bacciochis. The proud Mathilde was not sorry. Preferring to be first in her own village to being second in Rome, her casual treatment at the hands of Eugenie gave her a good excuse to shun the court. "The Tuileries . . . Saint-Cloud . . . how dull is the château of Saint-Cloud!" she scoffed. "It is odd how glad I always am to get away from both places. I am not at home at court. There is a difference both in feeling and language there. I cannot explain it. But I know myself to be quite another person, and I am always anxious to get away and be my own dear self once more." Some of this was true: Mathilde was much happier amongst her literary friends than amongst the simple-minded frivolities of Eugenie's circle.

The Emperor's half brother, Auguste de Morny, was far too shrewd to quarrel openly with the Empress. From the very first, when he had sensed that Napoleon, in spite of all opposition, would marry Eugenie, he had placed himself, as always, on the side of the broom handle. Since then, appreciating her growing lust for power, he had treated her very carefully. Whenever his opinions clashed with hers, he would try to change her mind by flattery, by cajolery, by sweet reasonableness, but never, like Plon-Plon, by trying to shout her down. As a result, Eugenie always retained a very favorable opinion of Morny, and this in spite of his decadent life. "You may guess, of course," she said in later years, "that he often shocked my puritan sense . . . (but) as a man he was charming; his ease and distinction of manner were perfect."

With Napoleon I's son Walewski she also remained on very good terms. His solemn, formal manner appealed to her. They often saw eye-to-eye of affairs of state; like her, Walewski was pro-British, anti-Russian, an ardent champion of the Papacy, and an advocate of an alliance with Austria. Unlike her, he favored a gradual liberalizing of the Empire. Only by increasing the power of the Chambers could Napoleon hope to secure the future of his dynasty, reckoned Walewski; only by continuing to rule autocratically could the throne be made safe for her son, argued Eugenie. In the end, neither was proved right.

With the exception of young Anna Murat, who was devoted to her, the rest of the family was not very enamoured of Eugenie. Nor, as was perfectly clear, she of them. But they accepted all her invitations to the Tuileries, Saint-Cloud, Fontainebleau, and Compiègne, and kept their real opinion of her to themselves or for publication in their memoirs.

That the Bonapartes did not care for her bothered Eugenie not one scrap; what did worry her was her unpopularity with her subjects. Try as she might—and she did try—Eugenie never won the love of the French. In vain did she show herself in public, visit slums and hospitals and orphanages; in vain did she grant audiences and give large sums to charity. It was for her less attractive features—her arrogance, her impetuosity, and her pride—that she became renowned. As the French had called Marie Antoinette "The Austrian Woman," they now called Eugenie "*l'Espagnole*." And she, who so desperately wanted to win their hearts, who longed to be loved as Josephine had been loved, had to accustom herself to their coldness, and in time, their hatred.

"If they knew," she once cried out in anguish, "what I would give to be really loved!"

CHAPTER THIRTEEN

☙ ☙ ☙

By the year 1865 the liaison between Princess Mathilde and Count Nieuwerkerque had worn very thin indeed. During their twenty years together Nieuwerkerque's treatment of her had become increasingly offhand, while she proudly pretended that she had not lost his love. It was only when the affair was finally over that she was to admit that he had loved her for perhaps three weeks and that he had deceived her after two months. Having made such a show of being his mistress, she was too ashamed to break with him, and was obliged to content herself with his occasional favors. They seem to have been occasional indeed. Handsome, high-handed, and conceited, Nieuwerkerque accepted all she had to give and gave practically nothing in return. She had him appointed superintendent of the Académie des Beaux-Arts (a post which allowed him to live in indolent luxury in the Louvre) and encouraged him to play the host at both her magnificent town house in the Rue de Courcelles and at her country place at Saint-Gratien. His massive chest was crowded with decorations, and she saw to it that he was treated with a respect out of all proportion to his talents. Yet she could not buy his fidelity. His innumerable affairs were the talk of Paris. She who longed so passionately for an all-consuming, unconditional romance had to settle for a very shoddy second best. She closed her eyes to his philanderings and hid her disillusion behind a vivacious, authoritative manner.

Frustrated in love, she flung herself, hardly less passionately, into friendships. Having little time for women (one always had to change the subject when a woman came into the room, she complained), she surrounded herself with a court of adoring men friends. Notable amongst these devotees were the Goncourt brothers. "Here," they wrote in their famous journal, "is the true salon of the nineteenth century, for its mistress is the perfect type of modern woman." No hostess, they said, was less formal yet more attentive than she. "We thought of her easy ways, the charm of her abruptness, her passionate speech, her colorful choice of words, the immediacy of her attack upon everything stupid, that fusion of virility with little evidence of feminine thoughtfulness, of the sum of her qualities, and even her defects, all of them of our time and all novel in a Highness—and we said to each other that she was the

281

archetype of a nineteenth-century princess, a sort of Marguerite of Navarre in the body of a Napoleon."

Of all Mathilde's many friendships, her association with the famous critic, Charles Augustus Sainte-Beuve, was undoubtedly the most ardent. Squat and ugly, Sainte-Beuve was the very antithesis of the magnificent Niewerkerque; and unlike Nieuwerkerque, who always treated Mathilde in a very cavalier fashion, Sainte-Beuve was attentive to the point of obsequiousness. A sensitive if self-centered man, Sainte-Beuve was grateful for the friendship of this proud princess; she, on the other hand, was flattered by the interest of so brilliant and celebrated a writer. Always wholehearted, she almost stifled him with attention. She became his champion, he, her mentor. Through her efforts he was nominated Senator in 1865, and as a result, devoted himself to her more than ever.

During the second half of the Empire, Sainte-Beuve was the brightest star in Mathilde's star-strewn sky. Seated amongst the self-consciously Bohemian furnishings of her house on the Rue de Courcelles, or waddling slowly along the flower-bordered paths at Saint-Gratien, Sainte-Beuve was her chief delight. He advised, he encouraged, he philosophized. Although by nature a reserved man, there were times when his conversation could hold the company enthralled. If his heart and his brain were to be taken from her, vowed Mathilde on one occasion, she would be left in the most pitiable state.

The durability of this passionate friendship between the Junoesque Mathilde and the gnomelike Sainte-Beuve was first put to the test soon after he became a Senator. The Marchioness Roccagiovine, formerly Julie Bonaparte, daughter of the ornithologist Charles Bonaparte (Lucien's eldest son), also presided over a literary salon during the Empire. Though her circle was not as illustrious as Mathilde's, her pretensions were no more modest. A tireless scalp-hunter, Princess Julie was eager to include Sainte-Beuve among her regular guests. She sent him some pages of a diary, begging him to comment on the style and content. As expected, Sainte-Beuve was very flattered, and read them immediately. Amongst this collection of gossipy anecdotes and commonplace maxims he came across a passage referring to himself. Princess Julie, in her somewhat scatter-brained way, had probably forgotten all about it. The passage was anything but complimentary. It mentioned his dissolute life (three mistresses, no religious beliefs, and "but one god—pleasure"), and claimed that he had left cards at her home in the hopes of being invited to her salon.

That Sainte-Beuve was enraged can be appreciated. He wrote an extremely sharp letter to Princess Julie, and then sent a copy of the offending remarks to Princess Mathilde. Mathilde, torn between family and friend, unhesitatingly chose the friend. Abandoning herself to what Sainte-Beuve used to call her "magnificent rages," Mathilde lashed out mercilessly against her cousin. In private letters to Sainte-Beuve, and in public to anyone who cared to listen, she poured a never-ending stream of vituperation onto the head of poor Julie. She was a hussy, a viper, a hypocrite, a liar; she was jealous of the intimacy between Sainte-Beuve and herself; a well-organized society, raged Mathilde, should be able to rid itself of so "vile a member." She would not rest until the story of Julie's infamous behavior had been spread throughout Paris.

The only sensible comment to emerge from this storm in a teacup came from the Emperor. "How could anyone be silly enough," he said laconically, "to write what they really think about people."

The contretemps tightened the bond between princess and critic considerably. She felt that she could now expect absolute loyalty from Sainte-Beuve, while he imagined that he could get complete understanding from her. They were both wrong. If one thing counted for more than friendship with Mathilde, it was Bonapartism; for Sainte-Beuve, independence of mind was always the prime consideration. Already she was beginning to find his views a little too radical; it was one thing to be liberal within the framework of the Empire; it was quite another to attack the Imperial regime itself. Things came to a head quite suddenly in January 1869.

Sainte-Beuve had written an article for the Emperor's mouthpiece, *Le Moniteur Universel,* in which he attacked a certain reactionary bishop. The article was refused. He then offered it to an opposition paper, *Le Temps.* He was welcomed, and his first piece appeared in *Le Temps* early in January. To Mathilde this was nothing less than treachery. Never one to mince matters, she drove straight over to Sainte-Beuve's house in the Rue de Montparnasse, and strode into his astonished presence. Giving vent, once again, to one of her "magnificent rages," she accused him of the very things of which he had been accused by her cousin Julie not long before. Trembling massively, she attacked him, "the vassal of the Emperor," for his desertion of the Bonaparte cause. With all the violence of a frustrated and disappointed woman, she hurled abuse at his round and balding head. "What are you, after all?" she screamed. "An impotent old man! . . . Let me tell you, I wish that you had died a year ago, so that you might at least have left me the memory of a man who was my friend." Unable to bear her wildcat fury a moment longer, Sainte-

Beuve escaped the room, leaving one of his companions to calm her down. They never saw each other again.

A few days later, in more sober mood, Mathilde wrote him a letter in which she made it clear that by offering his services to the opposition press, he had forfeited the right to her friendship once and for all. Any close association with Mathilde, be it sexual or platonic, meant complete identification with her interests. When Sainte-Beuve, who had given her almost everything else, had insisted on keeping his literary integrity, she had refused to compromise.

Disillusioned in both love and friendship (she and Nieuwerkerque finally parted that same year), Mathilde fell back on her worship of the First Emperor. Napoleon, in fact, was little less than a god to Mathilde. A blind admirer of his extraordinary character, she tried to model her own far more impetuous personality on his. To point to some trait in which she resembled him was the surest way to flatter her. The cane he had used at St. Helena was one of her dearest possessions; the bust by Canova had pride of place in her house in the Rue de Courcelles; often she would ask for the key to the Invalides and go and kneel beside his tomb. Once, when one of her men friends was paging through the Almanach de Gotha, counting the number of kings to whom she was related, Mathilde cut him short. "That is all very well," she said proudly, "but what does it amount to when compared with being Napoleon's niece?"

♛   ♛   ♛

In the year 1865 the Second Empire, already swaying in dangerously adverse winds, lost one of its stoutest supports. In March the Emperor's half brother, Auguste de Morny, died.

Ever since his return from Russia, where he had represented France at the coronation of the new Czar, Morny had done valuable service for the regime. As President of the Legislative Chamber, he managed this body (which, as the years went by, became less and less amenable) with all his customary skill. But he never allowed them to forget who was master. A contemporary asserts that "his amiability, his smiles, and his jests were, in reality, similar to those of a wild-beast tamer, whose *belles manières* are assumed to curry favor with the gallery, and who, in dealing with his beasts, neither forgets that he has a whip in his hand nor hesitates, when occasion arises, to use it." As much as Morny favored a strong hand at the helm, his experience in the Chamber convinced him that the Empire could only be saved by the granting of concessions. Always sensitive to the way the wind was blowing, Morny realized that if the regime was to endure, it would have to be liberalized. It would be better to introduce reforms now than to be forced into granting them later. In this he had the unequivocal support of Walewski and the somewhat less enthusiastic support of the Emperor. It was Eugenie and the reactionaries who were so bitterly opposed to these moves towards a Liberal Empire.

In the year 1862 Morny's services, both in the public of the Legislative Chamber and in the privacy of the Emperor's study, were rewarded by the title of duke.

A position of responsibility had made the Duke no less corrupt and pleasure-loving. His name was mentioned in connection with some shady financial speculation in the newly created Empire of Mexico, and the fortune which he won on the Bourse was remarkable even by Second Empire standards. As a *bon viveur* he had no equal. He was an inveterate gambler, a dedicated theater-goer, an enthusiastic playwright, a patron of writers and painters, and a lover of considerable reputation. Amongst the scores of women who contributed towards the achieving and upholding of this reputation was Hortense Schneider, the golden-haired actress who had created the role of *La Grande Duchesse de Gerolstein*. Renowned for her talents both on and off the stage, the voluptuous Hortense was usually referred to, quite simply, as Schneider. On one occasion when Morny felt the need for female company, he gave orders for Schneider to be brought to his rooms that evening. Schneider was fetched, ushered into a room filled with flowers and heady with perfume, and while waiting for the arrival of Morny, was offered a bath in the no less seductively scented bathroom. It was only when Morny himself, aglow with pleasurable anticipation, arrived on the scene, that the mistake was discovered. His servent had fetched M. Eugène Schneider, owner of the great iron and steel works of Le Creusot.

One would have imagined that so rakish a personality as Morny would have been immensely popular in Second Empire Paris, but this was not the case. There was an unnerving coldness in his glance; his hardness of heart was apparent in even his most relaxed and expansive moments. A contemporary, discussing whether or not Morny had a claim to his title of *grand seigneur*, remarked that if "a kind of quiet impertinence to some of one's fellow creatures, and a tacitly expressed contempt for nearly the whole of the rest, constitute a *grand seigneur*, then certainly Morny could have claimed the title." The opinion of

Lord Cowley, the British ambassador, is perhaps more fair. "He had it in him, if he had been honest, to be a very great man."

On the evening of March 9, 1865, the Emperor and the Empress were hastily called to Morny's bedside. Although still in his early fifties, the Duke, having lived life to the full, and having worn himself out in the process, was dying. When Napoleon and Eugenie arrived, he was delirious and unable to recognize them. The Emperor burst into tears, while the Empress fell to her knees in prayer. As neither of their reactions seemed to be doing much good, they withdrew to an adjoining room. When Morny regained consciousness and was told that his half brother was there, he asked to see him. For a few minutes Hortense's two sons spoke to each other in private, and then the Emperor, shaken with sobs, rejoined the Empress. At one the following morning the Archbishop of Paris administered extreme unction, and within a few hours, the Duke de Morny was dead.

His death threw his wife, the temperamental Princess Troubetskoi, into a paroxysm of grief. She seems not to have shown the same concern while he was still alive. "Madame de Morny behaved like a brute throughout his illness," reported the British ambassador, "and to the last had dinners and parties, to the great scandal of everybody." She now cut off her long fair hair and laid it in his coffin, and although he must have been the most inconstant of husbands and the most nonchalant of fathers, she continued to have a place laid for him at table. Caroline Murat, who visited the Duchess de Morny soon after her husband's death, found the beautiful creature sadly altered. And as Caroline can always be relied upon to provide some spiteful anecdote against the Empress—whatever the occasion—she tells how grieved the poor Duchess was at the "things which took place immediately after M. de Morny's death, when breath was scarcely gone from him." Protesting that she could not possibly "venture to disclose" what these things were, Caroline then proceeds to do exactly that. By order of the Empress ("a woman's hand") all the Duke de Morny's papers were seized and carried off to the Tuileries. In vain, according to Caroline, did the bereaved widow revolt against this outrage—"nothing was respected."

But Caroline had a blacker picture to paint than this. On the afternoon of Morny's death she visited the Empress at the Tuileries. As it was Shrove Tuesday and Morny's death had necessitated the canceling of the customary *bal masque*, Eugenie, "who thought only of fetes and amusements," was wondering how the court could be entertained instead. She decided to hold a council in her study—"the same study which a few hours before had been littered with all the private papers of M. de Morny, seized by order of the Empress." Surrounded by a few intimate friends, Eugenie set to pondering this important problem.

"Suddenly, in her natural exuberance of spirits, her Majesty had a quaint idea; doubtless some fancy, a memory of her Bohemian youth, passed through her brain. Sitting astride a chair and grasping its side bars as if they were the reins of a horse, she by her looks invited the others to do the same. Soon ladies and gentlemen alike mounted their wooden steeds, and a regular Shrove Tuesday cavalcade ensued, going round and round the large room after the Empress, to the accompaniment of the trumpeting and boisterous calls of the hunting field."

And that, says the ostensibly disgusted Caroline Murat, was how Shrove Tuesday, the day of the Duke de Morny's death, was celebrated at the Palace of the Tuileries.

The account has one very important flaw. Shrove Tuesday fell on February 28 that year. On that day the Duke de Morny, very much alive, had gone out for a drive. It was only on his return home from that outing that he had first become really ill. He did not die until ten days later, when the "Shrove Tuesday cavalcade," if ever it did take place (and it is not unlikely), was nothing more than a memory.

Morny was succeeded in the presidency of the Legislative Chamber by Walewski. But as Walewski had neither his predecessor's shrewdness nor his strength, he cut a very poor figure in the post. Although himself in favor of liberalizing the Empire, he found the Chamber, which was becoming yearly more critical of Napoleon's authoritarian regime, too much to handle. His urbanity and his integrity, although admirable, were not enough; after two years he resigned. A year later, in 1868, he died, at the age of fifty-eight. Born when his father's Empire had passed its peak, he died when his cousin's Empire was likewise waning.

Having lived during one of the most corrupt periods in French history, Walewski had led a remarkably honest life. Thirty years later, when his wife, the once lovely Marie-Anne de Ricci, spoke of her husband, she would remember these qualities of integrity and disinterestedness. And she would compare him with the Duke de Morny. "Morny!" she would snort, "they talk only of Morny! One would think there was but one man, one head, one character—always Morny! He worked the *coup d'état;* that is conceded. He was very successful with women, so they say, and I am willing to believe it. He was distinction itself; I do not question the fact. What I am sure of is that he left twelve million, carefully invested, to his children. Everything else—the things which did not belong to him, but to others, to France for instance—weighed about as much with him as a grain of tobacco; while, on the other hand Walewski went out of office with empty hands, concealing nothing in his portfolio."

        ☙   ☙   ☙

As the prestige of the Empire waned, as the Emperor grew yearly more flaccid and the Empress became increasingly unpopular, so did hopes center on the heir to the throne, the little Prince Imperial.

In 1866, the year of Sadowa, when the Empire suffered so terrible a diplomatic defeat at the hands of Prussia, he was ten years old. He seems, by all accounts, to have been a charming child. In spite of the somewhat artificial, almost theatrical atmosphere which had surrounded him from the very moment of his birth, he was growing up into quite an ordinary, unspoiled little boy. This was largely Eugenie's doing. As the Emperor was hopelessly indulgent with him (he could not bear to see him scolded, let alone chastised), she felt obliged to take a firmer line herself. Naturally ill at ease with children, and determined to make a man of him, strictness came more easily to her than tenderness. There were times, in fact, when she seemed almost too hard; people began to whisper that she cared nothing for him, that she loved him as the heir to the throne rather than as her own son. "There are three of us who love that child," said Princess Mathilde, referring to the Emperor, the Empress, and herself, "two of us with our hearts, *et la troisième avec son devoir.*"

Like so many things which were said about Eugenie, this was not quite fair. Surrounded as little Louis was by a host of fawning, flattering, applauding courtiers, and petted outrageously by the Emperor, Eugenie was almost compelled to be severe. He could so easily develop into an idle, arrogant, conceited little prince, accepting adulation as a matter of course. That he did not was due as much to his own innate good sense as to his mother's firm handling. Very much his father's son in these early days, he was naturally kindhearted and well mannered. His charm, like the Emperor's, was prodigious, and he never displayed a trace of bumptiousness. But he seemed, unfortunately, to have inherited some of his father's failings as well. He was dreamy and lacked the power of concentration; if a problem proved too difficult, he would evade it. When he tired of his lessons, he would ask to be allowed to draw, and as he asked so sweetly and drew so prettily, his tutor never had the heart to refuse him. Like his father, he always meant well, but the results sometimes fell short of the intentions.

In one, possibly the most important, respect he fulfilled the expectations of both his parents. He was a born soldier. Almost as soon as he could walk, he had been bundled into a uniform, and at eighteen months he had started riding lessons. At the age of three he had attended a review on his own pony, and he was not yet four when he had sat on the saddle-bow of the Emperor's horse, watching the victorious Army of Italy file by. The following year he accompanied his father to the great military camp at Châlons, and there, among the bluff-voiced, fiercely mustached veterans, he had felt thoroughly at home. "*A l'Armée!*" he had shrilled when asked to propose a toast one evening, and the company had been enchanted. Raised on tales of the *Grande Armée*, encouraged to look upon soldiering as the only worthwhile profession, surrounded all day by gorgeously uniformed troops, he was becoming yearly more conscious of the name he bore. It was a name of which he was inordinately proud. Once, at Biarritz, when the boat in which the Imperial party was returning after a day's excursion struck a rock and started to sink, Eugenie cried out, "Don't be frightened, Louis!"

"A Napoleon is never afraid," the little boy had answered magnificently.

If Louis was beginning to behave like a soldier, he did not yet look like one. He was small, pale, and inclined to be delicate. Nor was he attractive enough for Eugenie's taste. "It's so important to a nation," she sighed, "that the prince should be handsome." She seemed to have forgotten that her own marvelous beauty had not swayed her subjects. Louis, having outgrown his infant chubbiness, was becoming pasty-faced and heavy featured; people were saying (as they always will about royal children) that he was a permanent invalid—perhaps even simple-minded. To combat these rumors, it was essential that he show himself in public as often as possible. Normally this presented very little difficulty. Louis loved nothing better than to be seen astride his pony at military reviews or to drive through the streets of Paris, escorted by a troop of spahis in their billowing white robes. He was extremely popular with the Parisians; they called him "the little prince," and he, in turn, avowed time and again how much he loved them. During his tenth year, however, he caught measles, and being delicate, his recovery was slow. Then, while convalescent, he had a serious accident. He had been swinging on his trapeze in the park at Saint-Cloud when his feet had slipped and he had tumbled to the ground. Although he seemed to recover very quickly, the fall left him with a slight limp, and he complained of pain when he walked. A doctor was called in, and he was found to have an abscess on the hip. He would have to be operated on.

The operation was successful, but the recovery was slow. Louis was seen very little that summer. By autumn Paris was seething with rumors that Louis's operation had left him permanently crippled. It was therefore essential, at the State Opening of the Chambers in November 1867, that the Prince show himself in public. Louis was by now quite recovered from his illness and more than ready to play his part in the important ceremony. They dressed him that day in a black velvet suit and red silk stockings, with the Grand Order of the Legion of Honor aslant his little chest. At luncheon, however, he suddenly felt ill, and was obliged to hurry out of the room. He was followed, posthaste, by the Emperor and Empress, in the full magnificence of their state robes, by his English nurse, Miss Shaw, and his tutor, young Augustin Filon. Corvisart, the doctor, was sent for immediately. Pale and faint, little Louis lay in his mother's arms. When Dr. Corvisart arrived, Miss Shaw, in a state of acute anxiety, claimed that the boy had received a violent blow from one of his little friends the day before, and that it was all Dr. Corvisart's fault for allowing them to play so roughly.

"Is this true?" the Empress asked Filon, Louis's tutor.

The young man replied that on the contrary, he always found the boy's playmates very gentle, and that in his opinion the Prince was suffering from a bilious attack.

The Emperor, usually so calm, had lost his head completely. Displaying a temper which Filon never imagined he possessed, he was heaping reproaches on the poor doctor. At this Eugenie, always more sensible where their son was concerned, rounded on him.

"You are stupid!" she shouted. "You must make sure of your facts before getting angry. Miss Shaw is talking nonsense."

At that moment little Louis, above whose wan form all these frenizied words were flying, suddenly lunged forward, and the Empress was just in time to hold a basin under his head. That the boy was the heir to the Imperial throne of France, that his mother in her velvet and ermine and diamonds was the most beautiful sovereign in all the world, that the basin she held was decorated with crowned golden eagles, made not the slightest difference for the following few minutes. Louis was well and truly sick. Afterwards he felt better, and with a little brushing and rearranging, he was soon ready to accompany his parents to the Salle des États.

Throughout the ceremony young Filon stood behind the heavy curtain which backed the throne. He could not see the Imperial family as they sat in state, but he could hear the Emperor's voice as he addressed the assembly. It was calm, clear, and strong, and was listened to with an almost religious respect. The young tutor could not help smiling to himself as he remembered that not fifteen minutes ago the erect, elegant Empress had been shouting to this solemn, dignified Emperor: "You are stupid!"

There was one person whom Louis's gracious manners and unaffected charm did not win over, and that, of course, was Plon-Plon. The passing years had done nothing to soften Plon-Plon's attitude towards the little boy whom he always considered had robbed him of the throne. He called him "that poor little brat" to anyone who cared to listen, and was quite sure that the boy was an imbecile. His attitude towards Louis was clearly illustrated one evening at Compiègne. Plon-Plon found himself alone with the little Prince Imperial in the salon in which the Imperial princes assembled before dinner. Not having anything to say to each other, they moved forward to join the guests in another room. At the doorway Louis, from politeness and from fear of Plon-Plon, stood back to let him pass.

"Go on," said Plon-Plon impatiently.

At the next door the same thing happened. Again the little prince hung back, and again Plon-Plon, but even more gruffly this time, motioned him forward.

"Go on, then," he barked.

At the third door, the last before the salon in which the rest of the company was assembled, little Louis made yet another attempt to let his cousin pass first. With a thrust of his great hand, Plon-Plon sent the boy hurtling headlong through the doorway and into the room. Just managing to save himself from slithering full length along the floor, Louis gave the company an embarrassed look and hurried to his father's side.

Incidents like this, however, could be ignored. Everyone knew that Plon-Plon was ungracious and ill-tempered; his opinion did not make much difference one way or another. Little Louis, although he always showed great respect towards Plon-Plon, realized that he was not very highly regarded. "Papa," said the Prince to the Emperor one day, "what is the difference between an 'accident' and a 'misfortune'?" The Emperor considered this for a moment. "Well, Louis," he answered wryly, "if our cousin (Plon-Plon) were to fall into the Seine, it would be an 'accident.' If someone pulled him out, it would be a 'misfortune.' " With this definition in mind, it is unlikely that the Prince Imperial cared about Plon-Plon's antagonism so very much.

He was soon brought up against more serious opposition, however. It happened at the prize-giving for the *Concours général,* held at the Sorbonne. As part of the scheme for accustoming Louis to public appearances, it was decided that he would distribute the prizes to the pupils. Accompanied by his governor and his tutor, Louis came up to Paris from Fontainebleau for the ceremony. From the very moment of entering the hall, the two adults felt a chill in the air, but the Prince Imperial seemed blissfully unaware that anything was wrong. He was politely if not enthusiastically applauded, and for a while things went quite smoothly. His naif charm seemed to be having its usual effect. It was when he rose to present the second prize for Greek translation to a boy named Cavaignac that the trouble started. Young Cavaignac was the son of General Cavaignac, the Emperor's opponent in the presidential elections of 1848. A dedicated Republican, Cavaignac had never forgiven Napoleon III for the *coup d'état* of December 2, 1851. When young Cavaignac rose to go towards the happily smiling Prince, Madame Cavaignac motioned him to keep his seat. His refusal to receive his prize from the hands of Napoleon III's son was enthusiastically acclaimed by his classmates. "*Vive Cavaignac!*" they shouted, and here and there was heard the dreaded cry, "*Vive la République!*"

Louis behaved splendidly. It seemed, in fact, as though he had noticed nothing amiss. But in the train home his two companions noticed that he kept his head turned away from them. They realized that the Prince was in tears. For Louis, who until that afternoon had led so sheltered, so secure a life, the incident had been a moment of truth. When they arrived back at the palace, the Emperor and Empress were told about the day's events. "What can you expect?" asked Napoleon quietly. "Sooner or later Louis will have to face opposition." The atmosphere at dinner that night was very subdued. Louis's normally bright-blue eyes were cloudy, and the Emperor repeatedly stroked the back of his head. Eugenie seemed preoccupied. After dinner the company scattered through the salons and the gardens; everyone was tense, apprehensive.

Suddenly a strident laugh shattered the still night air. It was followed by another, and another, until the terrible sound could be heard in all the rooms of the great palace. The Empress was in hysterics.

A doctor came scurrying up to her apartment, but it was some time before he could quiet that bloodcurdling, maniacal laughter. . . .

♔ ♔ ♔

One had to be fairly perceptive to realize that it was the late afternoon and not the nooday sun which now suffused the Second Empire in such a golden glow. Things might be going from bad to worse for the Imperial regime, but judging from appearances, no one would have believed it. France had never seemed more brilliant, and Paris was the capital of the world. The city itself had undergone an almost miraculous transformation. The Emperor had had mile upon mile of squalid slum districts cleared and wide tree-lined boulevards cut through them. He had taken the precaution of having the surfaces of these avenues (wide enough to allow a detachment of cavalry to sweep through them) covered in bitumen in order to put an end to the tearing up of paving stones for barricade-building by the mob. Thus, by the last years of the Empire, Paris was a city of elegant boulevards, long vistas, and triumphal arches; it was the matchless city one knows today. "*L'auberge de l'Europe*," they called Paris in those days, and if it was indeed the inn of Europe, then never did an inn have a more hospitable host and hostess.

The regime might be threatened by a resurgence of Republicanism from within and by the growing might of Bismarck's Prussia from without, but Napoleon and Eugenie continued with their accustomed grace to entertain all the crowned, and half the uncrowned, heads of Europe. The Empire during these years was *en fête* from morning to night. The opening of the *Exposition Universelle* in 1867 saw the climax of this brilliant decade; the Imperial couple kept open house to all Europe that summer. Royalties flocked to Paris by the score; one could hardly move, they said, for kings. By day they drove through the streets in splendid processions to the exhibition buildings, by night they danced their feet off at the Tuileries. Napoleon, looking tired and uneasy (this show of magnificence was meant to fool others, not himself), chatted quietly in corners to visiting princes; Eugenie, looking more radiant with the arrival of each new sovereign, seemed intoxicated by the never-ending round of parties. The disastrous Mexican campaign, the shame of Sadowa, the threat of Prussia, the dissatisfaction within France itself, was all forgotten amidst the kaleidoscopic splendors of this great exhibition. Who could doubt that France was the grandest, the most powerful nation on the Continent, and that the Empire would last forever?

Disillusionment came before the end of the summer. It happened on the day that the exhibition awards were to be distributed. It was to be an occasion of great pomp, with the Emperor, the Empress, and the Prince Imperial driving in state to the Palais de l'Industrie. Little Louis was to distribute the prizes.

On the evening before the great day Napoleon received a telegram to say that his protégé Maximilian, the newly created Emperor of Mexico, had been shot by the rebellious Mexicans. The news was upsetting enough for him, but it almost drove Eugenie out of her mind. The Mexican Empire had been her idea—"*une très haute pensée politique et civilisatrice*"—and she felt that it was she who had killed Maximilian. She already knew that the Empress Carlota, Maximilian's wife, had been driven mad by the disasters in Mexico; this latest news came as a further terrible reproach.

In the meantime there was the distribution of awards at the Palais de l'Industrie. What was to be done about that? Characteristically, Napoleon decided to go through with it and to keep the announcement of the terrible news until afterwards. So the following day, in a magnificent glass coach, the Imperial family set forth from the Tuileries. The ceremony was all that it was meant to be: the Emperor spoke well, the Empress looked superb, the Prince Imperial was charming. But as the awards were about to be presented, Napoleon received another telegram confirming the news of Maximilian's death, and before the afternoon was over, the audience seemed to know about it as well. The Austrian ambassador was seen to slip away before the end of the proceedings, but it was not until she had returned to the Tuileries that Eugenie herself gave way. Although the ceremony had been saved, the regime was lost. Mexico, in the opinion of the Austrian ambassador, was the Moscow of the Second Empire.

The year 1869 marked the centenary of the great Napoleon's birth. This event, which should have afforded the Empire the opportunity of staging one of its glittering pageants, was celebrated in a surprisingly modest manner. The celebrations were limited, for the most part, to the island of Corsica, and as Napoleon III was too ill, and probably too dispirited, to attend, he sent Eugenie and the Prince Imperial to represent him. The journey made her conscious of her unpopularity as never before. At Toulon she heard whistling under the officially induced cheering, and on Corsica itself her reception was distinctly cool. She had imagined that her verve, her beauty, and her stylishness would have appealed to the showy, high-spirited Corsicans, and that she would move in an aura of admiration. But instead of being pelted with flowers as she had hoped, she had to content herself with official bouquets.

With the thirteen-year-old Prince it was a different story. The Corsicans adored him. "The wild popular enthusiasm . . . leaped and gleamed about him like a fire," says his tutor Filon, and wherever he went, the people crowded forward to see him. On the day that he visited the house of Carlo and Letizia—the house in which Napoleon and his brood of brothers and sisters had been born—the enthusiasm of the crowd was almost dangerous. When an attempt was made to keep them from surging into the house, the little prince turned round and shouted in his young, excited voice, "Oh! Let them come in, they're part of the family."

"No words," says Filon, "can describe the delirious joy of that mass of humanity, already vibrating with passion, on which that speech fell like a spark upon a heap of powder." With one long, delighted cry, the Corsicans hurled themselves on the flushed, bright-eyed youngster. "I don't know how he got out alive!" one of his aides afterwards exclaimed.

Eugenie's disappointing reception was somewhat compensated for later in the year when she went to Egypt to open the Suez Canal. With so many of the projects championed by the Empress turning to dust, here was one which had turned to gold. For many years, like a latter-day Isabella of Spain, Eugenie had encouraged *her* Columbus—her cousin Ferdinand de Lesseps—in his determination to cut a canal through the isthmus of Suez. When the Khedive had come to Paris to invite her to open the completed canal, she had accepted without hesitation. The duty was very much to her taste. She was an enthusiastic traveler, and the ceremony itself would have the sort of dramatic quality she adored. It was decided that she would visit Constantinople en route. Accompanied, amongst others, by Prince Joachim Murat, Lucien Murat's soldier son, Eugenie set off for Venice, from where she would embark on the imperial yacht, *l'Aigle*. In Venice she floated down the Grand Canal in a rose-colored sunset ("*cette ville du silence, ou tout semble glisser*," she wrote), and, less romantically, received a visit from King Victor Emmanuel II, father of Plon-Plon's wife, Clotilde. Eugenie loathed Victor Emmanuel, not only for his opposition to the Pope, but because of the embarrassing coarseness of his manner.

Once the party had embarked on *l'Aigle*, however, Eugenie was in her element. She was one of the very few passengers not to succumb to seasickness. "She told me," wrote one of her young maids of honor, "that had she been fortunate enough to have been born a man, she would certainly have been a sailor, that she was made to sail on for ever, that for her all the palaces in the world were not worth a boat's deck. . . ."

At Athens they were met by the King and Queen of Greece and taken on a tour of the Acropolis. Eugenie seems not to have been particularly impressed by the achievements of the ancient Greeks or the behavior of the modern; she had, she said, "been greatly disillusioned by its poverty, and the misery of its ruins."

Constantinople was quite another matter. As she stood on deck, with the dawn flushing the minarets, the cupolas and towers, she cried out in admiration. Here was the East of her dreams! She was housed in the magnificent Beylerbey Palace on the Bosporus ("I felt almost crushed by the splendor of it all," wrote one of her suite), and the next few days were a time of almost unreal brilliance. One evening she was rowed from the Sultan's palace in his purple and gold caique. "It was a glorious night," remembered one of her ladies, years later; "the Empress, reclining on a raised seat, was wearing a white dress embroidered with gold, and on her head, a wonderful tiara of diamonds. Her arms and neck sparkled with precious stones, and a long tulle veil enveloped her. She was ravishingly beautiful, as beautiful as the wonderful night; as we saw her approaching over the water, she might have been an apparition from another world. . . ."

While Eugenie was winning gasps of admiration in the East, Napoleon had been taking advantage of her absence to devote himself to his two latest projects—the granting of liberal reforms and his love affair with the Countess de Mercy-Argenteau. The Liberal Empire, so long talked about, was on the point of being inaugurated; although the Emperor referred to these reforms, rather grandiloquently, as "crowning the edifice" of his Empire, it was, in some ways, the last throw of a desperate gambler. Having been unable to beat the opposition, he had decided to join it, or rather, to get it to join him; this, he reckoned, would be the only way to make the throne safe for little Louis. The Constitution was revised, and the authoritarian Rouher, known as the Vice-Emperor, was dismissed and replaced by the younger, more liberal Emile Ollivier. A nationwide plebiscite resulted in over seven million votes in favor of the Liberal Empire; it was, in effect, a vote of confidence in the Emperor. The Republicans had sustained a crushing defeat, and things suddenly began to look quite rosy again.

The Countess de Mercy-Argenteau used to refer to herself as the Emperor's last love, and this is probably true. Although Napoleon was only sixty, he was already a decrepit old man. Ten years of political misfortune and half a dozen years of agonizing pain had worn him out; he now asked for nothing more than to be left to live in peace and quiet until the Prince Imperial was old enough to take over from him. The one thing he still craved, however, was sympathetic female company, and in these sunset years of the Second Empire he had his last fling. The Countess de Mercy-Argenteau was a golden-haired beauty with a somewhat exaggerated idea of her own importance; but the Emperor seemed to take a very real delight in her youth and vivacity. And it is from her self-congratulatory memoirs that one gets a last glimpse of Napoleon as Emperor. He had an air, she says, "that was at once majestic and kindly, but sometimes he seemed to be sick of everything, and tired." His voice was soothing, his eyes "irresistibly charming," his hands beautiful. But it was for the mildness of his manner that he was chiefly remarkable; "Gentleness was the distinguishing feature of his character."

The two of them—the dreamy, pain-racked Emperor and the golden, high-spirited Countess—used to meet in the sacristy of a disused chapel, which the Countess would reach by means of a secret underground passage. The room was very simply furnished with two armchairs, a sofa, a table, and a screen; there is no mention, in the Countess's memoirs, of a bed. "One thing, however, I wish to state," she writes emphatically. "It has been said very often that I was his last love. Without any misconceived pride, I may admit that this is true. But his mistress I have never been." Was this true? One does not know. The Emperor was old and ill, and one must not doubt the word of a lady.

Meanwhile, in Egypt, Eugenie was sailing up the Nile on a dahabeah, like a latter-day Cleopatra. Purposely closing her mind to all painful thoughts ("I would wish to put out of my memory everything in my life which has tarnished the bright colors of my illusions"), she gave herself over to the enjoyment of her exotic journey. She rode a white camel under the hot desert sun; she sat talking on deck under a star-spangled sky; she wandered, entranced, among the colossal statuary of Thebes, Luxor, and Karnak. She wanted to drench herself in light and warmth and space. Paris with its troubles seemed a million miles away. Her mounting unpopularity, her apprehensions about the introduction of the Liberal Empire, her fears about the growing menace of Prussia, were almost forgotten. "Here, far from men and things, there is an atmosphere of peace which does good to the soul, and I am apt to fancy that all is well because I know nothing."

On November 16 she opened the Suez Canal. The ceremony was probably the crowning moment of her life. She was never to forget that day. "There was a real Egyptian sky," she used to say, "a light of enchantment, a dreamlike resplendence. I was awaited by fifty vessels, all beflagged. . . . My yacht, *l'Aigle,* at once took the head of the procession, and the yachts of the Khedive, the Emperor Francis Joseph, the Prince Royal of Prussia, Prince Henry of the Netherlands, followed at less than a cable's length. The spectacle was so supremely magnificent, and proclaimed so loudly the greatness of the French regime, that I could contain myself no longer; I was exultant! That frightful nightmare I had brought way from Paris suddenly vanished, as at the touch of some magic ring. *And then, for the last time, I believed that a great future was in store for my son. . . .*"

CHAPTER FOURTEEN

♔ ♔ ♔

If Napoleon III was celebrated for the mildness of his temper, most of his male relations were notorious for the violence of theirs. The history of the Second Empire is peppered with accounts of their riotous escapades. In the early years of the reign it was the Prince of Canino (Lucien Bonaparte's eldest son, Charles, the ornithologist) who gave the most trouble. He was, according to his cousin Mathilde, "a bad son, a bad father, and a bad husband," while Viel Castel considered him "the most manifest blackguard it is possible to meet." Not only, says Viel Castel, was he dishonest, cowardly, and ungrateful, but he surrounded himself—as did so many of Napoleon III's relations—with "revolutionists of the most disreputable kind." He seemed to be in hot water almost every other week. On one occasion he even challenged old Marshal Vaillant, the Grand Marshal of the Palace, to a duel. It appears that the Marshal, knowing Canino to be a notorious windbag, had granted him an interview with the Emperor, and in order to discourage him from keeping it, had made it for half past six in the morning. Instead of turning up at that unholy hour himself, the hotheaded Canino sent his seconds. Vaillant graciously but firmly sent them back, and the Emperor, who for once found the behavior of one of his cousins amusing, allowed the business to go no further.

On another occasion a young man by the name of Rossi stalked up to Canino as he was leaving the Café d'Orsay, and calling him a scoundrel and an assassin, spat in his face. It seems that the violent young man was the son of Count Rossi, for whose assassination Canino was rumored to have been responsible. Canino promptly challenged young Rossi to a duel. When Nieuwerkerque, whom Canino had asked to act as one of his seconds, declined the doubtful honor, Canino's equally quick-tempered brother, Pierre Bonaparte, felt obliged to defend his brother's name by challenging Nieuwerkerque. . . . "These sons of Lucien Bonaparte," says Viel Castel apropos this merry-go-round of family duels, "are all veritable ruffians, whose bad reputation is fully deserved."

In the second year of the reign Canino's foolish behavior obliged the Emperor to issue a decree limiting the use of the Imperial livery. The decree was promptly nicknamed "Rachel's decree." It appears that Canino (who in common with Plon-Plon and Walewski, was enjoying the favors of the celebrated actress Rachel) had lent her his carriage and horses with the Imperial livery for a drive to Longchamp. Rachel had swept through the Empress's private passage in the Arc de Triomphe, and had been acclaimed with cries of *"Vive l'Impératrice!"* by the unsuspecting public. Eugenie was furious, Canino was forbidden to use the Imperial livery, and Rachel complained that it was "extremely disagreeable to be mistaken for the Empress."

When Canino died, no one seemed particularly sorry. The government newspapers, hard pressed to find something complimentary to say in the obituaries, concentrated on his ornithological achievements. Viel Castel was more frank. "Reeking with every vice, capable of any crime or act of ingratitude, a passionate gambler, and disordered roué, he was spurned by his wife and suspected by his children."

The Murats were no less troublesome. Fat Prince Lucien Murat, who had bustled over from America at the fall of Louis Philippe, had never forgotten that his mother and father, Caroline and Joachim Murat, had once reigned at Naples. And he was determined that no one else would forget it either. On the death of his elder brother in Tallahassee in 1847, Lucien Murat considered himself pretender to the Neapolitan throne. At the inauguration of the Second Empire he sported the livery and arms of Naples in the carriage procession to Saint-Cloud. Renowned for his extravagance, and for very little else (Napoleon paid his allowance directly to his more thrifty wife, the former Caroline Fraser), no one took Prince Murat's claims very seriously. Even his family was embarrassed by his pretensions. In 1861, however, after Garibaldi had driven Francis II from Naples, Prince Lucien Murat decided that his hour had struck. He published letters asserting his claim to the throne, traveled to Aix-les-Bains to confer with Cavour and attempted to form a Murat party in southern Italy. This political activity was promptly discouraged by the Emperor. Whatever mistakes Napoleon III made, he did not repeat the first Napoleon's supreme error of setting up his relations as kings. Brought to heel, Prince Lucien henceforth confined his doubtful talents to social, rather than political, activities. Even here he did not seem to shine. A famous Second Empire cocotte who once had dinner with him complained that he spent the entire evening telling her about how he had once almost drowned in a fish pond; Prince Lucien Murat, she afterwards pronounced, was a bore.

Another person who had the doubtful pleasure of dining with Prince Lucien was Henry Greville, the diarist. He once attended a banquet given for Prince and Princess Murat and their daughter Anna. In spite of the fact that the Murats were members of the civil family only, these "demi-semi Royals and Imperials" were treated as royal highnesses, and were met in the entrance hall by their hosts. The entire company rose as they entered the room. Prince Lucien, says Greville, was a "hideous, fat, vulgar-looking man with jolly, good-natured manners." His wife was a simple unaffected creature who spoke indifferent French and "Yankee English." Anna Murat, he admitted, was lovely.

Lucien's eldest son, Prince Joachim Murat, cut a rather better figure than his father. Very popular at the Tuileries, this dashing young officer was often chosen to accompany the Emperor or Empress on their journeys. "I am at a loss to understand the reason for this special mark of favor," grumbled Viel Castel when Napoleon once took Prince Joachim with him to meet the Czar, "a distinction which the young prince's merits certainly do not entitle him to." He was, according to Viel Castel, a pleasant enough young man, but without brains or education, and one who always managed to keep well clear of any war. "When our soldiers were dying like heroes before Sebastopol, he was shooting at his father-in-law's at Grosbois." He was married to the Princess de Wagram, "the most disagreeable little minx it is possible to meet."

His brother Achille seems to have been a somewhat more fiery personality. At the age of seventeen he became the lover of the notorious courtesan, Cora Pearl, and through his infatuation for her, became involved in a public scandal. It seems that a horse dealer had started an action against Cora Pearl for some money she owed him, and that the besotted young Achille had signed a certificate stating that the debt had already been settled. Ordinarily, the fake certificate, signed by a member of the Emperor's family, might have put an end to the business, but when it came to the notice of a journalist by the name of Henri Rochefort, the trouble started. Henri Rochefort, an ardent Republican and a merciless opponent of the Empire, was renowned for his scurrilous attacks on the Imperial family, and in this attempted fraud by young Achille, he saw the opportunity of striking yet another blow at the Emperor. His public criticism of Achille's behavior led, as he knew it would, to his being challenged to a duel by the excitable young prince. The duel took place in the riding school in the forest of St. Germain. Legend has it that as the duel was about to start, Cora Pearl threw her arms about the Prince's neck and cried, "Don't kill him. He is the only man I ever loved." The fight, in fact, ended in a victory for Achille after he had given Rochefort a slight wound in the thigh. Achille's sister Caroline, who had always to give her own, somewhat suspect version of a story, claims to have been told by one of the seconds that Rochefort had "received his wound where the toe of a boot is the more usual weapon." To allow the affair to blow over, Napoleon III bundled the impetuous Achille off to North Africa for a while.

Another of Achille's duels was with the Marquis de Gallifet. Gallifet was an extremely popular figure at the court, but it appears that Achille had taken exception to a letter in which Gallifet had written slightingly of a member of the Imperial family. Achille promptly challenged him to a duel, and the challenge was accepted. Young Jerome Patterson Bonaparte was one of Achille's seconds on this occasion. As Gallifet, besides being popular, was a very accomplished fencer, Achille hurriedly took some lessons from the famous swordsman, Espeletta. His family was naturally apprehensive about the outcome of the fight, and were immensely relieved to hear that Achille was safe and that it was Gallifet who had received the wound.

Every bit as embarrassing, but in a quite different way, was the Duke de Mouchy, who was married to Anna Murat. Unlike his swaggering brothers-in-law, the young Duke de Mouchy had a taste for soldiers rather than for soldiering. But as he was a member of the old noblesse of France, and as such, a golden addition to Napoleon's somewhat silver-plated court, the Emperor tended to overlook the Duke's bizarre private life. It was said that whenever the good-looking young man was picked up by the police for some particularly outrageous bit of behavior, he would ask to be taken to the Tuileries rather than the police station, and the Emperor would always order his release. There is a story, possibly apocryphal, that his marriage to Anna Murat was the result of one of these escapades. The Duke, having been arrested for diverting the soldiers at the Pepiniere Barracks by dancing naked for them, was taken as usual to the Tuileries. This time Napoleon III threatened him with a public scandal unless he married someone of his, the Emperor's, choosing. Mouchy somewhat ruefully agreed, and Eugénie had the satisfaction of seeing her favorite *dame d'honneur* allied to one of the noblest, if most decadent, dukes in France.

Marriage to the lovely Anna Murat seems to have made precious little difference to the Duke de Mouchy's way of life. He remained as effete, and as appreciative of masculine virility, as ever. When two masked burglars broke into his bedroom one night, he is reported to have shrieked, "Please don't touch me. I've got nothing. But I'll show you where all the Duchess's jewels are with pleasure if you'll promise not to hurt me." The burglars, delighted with this offer of cooperation, agreed. Having handed over all his wife's jewelry, the Duke offered the two men a drink, and they, touched by this second generous gesture, unmasked and took advantage of his hospitality.

"You've no idea, *mon cher*," breathed the excited young man to his friend the Marquis de Contades a day or two later, "what good-looking burglars they were!"

Throughout the Empire, Napoleon III was pestered by Count Léon, Napoleon I's son by Eléonore Dénuelle. Having forgiven him for that duel in London in 1840, Napoleon, on becoming Emperor, had granted him a pension. This, of course, proved hopelessly inadequate. Not only was the Emperor compelled to pay his debts on several occasions, but he was obliged to put up with his harebrained schemes for making money out of new road and rail systems as well. In 1857 Léon sued the Minister of Works for 500,000 francs, which he claimed was due to him for draft plans of the Northern Railway; somewhat wearily, Napoleon III admitted his claims and paid up. When Léon finally died at Pontoise in 1881, he seems, by all accounts, to have been quite mad.

Plon-Plon, of course, gave trouble more or less continuously. No one was safe from his ill-natured tongue. At one stage he made a vicious attack on the Bourbons, which was answered by a no less insulting defense by the Duke d'Aumale, son of the late King Louis Philippe. The Duke d'Aumale fully expected Plon-Plon to challenge him to a duel as a result of his outspokenness, but Plon-Plon failed to do so. Napoleon's ministers, appalled at Plon-Plon's cowardice in the face of Aumale's insults to the regime, implored the Emperor to jolt his cousin into taking action. But although Napoleon was extremely upset by the affair, he replied that it was for Plon-Plon to make up his own mind, that he had no advice to offer. Eugenie did not show the same restraint. "If my son were in Prince Napoleon's (Plon-Plon's) place," she declared at dinner one evening, "I would myself conduct him to the field of honor and place within his hands the sword or pistol which was to avenge the slur upon his name." And when next she saw Plon-Plon, she had something no less cutting to say to his face.

In 1863 Plon-Plon made a speech in the Senate in support of the insurgent Poles. As this constituted a public denouncement of Russia, the Emperor was obliged to issue an equally public reproof. This was followed by a private letter from Napoleon, begging Plon-Plon to curb his tongue and to try and help, instead of hinder, the regime. Things reached a climax, however, in 1865, when Napoleon sent Plon-Plon to Corsica to unveil a monument to Napelon I and his brothers. The Emperor was on a tour of Algeria at the time, and Eugénie was acting as Regent in Paris. Plon-Plon took the opportunity of the unveiling to deliver a violently revolutionary speech. He claimed that the mission of Napoleon I, and therefore of Napoleon III, was to use dictatorship as a means of emancipation. Napelon III *had* promised something rather like this in pre-Second Empire days, but thus far he had departed very little from autocratic rule; this, of course, was before the introduction of the Liberal Empire. Plon-Plon now demanded sweeping reforms. His latest outburst earned him another, much more severe public rebuke from the Emperor. In a letter published in *Le Moniteur*, Napoleon threatened a strict disciplining of his family if they persisted in "serving the foes of my government." Plon-Plon promptly resigned his post as Vice-President of the Council of State and President of the Commission for the Exhibition of 1867. He retired, in a huff, to Switzerland.

♔   ♔   ♔

It was left to Prince Pierre Bonaparte, Lucien Bonaparte's violent son, to create an incident which all but toppled the Imperial regime.

Pierre Bonaparte had mellowed not at all since the days when he had brawled and drunk and gambled his way across America, the land he had left after stabbing a dog. Ever since his arrival in France, in fact, Napoleon had been trying to keep this pugnacious cousin in order. Somehow or other, at the elections of 1848, Pierre had got himself elected as a deputy, but his behavior in the Assembly was so uncontrolled (on one occasion he flung himself bodily on a much older member) that Napoleon decided to get rid of him as quickly as possible. He procured him a commission in the Foreign Legion and packed him off to Algeria. Here his conduct was no less brutal, and after he had returned to France without leave, he was cashiered. Home again, Pierre began pestering the Emperor for loans, advances, and extra allowances; Napoleon usually paid, but he consistently refused to grant him the official post for which he was always nagging.

During the 1850's Pierre married, morganatically, Justine Ruffin, a humble milliner's assistant seventeen years his junior, The union, at a time when Napoleon III was trying desperately hard to make his embarrassing family more respectable, did nothing to endear Pierre to his cousin, and neither he nor his wife were received at court. The simple Justine bore her husband two children, Roland, born in 1858, and Jeanne, born in 1861. In 1867 Pierre and Justine were married a second time, in Belgium; the second ceremony established the rights of their two children in Belgium, but not, apparently, in France. Four years later Pierre (who was steadfast in his affections, if nothing else) married his wife for a third and positively last time. Justine could at last call herself a princess, and her children became known as Prince Roland and Princess Jeanne. It was in January 1870 that the quarrelsome Pierre committed the crime which rocked the shaky Empire to its foundations. A certain Parisian journalist, a contributor to *La Marseillaise* (the notoriously anti-dynastic paper of Henri Rochefort), claimed to have been insulted in an article written by Prince Pierre Bonaparte. The journalist challenged the Prince to a duel. The seconds who carried the challenge to Prince Pierre were two fellow journalists named Fonvielle and Victor Noir.

Until that day Victor Noir was a pale, young, little-known reporter whose real name was Yvan Salmon. By that evening his name was on everyone's lips. When the two men arrived at Prince Pierre's home bearing the challenge, Pierre immediately lost his temper. He refused the challenge, claiming that his challenger was a mere tool of Henri Rochefort, who, in his opinion, was the champion of "*la crapule.*" When the seconds insisted that they fulfill their mission, a scuffle broke out among the three men. Whether Victor Noir did, as Pierre afterwards claimed, strike him across the face with a cane, is not certain; what is clear is that Pierre drew his revolver and shot Noir in the chest. Noir staggered out of the room, closely followed by Fonvielle. Pierre's bullet had struck Noir's heart; within a few minutes he was dead.

The affair created an enormous furore. Prince Pierre was arrested that evening, and imprisoned in the Conciergerie. The Republicans promptly turned the unknown Victor Noir into a martyr. Over twenty thousand people braved the five flights of stairs up to the little room where his body lay in state, and on the day of his funeral over a hundred thousand people crowded the streets leading to the cemetery of Père-Lachaise. As the hearse moved slowly through the dense, sullen crowd, there were cries of "*Vengeance,*" "*Mort à Bonaparte,*" and "*Vive la République!*" By the time the bier reached the cemetery, the mob was in a dangerous mood, and it was thought necessary to send a regiment of hussars cantering through the streets as a warning. A revolution was very narrowly averted that winter's afternoon.

When Prince Pierre faced trial, he pleaded not guilty, claiming that he had fired in self-defense. It was his word against Fonvielle's. Fonvielle swore that Pierre had flown into one of his well-known rages and had fired at Noir without any warning; Pierre claimed that Noir had struck him across the face and that Fonvielle had drawn a revolver on him. Nothing was proved, and the Prince was acquitted of murder. He was sentenced, however, to pay compensation to Noir's parents. He fled the country, leaving the Emperor, who had made a point of having nothing to do with him all these years, to bear the full brunt of his recklessness.

Henri Rochefort, in the meantime, was having a field day. Were they living under the Bonapartes or the Borgias? he wanted to know. "I was foolish enough to believe that a Bonaparte could be anything but an assassin," he thundered. "I thought an honest duel was possible in this family where murder and ambush are traditional. We weep for our dear friend Victor Noir, murdered by the bandit Pierre Napoleon Bonaparte. For eighteen years France has been in the bloody hands of these cutthroats, who, not content with shooting down Republicans in the streets, lay traps for them and murder them indoors. People of France! have you not had enough?"

    ♛   ♛   ♛

In the summer of 1870 the Spanish throne, recently made vacant, was offered to Prince Leopold of Hohenzollern. Bismarck, who had been longing to go to war against France (a war with France was necessary to complete his unification of Germany), and knowing that a German king on the Spanish throne would infuriate the French, championed Prince Leopold's candidacy. As expected, the announcement brought a hysterical protest from the French, and Prince Leopold withdrew, not wishing to be the cause of a conflict between France and Prussia. This should have satisfied even the touchiest of nations, but not France—at least, not a certain section of the French cabinet. Napoleon himself, who wished for nothing more than to be left in peace to get the new Liberal Empire working and to cope with his constant pain, was more than grateful for this easy way out. He seems to have been the only person in France to realize how pitifully unprepared that nation was for a war against Prussia. It was therefore with the utmost relief that he exclaimed, "C'est la paix!" on hearing of Leopold's withdrawal.

But it was not to be. The more aggressive element in his cabinet, encouraged by the Empress, insisted on something more. Not content with the withdrawal alone, they wanted the Prussian king's promise that the candidacy would not be proposed again. Only thus, they cried, would the honor of France be saved; only thus would the stains of Mexico and Sadowa be wiped out. The French ambassador was instructed to wait upon King William of Prussia at Ems in order to get this guarantee. The ambassador saw King William, and the King, firmly but politely, refused to give any such promise. The ambassador, under instructions from Paris, tried again; this time the King refused to see him. When King William reported the matter to Bismarck, the latter was delighted. He published a shortened, and therefore more abrupt-sounding, version of the report—known to history as the Ems dispatch—and France, considering herself insulted, declared war. It was an act of supreme folly. No one, however, with the exception of the Emperor, seemed to think so; as for Eugenie and the fourteen-year-old Prince Imperial, they were both beside themselves with excitement.

War was declared on July 19. From then until the end of the month the court was in ferment. It was decided that the Emperor, ill and incompetent though he was, would take command of the Army, and that the young Prince Imperial would go with him. Eugenie would remain as Regent. Plon-Plon, who happened to be cruising off the coast of Norway at the time, was sent for, as were the two Murat princes, Joachim and Achille, and the young Jerome Patterson Bonaparte.

During this whirlwind of preparations, the Emperor alone remained calm. "We are beginning a long and difficult war, . . ." he said to the assembled Senators who had come to bring him good wishes; his solemn manner put a temporary damper on their enthusiasm. His cousin Mathilde came to see him the evening before he set off for the front. Taking in his gray complexion, his puffy eyelids, and his unsteady walk, she told him, in her blunt cousinly way, that he was in no fit state to take command of the Army. "You can't ride," she snapped. "How will you manage on the day of battle?" With a sad half-smile he accused her of exaggeration. "Look in the glass," she commanded. When he did, he had to admit, with a shrug, that he did not look too good.

Eugenie was not nearly so concerned with the state of his health. The fact that he was a Napoleon going off to war was far more important to her. She always denied the rumor that she had once shouted, "This is my war," but it was no secret that she considered waging a successful campaign, the only way to strengthen the dynasty. Besides this, she was looking forward to her Regency; this time she could play her role of Roman mother, and Empress, for all it was worth. July 28 the Emperor and his son left for Metz from the station in the park of Saint-Cloud. Napoleon, followed by a doctor with a bag full of paraphernalia to ease his sufferings, clambered aboard the train. Eugenie, holding back her tears, made the sign of the cross on little Louis's forehead, and the excited boy scrambled aboard. As the train started to pull out, there could be heard, above the shrill of the whistle and the hissing of the steam, the the sound of the Empress's voice shouting triumphantly to her son, "Louis, do your duty!"

He did, or at least he did as much of his duty as he was allowed to do. The campaign, which was meant to be so swift, so glorious, was a fiasco from the very start. When the Emperor arrived at Metz, he found everything in hopeless confusion; any chance of a lightning thrust into enemy territory was impossible. But as some show of strength had to be made, the French decided to attack the little German town of Saarbrücken. In overwhelming numbers they bore down on the small Prussian force and captured the town. Young Louis was almost delirious with excitement at the "victory"; in a telegram to the Empress, Napoleon wrote of their son's admirable coolness at his baptism of fire. The Prince had even picked up a spent bullet to keep as a souvenir. There were men so moved at Louis's calmness, the Emperor assured his wife, that they "shed tears." Eugenie foolishly allowed the telegram to be published; the reaction was not, as she hoped, a wave of admiration for the brave young prince, but a flood of derisive laughter. It was going to take far more than a few picturesque details of the Prince Imperial's doings on the battlefield to save the dynasty; what they needed were spectacular victories.

What they got was a series of humiliating defeats: Wissenbourg . . . Fröschwiller . . . Forbach . . . each battle was more disastrous than the last. Somebody had to take the blame, and who better than the Emperor himself? It was decided that he would hand over the supreme command to Marshal Bazaine—whose only qualification was that he happened not to have been beaten as yet; lest he prove an embarrassing encumbrance to the new commander-in-chief, the Emperor retired to the camp at Châlons. Marshal MacMahon was there, and perhaps Napoleon would be of some use to him. "To your charge I commit the last army of France," said the Emperor as he took leave of Marshal Bazaine. "Think of the Prince Imperial."

Then, with this same Prince Imperial—now a broken, bewildered little boy—by his side, the Emperor headed for Châlons. Traveling in great style, with an escort of lancers, a host of liveried servants, and a long line of baggage wagons, the tired old man went lurching along the dusty roads towards MacMahon's headquarters. When his pain was too great, he would clutch his son's hand; in this terrible nightmare through which Napoleon was now living, little Louis was his one comfort. At Châlons he found that he was of no more use than he had been at Metz.

The troops, in fact, were openly hostile; it might be better if he could get away altogether.

At this stage Plon-Plon moved into the forefront of affairs once more. Consumed with jealousy by the increasingly important role his archenemy, the Empress, was playing in Paris, Plon-Plon introduced a plan of his own. If adopted, it would strengthen the Emperor's position while effectively clipping Eugenie's wings. Displaying all the tactlessness for which he was renowned, Plon-Plon confronted the irresolute Emperor. What, exactly, he asked, was Napoleon doing at Châlons? He no longer commanded the Army, he no longer governed France; what *was* his position? The only possible course open was for him to return immediately to Paris and for MacMahon's army to concentrate their strength around the capital. To help popularize this move, he should appoint the well-loved General Trochu as Governor of Paris. It was the best possible plan in the circumstances, and the Emperor, encouraged by MacMahon and his officers, agreed to it. Trochu was despatched to Paris as Governor, and the Emperor made ready to follow.

When Eugenie heard the news, she was appalled. Ever since she had heard of the first disasters, she had been behaving with exemplary courage. Exclaiming heroically, if not quite sincerely, "The dynasty is lost, we must think only of France now," she had thrown herself into her Joan-of-Arc role with gusto. Never one to shirk responsibility, she now assumed far more than she was entitled to. This, she decided, would be her finest hour. She would set a shining example, and France, touched by the sight of this brave, lonely woman, would applaud her stand and throw its full weight behind her. By her strength would she atone for her husband's weakness. With a complete disregard for the limitations of her powers as Regent, she issued proclamations, dispatched imperiously worded telegrams, convoked the Chambers, dismissed Ollivier's liberal ministry and chose a new and tragically reactionary cabinet. She hardly slept, she hardly ate, she hardly bothered to change her clothes. "She is as firm as a rock," wrote one admirer. "The woman is an ancient Roman," said another.

Thus, when Eugenie heard that Napoleon was considering returning with MacMahon's army to Paris, she launched into one of her impassioned harangues. The Emperor return to Paris? It was impossible It would look like desertion! It would be an admission of defeat. Come what may, he must not be allowed to return. Her new War Minister was equally adamant that MacMahon's army should not fall back on the capital. He insisted that MacMahon march in an opposite direction and join forces with Bazaine. Bazaine had recently suffered a crushing defeat; it was up to MacMahon to go to his aid. Eugenie, in full agreement, wrote a letter of instruction to her husband. When Filon, the Prince Imperial's tutor, who was now acting as her devoted secretary, read the letter, he begged to be allowed to soften its tone; he wanted it to be merely a list of views of the various ministers. Surely the once-mighty Emperor of France should be allowed to make up his own mind?

"Do you think," answered Eugenie, "that I am not the first to feel how horrible his position is? But the message that you propose sending wouldn't stop him, and he is lost if we don't stop him."

So the letter was sent, and the Emperor Napoleon III received, at the hands of his wife, one of the cruelest blows of his life. He did not have the strength to ignore her instructions; Plon-Plon, who might have backed him up, had been sent off to try and get some help from his father-in-law, King Victor Emmanuel II. So, clambering into his gilded coach once more, with his son at his side and his magnificent Cent Guards riding ahead and behind, Napoleon drove northwards in the dust of MacMahon's army. Racked with pain, insulted by his troops, stared at impassively by the peasants along the road, he was driving towards the final disaster, and he knew it.

There was one thing that he could do, and that was to spare the Prince Imperial the final inevitable humiliation. Sick at heart, he extinguished the last flicker of light in all the blackness of his sufferings. Father and son parted company; the Prince, with three aides-de-camp and an escort of Cent Guards, rode off in the direction of Belgium, and the Emperor, surrounded by his surly troops, lurched on in the direction of Sedan.

Once MacMahon's army had entered the small fortified town of Sedan, the end was not long in coming. When the French were all safely in the town, the Prussians encircled it. On the morning of September 1 the Emperor, his limp mustache waxed and his pale face rouged, rode along the French line. For five hours he cantered up and down the low hills; twice he was forced to dismount in pain. That he was openly courting death was obvious; one of the men in his party was killed and three of them were wounded, but Napoleon was not destined to die at the head of his troops. At noon he returned to the town. Here everything was chaos. Shells rained ceaselessly into the town, flames quivered from the bomb-shattered buildings, men lay dying by the hundreds, there was no more ammunition, no more food . . . it was all a useless slaughter. Assuming once again, and for the last time in his life, supreme responsibility, he hoisted a white flag. The actual carrying out of this painful order was delegated to young Prince Achille Murat. Napoleon then dispatched a letter to the King of Prussia, offering to surrender his sword in token of defeat.

At dawn the following morning the Emperor drove out of Sedan to meet Bismarck at a nearby cottage. Some Zouaves cheered him as he passed the gates of the town, but farther on some of his men had less complimentary things to shout. After a short preliminary talk with Bismarck, Napoleon drove on to the Château de Bellevue for the signing of the surrender. Afterwards, King William of Prussia drove over to see him. He remained for twenty minutes. It was decided that Napoleon would be imprisoned at Wilhelmshöhe, near Cassel, until the end of the war. The choice of Wilhelmshöhe as his place of detention was a strange one, for in the days that it had been called Napoleonshöhe, it had been the palace of Napoleon I's brother, the frivolous Jérôme. Here, where Jérôme and Catherine had lived that butterfly life, his nephew was to drag out the long days of his captivity. He set out on the morning of September 3.

As the Imperial carriages swung down the long autumn-bright road towards Wilhelmshöhe, Bismarck turned to a companion. "There," he remarked cynically, "is a dynasty on its way out."

♚   ♚   ♚

But the dynasty was not quite on its way out. In Paris, Eugenie, unaware of the surrender of Sedan, was still hanging on for dear life. She had come at last, well and truly, into her own. So sure was she that she could manage Paris alone that she had cold-shouldered General Trochu—whom the Emperor had sent as Governor of the city. Rebuffed, he sought solace with the Republicans. She kept in constant touch with the ambassadors for Austria and Italy, but since the first French defeats their vague promises of aid had melted like snow before the sun. She organized a hospital on the terrace of the Tuileries, and passed, each day, like some proud but dolorous angel of mercy, between the beds. She sent heroic messages to the men in charge of the Prince Imperial. "Remember this: I could weep for my son dead or wounded, but a fugitive! I should never forgive you. It is therefore, to your honor as soldiers that I appeal. . . . We shall stand firm in Paris if we are besieged, and out of Paris, we shall hold out to the end. There can be no question of peace!"

What she meant by all this, the Prince's poor aides did not know.

Louis had been on the run ever since that first pathetic victory at Saar-brücken; it was a bit late to talk of making stands and of duties "more urgent than security." The Prince's party galloped on towards Belgium, and MacMahon's army stumbled on into Sedan.

For all Eugenie's dauntless stand, the truth was that no one seemed to be taking the slightest notice of her. She was like some great tragedienne, playing to an empty house. Her frequently repeated vows that she would never "desert her post," her ideas for rallying the populace by showing herself on horseback, her nights without sleep and her days without food did not alter the situation in the least. She was magnificent, but she was expendable, though she never for a second suspected it.

It was on the afternoon of September 3 that she received the news of Sedan. It was given to her, not without considerable trepidation, by the Minister of the Interior. His apprehensions were more than justified. When Eugenie realized that her husband had surrendered to the enemy, her fury knew no bounds. Augustin Filon and Charles Conti (the Emperor's *Chef-de-cabinet*) were sitting dolefully in the Empress's study when Eugenie suddenly appeared at the head of the little winding staircase connecting the Emperor's apartments with her own. One look at her face told them that she, like them, had heard of the surrender. Her skin was paper white, her eyes were diamond sharp, her features were hideously distorted. In that voice which could be so hatefully strident, she screamed at the two hurriedly advancing men.

"Do you know what they are saying? That the Emperor has surrendered, that he has capitulated! You surely don't believe this infamous thing?"

Stunned by her vehemence, the two men kept silent. With increased, almost threatening, anger, she repeated the question.

"You don't believe it?"

The terrified Conti stammered out something about there being circumstances in which even the bravest . . .

But she cut him short. For five terrible minutes she stood there at the head of the stairs, pouring out such a torrent of abuse against her husband that the men could not bear to listen. It seemed that she would never stop her raving. Poor Filon was so shocked, so nearly paralyzed, by the things she was saying that it was the terrible sound of her words rather than their meaning that he afterwards remembered. And what he did remember, he tried his best to forget. "What she said then, Conti never repeated to anyone," he wrote years later, "and I shall die, like him, without repeating it."

Having had her say, Eugenie turned round and swept down the staircase. "We remained speechless and stunned," says Filon, "like men who have come through an earthquake."

By the following morning—the fateful fourth of September—all Paris knew about Sedan. From early morning the crowds were out in the streets. It was Sunday, it was as warm as midsummer; what better day for a revolution? Eugenie heard Mass at seven-thirty that morning. Exhausted from lack of sleep and from her outburst the day before, she seemed strangely calm; her one thought was still to remain at her post, come what may. Over half a century before, in this very palace, the Empress Marie Louise, timid, tearful, and bewildered, had allowed herself to be bundled into a carriage and driven away; when someone suggested to Eugenie that she too leave Paris and transfer the government to some other city, she answered that she would not budge an inch. When it was proposed that she abdicate in favor of a Council of Regency, she refused to discuss the idea. "The sovereignty does not belong to me. I will not abdicate."

By now the crowds were beginning to swarm round the Tuileries gardens; confident that the *déchéance* would soon be announced, the Imperial eagles were already being hauled down. At noon a delegation arrived from the Corps Legislatif to ask Eugenie to abdicate; she refused, but promised to abide by any decision her Cabinet made. Two hours later she heard that the crowd had broken into the Corps Legislatif and that the Tuileries would be invaded at any moment. In the meantime, unbeknown to the Empress, an excited mob was streaming towards the Hôtel de Ville to proclaim a Republic. Towards four o'clock the railings along the Place de la Concorde gave way and the crowd poured into the private garden. What was to be done? From the very first she had given instructions that no shots were to be fired in her defense. The alternative was to face the mob. "I had no fear of death," she afterwards said. "All I dreaded was falling into the hands of viragos, who would defile my last scene with something shameful or grotesque, who would try to dishonor me as they murdered me. I fancied them lifting my skirts, I heard ferocious laughter. . . ."

And so, urged by her friends, she fled the palace. Escorted by the ambassadors for Austria and Italy, and accompanied by her reader, Madame Lebreton, she made her way down the great staircase towards her carriage. But the crowd were already clamoring at the courtyard gates; it would be impossible to get out that way. They decided to climb back up the staircase and make their escape through the Louvre. The door was locked. As they stood in agonized confusion, they could hear the sealike roar of the crowd around the palace. Then someone arrived with a master key, and they hurried on. Passing through galleries, down flights of stairs, along halls filled with Greek and Egyptian statuary, the little party arrived at the entrance to the Place St. Germain-les-Auxerrois. The mob had reached it before them. Cries of *"Vive la République!"* and *"A bas l'Espagnole!"* filled the air. The fugitives stood rooted in the doorway. But the crowd surged past, and for a moment the square was almost deserted. Ignoring the pleas of the others to wait a little longer, Eugenie stepped out into the sunshine. Someone hailed a passing fiacre, but as Eugenie was about to scramble into it, an urchin recognized her and shouted her name. Before he could summon the crowd, however, the cab, containing the Empress and Madame Lebreton, had disappeared towards the Rue de Rivoli.

As they drove along, the cab bobbing like a cork on the river of excited people, Eugenie noticed the bees and eagles being torn down from shop fronts. "Already," she said, with a shrug, to Madame Lebreton. The first two houses in which the women sought refuge were closed; at the third, someone was at home. It belonged to the Empress's dentist, an American named Evans, and it was he who sheltered her and escorted her to Deauville the following day. Heavily veiled, and proceeding with more caution than was really necessary (France had lost interest in her by now), Eugenie made her way to the coast. Here Dr. Evans arranged for her to be taken aboard the yacht of a visiting Englishman, Sir John Burgoyne, and that night the two women sailed for England. The crossing was terrible; Madame Lebreton spent most of the night on her knees in prayer, but Eugenie bore up bravely. In fact, as in most of the crises in her life, she was almost enjoying herself. She arrived in England on the morning of September 7, 1870.

Although Eugenie did not yet accept it, the Second Empire had fallen.

PART FIVE

The Years After

1870–1920

CHAPTER FIFTEEN

♔   ♔   ♔

FOR the third time that century the Bonapartes were scattered pell-mell across the face of Europe. As after the Great Napoleon's first abdication, and again, after Waterloo, the family now saved what they could from the wreckage and got out of France as quickly as possible. Whereas Italy had been the place of refuge for the majority of the Bonapartes after the First Empire, it was to England that most of them fled after the Second. "London for the time being has turned into Paris," wrote Caroline Murat. "On every side a chatter of French was heard. The Faubourg St. Germain and the Faubourg St. Honoré, the old and the new aristocracy of Paris, filled London. There was not a house from end to end of Clarges Street and Half-Moon Street without familiar faces."

The Emperor himself, accompanied by Prince Achille Murat (Prince Joachim Murat was to join them later), arrived at Wilhelmshöhe on September 5. The day before, on the station platform at Libramont, he had chatted with his dissolute cousin Pierre Bonaparte, who had been living in Belgium ever since the Victor Noir incident. It was that same night that Louis-Napoleon heard of the overthrow of the Empire and the flight of the Empress; it was not until after his arrival at Wilhelmshöhe that he learned that she and the Prince Imperial had been safely reunited in England.

On the first day of his captivity the Emperor told young Achille Murat that he had once visited Wilhelmshöhe fifty-seven years before, when it had been the pleasure pavilion of his uncle Jérôme, and he wondered whether its present owner had left "some souvenirs of the past." They were strolling slowly through the great rooms, the Emperor seeming almost indifferent to their surroundings, when suddenly he stopped short. On the wall hung a portrait of a young woman in all the seductive grace of her First Empire clothes. She was his mother, Queen Hortense. Deeply moved, he motioned his companions away, and remained for almost an hour, standing alone in front of the painting. When he reappeared, he seemed, according to an eyewitness, "comforted, encouraged, resigned, calm and strong." Napoleon III had loved his mother very dearly; perhaps, with his strong streak of mysticism, he really had drawn comfort from this unexpected sight of her portrait.

317

Throughout the captivity, which was to last for six months, the Emperor was treated with the utmost respect. The King of Prussia had given instructions that Napoleon's captor, General Monts, had to be "very attentive to all the Emperor's legitimate wishes," and that the public attitude towards the Emperor was to be "decorous." The Queen of Prussia herself sent cooks from the palace at Berlin and made sure that none of the servants with whom the Emperor came in contact were German. The French were allowed any books or papers that they wanted, and were given permission to attend the theater at Cassel. The only one to take advantage of these visits to the theater was, of course, Prince Achille Murat.

If the Germans were proving to be very gentlemanly captors, Louis-Napoleon was proving to be a no less gentlemanly prisoner. Never had a captive given less trouble. "His whole attitude is characterized by a certain lassitude," noted General Monts, "which only disappears when he is talking about things which particularly interest him, such as the Empress's and the Prince Imperial's health. He then looked almost captivating."

For the first two weeks of his captivity, however, he was in complete ignorance about the state of the Empress's health; he had received no word from her. He must sometimes have wondered whether his capitulation had permanently estranged her. Her first letters came as a great relief. She had, it seems, written earlier, but the letters had been delayed. Forgiving her for her extremely highhanded treatment of him during the days before Sedan, he now answered her in his usually good-natured vein. Although neither admitted that their exile might be permanent (they were both involved in schemes for restoring the dynasty, and Eugénie still regarded herself as Regent), they did suggest possible places in which they might live when the war was over. The Emperor thought of Arenenberg, the villa of Lake Constance in which he had grown up; Eugénie mentioned Trieste, but that probably smacked a little too much of the aftermath of the First Empire. Napoleon, an expert in matters of exile, claimed that people like themselves were far better off in "free" countries such as Switzerland or England. "So when I am free," he wrote somewhat whimsically, "I should like to go to England, and live with you and Louis in a little cottage with bow windows and creeper."

Towards the end of October, Eugénie suddenly arrived to spend a few days at Wilhelmshöhe. Her first sight of her husband was disconcerting; he seemed so cool, so disapproving almost; but as soon as they were alone, he became his old affectionate self. As usual she poured out her news with great emphasis and at considerable length, while he listened, twirling the ends of his mustache and mumbling an occasional comment. "All her manner," noted General Monts, "convinced me that she had always known how to impose her views on her husband's policy. She spoke little to me, more to the Emperor, and displayed throughout great assurance in her observations. I derived the absolute impression that she was accustomed, not only to make herself listened to, but to have the last word. . . ." The General had to admit, though, that she was not quite the impulsive, unintelligent creature he had always imagined she would be.

Eugenie remained at Wilhelmshöhe for two days only; by early November she was back in England.

The house in which Eugenie and the Prince Imperial had settled was not the cottage of the Emperor's dreams, but a three-storied red brick mansion standing in a sizable park. Called Camden Place, it was situated in the village of Chislehurst, not far from London. As the house was inexpensive, secluded, and had a Catholic church nearby, it suited the Empress very well. By a strange coincidence the Emperor, when a young man, had visited Camden Place; it had been owned by people named Rowles in the 1830's and the daughter of the house, Emily Rowles, had been one of the dozens of women with whom Napoleon had imagined himself to be in love. The present owner, a Mr. Strode, had once been the trustee of one of Napoleon's mistresses. It is unlikely that any of these piquant details were known to Eugenie at the time she leased the house.

Set above the main entrance of the house was a clock, and over it, a motto cut into the light-colored stone: *Malo mori quam feoderi.*

"It might be my own!" exclaimed the Empress on first seeing it, while the Prince Imperial, less certain of his Latin, asked his mother's maid of honor, the young Marie de Larminat, how she would translate it.

"Well," she replied, "Death rather than desertion."

"Ah, that's fine," answered the fourteen-year-old Prince, "that is the kind of Latin I like."

It was not long before a small court had formed round the exiled sovereign. Amongst the faithfuls who had followed her from the Tuileries were the Prince's tutor Augustin Filon, the Emperor's physician, Dr. Conneau, and Marie de Larminat, her maid of honor. Conspicuous by their absence were any members of the Bonaparte family; they had found Eugenie trying enough when she had half a dozen palaces in which to spread herself. They were not going to risk being cooped up with her in a modest country house.

♚   ♚   ♚

When Plon-Plon, who had been in Italy at the time of Sedan, heard of the Emperor's surrender, he promptly offered to share his cousin's captivity. Napoleon very wisely declined the impulsive offer. Instead of going to Wilhelmshöhe, Plon-Plon went to England. He took with him, not his wife, the saintly Clotilde, but his mistress, the worldly Cora Pearl. His liaison with the outrageous cocotte was of some six- or seven-years' standing, and there had never been any attempt to keep it discreet. Cora had often spent the night in a room adjoining the apartments of Princess Clotilde's lady in waiting at the Palais Royal, and she had frequently dined in Clotilde's own dining room. Sometimes, during these meals, she could hear Princess Clotilde chatting to her children in the next room; this, said Cora a little testily, always embarrassed her.

In London the lovers rented a furnished house, but Cora found Plon-Plon sadly changed since the days of the Empire. Often surly before, he was now permanently steeped in melancholy, and none of her old extravagances or vulgarities seemed to amuse him. Yet she alone, of all his many acquaintances, found something good to say about him. He was so kind, so unpretentious; he liked to put his feet up on a chair; he hated tight waistcoats; he would sometimes buy himself a roll in a modest baker's shop and eat it in the street as he strolled along. . . .

Such vignettes, however much they might melt the heart of Cora Pearl, were lost on Eugenie. When Plon-Plon visited her at Camden Place, there was a row before the afternoon was out. The Empire's last ministry (chosen by Eugenie) had been *crétins*, claimed Plon-Plon, in his maddeningly self-righteous way. Eugenie, no less self-righteous, rose to the bait. If Plon-Plon had been in Paris on September 4, she said icily, he would doubtless have given them all the benefit of his good advice. But, as was usual in times of danger, he had been noticeably absent. Upon which Plon-Plon for the first, but by no means for the last time, left Camden Place in a huff. Eugenie issued a public statement about Plon-Plon's behavior. All this did was to earn her an equally public rebuke from the *Morning Post,* and a sage piece of advice about not forcing the "squabbles of a divided house" on the attention of British readers.

After a few weeks in London, Plon-Plon and Cora packed up and moved to Switzerland. Eugenie must have been glad to see them go.

Alone amongst the Bonapartes, Plon-Plon's wife, Clotilde, had left Paris unhurriedly and in great style. Having been brought up at a court, she was determined to leave Paris as a princess. With her three children, Victor, Louis, and Laetitia beside her, she drove through the wide-flung gates of the Palais Royal as though she were off to some official ceremony. Drawn by four horses and escorted by outriders, her barouche bowled down the Rue de Rivoli to the Gare de Lyon. Someone in the crowd, recognizing her, ran forward shouting, "The Chamber has been dissolved—the dethronement has been proclaimed!" but the carriage rolled serenely on. At the Gare de Lyon she caught the train for Italy; the demure Clotilde was on her way to join her loutish father, King Victor Emmanuel II.

Her sister-in-law, Princess Mathilde, was in Belgium. After September 4 she, too, had fled for England. At Dieppe, however, as her trunks were being loaded onto the packet, an angry crowd surged forward, claiming that she was absconding with valuable state property, including the crown jewels. Only the intervention of the mayor convinced them that she was not, and although her belongings were safely loaded, she herself was refused passage. The officers were too afraid of reprisals. Tired and disillusioned, Mathilde set up temporary house at Mons. Here, in a drab little villa, she had ample opportunity to take stock of the situation. "In spite of all the marks of affection and devotion that I received, and which I hardly had the right to expect, I am horribly sad, and my heart is broken," she wrote to her niece Caroline Murat. "I remain here, not knowing where to go, and not wishing to leave; besides I really do not care. Everything is indifferent to me, and I feel so overwhelmed in every way that I have not the courage nor the desire to form any plan." She blamed the *débâcle* almost entirely on Eugenie. "She, and she alone, has been the cause of all our misfortunes," she wrote bitterly. The Empress, whom everyone considered so virtuous merely because she had never taken a lover, had ruined both the Emperor and France. In the eighteen years of the reign she had worn out her husband by her arrogance, and her country by her extravagance and her lack of perception. . . .

Yet when Eugenie wrote to Mathilde a few days after arriving in England, the sincerity of her letter should have touched Mathilde's heart; Eugenie was so obviously distressed. Mathilde, like Plon-Plon, had offered to share Napoleon's captivity, and the Emperor had asked Eugenie to dissuade her from this generous impulse. She did so with consummate tact.

Like the majority of the family in these bewildering days, when the war was still raging and the future was so uncertain, Mathilde had high hopes of an Imperial restoration. Surely Bismarck would not want to treat with a republic? Surely the French, who only a year before had given Napoleon such a resounding victory in his nationwide plebiscite, had not changed their minds? The Emperor himself felt sure that if the people were consulted, he would be recalled to the throne. The cousins exchanged letters on the subject; they found that they were in complete agreement. What they could not realize was that whatever they discussed and agreed on was not of the slightest interest to France any more. The French had washed their hands of the Bonapartes once and for all.

At the end of the war in 1871, when the Emperor had been released from Wilhelmshöhe and passed through Belgium on his way to join Eugenie in England, he was met at the frontier by Mathilde and one of his old loves, the Countess Walewska. At the sight of her cousin, Mathilde burst into tears and flung herself into his arms. Her emotional behavior irritated the Emperor. He had much preferred the proud, statuesque, sharp-tongued Mathilde to this weak, weeping creature; but by displaying the utmost coolness himself, he managed to calm her a little. They stood together on the wintry station platform, a recently dethroned Emperor exchanging platitudes with the woman who might have been his Empress. Almost forty years had passed since the days when they had strolled hand in hand under the summer trees at Arenenberg. She had been so bright, so mercurial, in those days; he, so eager, so ambitious. Now they were an aging disenchanted couple, standing in the wind on a strange station platform. Unknown to either of them, this was to be their last meeting.

Although Mathilde had by now moved from Mons to Brussels, she still seemed to be leading a meaningless life. Her heart was in Paris, and she knew that she would never be happy until she could go back. She had never realized until now how French she really was. She bombarded her friends with letters, anxious to know how soon they thought she could return to Paris. They advised her to wait; defeat was still too bitter to the French for them to welcome home a member of the family whom they held responsible for all their sufferings and humiliations. Then, in March 1871, soon after peace had been signed between France and Prussia, civil war broke out in the capital. For two months bloody battle raged between the Paris Commune and the new French government, installed at Versailles. The Vêndome column, crowned by the statue of the Great Napoleon, was brought crashing to the ground, and the palace of the Tuileries, twice the home of Napoleon's dynasty, was set afire. It blazed for three days. The insurrection was not put down until the end of May. Three weeks later Mathilde arrived back home; as she walked through the silent streets towards her old house (there were no cabs to be found), her beloved Paris must have seemed little more than a mass of rubble.

The Murats, who had lived in America before the Empire, were obliged to fly to England as well. Fat Prince Lucien Murat and his devoted wife, Caroline, set up house in London; with them was their daughter, the acidulous Caroline Murat—now Baroness de Chassiron—and her little son Guy. Anna Murat—now the Duchess de Mouchy—was at Chislehurst with the Empress. "Send your maid with all I need. I have not even a pocket handkerchief," the Empress had wired to Anna on her arrival in England. The eldest Murat boys, Joachim and Achille, were with the Emperor at Wilhelmshöhe; the youngest son, eighteen-year-old Louis Murat, reached France from Mauritius only after the fall of the Empire, and had also come on to England.

Young Jerome Patterson Bonaparte had been stationed near Paris during the war, and no sooner had the dynasty fallen than the new regiment to which he had been assigned refused to serve under a Bonaparte. With a firmness that would have gladdened the heart of his grandmother, Betsey Patterson, he threatened to shoot any man who refused to fight. His show of strength worked, and his men served him loyally for the remainder of the campaign. He was in Paris throughout the siege, eating hard black bread and sewer rats with the best of them; the rats, he assured his squealing girl cousins after the war, were "far more delicate than young chickens." When peace was signed in 1871, young Jerome, not wishing to serve the Republic, resigned his commission and joined his relations in England. He remained there for a few weeks only, and then returned to America.

The majority of the Lucien Bonapartes, always rather more of an Italian than a French family, went to Italy. Rome, after the fall of the Second Empire, was as full of minor Bonapartes as it had been full of major ones after the First Empire. Caninos, Gabriellis, Primolis and Roccagiovines, all bearing the unmistakable Bonaparte stamp, settled down in the Italian sunshine to await events. Two exceptions were Lucien

Bonaparte's sons, Prince Louis-Lucien and Prince Pierre. Prince Louis-Lucien had been living in London, quietly and decorously, for many years, devoting himself to a life of study. He was now joined by Pierre, who, in order fully to legitimize his two children, had just married his wife, Justine, for the third time. The fall of the Empire had affected the financial status of both brothers rather drastically. Louis-Lucien solved it by hard work. Pierre alleviated it by sending his wife out to work.

♛   ♛   ♛

On March 20, 1871, the Emperor, released from Wilhelmshöhe, arrived at Camden Place. Eugenie and the Prince Imperial had gone to Dover to meet him. On their way back, as the reunited Imperial family was passing through a narrow corridor leading to Dover station, there occurred an incident of almost overwhelming significance and poignancy. The defeated Emperor, about to begin his exile, came suddenly face to face with some members of the Orléans family, about to end theirs. It was his reign that had prolonged their exile; now that he had fallen, they were able to return to France. For a few seconds the two opposing groups of royalties stood rooted to the ground in embarrassed silence. It was Eugenie who made the first move. Always a Legitimist, and with her strong sense of occasion, she moved slowly to one side, and then dropped one of her magnificent curtsys. She straightened, and followed by the Emperor and her son, swept on without a word.

The gates through which Napoleon III drove into the park of Camden Place had once been the entrance gates of the *Exposition Universelle* in Paris in 1867; Mr. Strode, the owner of Camden Place, had bought them and re-erected them here. Four years ago the Emperor had driven through them in triumph to open his great exhibition; now he passed through them into exile. Nor, of course, was the house new to him. "I used to be here frequently in former years," he would say, remembering Miss Rowles, the English girl who might have been his Empress. Another link with this happier past was in the form of a little circular building which his fellow exiles had discovered half-buried in a hollow at the back of the house; it was an exact copy of a monument which had once crowned a hilltop at Saint-Cloud. "It struck," thought one of his companions sadly, "an incongruous note under the misty sky and the unceasing rain in the melancholy sadness of that drab country."

The ease with which the Emperor settled into exile amazed his companions. Renowned for his generosity, his charm, and his patience during the good years, the years of exile revealed him to be no less amiable. Life at Camden Place, Chislehurst, after the fall of the Second Empire was a far cry from Longwood, St. Helena, after the First. At no time, in fact, were the differences between Napoleon III and his uncle, the Great Napoleon, more apparent than during their respective exiles. The circumstances of these exiles were, of course, rather dissimilar: Napoleon I was a prisoner and housed in some discomfort; his nephew was a deposed monarch living in modest state. But it is almost certain that had their roles been reversed; and Napoleon I been imprisoned (as he had hoped) in some English country mansion, and Napoleon III exiled to Longwood, their respective behavior would have been almost exactly the same. The Great Emperor would have skulked about Camden Place, raging against his generals, making life unbearable for his companions, cursing the weather; Napoleon III would have accepted Longwood with that sublime resignation and have settled down to writing a paper on the growing of flax. Napoleon I at St. Helena was troublesome, truculent, selfish, unforgiving, unbelievably demanding; he blamed his misfortunes on everyone but himself, he expended almost every ounce of spare energy on making complaints, he crushed the long-suffering spirits of his companions one by one. . . . Where exile brought to the surface all the smallness of his highly complex character, it revealed all the nobility of his nephew's less brilliant mind. Napoleon III's philosophical acceptance of his misfortune was something to marvel at. He never complained. Never a word against those who had dragged him into the war against Prussia; against those who had misled him as to the state of unpreparedness of the Army; against those (Eugenie chief amongst them) who had forbidden him to return to Paris after the first defeats; against those who had deserted the Empire in its greatest hour of need; against those who had since heaped insult after unbelievable insult on the fallen dynasty. Nor did he complain about little things: about the food or the weather or the boredom or the same sad faces. His control, his courage, his kindness, were an example to them all. "The Emperor was like an oak tree, round which everybody gathered, listening to wise words," wrote one of the exiles after his death.

One day the Empress was going through a box of papers recently arrived from Paris. It contained private letters belonging to the Imperial family, which had somehow escaped the prying eyes of the Republican government. For the most part they were unimportant. Suddenly

Eugenie, who had been on her knees beside the box, leaped to her feet and pressed a letter into his hands. "Look," she shoutd in triumph, "I have been searching for this for hours. Read it!"

It was a letter from M. Guizot, who, since the fall of the Second Empire, had spared no effort to defame the late regime. While Napoleon III had still been in power, Guizot—although hostile to the Empire—had one day come to him with a woeful tale of a son's debts which he found himself unable to pay. The Emperor, without question or comment, had placed the whole of his personal wealth at Guizot's disposal, saying simply: "Take what you need." The grateful father had taken immediate advantage of the offer, and had subsequently written a flowery letter of thanks, saying, "Sire, you have saved more than my life, you have saved my honor." It was this letter which Eugenie had discovered. The Emperor read it in silence, and then murmured, "I had forgotten all about it."

He was about to crumple it when Eugenie, flushed with elation, snatched it from him, crying, "Let me have it; it will be my revenge!"

Napoleon fixed her with that impenetrable gaze. "No," he said softly, "no, Eugenie, one does not take that kind of revenge."

And he left the room.

However much Eugenie might try, she could never match Napoleon's great qualities of forgiveness. Exile was proving especially difficult for her. For Napoleon, who had spent more of his life in exile than out (and unbeknown to Eugenie in 1870, so would she), it was not really so hard. He was by nature phlegmatic, whereas she had always been restless, highly strung, ill controlled. She could not adjust herself to the tedium of life at Camden Place. Her story during the last eighteen years had been one of a gradual ascent to power over her physically declining, mentally weakening husband; this flight to greater and yet greater glories had now suddenly been checked in mid-air. In the unbroken boredom of Camden Place she stormed, she ranted, she talked on and on, railing against the treachery of those who had deserted her on the fatal fourth of September, against those who now spared no effort to besmirch the memory of the fallen regime. Sometimes the Emperor, exhausted by this never-ending tirade, would say wearily, "Eugenie, you do not possess an idea, the idea possesses you." Then she might cease her rantings for a while (she had learned to respect his opinions since the trials of 1870), but before long her robust unforgiving nature would reassert itself, and her companions would be subjected to another long diatribe against the traitors of the Empire.

The infamy of General Trochu was her pet subject. After being appointed Governor of Paris by the Emperor, Trochu had sworn to the Empress that come what may, he would die at her feet rather than desert her. On the fourth of September, when it began to look as though he might have to make good his expansive promise, Trochu refused to answer the Empress's summons. Twice she appealed to him to come to her aid, and twice he ignored her requests; when he did finally emerge, it was to go to the Hôtel de Ville and help proclaim the Republic. This treachery Eugenie could never forget, and she was determined that no one else would, either. Night after night, hour after hour, she would discuss every nuance of Trochu's behavior, working herself up into a state of almost hysterical indignation. One evening at about midnight, when she had, as usual, spent several hours re-examining Trochu's treachery, she noticed poor Marie de Larminat, her maid of honor, struggling to keep her eyes open.

"Good heavens, what time is it?" demanded the Empress.

"Madame," answered the exhausted Marie, "it is forty-five minutes past Trochu."

But in spite of all her irritating, and at times almost maddening, qualities, they loved her. For they understood the essential honesty of her character. "Her impetuous, passionate nature must have made her suffer more intensely than many . . ." said Marie, "and I pitied her with all my heart."

There were days when the Empress was too depressed even to rail. Then she would walk up and down the long gallery at Camden, the rustling of her dress blurring against the rhythmic *tick-tock* of the clock in the hall, the bust of Machiavelli grinning wickedly at her as she passed to and fro. Sometimes she might pause and pressing her forehead against the windowpane, look out into the drifting fog or the never-ending rain. "The pearly-gray English sky," she sighed on one occasion, "is like a dish which has been cooked without salt. One must be very hungry to appreciate it." When she tired of walking, she would return to the drawing room and take up her embroidery, and then the Emperor, rising heavily from his chair, would motion the Prince Imperial to his side and start his promenading. Down the gallery he would go with languid steps, his body swaying from side to side above his short legs, his head always drooping to the left. Beside him, his springing step slowed down to match his father's pace, would be the young Prince. "Ah! how many thousands of miles have we walked on this poor carpet which led us nowhere!" said Eugenie one day. "Our impatient restlessness has worn it out."

It took these years of exile at Chislehurst to reopen Eugenie's eyes to her husband's many good qualities. In this afterglow of the Empire she gave him back her affection and her respect; her love he had never had. Eugenie, they say, loved only two people in her life—her sister, Paca, who had died during the Empire, and her son, the Prince Imperial. Physical love for a man was something she had never known. She seemed, in truth, to be more inclined towards the company of women than men; she certainly carried her delight in beautiful young women to excess. She had only to see a pretty face to become immediately interested. "Who in the world is that?" she once demanded on catching sight of the exquisite Madame de Pourtales. "I *must* know her! She must be presented immediately." And in this way she built up that court of beauties with which she adored surrounding herself. In these days, her passion for lovely young women would have been almost suspect, but this aspect would never have occurred to Eugenie. There was an innocent, adolescent quality about Eugenie's relationship with her women friends; the part-sentimental, part-hoydenish, atmosphere of an upper-class girls' school pervaded the Imperial circle. Any implication that there might have been something more would have shocked the Empress. Years later, after the death of the Emperor, the conversation turned one day to Sapphism. "*Voilà une chose que je ne comprends pas!*" exclaimed Eugenie dogmatically. "*Moi je suis vieille, mais je vous donne parole d'honneur que si l'un me donnerait une femme je ne saurais qu'en faire! Je dirais 'tres bien.' Mais . . . je . . . ne . . . sais . . . qu'en . . . faire!*"

Eugenie might have become easier to live with, but the young Prince Imperial was the one source of unqualified happiness to the aging Emperor. He adored him. Filon might complain of the boy's lack of concentration; the Empress might fear his fits of reckless generosity; to the Emperor his son was perfection. And Louis returned his father's love with all his heart. Never, not even during those terrible days before Sedan, when, powerless, unwanted, and ill, Napoleon had floundered along towards the final tragedy, had Louis once questioned his father's capabilities. Humiliated before his generals, the Emperor remained a hero to his son. That his father might be unequal to the task of leading his country to victory never occurred to the boy, and even after the surrender at Sedan had opened his eyes, his love for his father remained as powerful as ever. Nor, in his turn, did Napoleon doubt that Louis would be equal to the task he had bequeathed him—that of re-establishing the dynasty in France. No, the son would live to consolidate the father's work. Secure in their confidence in each other—the son, in his father's wisdom, the father, in his son's capabilities—they would talk for hours together, about the past which had been so glorious, and about the future, which for one of them, was to be more glorious still.

These had been the very dreams of the first Napoleon for his only son.

      ♛   ♛   ♛

Very much the odd man out amongst the high-spirited, intemperate, Anglophobe members of the family was Prince Louis-Lucien Bonaparte. Having inherited from his father (Napoleon I's brother Lucien) strong literary interests and a certain independence of mind, Prince Louis-Lucien had held himself aloof from his family. In the early days of the Empire, after he had been made a Senator, he had spent a few years in France; but by now he was permanently domiciled in Bayswater, London. He owned two semidetached houses; one in which he lived, the other in which he had his library and his laboratory. Literature and chemistry, he said, were the two great loves of his life. If he had any other, less academic, loves, no one seemed to know about them. He might not have been celibate, but at least he gave no cause for scandal. This could be said of very few Bonapartes.

A great collector of books, he spent every spare shilling on them. He had seven or eight large rooms crammed with books—the majority scientific studies, many of them written by himself. He was said to be one of the greatest authorities on the Basque language and on English dialects (he once erected a monument to the last woman known to have spoken Cornish), and wrote or edited over two hundred volumes himself. His collection of Bibles ran into thousands.

Unlike the majority of his relations, he never interested himself in political affairs; he had for politics, he said, an "intense repugnance." Having discarded the liberal principles of his youth, he often found himself at odds with his Bonaparte relations, a great number of whom, despite the fact that they had lived for years off the Emperor's civil list, considered themselves very much men of the Left. Prince Louis-Lucien, said his friend Sir Drummond Wolff, "deplored the political tendencies of advanced liberals." One day, when the Prince was visiting Camden Place, Mr. Gladstone was one of the guests. As the Prince had arrived too late to be introduced, he was obliged to ask the Empress, in a very loud whisper, the name of the tall gentleman talking to the Emperor. On being told that it was Mr. Gladstone, he exclaimed, *"Mais comment donc! I didn't know that a Liberal could be a true gentleman."*

Whether Mr. Gladstone heard him or not, one does not know, but it in no way lessened his respect for the Prince's achievements. Prince Louis-Lucien, who since the fall of the Empire had been in grave financial difficulties, was awarded an English pension by Mr. Gladstone for his contribution to the worlds of science and literature. As the Prince had actually been born in England (his father Lucien had been living at Thorngrove at the time), he now considered himself almost an Englishman. And he always claimed that although only a member of Napoleon III's civil family and therefore not entitled to call himself Imperial Highness, he was an Imperial Highness by the courtesy of Queen Victoria, who always addressed him as such.

And yet, for all his Englishness, he looked the perfect Bonaparte. Dark-haired, dark-eyed, sallow-skinned, he bore a stiking resemblance to his uncle Napoleon I. Whereas the Prince Imperial often passed unnoticed in the streets of London, Prince Louis-Lucien's typically Bonaparte features always attracted attention. Whether rummaging through a stall of books on a pavement in the West End, or waiting in his somewhat abstracted way for a train to take him to Chislehurst, he was always pointed out and stared at: "Looking at him as he faced you in the library at his Bayswater residence," wrote one of his vistors, "you might almost have imagined that it was the 'Little Corporal' who stood before you."

Prince Louis-Lucien, almost alone amongst the Bonapartes, was very highly thought of by the Emperor Napoleon III, and was appointed by him as one of the guardians of the Prince Imperial.

Quite another proposition was his brother, the impossible Prince Pierre Bonaparte. With his wife, Justine, and his two children, the fourteen-year-old Roland and the eleven-year-old Jeanne, he arrived in England from Belgium in 1872. He was, as usual, penniless. Despite the fact that he had never been welcomed at the Tuileries by Napoleon III, he now wrote to Camden Place, hoping to be received by the Emperor and to get some more money from him. In his letter he issued his cousin an ultimatum. Either the Emperor must come to his assistance or else his wife, Justine—an ex-milliner—would be forced to open a hat shop. He should never have presented the Imperial couple with this alternative. The Emperor no longer had a civil list at his disposal, and primed, no doubt, by the more realistic Eugenie, Napoleon refused to help. Rebuffed, Princess Justine opened her hat shop. A handsome woman with, according to Caroline Murat, all her wits about her, the Princess started "a large dressmaking and millinery business in Bond Street under her husband's name, much to the indignation of the Empress." It was an immediate success; society, intrigued by the idea of a Bonaparte princess making a living by her needle, flocked to the Bond Street shop.

The enterprise turned out to be something of a nine-day wonder. Once the world of fashion discovered that a hat made by a princess was very like a hat made by anyone else, business deteriorated, and one may be sure that whatever profits were made were quickly squandered by Prince Pierre. In spite of all Justine's courage and resource, she was obliged to give up the shop, and the family returned to France. Life was no less difficult there. Prince Pierre had never been popular; now that the Empire had fallen, he was openly snubbed. However hard Justine might try (and Pierre would have made very little effort himself), the family could barely scrape along. On one occasion Pierre wrote a pathetic letter to his brother, Louis-Lucien, begging him to go to Camden to ask the Empress's aid. His family, Prince Pierre assured his brother, were almost without bread, and unless Eugenie helped him, he would shoot himself. This melodramatic threat threw the earnest Prince Louis-Lucien into a state of panic. "We must get help!" he exclaimed to Caroline Murat. "My God!" he added, on second thought, "if my brother kills himself, I will be refused admittance to my club!"

"As I had foreseen," said Caroline, who had accompanied Louis-Lucien on his mission to Camden, "nothing was to be obtained from the Empress." Eugenie, according to Caroline, was very angry, particularly with her. She invited Prince Louis-Lucien to remain at Camden for dinner, but not Caroline. "My dear," Eugenie is reported to have said, "I can't ask you to dinner because that would make thirteen of us." Caroline returned to London late, tired, and hungry, but not, she says, one jot wiser.

Needless to say, Prince Pierre did not commit suicide. In fact, he lived just long enough to see his son Roland marry Mademoiselle Marie Félice Blanc, the daughter of François Blanc, the one-time Savoyard waiter to whom Monte Carlo owes its fame as a gambling resort. As Marie Blanc is rumored to have brought her husband a mansion in Paris, a palace in Italy, and a dowry of a million pounds, one presumes that her father-in-law, Prince Pierre, died satisfied. He would have died more than satisfied had he known that the only child of this marriage, his granddaughter Princess Marie, would one day marry the second son of the King of Greece. The family had come a long, long way from the days

when Justine Ruffin, the humble milliner's assistant, had married Prince
Pierre, black sheep of the Bonapartes.

♛ ♛ ♛

Life at Camden Place was not entirely confined to pacing up and
down the long gallery. Some relief from this caged atmosphere was provided by the almost daily visits from the faithfuls, now living in Chislehurst, and from the relations, living, for the most part, at a safer distance. There would be calls from members of the party over from France
and the arrival of an occasional opportunist ready to turn the misfortunes of the family to his own advantage. Queen Victoria visited them
(a hint was dropped that she found the rooms too stuffy), and once the
royal call was over, county society and the Emperor's old English friends
followed her example. Sometimes the routine was varied by holidays; in
September 1871 the Empress went to Spain to visit her mother, the
aging Countess de Montijo, while the Emperor and the Prince Imperial
spent a month at Torquay. The following summer Eugenie, the Prince,
and a party of young Spaniards did a lightning tour of Scotland, during
which time the Emperor was enjoying a more leisurely holiday at
Brighton and Cowes. These outings, however, were the exception rather
than the rule; during most days of the year, while the trees in the park
dripped with rain, the handful of exiles fell back on each other's company. There were amongst them, says Filon, "divergencies of thought,
rivalries and antipathies which beneath the outwardly calm surface produced whirlpools and eddies."

Marie de Larminat was less poetic. "By degrees," she says, "we
began to rasp one another's nerves."

A further cause for gloom was the departure of the Prince Imperial.
Towards the end of the year 1872 he entered the Royal Military College
at Woolwich as a cadet. Now sixteen years of age, it was important that
he begin his military training. If Louis was to be Emperor of the French
one day (and the household at Camden was optimistic), he must, as a
Napoleon, prove himself a soldier first. For the next few years he would
by living at Woolwich and coming home on weekends only. The Emperor
was heartbroken at the wrench, but Louis, despite the fact that he loved
his parents dearly, could not help being excited at the prospect. He began,
almost for the first time since his arrival in England, to look to the future
again. Life, after all, was not really so bad.

At Camden, however, they were not prepared to wait until Louis felt ready to restore the Empire. They were busy with plans of their own. None of them had ever imagined that the Republic would last for long; nor did they imagine that when they did return to France, they would not be welcomed with open arms. Sedan had, of course, been unfortunate, but the Emperor had written a pamphlet explaining the *débâcle*. French political memories, anyway, were commendably short, but as their economic memories tended to be longer, it was unlikely that they could have forgotten the very real prosperity they had known under the Empire. The Republicans were ineffectual, the Monarchists, divided, and the Army, surely, would always be loyal to a Napoleon. Things, at Camden, seemed to be looking brighter every day. And then, early in 1872, Rouher—the minister who had been known as the Vice-Emperor during the Empire—was elected member for Corsica in the National Assembly. The exiles were beside themselves; a restoration was inevitable.

It was, of course, to be another return from Elba; another bloodless march to Paris. Napoleon III had spent too much of his life emulating the first Emperor to forsake him now. He would slip out of England and meet up with a handful of adherents in Switzerland. From there he would cross the border, and acclaimed by his loyal troops, would ride at their head into a welcoming Paris. Details of where the Imperial family would live, of how they would live, and of who their ministers would be were all decided, and a date set for the spring of 1873.

Plon-Plon was up to his neck in this conspiracy. An avowed Republican throughout the Empire, he now supported—in fact, urged—the overthrow of the Republic and the restoration of the Imperial regime. He came hurrying across to England to discuss the plan more fully. The sight of Napoleon appalled him. Was this shambling gray-faced creature the man who hoped to rally France once more to the Empire? How was this poor pain-racked figure going to ride in triumph into Paris? Chances were that he would not even be able to drive into his capital, let alone ride. The two of them decided to put things to the test. On the morning after Plon-Plon's arrival, he and the Emperor set out in a carriage for Woolwich. Plon-Plon observed his cousin carefully during the drive—his face showed no signs of suffering, he never complained. But that was never any guide to Napoleon's true feelings; that evening, when he was alone with the Empress, he admitted that he had suffered a little.

Something had to be done. Loath as the Emperor was to be examined, he consented to put himself in the hands of the doctors. "My health will never stand in the way," he declared heroically, "I will do what it is my duty to do." Later, with less heroism and an eye on that triumphal ride, he exclaimed, almost jauntily, "In a month we shall be on horseback." The doctors were sent for.

They met at Camden on December 24, 1872. In the Emperor's bladder was discovered a stone the size of a large date. "What!" exclaimed one of the doctors after the examination, "did that man actually endure five hours on horseback on the battlefield of Sedan? He must have suffered agonies!" An operation was considered imperative, and Sir Henry Thompson, the renowned urologist, was installed at Camden Place. The first operation took place on January 2, 1873. The stone was found, crushed, and as many fragments as possible removed. Throughout the next two days the Emperor experienced considerable pain. A second operation was performed on January 6. After careful manipulation, a further fragment was removed. For all the following day and the day after, the patient was sleepy and semidelirious. The presence of yet another obstructing fragment was suspected, and a third operation decided upon.

Once during that delirium-dazed day Napoleon asked Eugenie where Louis was.

"He is at Woolwich," she answered. "Do you want me to send for him?"

"No," he said. "His work mustn't be interrupted."

That night, January 8, the Emperor was given a dose of chloral to induce sleep. The administration of this dose of chloral was to give rise to strong rumors regarding the real cause of the Emperor's death. There were whispers that, as he had refused to take the chloral that evening, Eugenie had, in her impulsive way, poured out a too-liberal dose and entreated him to take it for her sake. He had obliged her, and had fallen asleep—never, affirmed the gossips, to wake again. The Countess de Mercy-Argenteau, Napoleon's last love, claimed to have heard this story from the Emperor's doctor himself, and the Count de la Chapelle, a friend of Napoleon's, swears that he was dragged into a private room at Camden and begged, by "a person in authority," not to reveal the truth about the Emperor having been "poisoned by inadvertence." Caroline Murat, of course, has a field day on the subject; her insinuations that Eugenie had murdered the Emperor fill several pages of her memoirs.

The rumor is without a grain of truth. Napoleon, with his doctor in attendance, took the dose of chloral; he slept well, and when Sir Henry visited him at six the following morning, he woke and answered the surgeon's questions. In fact, when Sir Henry saw the Empress at eight, he was able to report that the patient was so much better that it had been decided to perform the third operation at noon. Eugenie, reassured, put on her hat and prepared to drive to Woolwich to visit the Prince Imperial. Sometime during that morning, when Napoleon's old friend Dr. Conneau came to lean over his master's bed, the Emperor uttered his last coherent words.

"Ah! It's you, Conneau . . ." he breathed. "Were you at Sedan?"

No words could have been more poignant.

At twenty-five past ten Sir Henry Thompson, looking into the Emperor's room, was startled to see a marked change in the patient's appearance. They revived him with a little brandy and called for the Empress. She was warned that he had not long to live. She sent for the Prince Imperial and hurried to the bedside. "*Voilà l'Impératrice, Sire,*" said someone as she leaned over her dying husband.

"Louis is coming," she whispered, knowing that this would give him the greatest comfort. He moved his lips, as though wishing to kiss her. At a quarter to eleven Napoleon III died. Eugenie lifted her arms and uttering an ear-piercing cry, fell across the bed and kissed the dead face. Then, fainting, she was carried to her room.

It had been so simple, so sudden, so pedestrian, almost, this deathbed scene of the Emperor Napoleon III. Where the first Napoleon's last days on St. Helena had been notable for their poignant simplicity, and those of the second Napoleon at Schönbrunn, for their theatrical splendor, Napoleon III died in ordinary, almost suburban surroundings, attended to the last by his wife and doctors. In two respects only did the passing of Napoleon III match that of Napoleon I and Napoleon II. He died in exile, and he died, this bearer of a name synonymous with all the glories of the battlefield, in bed.

Half an hour after the Emperor's death the carriage bringing Louis came clattering from Woolwich. It was met at the front door by several members of the household. The Prince guessed from their expressions that all was over. Pushing past them, he ran through the hall, across the gallery, up the broad flight of stairs, stumbling and falling as he ran. On the landing he met his mother. "I have nothing left but you, Louis," she sobbed. He went into his father's room. At the sight of the motionless figure on the bed, he fell to his knees, and in a firm, fine voice, recited the Pater Noster.

"He knelt down a boy," says Augustin Filon, "and rose a man."

For the next few days everything was in a state of utter confusion. The house, besides being prepared for the lying in state, was rapidly filling up with members of the family and friends of the Empire. The

Bonapartes were all there, bickering, complaining, insinuating, accusing. It was against Eugenie, of course, that their churlishness was chiefly directed; the sight of her veiled in black and awash with tears, almost relishing her role of the heartbroken widow, irritated rather than distressed them. They even tried to blame her for the fact that one could go nowhere in the house without catching a glimpse of the Emperor, lying in his coffin in the hall. Whatever Eugenie's shortcomings might have been, however, she was not responsible for the design of the house.

On January 14 the Emperor lay in state. He was dressed in the uniform of a French General of Division—red trousers, blue tunic, and gold sash. Across his breast slanted the broad red cordon of the Legion of Honor. His mustache was jauntily waxed and his thinning hair combed flatteringly forward. His expression was his usual one of aloof serenity; it was a pity that the embalming process had turned his face that unfortunate shade of yellow. Once the Prince of Wales had paid his respects, the defile began. It started at noon and lasted until nine o'clock that night; they say that twenty thousand people passed through the house that day. When the last mourner had shuffled out into the winter's night and the coffin had been closed, Eugenie came downstairs. She remained on her knees in prayer all through the night.

They buried the Emperor in the little Catholic church on Chislehurst Common the following day. St. Mary's had never known such splendor. Not only was a dead Emperor lying at the foot of the chancel steps, but a host of live royalties was crowded onto its little wooden chairs. Besides the Prince Imperial and the Bonaparte and Murat princes, there was Princess Mathilde, recognizable by her bulk, and her sister-in-law Clotilde, notable for her devout air. And there were lesser members of the family almost without number. At the end of the service the coffin was put to rest in a little side chapel, and the Prince Imperial, whose behavior throughout the trying ceremony had been exemplary, laid two wreaths on it. He sprinkled it with holy water and left. Arriving back at Camden Place, he had to receive the mourners. This was almost worse. Towards the end of the reception, as a group of French workmen moved towards him, their leader suddenly shouted: "*Vive l'Empereur! Vive Napoleon IV!*"

"The Emperor is dead," said the startled Louis, "but France lives. You should say '*Vive la France!*'"

But his words were lost as the great crowd took up the cry, "*Vive l'Empereur!*" The mass of people, a moment before so restrained by grief, suddenly pressed closer, shouting his name with such gusto that those who had started leaving came dashing back to join in the excitement. It was only with difficulty that Louis's companions managed to get him safely into the house.

Eugenie, as she heard the commotion from behind the shuttered windows of her room, must have felt very proud.

♔   ♔   ♔

It was during these sorrow-steeped days, when the house was still wrapped in gloom and the exiles were tiptoeing about, talking in whispers, that Eugenie and Plon-Plon staged one of their periodic rows.

Napoleon's death had improved Plon-Plon's position considerably. With Louis not yet of age, Plon-Plon considered himself, without any doubt whatsoever, the head of the house. He had waited many years for this moment. At one time only Napoleon III had stood between him and the coveted position; then the birth of the Prince Imperial had shifted him down to third place. Now, at one stroke, both obstacles had been removed, and until March 1874, when the Prince Imperial would turn eighteen, Plon-Plon would be the head of the family and in complete control of the Imperialist Party. It was thus with hopes running high and an expectant gleam in his usually somber eye that he arrived at Camden after the death of his cousin. He was in for a shock.

On demanding to see the Emperor's will, he discovered that it had been drawn up in 1865, and as such bore no relation whatsoever to the present position. It was a political testament drawn up during the Empire and full of high-flown phrases about "the writings of the prisoner of St. Helena" and the burdens and duties of sovereignty. To Louis was left the seal which the Emperor had always carried on his watch-chain. That was all. Everything else went to Eugenie.

When Plon-Plon read it, he could hardly believe his eyes. He demanded a second will. He was quite sure that Napoleon had made another will, more in keeping with the changed circumstances. Certain that Eugenie would stop at nothing to keep absolute control of her son as well as the whole of the Emperor's fortune in her own hands, Plon-Plon insisted on going through the Emperor's papers himself. Pietri, the late Emperor's secretary, led Plon-Plon into Napoleon's little study. He found the drawers of the Emperor's desk fastened with bands of linen on which were affixed Pietri's seal. Plon-Plon muttered something about the seals not being official ones, and Pietri explained that they had simply been placed there as a precaution during the Emperor's illness. Napoleon had not wanted to have anyone tampering with his papers. Whereupon Plon-Plon broke the seals and started rummaging through the drawers. He afterwards claimed that the papers, amongst which nothing of importance remained, were in great disorder and that they had obviously been hurriedly gone through before his arrival.

This convinced him that there had been a second will and that the Empress, with the connivance of Pietri and Rouher, had destroyed it. This was his theory, and he thereafter never hesitated to voice it, both privately and in public.

It did seem strange that Napoleon had made no second will. But then he had never really accepted his exile as permanent, and although he was ill, he did not think he was dying. The return from Elba would have put everything back to where it had been in 1865. Nor was Napoleon III a man to concern himself with material things; the making of a will, as Pietri afterwards said, was a task "not to everyone's taste," and having no less confidence in the Empress now than he had had in 1865, he had let the will stand. He had felt sure that whatever she did would be in the best interests of their son.

As far as Plon-Plon's affirmation that Eugenie had destroyed the will, it was preposterous. Whatever her faults, Eugenie was honest. Not even her bitterest critics (except, of course, Plon-Plon) ever accused her of deceit. If anything, their complaint was that she was too honest—she had no control over her emotions, she said exactly what she thought, she lacked tact. Nor would Pietri or Rouher, both upright men, have given their support to this scheme; they were both too devoted to the Emperor ever to disregard his last wishes in such a fashion.

Eugenie, in fact, far from wishing to discard Plon-Plon, wished for a reconciliation. The Imperial Party was far too weak to stand an open breach between its two leading figures; she wanted to make a fresh start. In this spirit, she sent for him. Gritting his teeth, he allowed himself to be ushered into her dark little drawing room. As always, the sight of that pale, lovely face, paler and even lovelier now in its halo of black net, irritated him beyond endurance. She held out a small white hand.

"Come now," she said, "you know that I am not a vindictive woman; let us forget our disagreements, put your hand in mine, and let the past be forgotten."

It was a pretty speech, but it was lost on Plon-Plon.

"Madame," he replied stiffly, "I will shortly acquaint you with my intentions."

With that he left, and a day or two later he sent an aide-de-camp to give her his terms for a reconciliation. They were two. First, he was to be given absolute control of the Imperialist Party; and second, the Prince Imperial was to be entrusted to his sole guardianship. Eugenie's reaction may be imagined. "He dared . . ." she would afterwards exclaim, "he *dared* demand that the person of the Prince Imperial should be confined to his sole surveillance! . . . Do you realize the insult and all the threat of such a message?" Eugenie could never tell the story without bursting into tears. Did Plon-Plon expect her to admit that she was unworthy of bringing up her own son? What had she done to deserve such an insult?

So powerful was Eugenie's upsurge of anger against Plon-Plon that it quite eclipsed her grief. There was nothing like a good fight for shaking Eugenie out of herself. Grief, she admitted in a letter to her mother, might have crushed her, but Plon-Plon had roused "*sa fibre un instant endormie.*"

And for the next few weeks, of course, everyone was treated to the tale of Plon-Plon's infamous behavior. Even Queen Victoria had to sit through it. Not that the Queen minded; she had always found Plon-Plon extremely unpleasant, and she adored Eugenie. Playing down her own anger in the affair a little, Eugenie told the Queen how Plon-Plon had wished to take Louis ("*tout ce que j'ai*") away from Woolwich and away from her. He had told her that the Prince of Wales disapproved of Louis being at Woolwich (this Victoria denied hotly), and that he, Plon-Plon, intended taking Louis away from England. But Eugenie remained firm; she was not going to allow Plon-Plon "*faire l'aventure*" with her son and Louis himself was just as determined not to yield to his cousin. Plon-Plon had, noted the Queen, "behaved very badly."

On the same day that Victoria had paid this visit of condolence to the Empress, she and her youngest daughter, Princess Beatrice, had stopped at St. Mary's church to see the Emperor's coffin. It was, she noted in her *Journal*, "a pretty, rural little place, quite a village church. . . . To the right of the altar, or rather below it, behind a railing, in the smallest space possible, rest the earthly remains of the poor Emperor, the coffin covered with a black velvet pall, embroidered with golden bees. . . ."

In order to provide the Emperor's coffin with a more seemly resting place than the one in which the Queen had seen it, Eugenie had decided to add a chapel to the little church. It would be a far cry from Napoleon I's grandiose tomb in the Invalides, but what else was there to do? The chapel was completed that summer, and if its elegance did seem a little pretentious beside the unadorned gray bulk of the parent church, no one thought to mention it. Towards the end of the year an enormous granite sarcophagus arrived from Aberdeen. It was the gift of the Queen. On the first anniversary of Napoleon III's death, at a small family ceremony, the coffin was deposited in its new granite bed. The Prince Imperial, who had behaved so admirably during his father's first official funeral, gave way to his heartfelt grief on this occasion. His sorrow, they say, was pitiful to see.

The chapel is hardly changed today. For all the professed French Gothic of its style, its atmosphere is frankly Victorian. Its dark, too-slender columns topped by flowery, too-fulsome capitals, the unnecessarily involved vaulting of the ceiling, the predominant use of black and red, the insistent pattern of crowned *N's* and eagles in the pavement, give it that gloomy mock-medieval air so beloved of the Victorians. In the center of the tessellated floor is a dark marble slab. On it are inscribed these words:

ON THIS SPOT RESTED
FOR MANY YEARS
THE REMAINS OF NAPOLEON III
R.I.P.

For like the first burial places of Napoleon I and Napoleon II, the first tomb of the Emperor Napoleon III is empty.

CHAPTER SIXTEEN

✦ ✦ ✦

PRINCESS Mathilde Bonaparte, at the age of fifty, embarked upon yet another love affair. The name of her new lover was Claudius Popelin. Like his predecessor, the faithless Nieuwerkerque, he was tall, golden-haired, and artistic; unlike him, he was gentle and somewhat self-effacing. Five years younger than Mathilde, he had been a member of her circle for some years during the Empire; now, on her return to Paris after the war, he was one of the few who hurried back, unhesitatingly, to her side. Mathilde, still reeling from the blows she had sustained during the last two years—the loss of Nieuwerkerque and the fall of the Empire—was grateful for the web of adoring affection which Popelin wove round her. Disillusioned and sick at heart, she allowed herself to drift into this new love affair. Popelin, who during her brilliant years had had to content himself with a position on the fringe of her circle, was now gratified to find himself in the place of honor. It gave him confidence, but it never made him arrogant.

Mathilde, however, was never one to conduct a half-hearted affair. Anything she did had to be done passionately, wholeheartedly; she was incapable of keeping her affections down to a sane, comfortable level. If Popelin loved her, then she would return his love with all the robustness of her nature. She would make this the *grande passion* of her life. Popelin would be what the brutal Demidov and the egotistical Nieuwerkerque had never been; together they would make their love a complete, a vehement, an almost heroic thing.

This was all very well, but although Popelin loved her, he was not of the stuff of which heroes are made. Of middle-class birth, he was a shade too anxious to emulate his betters; of mediocre talent, his achievements paled beside those of her more brilliant friends; of a gentle disposition, his humility could be a little irritating at times. Nevertheless, Popelin was appointed superintendent of her private museum and acted as host at all her parties. He seems to have acquitted himself very well. When Frédéric Masson, the famous Bonapartist writer whose veneration for the first Napoleon almost matched Mathilde's own, visited her at Saint-Gratien, he was full of praise for Popelin. He called him a "universally-minded artist capable of conceiving, expressing and carrying out everything well."

As Prince Demidov, Mathilde's husband, from whom she had been separated for some twenty-five years, died in 1870, and as Popelin's wife died a year or so later, there was nothing to stop these two from getting married. As a matter of fact, several papers had hinted at a morganatic marriage between Mathilde and Popelin. However, it is unlikely that she ever considered it; she might have loved Popelin, but she was too conscious of her position as a Bonaparte to ally herself legally with a bourgeois artist. Once, when a woman friend of hers contemplated marrying a man poorer and of more humble birth than herself, Mathilde gave her this advice: "You are in love with him; he is good-looking and he pleases you; keep him at your side, but do not marry him."

As well as a new lover, Mathilde got herself a new house. Although she still retained her famous country place at Saint-Gratien, she now replaced her Paris house in the Rue de Courçelles by one in the Rue de Berri. She filled it with haphazard Bohemian furnishings—the multicolored cushions, the Eastern vases, the Chinese lanterns, the crimson silk hangings, the dozens of paintings, the scores of knickknacks. The fall of the Empire made not the slightest difference to her proud display of Napoleonic souvenirs. At every turn there were marble busts of the members of the family; a bronze eagle spread its wings across her dining table; a silver statue representing the young Napoleon at Brienne rose proudly from a bed of foliage in the dining room. One glance around her rooms was enough to give the lie to the whispers that she was consorting with the Republicans, that she had deserted the Bonapartist cause. Nothing made her more indignant than the suggestion that for the sake of personal convenience she had turned her back on her Imperial past. She always maintained that by returning to Paris and living in the midst of things she was doing the Bonapartist cause more good than by skulking in the fogs of England or the sunshine of Italy. By reopening her salon, she hoped to keep in touch with the old adherents and to win over some new ones. A fresh generation was growing up—young men nearer the Prince Imperial's age than her own; surely it was only right and sensible that she should win their friendship. Surely the role that she was now playing was no less important than the role she had played during the Empire. Surely she could still be *Notre Dame des Arts.*

She could not. But it took her some years to realize it. At first her old friends had come flocking back, and there were nights when she seemed to have recaptured the magic of those prewar gatherings. But one by one they dropped out: they died, or they became too old, or they simply lost interest. And when she did manage to fill her rooms with members of the new generation and the new society, they came in order to get a glimpse, not of the future, but of the past. Napoleon's niece, with her noble head and her white shoulders, her queenly dignity and her intense family pride, was as much a museum piece as the marble busts and the bronze eagles. She was magnificent, but she was of no more significance than a reflection or an echo.

            ♕   ♕   ♕

On March 16, 1874, the Prince Imperial came of age. To mark the occasion the Bonapartists decided to stage a vast Imperial rally in the grounds of Camden Place. Although neither the Empress nor the Prince were very eager for it to take place (Eugenie was afraid of embarrassing the British government and Louis wanted to finish at Woolwich before doing any serious pretending), the Party would not hear of them letting the occasion go by without a celebration. France, said the Bonapartists firmly, needed to be reminded that the Empire had an heir. So the plans went forward and the invitations went out.

Amongst those to receive a personal letter of invitation from the Prince was Plon-Plon. This was the day that Plon-Plon had been dreading for years; with Louis of age, any chance of his claiming the leadership of the Party was gone. The thought of Louis being acclaimed by the Bonapartists and of Eugenie queening it under the cedars of Camden Place was too much for Plon-Plon to bear. He refused to come. In public statements in both England and France (the Bonapartes could never keep their family squabbles out of the papers) he made clear his reasons for not attending the Camden jamboree. Having always been democratic and anticlerical, he said, he disapproved strongly of the men now surrounding the Prince Imperial. As these same men (and in "men" he certainly included Eugenie) had by their reactionary policies brought about the downfall of the Second Empire, he did not wish to be associated with them at Camden. The happiness of France had always been of more importance to him than any narrow dynastic interests. . . .

The celebration went very well without him. The weather was perfect, the crowds were enormous, the applause was deafening, the enthusiasm was almost hysterical. Louis's speech brought tears to every eye ("Did you hear him? How well he speaks, the little Prince"); his reference to his mother brought a wave of prolonged cheering; at the end there was such a scene of rapturous frenzy that the Imperial couple were all but torn to pieces as they made their way back to the house. And when

Louis made his final appearance at the window, standing suffused in the rose-gold glow of the setting sun, he seemed little less than a god to the delirious crowd in the garden.

But all this brought him no nearer to the throne of France. Very wisely, Louis decided to ignore the hotheads who urged him to "do something" immediately, and to get on with his work. There would be time enough for attempts on the throne when he had graduated from Woolwich. He happened, in fact, to be doing extremely well at the military academy; he was hard-working, he was popular, he was highly thought of. If he did have a fault (and it was a fault in the eyes of the more reticent English only), then it was that he tended to "show off," to make no bones about his ability to do certain things better than his colleagues. But he always did it so charmingly, so unself-consciously, that he was easily forgiven; one had to remember, his fellow cadets murmured, that he was French.

He graduated from Woolwich at the beginning of 1875 with considerable distinction. Queen Victoria, who had kept a friendly eye on his career, wrote to the Duke of Cambridge, Commander-in-Chief of the Army, expressing her delight in "the success of the dear young Prince Imperial." How glad they must be, she said, that he had *behaved* so well.

His graduation from Woolwich was by no means the end of his association with the British Army. Much to the bewilderment of his Bonaparte relations (they never could accustom themselves to the idea of a Napoleon in an English uniform), he promptly joined the autumn maneuvers at Aldershot. Again, as at Woolwich, his simplicity, his good humor, and his adaptability won all hearts, and the P.I. (as he was inevitably called) was very quickly accepted by his fellow soldiers. "In the five days we have been under canvas it has done nothing but rain . . ." he wrote gleefully to Eugenie. "Our misfortunes have had no effect on the morale of the troops; they are resigned to the weather now that they have a French cook to make up for it. This cook is a charming young man, endowed with the most exquisite graces of mind and body. . . . This cook, as you will have guessed from my description, is myself. . . ."

But his life was not all soldiering. To escape the vagaries of the English summer, the Camden household spent a few months each year at Arenenberg, Queen Hortense's old villa on Lake Constance. The Emperor had always refused to revisit his old home; it would have seemed too much like a wounded animal crawling back to its lair to die. But now that Napoleon was dead, the family felt free to spend their summers amidst its fairy-tale beauties. The house itself had hardly been altered since Hortense's day; the atmosphere of the sad-eyed sentimental queen seemed to pervade every room. The graceful Empire décor looked merely stiff and cold to a generation accustomed to lush overcrowded rooms; they found the highly romantic paintings (Hortense chasing butterflies, Eugène de Beauharnais "brandishing a saber," Louis-Napoleon climbing the Alps) faintly amusing. It was for its outdoor diversions that Arenenberg was chiefly appreciated by the exiles. With its lake and its forests and its mountains, it afforded endless opportunity for amusement. Those tensions which were such a feature of life at Camden seemed to melt away in the warm pine-scented air of Arenenberg. The family noticed this, too; loath to visit the Empress in England, they flocked to see her in Switzerland. Mathilde came one year, and left entranced with the Prince Imperial. Another year saw Prince Joachim Murat as well as a host of Lucien Bonapartes—Prince Charles Bonaparte, the Roccagiovines, the Primolis, the Gabriellis. . . .

Conspicuous by his absence from these friendly family gatherings was Plon-Plon. Louis, along with everything else that had come to him from his parents, had inherited their quarrel with Plon-Plon. And it was not Eugenie's nudging alone which encouraged him to continue it; Plon-Plon's atheism, liberalism, and general pigheadedness were just as abhorrent to Louis as ever they had been to the Empress. In a way it was the old Bonaparte-Beauharnais feud manifesting itself in the fourth generation. Just as Josephine and her daughter Hortense had been despised by the Bonapartes during the First Empire, so were Hortense's son Napoleon III and his son Louis despised by Plon-Plon in the Second Empire. Throughout these years the war between Louis and his cousin raged unabated. At one stage Princess Mathilde tried to make peace by getting Filon, as Louis's representative, to have a talk with Plon-Plon. Needless to say, Plon-Plon did most of the talking (he "sparkled with eloquence and wit"), and refused to believe that Louis was anything more than a puppet in the control of his overbearing priest-ridden mother. Filon's report of the conversation did nothing to endear Plon-Plon to the Prince Imperial, and when, in 1876, Plon-Plon decided to stand in Corsica for election to the Chambre des Deputés, Louis put Rouher up against him. Rouher won (helped by a published attack by Louis on Plon-Plon), but the fact that his supporters had had to fight against a Bonaparte left the party feeling a little uneasy. When Napoleon III's old friend Queen Sophie of Holland wrote to Louis, begging him to make a fresh start with Plon-Plon, Louis's reply was charming but firm. He had tried a reconciliation with Plon-Plon three years ago, he told Queen Sophie; "since then, our dissensions have grown greater. . . ."

Was there, in fact, any truth to Plon-Plon's assertion that Louis was a mere tool in his mother's hands? That he had no will or intellect of his own? Actually, nothing could have been more inaccurate. No one, devotee or disinterested acquaintance, had anything but the warmest praise for the young Prince Imperial at this time. Of all the Napoleons, none was a more engaging personality than he.

In the year 1878 he was just twenty-two years old. Like his father—and the first Napoleon—he was small, and like them in their youth, slight and sallow skinned. His hair and his mustache, both of which he kept clipped short, were dark. With this, however, his resemblance to the Bonapartes ended; if Plon-Plon's was the typical Bonaparte face, then Louis did not have it. The Montijo strain was far stronger. "In features," noted someone who knew him at this time, "with his long oval face and black hair, attributes of neither of his parents, and his lean shapely head, he was a Spaniard of the Spaniards. One recognized in him no single characteristic of the Frenchman, he was a veritable hidalgo. . . ." For all this observer's denial of any resemblance to his parents, Louis had inherited much of Eugenie's rather special beauty, and some of Napoleon's faint air of melancholy. He had his mother's sad pale eyes, her straight nose, and her firm jaw; from his father came what Madame Octave Feuillet has called the "grace of a perfect gentleman." But it was obvious after a few minutes in his company that his somewhat grave air was an acquired one; it was a façade affected in imitation of his adored father, and screened a nature far more like his mother's. For Louis had inherited, along with her looks, all Eugenie's more commendable characteristics— he had her enthusiasm, her vivacity, her vitality, her honesty—and it was these not altogether regal qualities which he tried so hard to keep in check. When he did let himself go, people found him utterly charming. Such was his charm that even when he was at his most raucous (and at times his behavior could be high-spirited to the point of madness), he was forgiven.

But there was more to him than this—much more. For not only was he dedicated to winning back the Imperial throne, he was eminently suited to fill it. Even Eugenie, who had been loath to abdicate her leadership of the Bonapartist Party when Louis came of age, finally did so because of his capabilities rather than because it was expected of her. His dealings with the senior men of the party had given him, by this time, an air of authority, and after an interview with him they would return to France confident that in him they had a leader indeed.

Inevitably, Louis's life story has been compared with that of Napoleon I's son, the Duke of Reichstadt. The broad pattern was very similar; it was in personality that the two were so unalike. Both were born the sons of reigning Emperors; both were the sons of adoring fathers; both in youth underwent a dramatic change of circumstances; both grew into manhood in exile, both devoted themselves to military careers; both cherished faintly biased memories of their fathers; both dedicated their lives to the fulfillment of their heritage—the re-establishment of the Empire in France. And they both died, with destiny unaccomplished, in their early twenties.

But here the parallel between them ends. Where, in the Duke of Reichstadt, the potency of Napoleon I's personality had been considerably diluted by the mildness of Marie Louise's character, in the Prince Imperial, Napoleon III's less powerful qualities had been greatly strengthened by those of the strong-willed Eugenie. Reichstadt, although driving himself mercilessly, possessed more willfulness than strength of will; his rather theatrical dedication to his destiny was more the result of a restless, highly emotional nature than of any firmness of purpose. His ambitions were a shade too flamboyant and ill defined. The Prince Imperial, on the other hand, was more realistic; every bit as dedicated and ambitious as his cousin, his approach was less hysterical, less showy; his common sense had kept him from flinging himself into the French political whirlpool when others had urged him to do so, and there is no doubt that had the time for his return to France ever seemed opportune, he would have been more than ready to take advantage of it. And had either of the two young men been called upon to assume the leadership of France, the Prince Imperial would most certainly have made the better Emperor.

But how were Louis's qualities of leadership to be brought to the attention of the majority of Frenchmen? "His more impatient partisans," says Marie de Larminat, "did not cease clamoring: 'Do something,' 'Make yourself known,' 'Land in France and everyone will rally to your cause.' " But Louis in the 1870s was not his father, Louis-Napoleon, in the 1830s. He wanted France to recall him, or at least to welcome him when he did make his return; his did not want to force himself on her. Until such time, he would have to prove himself worthy—and how to prove this, if not on the field of battle? "He anxiously scanned the face of the earth, his sword burning in his hands," continues Marie, "and if there was one thing evident about him, it was that, although he might be an aristocrat in the finest sense of the word, and even though he already gave promise of being a remarkable political leader . . . he was first and foremost a soldier. He never forgot the insults and base calumnies which had been flung at his father's name after Sedan; he never spoke about it, but his intimate friends knew only too well that he would never have either respite or repose until he had, even at the cost of his own blood, attested to his courage, and shown to the whole world that a Napoleon knew how to fight and, if needs be, knew how to die."

⚜   ⚜   ⚜

Almost incredibly, Betsey Patterson Bonaparte was still alive. Born before the outbreak of the French Revolution, she had seen the rise and fall of two empires and the birth of three generations after her own. In 1878 she was ninety-four years old. It was three-quarters of a century since she had married the flighty Jérôme Bonaparte. Since that radiant wedding day, when all the world seemed to be unrolling at her feet, her story had been one of heartbreak and disillusion. The one candle glowing in the blackness of her Baltimore night was her faith in the future of her grandson, young Jerome Patterson Bonaparte, until recently a colonel in Napoleon III's army. This, too, was about to be snuffed out.

Young Jerome Patterson Bonaparte, having eaten his share of rats during the siege of Paris, returned to America in 1871. His father, Bo, had died the year before at sixty-five—like so many of the Bonapartes, of cancer. On the whole, his life had been a happy one. Unable to match his mother's grandiose schemes for him, he had been strong-minded enough to live a life of his own choosing and to settle down in Baltimore without hankering after the ephemeral joys of European society. Betsey, having become resigned, if not reconciled, to Bo's lack of social ambition, had long ago transferred her hopes to his son young Jerome, and refusing to believe that the fall of the Empire meant the end of the Bonapartes (she had seen an Empire fall before), she still dreamed of a brilliant Imperial future for her grandson. Had he not been a favorite at the Tuileries and a popular figure in the Army? And even if he himself did not rise to a position of power, he could at least marry a princess of the Imperial family. He must know so many eligible ones. . . .

Unfortunately for Betsey, he also knew a wealthy young American widow who had once visited Paris. She had been a Miss Caroline Le Roy Appleton (her grandfather had been Daniel Webster), and she was now Mrs. Newbolt Edgar. When young Jerome returned to America after the war, the Le Roy Appletons arrived in force to welcome him home. Although he could not make the young widow a princess ("The air of her manners was one of quiet royalty," enthused a local paper), he could at least make her a Bonaparte. Within a few months they were married. To Betsey this foolhardy match was almost the last straw; her grandson's rash action, she did not hesitate to tell reporters, had injured his "prospects of a throne." That Betsey could still dream of young Jerome mounting the Imperial throne of France was some indication of her resilience. Seventy-five years of disillusionment had not crushed that tenacious spirit.

Disappointed in young Jerome, she turned more and more towards his brother. Charles, born a full twenty years after Jerome, was in his twenties during this last decade of Betsey's life. As this grandson had never, at any stage, shown an interest in associating himself with the family's Imperial fortunes, she could not look to him for the fulfillment of her dreams. But she was getting old, and with her own son dead and her eldest grandson married, it was good to have someone in whom she could take an interest. In 1872 Charles entered the Harvard Law School; on being admitted to the bar, he returned home to practice. Baltimore— Betsey's provincial, impossible, unspeakably boring Baltimore—was quite good enough for him. He married, in 1875, Miss Ellen Channing Day of Hartford, Connecticut. Betsey seems, by this stage, to have resigned herself to these American marriages; the days when she had considered any offspring of hers "too high in birth and connection ever to marry an American woman" had passed. She did not even bother to toss the reporters some disgruntled morsel on the occasion of this latest *mésalliance*.

Charles, however, was to make a name for himself quite independent of the one he bore. Unsuspected by Betsey, her grandson's future was to be nothing short of brilliant. She had hoped to give France an Emperor; she gave America a statesman.

Although Betsey had once assured her down-to-earth father that ladies never lived in lodgings, it was in a lodginghouse, on the corner of Lexington and St. Paul Streets in Baltimore, that she died. There was, in fact, not the slightest need for her to end her days in such modest circumstances. She was an extremely wealthy woman, but life had made her at first careful with money, then positively avaricious. Even when her failing powers made it imperative for her to engage a permanent nurse-companion, she did so under protest. Compared with her, her mother-in-law, Madame Mère, had been almost reckless. And how she would ever have coped with her husband Jérôme's extravagance is beyond imagining.

In spite of the fact that she was convinced that she would live to be a hundred (at the age of eighty-eight she had harangued a doctor for suggesting that she was at death's door), she died in April 1879, at the age of ninety-four. She was buried in a lone grave in Greenmount Cemetery—she had spurned the family vault—and with her passing disappeared the last link with the days of Napoleon's Consulate. For all her shortcomings, this woman whom Napoleon I had considered not good enough a bride for a Bonaparte had turned out to have been made of sterner stuff than the lot of them. It was Talleyrand who once said that Betsey was the only woman in the Imperial family to come anywhere near looking and behaving like a queen; and Talleyrand, as usual, was right.

♛   ♛   ♛

Another Bonaparte who had once been associated with America—fat Prince Lucien Murat, son of Napoleon I's sister Caroline—died at this time as well. Prince and Princess Murat (the former Caroline Fraser) had returned to Paris from their exile in London as soon as things had simmered down after the war. The Prince having played so nebulous a role during the Second Empire (except for that one spurt of political activity concerning the throne of Naples), nobody much minded their coming back, and they were allowed to resume their somewhat indolent life unmolested.

Always fat, Prince Lucien became positively grotesque in later life. Clambering with difficulty out of his carriage, he would be assisted to his seat at the Folies-Bergère. There, night after night (he engaged his seat by the month), he would sit like some stranded whale, avidly watching the legs of the dancers as they cavorted about the stage. The ballet over, he would be hoisted up onto his own two gouty legs and be shuffled out of the theater. He died in 1878. His devoted wife, who in the lean years had uncomplainingly run a girls' school in Bordentown, and in the good years had put up with all his extravagance and buffoonery, died a year later.

His sons, Joachim, Achille, and Louis, who had swashbuckled their way through the Second Empire, were aging, too (Joachim's eldest son, "Chino," was a contemporary of the Prince Imperial's), and all three had, of necessity, retired from active participation in the affairs of France. Anna Murat, the Duchess de Mouchy, was living on her husband's estate in France and visiting the Empress as often as she could brave the Channel crossing. The catty Caroline Murat had married a second time (Baron de

Chassiron had died in 1871), and now lived in England. Her complaints about her new country poured forth in a strong, never-ending torrent. "I am no hypocrite," she would say self-righteously, "I wish I were: I would pretend, as *some* of us do, that I love England. . . . No one who *really loves* France can honestly say that he is devoted to the English."

All this, of course, was directed at the Empress; none of them could understand how Eugenie could bear to continue living in England.

Another way in which Caroline could hit out at Eugenie was by an ardent and completely unnecessary championship of the Prince Imperial. His life at Camden, she assured the other Bonapartes, was a hell. Not only did Eugenie keep a close watch on his every move, but in order to prevent him from having any life of his own, she kept him in a state of absolute penury. In his will (or at least the will which was found at Camden) Napoleon had left everything to Eugenie and nothing to Louis; the Empress was determined, claimed Caroline, to keep it that way. She had been told that the Prince had once been acutely embarrassed in the public rooms at the St. James's by not having enough money to pay for a luncheon which he had given for some friends. On another occasion Caroline herself had invited him to Greenwich for a fish dinner one Sunday; he had regretfully refused the invitation. On being asked whether he had another engagement, he said no, but felt sure that the Empress would not allow him to go. When Caroline offered to ask the Empress herself, Louis blushed furiously and cried out, "No, my cousin! I never ask for anything, *parce que je n'admets pas qu'on me refuse.*"

When the ostensibly shocked Caroline told her uncle, the studious Louis-Lucien, he tactfully suggested that she forget the whole thing and not spread it about. The Prince, he assured her, could be "wonderfully young and gay" at times, and her disclosure of these domestic troubles would serve no purpose whatsoever. "It was good advice," says Caroline piously, "and I strictly adhered to it." Until, of course, it was published in her memoirs while the Empress was still alive.

Something which this sensuous brood of Bonapartes must have found faintly puzzling was Louis's sex life—or rather, his lack of one. When they remembered his father's record (while still adolescent, Louis-Napoleon had slipped into the room of his married mistress disguised as a flowergirl), and the sexual prowess of most of his cousins (Achille Murat, at the age of seventeen, was keeping Cora Pearl), Louis's celibacy seemed almost unnatural. Healthy, high-spirited, and a prince, the world—sexually speaking—was his oyster; he must surely be interested in *someone.* The truth was that the Prince, like his mother, had a high moral code; this was a reason which would not have readily occurred to the majority of Bonapartes. Once, during a discussion on sexual morality in Camden, one of the young men present claimed that no man led a completely virtuous life. The passion with which Louis supported the opposing view startled them all; a man with no control over his sexual desires, he argued, was no better than an animal.

As there was no evidence of a love affair, one had to be invented. Some years later a batch of "love letters," supposedly written by Louis to a girl named Charlotte Watkyns, was produced. The story of the Watkyns affair, which appeared in *Le Figaro* in 1887, was widely believed, and it was even rumored that Charlotte had arrived at Camden Place after Louis's death, to present Eugenie with his baby. As the child would have had to have been in its mother's womb for something like eighteen months, Eugenie had sent the girl packing.

The only woman with whom Louis's name was ever seriously coupled was Queen Victoria's youngest daughter, Princess Beatrice. Despite various snags (Victoria was on the lookout for a tame stay-at-home son-in-law, and Louis was a Catholic), it would have been a very suitable match. But nothing was decided. Princess Beatrice kept the Prince Imperial's photograph on her desk, they say, until the day she died.

♚   ♚   ♚

It was after dinner one February evening in 1879 that Eugenie noticed a restlessness about the Prince Imperial's behavior. He seemed unable to sit still. He would get up, move the chairs about, leave the room, come back, sit down for a few minutes, get up again to tap out a military call on the piano, then rejoin his mother in the drawing room. There was an air of scarcely suppressed excitement about him. He seemed to be in tearing spirits.

"What is the matter with you tonight?" asked Eugenie when she could bear it no longer.

"If I told you, you wouldn't sleep all night," he answered tantalizingly.

"Do you imagine that I shall sleep after what you have said?" she asked. "I shall conjure up terrible things: for instance, that you have asked to go and serve in Africa against the Zulus."

Her conjecture had been correct. Louis, with a boyish delight in being found out, admitted that he had sent just such a request to the Commander-in-Chief. Eugenie, appalled, broke into a flood of objections.

But he cut her short. Knowing her impulsive nature so well, he begged her to sleep on it and to discuss the matter with him the following day. Reluctantly she agreed; there was an increasing air of authority about Louis these days, which even she could not ignore. Worried almost sick, she went to bed. That she got any sleep is unlikely.

This campaign in which Louis was so eager to serve was an obscure South African skirmish which had suddenly been blown up into a full-scale war. The British, having somewhat nonchalantly invaded Zululand, had suffered a terrible reverse at the battle of Isandlwana; this unexpected blow to imperial prestige had demanded instant revenge. Amongst the reinforcements which were being rushed out to Natal were members of the battery with which the Prince Imperial had served at Aldershot. Almost beside himself with envy of what he considered their good fortune, he wrote the Commander-in-Chief, begging permission to go with his battery.

When, the following morning, Eugenie came downstairs armed with her reasons why Louis should not risk his life in this foolhardy adventure, he was more than ready for her. God, he claimed earnestly, had chosen him as heir to the French Empire, yet what did France know of him? Having spent all his young manhood at Camden Place, he was nothing more than a name to the people of France. To the Bonapartists he was still looked upon as a child. It was imperative that he do something to assert himself, to show what sort of person he was. . . .

For hours he buffeted Eugenie with his arguments until her disapproval dissolved into pleading, and her pleading, into tears. But it was hopeless.

"Do you want me to be 'the little prince' all my life?" he cried out. "Do you want me to pine away and expire of boredom like the Duke of Reichstadt?"

There was nothing more that she could do except hope that his request to join his battery would be refused. It was. When Louis received the letter of refusal, he burst into tears. The sight of him—usually so calm in misfortune—standing before her, sobbing bitterly, melted Eugenie's heart. In a twinkling, she was completely on his side. She had, in fact, understood his attitude from the start; now she came out openly and supported him. He did not intend to let the matter rest with a refusal. He wrote a second, far more persuasive, letter to the Duke of Cambridge; Eugenie herself, veiled in black, went to the War Office to speak up for him; Queen Victoria, understanding his desire to repay *her* hospitality by fighting with *her* troops, added her voice. Thanks to the efforts of the

Queen and the Empress, he got his way. He was allowed to join the forces in Zululand, but in the capacity of a spectator only. In their letters to South Africa, the Government made this abundantly clear. "Well," Disraeli was afterwards to say, "my conscience is clear. I did all that I could to stop his going. But what can you do when you have two obstinate woman to deal with?"

For a few days Camden Place was in a state of uproar. Rouher, as leader of the party in France, came dashing over to England to try to get the Prince to change his mind, while a group of younger, more romantically minded members of the party (led by young Prince "Chino" Murat) offered to accompany him. But Louis would neither alter his decision nor take anyone but a valet, and by the morning of the twenty-seventh he was ready to set off. At dawn that day he went to the little church of St. Mary to pray by his father's sarcophagus, and then, accompanied by Eugenie, he traveled by train to Southampton. The journey down was a triumphant progress, and Eugenie had the bittersweet consolation of seeing her son feted all the way. At Southampton itself things were no less enthusiastic, and there was a vast crowd assembled to see him board the *Danube*. Clutching a posy of violets and sobbing bitterly behind her black veil, Eugenie kissed him good-by and then withdrew to a waterside hotel to watch the departure of the ship. And she did not move from the window until the *Danube* (a tricolor fluttering from its mainmast) had disappeared into the gray mist-blurred distance.

Back again at Camden, Eugenie dedicated herself to the anguish of waiting for news. "This state of waiting reminds me of 1870," she said, remembering the last agonizing days of the Empire. "All the old sensations are renewed under the influence of fear." To quiet these "old sensations" which now came surging into the void left by Louis's departure, she thrashed about for some sort of distraction. Very characteristically, it took the form of an attack. Her victim was Princess Mathilde.

"Would you believe," she wrote to Marie de Larminat, "that Princess Mathilde, to whom I wrote, announcing my son's departure, has not attempted to wish him good-by, nor to send me a word of consolation! She may not approve of the step, but I don't think it can be fear of the dangers which he may encounter which robs her of any sleep." And a few days later, in a further letter, she renewed the attack. "At last I have heard from Princess Mathilde; she also felt the REACTION; she might have had a little more feeling and have telegraphed a few words of farewell to my son; *he* thought so, too! Besides," continued the Empress, in her usual unforgiving strain, "since she went to the Crystal Palace when the Emperor was dead and not yet buried, she might just as well have continued to behave as callously as she has always done; it is impossible to believe that she has ever had any consideration for others."

What Eugenie seemed unable to realize was that Mathilde, stanch Bonapartist that she was, simply could not reconcile herself to the fact that a Napoleon had gone to fight *for* the British Army. Her attitude mirrored that of most members of the family and the party—they looked upon Louis's action as sheer madness, and it was Eugenie they blamed for allowing him to go. Louis was young, hotheaded, inexperienced; it was only natural that he should want to go to war, but it was nothing short of criminal of Eugenie to let him have his way. What had she done, they demanded of each other, to dissuade him from going? When this line of argument was exhausted, they tried another. Louis's only reason for going to war was to get away from the Empress. He could stand her dictatorial manner and parsimonious ways no longer. Things had come to a head, some claimed, when Eugenie learned of the Charlotte Watkyns affair. When he had refused to break with the girl, Eugenie's shrill disapproval had driven him from home. . . .

And so, while Louis sailed off to Africa in search of glory (and that was his only reason for going), Eugenie remained in England, to be covered with ill-informed abuse.

❧   ❧   ❧

Eugenie was fighting her battles at Camden; Louis was itching to be allowed to fight his in Natal.

No sooner had he landed in Durban (he had been greeted with all the honors due to a crowned head) than he came down with fever. He was confined to bed, and his forced inactivity almost drove him mad. "My regret is not to be with those who are fighting," he wrote querulously to Eugenie. "You know me well enough to judge how bitter that is. But all is not over and I shall have revenge upon my bad luck."

He never really did have revenge on what he called his bad luck. On his recovery from fever, the Commander-in-Chief of the British forces, Lord Chelmsford, not quite certain of what to do with this eager young man, attached him to his staff. As Chelmsford's instructions were that Louis was to be treated as a spectator and not as a combatant, he decided to keep him well out of harm's way. This did not suit Louis at all. But for the moment, while they were jogging north towards the borders of Zululand (Chelmsford was busily assembling his forces for a massive offensive), the Prince was happy enough. If anything, he took to army life almost too enthusiastically. He nosed about the camps asking questions, taking notes, examining everything. "He was very keen to learn all he could," commented a certain colonel with just a hint of exasperation, "of the manner in which we conducted our wars. . . . He was also anxious to take part in anything that was going on, and was only too eager for employment in the face of the enemy."

When he was not battering his superior officers with questions, he would be showing off—in the nicest way possible—for all he was worth. One of the ways in which he exhibited his skill was in feats of horsemanship. In Durban he had bought a horse called Fate, a big gray with a tendency to resist being mounted. It was a trait which suited Louis admirably; there was nothing he liked better than to prove his agility when it came to mounting a difficult horse. Running beside her, he would grasp the strap round the holster in front of the saddle, and ignoring the stirrups, vault into the seat. It was an accomplishment which had always won him the admiration of his colleagues at Woolwich.

But diverting as all these camp activities might be, they did not console him for the lack of any more active or dangerous employment. Once or twice, with Chelmsford's grudging permission, he was allowed to go out on reconnaissance. On one occasion he went careering after a solitary Zulu, and on another he led a charge on an all but deserted kraal. He was delighted with this taste of action, and when the commander of the little scouting party tactfully had the place entered on the map as Napoleon's Kraal, Louis flushed with pride and pleasure. When Lord Chelmsford heard about the Prince's somewhat reckless behavior on these reconnaissances, he took fright; from now on Louis was to be given employment which would keep him in the camp. He was ordered to draw up plans for a fort. As Louis was an obedient as well as a brave soldier, he resigned himself to this more sedentary life. But it was not easy.

On the morning of June 1, 1879, he was entrusted with a slightly more interesting mission. This was to be the first day of Chelmsford's big offensive. As the Prince was so obviously longing for an opportunity to get away from the confines of the Q.M.G. tent, his superior officer commanded him to select the site for the next day's camp. It was so tame, so safe, an assignment, that Louis was not especially pleased to be doing it, but it was better than nothing. So at nine in the morning, with an escort of six troopers and a Basuto guide under the command of a captain named Carey, Louis rode out from camp across the open grasslands. Just before leaving he scribbled a note to the Empress. "This will be my

last chance to get news to Europe," he remarked airily to the man who
was going to dispatch the letter for him.

By noon they had chosen the site for the camp, and on their way
back they decided to dismount for a little rest. It must have been about
three o'clock when the party of horsemen rode into a little kraal which
stood on the banks of a tributary of the Ityotyozi River. This kraal was
a collection of four or five huts, with a roughly fenced enclosure for
cattle, surrounded on three sides by grass and mealies growing to a
height of over four feet; on the fourth side the open ground sloped down
to the khaki-colored stream. The men dismounted. There were a few
lean dogs sniffing about and someone found a mound of ashes, still warm,
in the clearing between the deserted huts. It seems incredible that the
party should have chosen a spot so obviously recently abandoned, and so
clearly vulnerable to attack, in which to bivouac. More incredible still,
no sentry was posted. The men off-saddled, the horses were let loose
in the corn to graze, the Basuto guide went off to fetch water, and while
Louis and Carey stretched themselves on the ground, the troopers
prepared the coffee.

Having had their coffee, Carey suggested that it was time to go. "Not
yet," said Louis, "let's give the horses ten minutes more." It was five
minutes later that the order was given to saddle. As the men made ready
to mount, the terrified Basuto guide came tearing up with the news that
he had seen the head of a Zulu in the grass beyond the kraal. In a flash
Carey was in the saddle. Louis waited for the men, and when they were
ready, gave the order to mount. As the men mounted, the Zulus opened
fire. Howling their war cry and shooting a volley into the bewildered
group, the Zulus leaped out of the grass. From now on everything was
a confused blur of gleaming black bodies, of thrusting assagais, of echoing
gunshot, of rearing horses, and of swirling dust. Carey, not waiting to
see what was happening to the others, urged his horse forward, and
spurted away. Two of the troopers were assagaied soon after mounting; the
rest, with the exception of Louis and a man named Le Tocq, galloped
after Carey.

Fate, the Prince's high-spirited gray, had been panicked by the
shooting. She pranced and circled as her rider made desperate efforts to
mount her, and as Louis stumbled beside the jerking animal, his sword
slid from the scabbard and tumbled to the earth. By now Le Tocq, who
had managed to hoist himself sideways across his saddle, thundered past,
shouting, "*Dépêchez-vous s'il vous plait, Monsieur.*" As he passed, Fate
wrenched herself free of Louis's frantic grasp and galloped after the other

357

bolting horses. Louis dashed after her. There was nothing for it now but to try to vault into the saddle. He had done the trick so often before; surely he could manage to do it again. With his left hand he grasped the holster strap and with his right the pommel of the saddle. With a gigantic effort, he sprang forward.

The holster strap broke in his hand and he crashed to the earth. The strap had been paper-faced.

When he staggered to his feet, Fate was already some fifty yards away. Weakly he stumbled after her. Even now, at this late moment, he could have been saved. Everything had happened so suddenly, so simultaneously, that at the time Louis was racing after Fate, the others could not have been more than a hundred yards away. It would have needed only a minute or two for them to gallop back, drag the Prince onto one of the horses, and then make off again. True, there were about thirty Zulus in the kraal, but they were notoriously bad shots and had probably got rid of most of the throwing assagais by now and would have been left with only their shorter stabbing spears. And Louis was still some distance from them; some sign of help would have made him run all the faster. . . .

But there was no help coming. "The Prince is down," screamed Le Tocq to the scurrying Carey as he drew level with him, but Carey did not seem to hear. The four men thundered on.

By now Louis had stumbled into a small saucer-shaped island between two shallow streams. Fate was no longer to be seen and the Zulus were panting close behind him. There was nothing to do but to face them. With his left hand (his right had been trampled by Fate) he fumbled for his revolver, and turning, watched them come over the edge of the hollow. Then he walked towards them. There were about twelve Zulus who attacked him. Silently, the sun gleaming on their dusty black bodies, they watched him come towards them. He fired three cartridges—all that he had in his revolver—but the Zulus darted aside and avoided the shots. Then one of them threw an assagai. It hit the Prince in the thigh, and wrenching it out, he lunged towards his attackers. He fought, they were afterwards to tell, "like a lion," and it was not until his foot had been caught in a hole and he fell backwards that they closed in on him. The sharp-pointed assagais lifted and plunged, lifted and plunged, until his left arm was ripped to shreds from warding off the blows and there were eighteen wounds in his body.

When he was dead, they tore the clothes from his lacerated corpse, leaving only a gold chain round his neck. This chain, hung with several medallions, they refused to touch, having a deep fear of anything which might be magic. For some reason they did not disembowel the body as was their custom (perhaps they feared that magic chain), but did make a nick in the abdomen as a precaution against his ghost. Then, gathering up his scattered belongings—his revolver, his sword and his helmet—they wound their way through the surrounding mealie fields and disappeared.

It could not have been more than half past four. Half an hour before Louis had been sprawled in the sunshine, chatting to Carey; now he was dead.

He lay in the hollow on his back. Except for the golden chain, he was stark naked. His arms, the left one hacked to pieces, were crossed lightly over his chest; his body was a mass of oozing wounds. His head was turned to the right so that his cheek touched the ground. His right eye had been gouged out by an assagai; but apart from this, his features were in no way distorted, a faint smile parted his lips. . . .

Later the moon rose, and mounting into the wide, star-strewn African sky, washed the quiet grasslands with its white light. In the hollow beside the kraal the medallions glittered round the neck of the little corpse of Napoleon, Prince Imperial of France.

⚜   ⚜   ⚜

The news, which reached Europe three weeks later, brought the family flocking to Camden Place. The Empress was in a terrible state. On first hearing of her son's death, she had collapsed in a coma from which it seemed that she would never wake. When she did, it was into a state even more frightening; she appeared more dead than alive. She would not eat, she would not sleep, she would not even cry. Day after day she sat in her little boudoir with the windows closed and the curtains drawn, completely still, utterly alone. When she did consent to see the members of the family, it was for a few seconds only. One by one they groped their way towards that tragic figure, and throwing themselves at her feet, kissed her ice-cold hand. "My heart was full of sorrow and pity," wrote one of them; "such utter hopelessness, such anguish, was in every feature of her face, in every movement of her hands, in the few words she spoke." She was preserving "what little strength remains *for his return*," she said. Louis's body was being sent home for burial; it was due to arrive in England towards the middle of July.

At the end of June she wrote to her mother for the first time since hearing the news. "I have today the courage to tell you that I am still alive and that sorrow does not kill," she said.

A day or two after the recovery of Louis's body in Zululand and its dispatch back to England, Carey faced a court-martial. He was tried on the grounds of having deserted the Prince. At the trial, instead of simply admitting that he had lost his head and had tried to get away as quickly as possible, Carey tried to shift all the blame onto Louis. It was the Prince, he said, and not he, who had been in command of the party. It was the Prince who had chosen that fatal halting place. It was the Prince who had lost his head when attacked by the Zulus. And as for his deserting the Prince, he had, on the contrary, done everything to save him. The evidence of the troopers who had been with Carey at the time did nothing to support this claim. Carey's only orders, they said, had been for them to hurry on and get away.

Carey was cashiered and sent back to England to face a fresh trial. In fact, it is exceedingly likely that he was being made a scapegoat for the sins of his superiors, and that by playing up his undeniably cowardly behavior, they were able to emerge from the business with reputations intact. Eugenie, by demanding to see all the newspapers, both English and French, came to understand fully the circumstances of her son's death. And she had access to less public information as well. Three letters, written by Carey to his wife in the days after Louis's death, had been sent to her by Mrs. Carey. Perhaps Carey's wife hoped that her husband's wretchedness, so evident in these letters, might win the Empress's sympathy, or perhaps she thought that they absolved him from guilt. Whatever her reason for sending them to Camden, these letters did nothing to endear Carey to the Empress. Every other word confirmed his guilt and his despicable cowardice. The household at Camden begged Eugenie to publish the letters, but she refused. The time for revenge had passed. "I do not know anything," she cried out in her anguish. "I know that he has been killed, that is all!"

And when the Queen visited her (Victoria was the only person with whom Eugenie would spend any length of time), she suddenly exclaimed: "Tell me, they'll do nothing to that poor man? Oh no, I beg of you! He may have a mother!" Victoria replied that although Carey's fate was not in her hands, she would do her best to comply with Eugenie's wish. And then, as the commission was about to sit in judgment on Carey, the Empress issued an impassioned statement in which she begged that no one be allowed to suffer as a result of Louis's death.

These moves by Eugenie—the suppression of the letters and the written intervention on his behalf—saved Carey. The commission, hamstrung by Eugenie's pleas and Victoria's promise to do all that she could to help, was obliged to let him off. The sentence of the court in Natal was revised, and he was restored to his rank. But the affair was the finish of him. No one ever forgave him for his desertion of the Prince. Despised and ignored, he drifted from regiment to regiment, and died, six years later, in Bombay.

Louis's body reached home on July 11. It was carried ashore at Woolwich and placed in a specially prepared mortuary chapel for identification. Amongst the handful of persons present at this ceremony were Prince Joachim Murat, Prince Achille Murat, Prince Louis-Lucien Bonaparte, and his nephew Prince Charles Bonaparte. Eugenie had expressly asked for the body to remain undisturbed, but M. Rouher claimed that in order to scotch the mounting rumors about Louis's death, it would be best for the body to be identified. The coffin was unscrewed. What faced the horrified group was a hideously decomposed mass, completely unrecognizable as the Prince Imperial. It was only by holding the head at different angles and by recognizing certain scars on the body and certain fillings in the teeth that the body was identifiable. The group declared themselves satisfied and the coffin was closed.

If the identity of the corpse had satisfied the handful of mourners in the chapel, it satisfied hardly anyone else. As with the death of his three predecessors, the death of this latest Napoleon gave rise to endless speculations. The corpse had not been that of the Prince Imperial at all, they said: some other body had been put in the coffin, and somewhere in the world the Prince lived on! Exactly what the point of this deception would be was never explained.

The cortege, with the Prince Imperial's coffin on a gun carriage reached Camden Place late that afternoon. As a tribute to the Prince's blameless youth, the main hall of the house had been hung with white. In the center of the room, on the very spot where his father's coffin had rested six years before, was a mound of violets. On it they placed the Prince's remains. "We had given them our Prince in all the splendor and beauty of his youth," wrote Marie de Larminat of the departing English escort; "they gave us back his coffin."

Alone, dressed in black and heavily veiled, Eugenie descended the stairs. Suddenly, with a piteous cry, she sprang forward, dashed towards the coffin, and flung herself across it. With both arms she embraced the bier. Then she fell to her knees and rested her head against it. Tearless, motionless, she remained kneeling there throughout the night. About her, keeping watch over the coffin through the long hours, stood Louis's friends and various members of the family. No one moved. All eyes were fixed, as though dazed, upon that black figure slumped against the coffin.

And so the night passed. Towards dawn Anna Murat stepped forward, and motioning Marie de Larminat to help her, lifted Eugenie to her feet. Then, half-supporting, half-carrying her, they led her upstairs to her room.

That morning Louis was buried beside his father in the little church of St. Mary's on Chislehurst Common. Queen Victoria, who was determined that Louis should go to his grave with all possible pomp, honored Camden with her own presence that day. Accompanied by the Princess of Wales and Princess Beatrice, she was met at the door of the house by an impressive array of Bonaparte princes and princesses. The royal ladies each placed a wreath on the coffin and then knelt for a moment in prayer beside it. The sight of young Princess Beatrice kneeling by Louis's remains was especially poignant, in view of the rumors that she might one day have married him.

Having paid their homage, the royal family were ushered into the room which had been Louis's study and were introduced to the various members of the Bonaparte clan. Victoria, in her quick, observant way, had telling comments to make on each member in turn. It fell to Plon-Plon, as head of the Bonapartes, to effect the various presentations. Victoria found him "very civil, and very subdued and embarrassed." He had aged, she thought, and grown balder, but looked more like Napoleon I than ever. When she spoke to him of the dreadful event, he answered, "*C'est bien triste. . . . Votre Majesté a été si bonne.*" For Plon-Plon this was almost unbelievably civil.

His sister Princess Mathilde she found hardly altered at all. She was still the same handsome, impressive-looking woman she had always been. When Victoria offered her condolences, Mathilde, only just concealing her lack of sympathy with Eugenie's side of the family, answered, "*Il s'est précipité,*" and he must have had "*l'esprit malade.*" Victoria countered a trifle sharply to the effect that she thought it only natural that Louis had wished to distinguish himself and "*de faire quelque chose.*"

Plon-Plon's eldest son, the seventeen-year-old Prince Victor, was "tall and nice and intelligent-looking, very like the Italian family, but with the fine Bonaparte brow and complexion." His second son, the fifteen-year-old Louis, was shorter and darker, "and has quite the Bonaparte features. . . ."

When the introductions were over, Victoria left the house and took up her position on a specially erected dais in the driveway. From here she watched the cortege pass by. It seemed endless, and she had the satisfaction of seeing for herself that it was every bit as impressive as she had meant it to be. It was, she decided, "a most beautiful, touching, solemn procession, and yet not at all gloomy."

The cortege crawled through the vast bareheaded crowd on the Common towards the little church. For the second time in its history St. Mary's was filled with royalties. After Mass had been celebrated, they laid the coffin in a side chapel. From noon to sunset something like ten thousand Frenchmen filed past the chapel to pay homage to the Prince. Not five months had passed since Louis had knelt in prayer beside the sarcophagus of his father; now their bodies lay once more united beneath the black rafters of that steeply pitched roof.

Today, after the passing of over seventy-five years, the dim interior of the little church is hardly altered. It is still rich in Imperial souvenirs. Let into the right wall of the nave is a squat archway, below which lies an effigy of the Prince. It shows him in full uniform, with hands piously clasped, against a background of Imperial bees. A barely legible inscription tells one that it was erected in his memory by Father Goddard, the parish priest during the years of exile at Camden.

The chapel in which his coffin was laid is still there. But the coffin itself has gone.

CHAPTER SEVENTEEN

❦   ❦   ❦

THE day for which Plon-Plon had waited so long, and so impatiently, had dawned at last. He was now the pretender to the Imperial throne. Keeping his satisfaction down to a decent level, he played the part of chief mourner at the funeral with commendable dignity. That over, he returned to Camden Place to claim his heritage. He asked to see Louis's will.

This will had been drawn up by the Prince during his last night at Camden before setting sail for Africa. Unlike the Emperor's will, it was very relevant to the present circumstances. There were some conventional clauses dealing with his love for his mother, his gratitude to the Queen of England, and his deep affection for France. There was a request for his body to be laid beside that of his father. These clauses were followed by the expected list of bequests. It was in a codicil that Louis had planted his bombshell.

"I do not need to remind my mother to take every necessary step to preserve the memory of my great-uncle and of my father. I beg her to remember that so long as there are Bonapartes, the Imperial cause will have representatives. The duties of our house will not end with my life. When I am dead, the task of continuing the work of Napoleon I and of Napoleon III will devolve upon *the eldest son of Prince Napoleon,* and I trust that my well-beloved mother, by supporting him to the best of her ability, will give us, who are no longer of this earth, this last supreme proof of her affection."

In other words, Plon-Plon had been cut out. The succession had been passed on to his eldest son, Prince Victor. The news left Plon-Plon, for the first and only time in his life, speechless with rage.

Eugenie, in what she called a "spirit of sacrifice," offered to receive Plon-Plon and Mathilde for a few minutes after the funeral. Mathilde came but not Plon-Plon. He ordered his carriage and drove back to London without a word. "I think that my son's soul, pleased with the sacrifice I had made, delivered me from the sight of him by leaving him to the perversity of his instincts," wrote Eugenie later.

Because it was she, of course, whom Plon-Plon blamed for the will. He had always considered Louis little better than an imbecile; Eugenie and Rouher had obviously drawn up the document and had got Louis to sign it. And there were plenty of Bonapartes who agreed with Plon-Plon.

"No one who knew the Prince as we did," said one of them, "could believe him capable of expressing sentiments and having a successor which would, and must, fatally disunite a party and separate a father and son."

But Eugenie had had nothing to do with it. It had been Louis's decision alone. Being younger than the Empress, his hatred for Plon-Plon had been much more uncompromising than hers; Eugenie had even tried to make things up with Plon-Plon occasionally; Louis never had. For the Empress, moreover, the hereditary principle was far too sacrosanct for such cavalier treatment. A few weeks before Louis's death Eugenie, unaware that Plon-Plon had been disinherited, had been chatting to M. Duval, Public Prosecutor during the Empire. Her visitor had expressed a fear that if anything should happen to the Prince, the Imperialist party would disintegrate. When Eugenie reminded him that Plon-Plon was more than ready to assume the leadership, M. Duval assured her that the party would never accept him as a leader. When they spoke of Prince Victor, Plon-Plon's eldest son ("a charming young man whom my son likes very much," said Eugenie), they agreed that he could only follow, not supersede his father. "One cannot," said Eugenie, albeit with regret. "pass over Prince Napoleon (Plon-Plon)." And it is certain that had Louis ever consulted her on the matter, she would have advised him against such an action. Within a very few years, in fact, her attitude towards Plon-Plon and the succession would be made crystal clear.

At the moment, however, nothing would convince Plon-Plon that she had not been responsible for having him cut out. And the family was accusing her of worse things than that. Mathilde, writing to young Primoli, declared emphatically that Eugenie had killed her son, just as she had killed his father. Louis could not bear living with her. It was she who had urged him to go to war. With his "strength spent and his spirit crushed," he had gone to meet his death. She was, wrote Mathilde with more than a touch of hysteria, "an unnatural wife and mother."

Caroline Murat's contribution to the accusations, other than the usual ones about Eugenie making life impossible for the Prince, was that the Empress had insisted on Louis getting his equipment from a well-known London store and not having it especially made. The result, of course, was that the shoddily made holster strap had ripped apart when he had tried to mount his horse. "Now, when too late, it was recognized and bitterly deplored, that had the Prince's equipment been of a different make, he might have escaped. . . ."

That the paper-faced holster strap had contributed to the Prince's death is undeniable; that Eugenie had had anything to do with its selection was nonsense.

Whether or not any of these accusations reached the ears of the Empress, one does not know; but even if they had, it is doubtful if they would have been enough to shake her out of her terrible grief. "Her eyes," said Marie de Larminat, "worn out with weeping, could see nothing on the horizon, her thoughts could imagine nothing but a hopeless void; nothing seemed able to awaken her interest, and I began to fear that nothing would arouse her from this state of coma."

"'The entire universe could disappear and I would be quite indifferent," wrote Eugenie to her mother, "nothing more interests me . . . if you only knew what an empty desert the world is to me!" There was one thing, however, which kept her interest alive; she wanted to see the place where Louis had died. She wanted to make a pilgrimage to Zululand.

"I feel myself drawn towards this place of pilgrimage as strongly as the disciples of Christ must have felt drawn towards the Holy Places," she wrote. "The thought of seeing, of retracing the stages of my beloved son's last journey, of seeing with my own eyes the scene upon which his dying gaze rested, of passing the anniversary of the night of the first of June watching and praying alone with his memory, is for me a spiritual necessity and an aim in life. . . ."

Encouraged and assisted by Queen Victoria (this cult of the dead was very much to her taste), Eugenie was able to undertake her journey to Natal. Ignoring the whispers of those who considered it to be nothing more than one of her typically melodramatic gestures, she sailed from England towards the end of March 1880. Two months later, after four weeks at sea and a further four weeks of jolting along the rutted tracks of northern Natal, she reached the place where her son had been killed. The first sight of it disappointed her bitterly. She had expected some dark steep-sided ravine; what she found was a neat shallow dip, about as dramatic as an English country churchyard. Queen Victoria had arranged for a cross to be erected on the spot, and the party of men responsible for its erection had spruced up the site to such an extent that all traces of drama had been completely eliminated. Earth, once wet with the blood of the fourth Napoleon, had been carefully cemented over, and the surrounding area conscientiously raked and enclosed by a white-washed wall. Cedars had been planted at regular intervals. Eugenie lost no time in getting some of the more offensive improvements removed. Then she planted a willow shoot cut from a tree at Camden, which in turn had been grown from a shoot of a willow growing by the grave of Napoleon I on St. Helena.

Eugenie spent the day and the night of June 1, 1880, in prayer beside the cross. Of those long hours only the following characteristic description remains. "More than once, I noticed black forms on the top of the banks, which moved silently about and watched me through the tall grasses. This scrutiny was full of curiosity, but it was not hostile. I believe these savages wished rather to express their sympathy and their pity . . . and doubtless they were the very men who had killed my son on the same spot. . . .

"Towards dawn a strange thing happened. Although there was not a breath of air, the flames of the candles were suddenly deflected, as if someone wished to extinguish them, and I said to him: 'Is it indeed you beside me? Do you wish me to go away?' "

Whereupon she rose and went back to her tent.

The cedars which had been planted around the cross are now full-grown trees. They make a dark green oasis in the pale desert of the surrounding veld. A little gate, set in the low wall of whitewashed stones, leads one into the hollow of cool darkness under the spreading branches. There is a sudden clatter as two or three goats scramble over the wall at one's approach, and a flash of silver as the long-tailed lizards dart back between the sun-baked stones. But once this activity has subsided, it is very still, and the branches of the cedars diffusing the sunshine make the place a pool of green and quiet light. In the center of the hollow is a neat rectangle of stones, and at its head, rising from a whitewashed mound, is a simple cross. On it are inscribed these words:

THIS CROSS IS ERECTED BY QUEEN VICTORIA
IN AFFECTIONATE REMEMBRANCE OF NAPOLEON EUGENE LOUIS JEAN JOSEPH
PRINCE IMPERIAL
TO MARK THE SPOT WHERE
WHILE ASSISTING IN A RECONNAISSANCE WITH THE BRITISH TROOPS
ON THE 1ST OF JUNE 1879
HE WAS ATTACKED BY A PARTY OF ZULUS
AND FELL WITH HIS FACE TO THE FOE

On her way back to England, Eugenie spent a day at St. Helena. Her ship dropped anchor off the island on the morning of July 12, and this last of the Napoleonic empresses stood gazing at the black pile which had been the prison of the first Napoleon. It was his legend, so carefully fostered during the exile on St. Helena, which had made possible the restoration of the Napoleonic dynasty, and which had led to the whole glorious adventure of the Second Empire. So much had happened in the years since Napoleon's death. Sixty years ago, dethroned, exiled, and deserted, he had died on this island; now, similarly dethroned, in exile, and alone, the last Empress to bear his name came back to see the place where he had been buried. The drama of the situation was not lost on her.

Escorted by the Governor, she visited Longwood. The house, which had fallen into disrepair after the death of Napoleon, had been ceded to France during the Second Empire, and Napoleon III had had extensive repairs carried out. Eugenie thought the house "very like the officers' camp-huts at Aldershot, and wretchedly furnished." She wandered through its six small undistinguished rooms, and seems to have been affected only by the sight of the little drawing room in which Napoleon had died.

From Longwood she drove to Geranium Valley, the exquisite little dell in which the body of Napoleon had lain buried for twenty years. The grave, like the house, had been given to France during the Second Empire, and now looked as pretty as when Napoleon had first chosen it as his resting place. Eugenie picked a bunch of violets, and then cut several shoots from the willows growing around the grave. She sailed from the island at midnight.

Some two weeks later, towards the end of July, Eugenie stepped ashore onto English soil once more. With her sad white face lifted towards the little crowd that had gathered to welcome her home, she returned to the country that loved her so well. She was to be known, henceforth, as the Tragic Empress. "She to whom God has given so much," she would say of herself, "yet from whom He has taken, one by one, all those gifts which He had bestowed, leaving her the heart's bitterness as her only companion. . . ."

⚜ ⚜ ⚜

In the year 1880 Prince Victor Napoleon, Plon-Plon's eldest son and the new official pretender to the Imperial throne, was eighteen years of age. If typically Bonaparte features counted for anything, Prince Victor stood a good chance of succeeding. Like his father, Plon-Plon, and his grandfather Jérôme, he had the cameolike complexion and the high forehead of the Bonapartes; he had also the fine dark family eyes. Taller than average, he was, in these early days, quite slender. In looks, he would have made an admirable Emperor.

But it was not as easy as that. For one thing, while he had not inherited Plon-Plon's more pernicious characteristics, he had not inherited his driving ambition, either. Somewhat indolent by nature, and having been projected so unexpectedly into the position of Pretender, he had as yet no real sense of dedication to the Imperial cause. And, of course, with Plon-Plon still so very much alive, he had very little chance of developing one. Inevitably, the two of them fell out. The quarrels which had always characterized the family—be they between brothers, sisters-in-law, or cousins—now developed between father and son. Just as the family had always been split between the Bonaparte and Beauharnais factions, so did the remaining legitimate Bonaparte branch break into two. And this, quite naturally, led to a division in the party as well. From now on there were to be two factions, Plon-Plon's crowd, the *Jeromistes*, and Victor's adherents, the *Victoriens*.

Not that Plon-Plon ever took his son's claim to the throne seriously. In 1882 Plon-Plon drew up a letter for him to sign. In it, Victor would renounce the rights conferred upon him by the Prince Imperial. Had it not been for the impassioned intervention of a group of journalists (Frédéric Masson, that ardent Bonapartist, chief amongst them), Prince Victor might well have signed the paper and left the field to his father. Deciding that some show of solidarity was necessary, the pro-Victor faction (in reality, the bulk of the Bonapartists), held a vast meeting in which they resolved to unite behind the young pretender. It was thanks to the late Prince Imperial, claimed the zealous M. de Cassagnac, that the party had not perished. His death in Zululand had provided the Second Empire with a legend every bit as powerful as the legend of St. Helena which had followed the First Empire. And it was thanks to the Prince Imperial's naming of Prince Victor as his heir that the party would continue and flourish. One of the principles of the Empire was respect for religion, and as Plon-Plon had no more respect for religion than he had for anything else, he had forfeited his right to the Imperial throne. That Victor had not followed his father's shameful example was due entirely, declared Cassagnac, "to a saint." The saint, of course, was Prince Victor's mother, Clotilde, and at the mention of her name, the assembled Bonapartists burst into hysterical applause and the meeting broke up with heartfelt shouts of *"Vive Victor!"*

It would have needed more than this emotional outburst, however, to discourage Plon-Plon from behaving as though he were in fact the pretender. The following year, when Gambetta, head of the Republican government, died, Plon-Plon imagined that his hour had struck. He published a violent indictment against the Republic in *Le Figaro*. Copies of this manifesto, in which Plon-Plon (posing as—of all things—a champion of the Church) demanded a plebiscite, were pasted all over Paris. "Frenchmen," ran a typical phrase, "remember the words of Napoleon I— 'All that is done without the people is illegal!' " Instead of being hailed as a hero, Plon-Plon was arrested and imprisoned in the Conciergerie for a few days.

"As for Prince Napoleon (Plon-Plon)," noted one English paper dryly, "he has arrived at a time of life when Pretenders cannot afford to make blunders. . . . Now that he has only succeeded in making himself ridiculous, and in making the rift in the Imperialist Party deeper than ever, he will probably give France little further trouble for some time."

When Eugenie heard about his imprisonment, she was extremely upset. She lost no time in writing to Princess Mathilde, begging her to convey her sympathy to Plon-Plon and to tell him that she ranked family unity far above personal differences. Not content with this, she crossed to Paris to consult with the leaders of the party. This was her second visit to Paris since the disasters of 1870 (the first time had been the year before, en route to Nice), and she remained for one day only. She stayed at the Hotel du Rhin in the Place Vendôme, the very hotel where Queen Hortense and Louis-Napoleon had once stayed over fifty years before. What Eugenie's thoughts were at the first sight of the blackened ruins which were now all that remained of the Tuileries, one does not know, but they must have been poignant indeed.

She called this flying visit to Paris her "last political act." In spite of all rumors to the contrary, she had never championed Prince Victor in his fight against his father, and she now attempted to unite the rival factions. She wanted the leaders of the orthodox party to rally round Plon-Plon. "I have forgiven him, why can't you do the same?" she pleaded. "It is the only way to preserve our party, its unity and even its existence." But they would not listen. To accept Plon-Plon's leadership, they said, would hasten the end of the party, not preserve it. Defeated in her mission, Eugenie returned home.

She had won one thing, though—and that for the first time in her life: Plon-Plon's gratitude. The following year, wearing the Grand Cordon of the Legion of Honor, he crossed the Channel and attended the Mass on the anniversary of the death of the Prince Imperial. And Eugenie, spotting him standing a little shamefacedly in the dim interior of the church, whispered to one of her suite: "There's Prince Napoleon; go and pay your respects to him; we must be nice to him."

Eugenie and Plon-Plon might have patched up their quarrel, but the fight between father and son raged as bitterly as ever. In 1884, at the age of twenty-two, Prince Victor left his father's home and went to live on his own. Always ready to wash their dirty linen in public, both sides now published letters defending their relative positions. This well-publicized family bickering did nothing to strengthen the already pitifully weak Bonaparte cause; the two more responsible members of the family—Eugenie and Mathilde—were particularly sensitive to the sordidness of the affair. The Empress wrote a strong letter to Mathilde, blaming both Plon-Plon and Victor; and Mathilde wrote an even stronger one to Victor, telling him—as only she could—to pull himself together and to treat his father with more respect. But Victor, egged on by his truculent followers, was in no mood to retract. He assured his aunt Mathilde that since his father had proved himself incapable of re-establishing the dynasty, it would be up to him to do it. The name he bore demanded it of him, he declared earnestly. His heroics did not fool Mathilde; she pronounced him egotistical, and at the same time lacking in any real enthusiasm. She was not, she said, at all impressed by him.

A year or so later Republican France, heartily sick of the intrigues of the various pretenders to the throne (the royalists had recently broken out in rash of manifestoes as well) exiled all heads of formerly reigning families and their direct heirs. This meant that both Plon-Plon and Victor had to leave. Although the law did not apply to Plon-Plon's second son, Louis, he too decided to leave France. What this compulsory exile did was to put an end to the public dissensions of the family; in private, however, they continued at full strength.

When, in 1888, Plon-Plon's only daughter, Laetitia, married her uncle, the Duke of Aosta, at Turin, Plon-Plon refused to allow Prince Victor to attend the ceremony. Nor was this the only embarrassing incident to mark the festivities. As the Duke of Aosta was almost twice Laetitia's age, and a widower besides, his grown-up daughters did not much relish the idea of such a young stepmother. Their undisguised frigidity augmented the existing coolness between the houses of Savoy and Bonaparte. Neither Plon-Plon nor his youngest son, Louis, were invited to stay with the other wedding guests (including Plon-Plon's wife, Clotilde) at the Castle of Cisterna; and when father and son arrived at Turin, there was no one to meet them. It seems that an official reception had been planned, but that for some reason or other the orders had been countermanded at the last moment. The result was that Plon-Plon and Louis were obliged to make their way to a hotel unattended. Fortunately, the presence of Princess Mathilde added some much-needed dignity to the Bonaparte side of the family; dressed in white, with seven rows of pearls gleaming on her still lovely *décolletage*, she moved through the ceremony like a queen. No one could believe that she was almost seventy years old.

In March 1891, when Plon-Plon himself was just a year off seventy, he fell seriously ill. Mathilde, who had drawn nearer to him during these last few years, hurriedly left Paris to join him in Rome. She found him, obviously dying, at the Hotel de Russie. With him was his long-suffering wife, Clotilde, and his daughter, Laetitia. Princess Mathilde, realizing that the end was near, decided that this would be a good time to effect a reconciliation between father and son. She should have known Plon-Plon better. Fetching Prince Victor, she led him into the darkened sickroom. At the sight of his rebellious son Plon-Plon fell back on his pillows, growled something incomprehensible, and motioned him out of the room. Vindictive in life, Plon-Plon was no more forgiving as he neared death.

The only result of Mathilde's well-meaning gesture was that the doctors blamed her for exciting the dying Prince. Victor himself rushed into the night, crying out that there was a curse on his race.

Princess Clotilde's mission seemed to have been rather more successful. As devout as her husband was irreligious, she was determined that he should make what she called "a good end." She sent for Cardinal Mermillod, and together they seem to have worn down Plon-Plon's resistance. When the Cardinal emerged from the sickroom for the last time, he seemed "relieved of a great weight," while the gratified Clotilde looked almost radiant. "Her perseverance," wrote one reporter admiringly, "triumphed on that melancholy occasion." It must have been the only time that it had. Plon-Plon died the next day.

🐝   🐝   🐝

Princess Mathilde, who at the age of seventy was capable of loving as passionately as a girl of twenty, now experienced yet another emotional crisis. She discovered that her lover, Popelin, was deceiving her. Although they had been together for almost twenty years, such was Mathilde's nature that the affair had never really mellowed and grown supple; she loved him as vehemently now as she had in those first bleak months after the fall of the Empire. As with his predecessor, Nieuwerkerque, she devoted herself to him, and considered it only natural that he, in turn, should devote himself exclusively to her. Popelin, at sixty-five, had neither Nieuwerkerque's attractiveness nor aplomb, nor did he have his ability to go out and bowl women over like ninepins. But he did not have to; there was a young and attractive woman on hand to satisfy his wants. For years, under Mathilde's very nose, Popelin had been carrying on with Marie Abbatucci, Mathilde's protégée.

Marie Abbatucci was the daughter of the man who had been *chargé d'affaires* to the late King Jérôme, Mathilde's father, and it was in gratitude for the father's services that Mathilde had taken charge of the girl. Fair, fragile, and vivacious, Marie was a joy to have in the house. Mathilde came to look upon her as a daughter, and fondly imagined that Popelin, who was at least twice the girl's age, was doing the same. The three of them became inseparable. In the Rue de Berri, at Saint-Gratien, during the annual holiday at Dieppe, Mathilde, Popelin, and Marie were always together. The girl seemed to have given Mathilde a new lease of life, and it was soon being rumored that to Popelin she seemed to be giving something more.

When it was first suggested to Mathilde that there might be something between Marie and her lover, she refused to believe it. But once the seed had been planted, it began to germinate. She began to look for signs, she began to suspect their every move, and as she was incapable of concealing her jealousy, she began to question Popelin. He denied her accusations, and she was thrown back into an agony of suspicion. Her friends advised her to leave things as they were; she should believe Popelin and rest content with the situation. But this was not Mathilde's way. She was no more capable of compromise at seventy than she had ever been. She did not rest until she had convinced herself that the rumors were true. When she thought that she had discovered the evidence she needed, she treated Marie Abbatucci to one of her well-known rages. Like a female Napoleon she confronted the terrified girl, subjecting her to a seemingly endless torrent of abuse. The scene over, she drove Marie out of the house.

When the girl had gone, she and Popelin patched up their liaison. But it could never be anything more than a makeshift affair now. She could not forget his duplicity, and suspected that he was still in love with Marie. Before long all her resentment rose to the surface and she reopened the whole wretched question. In vain did Popelin protest that his continued interest in Marie was merely platonic, that he wanted to see her well married. Mathilde decided that if she was to have any peace of mind, she must break with him once and for all. She wrote, putting an end to the affair. He came hurrying back, and she forgave him. But the reconciliation could not last. In August 1890 she steeled herself for the final break, and having made it, fell sick with grief for six months.

Two years later Popelin was found dead in his room. When they called Mathilde to his bedside, she made an unusually magnanimous gesture. She instructed Popelin's son to tell Marie the news. Unfortunately, her gesture misfired; Marie, who had already been told, had reached the house before her. The girl had retired to another room on Mathilde's arrival. When Popelin's son, hoping that this would be a good moment for a reconciliation, fetched Marie and led her into the room, Mathilde ignored her. Her magnanimity forgotten, Mathilde, running far more true to form, gave Marie a withering look and swept out of the room.

Princess Mathilde never really recovered from her break with Popelin. Although she lived for another twelve years, her life seemed to have been stripped of all its meaning. She now lived, she would say, as a shadow. Despite the fact that her last years were somewhat comforted by the presence of her nephew Count Primoli (he was a great favorite with Eugenie, as well) she was never to recapture her old lust for life. Instead of that vigorous, quick-witted personality, speaking her mind and crowding her days with activity, she became a dependent, sorrow-steeped figure.

The one thing she never lost was her intense family pride. She who had sought love so passionately, and in vain, could still love the first Napoleon without fear of disenchantment. Once, on catching sight of someone who had written an uncomplimentary piece about the Emperor, she hissed, "That beast"; when her companion hinted that she should let bygones be bygones, she answered proudly, "Never!" On another occasion, when some sycophant suggested that she might be descended from Charlemagne, she scoffed. Charlemagne, she answered sharply, was not nearly good enough for a Napoleon.

♛   ♛   ♛

"I desire my body to be laid by that of my Father," the Prince Imperial had written in his will, "until such time as both are transferred to the resting place of the Founder of our House, in the bosom of that French people which was so dear to us, as to him."

Louis's wish to be laid beside his father had been granted, but the chances of the bodies being taken back to Paris and buried in the Invalides were remote indeed. And yet it was clear that they could not remain in St. Mary's church, Chislehurst, indefinitely. The side chapel which Eugenie had added to the church for the Emperor's sarcophagus had been meant as a temporary resting place only; it was hardly grand enough for an Emperor of the French. Nor was it big enough to accommodate Louis's coffin; as a result, his remains had been lying in a dark and almost inaccessible side chapel ever since his funeral. Eugenie, realizing that she would have to do something if her dead were to be provided with a more splendid tomb, set about making plans. The obvious thing to do would be to extend St. Mary's, and to this end Eugenie tried to buy the land adjoining the churchyard. But here she met with unshakable opposition. The property belonged to a toy manufacturer by the name of Eldmann, a man of such strong Protestant convictions that nothing would induce him to sell it for the erection of any Roman Catholic building. And supporting these religious prejudices were national ones—Eldmann was a German, and consequently did not relish the idea of providing the site for the grave of his late enemy. Faced with this hostility, Eugenie decided to leave Chislehurst and take her illustrious dead elsewhere.

She moved, in the autumn of 1881, to Farnborough Hill in Hampshire. The house had belonged to a Longman, a member of the publishing family, and looked like nothing so much as an immense cottage—a riot of gables and chimneys and imitation beams, very much in the semi-Tudor, semi-Swiss style of the period. Filon thought it "a magnificent residence, worthy of comparison with those noble ancestral homes which are the glories of the English countryside;" Eugenie, whose own taste was rather uncertain, was anyway more concerned with a home for the dead than one for the living. Even before taking up residence at Farnborough, she had climbed the pine-covered hill opposite her new home, and there marked the place where the mausoleum should rise. It was to be so placed that from the windows of her rooms she would be able to see its cross rising above the trees.

The foundations of St. Michael's Abbey were laid in 1883, but it was not completed until four years later. The finished building had a distinctly French look about it. With its leaping gargoyles, its flying buttresses, its slender pinnacles, its lacelike balustrading, it had a delicacy unusual in English ecclesiastical architecture. Even its honey-colored stone seemed somehow un-English. In the crypt, on a pavement which was an exact copy of the floor in the crypt of the Invalides, stood identical sarcophagi, ready for the coffins. The date chosen for the re-interment was January 9, 1888. It would be the fifteenth anniversary of the death of Napoleon III.

At ten that morning two gun carriages, in the charge of the Royal

Horse Artillery, came rumbling up the roadway towards St. Mary's church on Chislehurst Common. The coffins, each wrapped in a tricolor, were carried out of the church, laid on the gun carriages, and taken to the station. Here they were put in a specially prepared mortuary car and transported to Farnborough. This second funeral of Napoleon III and his son was remarkable for two things: its unpretentiousness and its Englishness. With the exception of the military escort, there was very little in the way of display, and almost the only notable Frenchman present was Prince Louis-Lucien Bonaparte. Eugenie herself did not attend. The days when the Imperialists had flocked to England in their tens of thousands were over; the Bonapartist cause was dying, and Eugenie had done with fanfares. As a result, the ceremony in the crypt of St. Michael's was simple and subdued. Mass over, the coffins were deposited in the waiting sarcophagi, and the priest having pronounced the blessing, the company dispersed, murmuring, into the darkening afternoon.

It had all been a far cry from the flamboyant funerals of the First Emperor and his son.

♛   ♛   ♛

Of all the dozens of great-nephews and great-great-nephews of Napoleon I, it was an extraordinary fact that by the end of the nineteenth century only two were eligible for the Imperial succession. These were Plon-Plon's sons, Prince Victor and Prince Louis. Although both men were nearing forty, neither was married. Victor, being in direct line of succession, had been banished from France in 1886 and was living in Belgium; Louis had left the country of his own accord and had become a general in the Russian Army. Except for an occasional spurt of activity —a manifesto here, a round of royal visits there, an article somewhere else—Prince Victor seemed to be making no serious attempt to win the throne, while Prince Louis seemed more than happy as an officer in the Czar's army. In the year 1906 the pretender's somewhat retired life had given rise to the rumor that he intended renouncing his rights in favor of his younger brother; Victor quickly authorized a Bonapartist journal to publish a denial of the story. He had no intention, he protested, of "renouncing all political ambition." That done, he resumed his quiet life in the Avenue Louise in Brussels, contenting himself with presiding over an occasional Bonapartist meeting or with the issuing of some high-sounding statement. When asked about the "program" of his party, he would make the lofty, if somewhat obscure reply: "The name of Bonaparte is a program."

There was, in fact, very little else that he could do. The time for *coups d'état*, he admitted, were gone. "The Empire!" he would say. "Do you really believe that France could still exist under all the laws of the First, and even the Second, Empire? The times have progressed. . . . I am of my time; I am a man of progress. I do not live in the past, with old-fashioned sentiments. I desire above everything the well-being of my country." Pressed to talk less obliquely about his hopes of a restoration, he would claim that he did not believe in "adventures," that in a modern country an army could no longer bring about a change of regime without the assent of the country. "One must know how to await opportunities," he would say tritely, "and never attempt to precipitate events."

"Prince Napoleon is a Pretender who seems to have no pretensions," they quipped in Brussels.

Although Prince Victor lived discreetly, he lived, as had all the Bonapartes, in great style. A visitor to the house would be ushered into one of several drawing rooms by a liveried footman, and would remain there until the Prince was ready to receive him. He would then be led through a white marble vestibule and along a vast corridor to the Prince's study. At every turn would be souvenirs of the First and Second Empires: a bronze statuette of the young Napoleon, portraits of every member of the family, busts of the two Emperors, an assortment of sabers, swords, crosses, and medals, and a six-thousand volume Napoleonic library. "I live my darkest hours in the midst of souvenirs of the First Emperor," the Prince once wrote to a friend. "Each one of these, in recalling a period of his life, teaches me a lesson. . . . I take refuge in his thoughts. To him alone I go to ask for inspirations."

On the visitor's being ushered into the Imperial presence, the Prince would rise and shake his guest firmly by the hand. Prince Victor was tall for a Bonaparte, and somewhat stout; he was, it has been claimed, "an imposing figure." His receding hair was more than compensated for by a luxuriant handlebar mustache; his eyes were dark and piercing; his manner, dignified and urbane. If the Bonaparte flame which had burned so brightly in Napoleon, Lucien, Louis-Napoleon, the Prince Imperial, and Mathilde merely flickered in Prince Victor, he did at least have something of the *grand seigneur* manner of Carlo Bonaparte and King Joseph about him. "By his admirable fulfillment of the role of a silent and studious exile," enthused one of his intimate friends, "by the charm of his conversation—the talk of an erudite and an artist—and by his sportsmanlike qualities,

Prince Napoleon has made, in the royal family and in the 'high society' of Belgium, friends whose circle he has restricted only from a sentiment of proud reserve. . . ."

His association with the royal family of Belgium went, in fact, beyond friendship. In 1910, at almost fifty years of age, Prince Victor married Princess Clémentine, youngest daughter of King Leopold II of the Belgians. They had waited something like ten years for this day. The Princess's father, King Leopold, had always been strongly opposed to the match. It was bad enough, he reckoned, that Princess Clémentine, the great-granddaughter of King Louis-Philippe, should wish to ally herself with a Bonaparte, but it was positively dangerous for the Belgian royal family to get itself entangled with the pretender to the throne of France. King Leopold might not approve of the French Republic, but he was hardly in a position to risk annoying it. Princess Clémentine, a dutiful— and a favorite—daughter, respected her father's wishes in the matter, and it was only on his death in 1909 that she felt strong enough to disregard them.

Prince Victor and Princess Clémentine were married just less than a year after King Leopold's death. The Prince's mother, Princess Clotilde, emerging from the gloom of her cloistered life for a few days, allowed the ceremony to be performed at her home, the castle of Moncalieri, near Turin. The Princess had lived in this somber pile, at first with her daughter Laetitia and then alone, ever since Plon-Plon's return to France after the fall of the Empire. It was here, in the words of some lyrical biographer, that she had "unrolled the autumnal stages of her saintly existence, divided between penance and charity." The decidedly musty interior of the castle had been spruced up for the forthcoming marriage (the King of Italy had sent flowers, curtains, carpets, furniture and plate), and for a week or two that November the place looked almost festive. Royalties flocked to the ceremony by the dozen but the Bonapartes seem to have been limited to Princess Clotilde and her children, Laetitia (now Duchess d'Aosta) and Louis. The bride, who, according to one witness, was "exceptionally accomplished, beautiful, *spirituelle*, cultivated, endowed with a taste for the arts, and a fervent Catholic," looked, as was to be expected after such a paean, "radiant in beauty and charm . . . majestic and amiable." The honeymoon was spent in Italy. As the guests of the King and Queen of Italy in Rome, the newly married couple were precluded from visiting the Pope—still considered "the prisoner of the Vatican." This earned them the condemnation of the Belgian Catholics and the applause of the Belgian liberals. "Let the Prince become a real liberal," advised one newspaper, "and he will not have to complain of lack of sympathy."

Prince Victor, however, was not contemplating any such thing. On his return to Brussels he retired once more behind the pale blue façade of his palatial home in the Avenue Louise to "await opportunities." Princess Clémentine, in fact, seemed to be a more fervent upholder of the Napoleonic legend than he. She immersed herself in the works of Frédéric Masson, Emile Ollivier, and other imperial historians, and surrounded herself with souvenirs of the First and Second Empires, The Princess, her friends would say smilingly, was *"plus Bonapartiste que le Prince."*

The Imperial couple had two children; a daughter, Clotilde, born in 1912, and a son, Napoleon, born in 1914. Twelve years later, on the death of Prince Victor, in 1926, this son became the pretender to the Imperial throne. He remains so to this day.

Prince Victor's brother Louis never married. Of Plon-Plon's three children, Louis was undoubtedly the richest. Plon-Plon, determined to leave as little as possible to his wife, Clotilde, or to his other children, Victor and Laetitia (Laetitia was supposed always to have "sided" with her mother), left the bulk of his fortune to Louis. And when Louis's aunt Mathilde died in 1904, she, too, left him most of her money. Handsome, eagle-eyed, and very military in his bearing, Prince Louis seemed to some a far more likely candidate for the Imperial throne, but in deference to his elder brother, or perhaps for want of ambition, he never pushed himself forward. Hunting bears with the Czar, waltzing in the drawing rooms of St. Petersburg and putting down revolutionary movements in the Caucasus were probably far more to his taste.

Prince Victor's mother, Princess Clotilde, died a few months after his marriage. The life of this docile princess could not have been a very enviable one. Married when hardly more than a girl to the turbulent Plon-Plon, she had suffered his cantakerous behavior with an almost sublime resignation. A devout Catholic and a dutiful daughter, the long struggle between the Pope and the King of Italy—her father—had almost broken her heart. The year 1870 had seen the collapse of the Empire and flight from Paris; the years following had been marked by those terrible quarrels between Plon-Plon and Victor. The last three decades of her life had been spent in almost nunlike seclusion at the castle of Moncalieri; she left it only to attend the deathbeds of her various relations. She died there, on June 25, 1911, at sixty-eight years of age.

"She was not pretty," summed up the usually acidulous Maxime du

Camp, "but she was gentle, absolutely virtuous, and devoted to her husband. . . . Her certainty of an eternity of bliss inspired wide charity and unfailing kindness. She was the most saintly woman I ever knew."

♔　　♔　　♔

While, in Europe, old Jérôme's legitimate grandson, Prince Victor, was leading an increasingly retired life, in America his illegitimate grandson, Charles Patterson Bonaparte, was leading an increasingly public one. Charles, the second son of Bo Patterson Bonaparte (and grandson of the redoubtable Betsey), was displaying an almost Napoleonic flair for politics. After busying himself for some years with the politics of his native Baltimore (an opponent once dubbed him a "professional reformer"), he was appointed Secretary of the United States Navy by Theodore Roosevelt in 1905. If he was aware of the fact that his grandfather, the giddy Jérôme, had also been connected with the Navy at the time of his marriage to Betsey, it is unlikely that the diligent Charles gave the coincidence much thought. Indeed, with his burning interest in the Catholic Church and the Society for the Suppression of Vice, Charles probably preferred to give his dissolute grandfather as little thought as possible. Where King Jérôme's life had been dedicated to the pursuit of pleasure, his grandson's life was dedicated to the cleansing of political life and the improvement of social conditions. After a year and a half as Secretary of the Navy, he was appointed Attorney-General of the United States. That this important position would have impressed the socially ambitious Betsey is unlikely; her dreams had been exclusively of kingdoms and empires; she would have looked upon Charles as nothing more than a civil servant. Nor, come to that, would Charles have bothered himself about Betsey's Imperial aspirations; "He who serves his country well need not boast of ancestry," was one his favorite sayings.

Charles had married Ellen Channing Day in 1875, but as they had no children, his nephew, Jerome-Napoleon, would one day be the only surviving male descendant of King Jérôme and Betsey Patterson. This Jerome-Napoleon was the only son of young Jerome, once a colonel in Napoleon III's army. Born in 1878 and educated at Harvard, Jerome-Napoleon led a singularly unspectacular life. He married a Mrs. Blanche Strabegh, and as there were no children of this marriage either, the male line of the Patterson Bonapartes petered out with his death in 1945, at the age of sixty-seven. His only sister, Louise-Eugenie, married Count Moltke-Huitfeld.

The story of Jérôme and Betsey, which had begun so romantically with their marriage in 1803, ended, almost a century and a half later, when their great-grandson, taking his wife's dog for a walk in Central Park, tripped over its lead and died from the resulting injuries.

Except for the achievements of Charles Patterson Bonaparte (who died in 1921), such distinctions as were won by the family during the twentieth century tended to be social and literary rather than political or military. The spectacular marriage of Princess Marie Bonaparte (daugher of Roland and granddaughter of the irascible Pierre) to Prince George of Greece in 1907 linked the family to practically every royal house in Europe. From her father, Prince Roland, who was a savant of very real distinction (he was a member of the Académie des Sciences and a keen anthropologist), Princess Marie inherited a taste for study. She became first a pupil and then a great friend of Freud's and was responsible for translating several of his works. Among her own writings was a psychoanalytical study of Edgar Allan Poe. She died in September 1962 at the age of eighty-one.

As for the rest—the scores of descendants of Napoleon's brother Lucien and his sister Caroline Murat—they lived, for the most part, sumptuously and discreetly. Occasionally a Murat prince would distinguish himself by his bravery in battle, or a Bonaparte princess consolidate her position by a good match. One of Lucien's grandsons even became a cardinal. Very few of the Second Empire Bonapartes lived long into the new century. The studious Louis-Lucien died in 1891; his coffin was so designed that having been placed in the sarcophagus, its sides and lid could be removed, and the Prince revealed in court dress, lying on a mattress of violet satin fringed with gold. His chest was aglitter with orders. Achille Murat committed suicide in Russia in 1895; his brother Joachim died in 1901; his sister Caroline, rancorous to the last, died in England the following year. And in 1904, at the age of eighty-three, Princess Mathilde died.

In July the year before, when coming downstairs at Saint-Gratien one morning, Mathilde had fallen and fractured her femur. Although she lived for another six months, it was obvious that her days were numbered. She herself never pretended otherwise, and despite the terrible pain in her hip, retained something of her unconquerable spirit to the end. On being visited one day by a young and handsome priest, she sighed for the fact that so virile a man would never know the joys of physical love. Such robust sentiments were very much in the tradition of the Bonaparte women of the First Empire. As the winter approached, Mathilde's nephew Count Primoli decided that she should be removed to Paris, and it was here, in her house in the Rue de Berri, that she died on the evening of January 2, 1904. Almost all surviving members of the Imperial family, including the Empress Eugenie, attended the private mass at the church of Saint-Gratien, and the funeral was celebrated with great pomp in Paris the following day.

"You only knew her in her decline," said Eugenie to a friend a day or two after Mathilde's funeral, "and so you can hardly imagine how beautiful she was in the great days of the Empire: the profile of a medallion, sparkling eyes, a Venetian head of hair, and shoulders like a piece of sculpture. Her ways, her charm, her speech, everything about her was redolent of grace and wit, independence and frankness, ardor and health. . . ."

In Mathilde's coffin, by her express wish, they placed a portrait of the one man from whom she had never known disappointment—The Great Napoleon.

◈   ◈   ◈

"I am left alone, the sole remnant of a shipwreck," wrote the Empress Eugenie in her old age, "which proves how vain are the grandeurs of this world. . . . I cannot even die; and God, in His infinite mercy, will give me a hundred years of life."

And He almost did. She, who after the death of her son desired nothing more than her own death, lived on for another forty years. It seemed as though she would never die. Born a mere five years after the death of Napoleon I, she lived to see the birth of the boy who could have called himself Napoleon VI; contemporary with Queen Victoria, the great-grandsons of the Queen grew to manhood during her lifetime. "I died," the Empress was fond of saying, "in 1870"; her life, in fact, had not run even half its course at the fall of the Empire.

Her "forty years of silence" was what Augustin Filon called this period during which the Empress turned her back on all those things which had hitherto made up her life, and resigned herself to a withdrawn and solitary existence. The grandiose schemes, the taste for power, were things of the past now; misfortune had humbled and at the same time ennobled her—it was almost as if she had replaced her Imperial crown by a crown of thorns. And with this loss of her old ambition, she lost some of her less commendable characteristics as well. The impetuosity, the vindictiveness, the arrogance, now likewise fell away, and with their going came discretion, forbearance, and a very real concern for others.

She very seldom spoke about her son. When she did, no one could forget the heartrending phrase by which she always referred to him, *"mon petit garçon."* A visitor tells of the occasion when, on returning from a visit to Paris, she mentioned to the Empress that France seemed ripe for a dictator.

"If he had been alive," answered Eugenie slowly, "he had every quality they needed . . . now might have been his chance . . . but I often say to myself that I would rather he is dead than think of him as Emperor. . . ." She went on to tell her listener something of the hardships she had endured while still Empress of the French. "Not for one second have I regretted losing my throne," she declared. "To think of his perhaps going through it all—to endure what I had to endure. . . . Ah!" Then, her face contracting "with an indescribable pain and horror which pierced one to witness," she cried out: "I thank God that he has, at least, been spared that!"

For all her new-found sense of resignation, Eugenie was never able to shake off her habitual restlessness. She could not, like Madame Mère and Princess Clotilde, spend the rest of her days in gloomy confinement. Travel was still essential to her; inactivity would have stifled her passionate nature. She bought herself a yacht, and every year, or several times a year, she would go off on a cruise. She explored the coasts of Scotland, Ireland, and Norway, of Italy, Greece, Asia Minor, Africa, and Spain. She loved the Mediterranean, and in 1889 she built herself a villa at Cap Martin in the South of France. She visited Egypt again, and in order to go sightseeing, rode on donkeys in the scorching desert sun at the age of eighty. The following year she visited the aging Emperor Franz Joseph at Ischl. On another occasion she took the mail boat to Ceylon, sailing once more through the Suez Canal which she had opened in 1869, and spent six weeks on that humid island. She was eighty-three years old at the time.

She frequently visited Paris. When she was there, she always stayed at the Hôtel Continental, overlooking the Tuileries Gardens. Although the palace itself had been burned down, the formal garden, with its statuary and its fountains and its chestnut tress, was still exactly as it had been during Eugenie's heyday.

"How can your Majesty endure this spectacle?" a friend had asked the first time he visited the Empress at her hotel.

"What! Do you, too, ask me that?" she had replied. "Oh, yes! I know they think me insensitive because I take rooms at this hotel where I have the Tuileries constantly before my eyes. But after all, nothing makes the slightest difference to me any longer! What matters one spectacle or another, compared with the memories I bear in my innermost heart? Why, there are times when I feel as if I had been dead for a long, long time! I only live now amongst shadows, so even of myself I fashion the image of a shadow. . . ."

She went, accompanied by Count Primoli, to Fontainebleau. She had not been there for forty-four years. "Ah! there is my box!" she cried out, seeing a little ivory casket in one of the rooms. When her companion pointed out that the box was known as the casket of Anne of Austria, she answered, "That may be, but it was given to me, filled with gloves and fans, by the Emperor for my marriage." She visited the ruins of Saint-Cloud (likewise destroyed during the Franco-Prussian War), and noticing a slab of marble through which a tree had thrust its way, recognized the chimney piece of one of the salons in which she had often entertained her court. At Compiègne, accompanied this time by Princess Eugenie Bonaparte (a great-granddaughter of Lucien's), she toured the palace incognito. When she reached the Prince Imperial's bedroom, she crossed directly to the inner shutter of one of the windows. Here she found the marks and dates which she had made when measuring her son's height. The sight of these faded scribbles was too much; she broke down, and the bewildered attendant went dashing off to find the keeper. When they returned, the unknown old lady in black had stopped her sobbing, but felt unable to continue her tour. She left the palace immediately. On another occasion, while walking in the Tuileries Gardens, she stopped to pick a rose. A caretaker, appalled at this vandalism, hurried up. "It is forbidden to pick flowers here, madame," he grumbled officiously. "I shall have to report you. What is your name?"

"Eugenie," answered the sad-eyed old lady, and passed on.

But however much the Empress felt the need to travel, she was always pleased to get back to her home at Farnborough Hill. In this sprawling house, which someone once called "a mansion in mourning," Eugenie had arranged her hundreds of Imperial souvenirs. Here, in these pictures, statues, busts, tapestries, ornaments, and furnishings, was the century-long history of the Bonaparte family. On one of the terraces was a statue of the young Napoleon at Brienne; David's heroic picture, "Napoleon crossing the Alps," dominated the grand staircase; in the vestibule were various pieces of furniture belonging to Queen Hortense; there were cabinets crammed with First Empire Sèvres in the long gallery; portraits of every member of the family crowded the walls of the drawing rooms.

In the conservatory was Carpeaux's statue of the young Prince Imperial with his dog Nero; on the wall opposite was Cabanel's painting of the Emperor Napoleon III. In the entrance hall hung Winterhalter's sugar-sweet picture of the Empress and her ladies in the park of Saint-Cloud. Unable to accommodate all her relics in the house, Eugenie built a museum in the grounds. Here stood the magnificent carriage in which she had driven to her wedding at Notre Dame; there stood the state coach used by Napoleon III at the opening of the Corps Législatif; between them stood the tiny brougham in which the little Prince Imperial had taken his outings. . . .

Farnborough Hill constituted, said Augustin Filon, "an incomparable record in history." By day the deserted drawing rooms and dimly lit galleries were wrapped in gloom, but in the evening, when the lights glanced off the painted canvases and gleamed whitely on the many statues, "the vanished world springs again into life, peopled with those once well-known figures who are the real inhabitants of the dwelling." And when the Empress, with her pale, still lovely face, moved slowly amongst these lamplit souvenirs, one was almost tempted, said Filon, to believe that she, too, was "a shadow of the past."

Of that host of Second Empire Bonapartes, only Anna Murat (herself an old lady in her seventies) was still alive. Although there had never been much love lost between Eugenie and the rest of the family, she felt each death very keenly. "A fresh bereavement is to me not only a fresh wound," she said, "but also the recollection, and as it were the concentration, of all my previous bereavements. . . ."

She was obliged to turn, more and more, to the younger generation of Bonapartes for companionship. Not that she minded; Eugenie had always adored young people, and even in her nineties she preferred the company of those half her age or less to that of her contemporaries. Her niece Madame d'Attainville (later Countess Bacciochi), Princess Eugenie Bonaparte (Princess de la Moskowa), and Count Joseph Primoli often accompanied her on her travels, and frequent vistors to Farnborough Hill were Prince Victor and Princess Clémentine. The outbreak of the Great War in 1914 forced the pretender to leave Brussels, and for the next four years he, his wife, and their two children, Napoleon and Clotilde, lived with the Empress in England. It is interesting that the present Prince Napoleon spent the first few years of his life in the company of one in whose own youth Letizia Bonaparte had still been alive. And not only Letizia, but Joseph, Lucien, Louis, Hortense, Caroline, Jérôme, the

Empress Marie Louise, and the Duke of Reichstadt. With her almost incredible lifespan Eugenie linked the world of pre-Revolutionary France with the present day.

She followed the course of the war with understandable avidity. Almost half a century after Sedan, France was once more fighting against Germany. "I must do the Republic this justice," she would say, "it was better prepared for the events of 1914 than we were for those of 1870; it had good military equipment and strong alliances. . . ." Again and again she compared the present conflict with the war of 1870. The *Union Sacrée*, the working together of all Frenchmen regardless of political beliefs, awakened all her old regrets. "Why was not the same truce made round the Emperor and myself, under the shock of our first disasters?" she cried. "Why were public passions let loose against us after Fröschwiller and Forbach? . . . Why, in fact, was I not listened to on September 4, when I implored them to call a truce to domestic quarrels and to think only of France . . . ?"

She turned a wing of Farnborough Hill into a hospital; she gave her beloved yacht, the *Thistle*, to the British Admiralty; she contributed generously, but anonymously, to French charities. When an enemy Zeppelin flew overhead and the household was warned to put out all lights, she called her niece, Madame d'Attainville, and hurried out into the night to see it. Pietri, her faithful secretary, died in 1916, and in spite of the fact that her sight was failing, she wrote out her own will. She left Farnborough Hill, with its priceless family collections, to Prince Victor; she left her villa at Cap Martin to his sister, Princess Laetitia. When, late in 1918, the Germans began to give way before Foch, she cried out again and again, "If Foch could only catch them at Sedan!"

The final victory filled her with elation. With almost hysterical pride and gratitude she thanked God for allowing her to live long enough to see this day. "It makes up for everything," she exclaimed, "it obliterates everything, it repays me all my grief, it allows me to die with my head held high, in peace with France, which will have nothing to reproach us for. . . ."

And in a less effusive moment she would wish that her son had been there; the news, she said quietly, would have made him so happy.

The end of the war allowed Prince Victor and his family to leave Farnborough, but although Sedan had been avenged, he was not allowed to return to France. It would take another war against Germany and the valor of another pretender—Victor's son—to abrogate the law of exile against the Bonapartes. It would not be until 1950, after the present Prince Napoleon had distinguished himself in the Resistance forces, that the Bonaparte pretender would be allowed to return to France. With his wife, the former Mademoiselle Alix de Foresta, he settled in Paris. His twin son and daughter, Charles and Catherine, and his daughter Laura-Clémentine, were to be born on French soil.

In 1920, in her ninety-fifth year, the Empress visited her native Spain. Although, she told a friend smilingly, she felt more like a very old bat, she was determined—like the butterflies—to make for the sunlight. "Besides," she added, "before death takes me, I want to see my Castilian sky once more."

And it was here, in the Palacio de Liria, the home of her nephew the Duke of Alba, that she died. The day was Sunday, July 11, 1920. Her body was sent back to England for burial beside those of her husband and her son in St. Michael's Abbey, Farnborough.

A century before, when they had buried the first Napoleon in that little valley on St. Helena, he had been laid to rest, unmourned, in an unmarked grave. When Eugenie, the last Napoleonic Empress, was buried in the crypt of St. Michael's Abbey in 1920, there stood about her coffin (besides all the Bonapartes, Murats, and Bacciochis) a host of royalties, headed by the British sovereigns, King George V and Queen Mary themselves.

The remains of Napoleon III, the Empress Eugenie, and the Prince Imperial lie in the crypt of St. Michael's Abbey to this day. One follows a white-robed sandaled monk into that ice-cold cellar, and as he flicks the half-dozen switches, each wash of light reveals more clearly its bleak and damp-stained state. The floor is a pavement of dull Corsican marble; from its far end the altar rises like a small white island; above it, the ceiling is patterned with spreading stains and flaking paint. The damp seems to have penetrated everywhere. As one stands facing the altar, the sarcophagus of the Emperor is on the right, that of the Prince Imperial on the left, that of the Empress on a high archway above the altar. They are all immense and all of dark red dully-gleaming granite.

It is all so different from the massive glories of the Invalides. And it is ironic that while the tomb which Napoleon III built for Napoleon I should be so lovingly preserved, his own should be allowed to crumble away. There, in the heart of that Paris which owes so much to Napoleon III, the tourists tramp by the thousands through Napoleon I's tomb; here, while the rain stains blotch the walls, a handful of visitors comes occasionally to stare at the sarcophagus of a forgotten Emperor. The

Prince Imperial, in his will, had asked for his body to be laid by that of his father until such time as both were transferred to the resting place of the founder of their house. Will they ever be taken to the Invalides? It does not seem very likely. Not, that is, until a Napoleon is once more in charge of the destinies of France.

Epilogue

Paris 1940

EPILOGUE

♔ ♔ ♔

ADOLF Hitler, by the winter of 1940, was firmly astride a cowering
Europe. From the North Sea to beyond the Vistula, from the Arctic
Circle to the Pyrenees, the roads of the Continent echoed to the clash of
German boots and to the rumble of German guns. Marshal Pétain, nursing
the shattered remnants of French pride, had retired to the palatial
obscurity of the Hôtel du Pare at Vichy, and from there set about
devising the best means of living in a Nazi-dominated Europe. For the
most part, opinion around the aged marshal was in favor of collaboration
with the conquerors, of consolidation of Hitler's New Order of Europe.
By the end of 1940, things looked black indeed for France; the conquest
of England seemed only a matter of time; it might be as well for France
to cut her losses and integrate herself in an efficient Nazi-run Europe.
Some argued even further. Was not Hitler's dream of a united Europe
Napoleon's very dream of a European Empire? Was not the *Führer*,
with his essentially European outlook, the true heir of the Great
Emperor? Were not the destinies of France and Germany, in fact, one?

In October 1940 Hitler, returning through France from a meeting
with Franco, sent for Marshal Pétain. This meeting of the all-powerful
Führer with the frail French marshal had been arranged by Pierre Laval,
one of Pétain's pro-German ministers, in the hope of enticing France to
support Hitler's proposed defeat of Britain. They met in the *Führer's*
armored train at Montoire, near Tours. There Hitler expressed his desire
to see France occupy a position in the New Europe to which she was
entitled; in exchange, he expected her cooperation in his fight against
England. To these shameful but loosely knit arrangements, Pétain agreed.
France, within certain undefined limits, would collaborate with the
conqueror.

To consecrate this *entente* at Montoire, Hitler decided that some
tangible gesture must be made towards France. He would present her
with the remains of the Duke of Reichstadt. The friendship and unity of
the two countries was to be symbolized by the return of Napoleon's son
from Vienna to Paris. The French Emperor and the German princeling
would be reunited. It was Benoist-Mechin, one of the Nazi sympathizers
surrounding Marshal Pétain at Vichy, who claimed to have first put
forward this idea. He had suggested it before the war to Abetz—the man

who was to become German "ambassador" in Paris during the Occupation—and doubtless reminded him of it when Hitler needed to make some token to crown the acceptance, by France, of his New Order in Europe.

That Reichstadt's remains were not his to give seemed not to have bothered Hitler especially. During the preceding hundred years there had been repeated requests for the body of Napoleon's son to be returned to France. Louis Philippe, encouraged by the fillip which the return of Napoleon I's ashes had given to his reign, sought permission for the son's coffin to be brought home; and Napoleon III, eager to make the most of any available dynastic relics, made several requests for it. He even went so far as to have a pamphlet prepared in which the details of a *grand fête funèbre* were set out. In 1911, on the centenary of the King of Rome's birth, France again asked for the body, and in 1932, on the centenary of his death, it tried yet another time. The most famous pilots in France, they said, would fly the King of Rome's coffin across the Alps to Paris. It would be a splendidly Napoleonic gesture. . . .

But Austria remained steadfast in its refusal. The Emperor Franz Joseph, who ruled Austria for the greater part of this period, would not hear of it, and even after Austria had become a republic and had rid itself of the live Hapsburgs, it showed a strange disinclination to part with the dead. Napoleon's son, encased in his copper coffin, remained undisturbed in the cold, ghostly crypt of the Kapuzinerkirche in Vienna.

And now, on a single order from Berlin, all this was changed. A hundred years of carefully timed and never satisfied demands were granted by one who had no right to fulfill them. This "generous gesture," as Pétain put it, was considered by the majority of recipient Frenchman to be melodramatic in the extreme ("What we want," cracked hungry Parisians bitterly, "is not bones, but meat"), but it did reveal a nice sense of historical timing. The ceremony was planned to take place exactly one hundred years after the return of the body of Napoleon I from St. Helena to Paris. The great day was to be December 15, 1940.

As it turned out, the ceremony was a dismal failure.

On Thursday, December 12, the coffin of the Duke of Reichstadt was taken from the crypt of the Kapuzinerkirche. A dozen men from a leading firm of Viennese undertakers trooped into the crypt, hoisted the coffin onto their shoulders (it weighed 900 kilograms), and staggered out into a bitter rain. An ornate horse-drawn funeral car was waiting in the square outside. Once the coffin had been positioned inside it, the carriage moved off in the direction of the Western Station. Not more than half-a-dozen passers-by had witnessed the removal; those who did probably had no idea of the identity of the coffin.

It was a pale echo of that day, over a century before, when in a red morocco hearse with gold studs glinting in the hot sunshine, attended by a galaxy of chanting choirboys, clanking cavalrymen, and well-tailored Imperial archdukes, the Duke of Reichstadt had been laid to what everyone had then imagined was to be his final rest.

Now the unattended black hearse drove slowly, by the shortest possible route, to the Western Station, from which it would leave for Paris. In the presence of "representatives of the Party, Army, and State," as the Neues Weiner Tagblatt so discreetly put it, the Duke's coffin was placed on a train. Over it was flung an embroidered pall, and as it lay, prior to its departure for France, in some sort of state in an empty truck, two helmeted German soldiers stood guard over it.

The King of Rome, by the grace of Adolf Hitler, was going home to join the Emperor of the French. His arrival was to precipitate a crisis within Vichy France which would rob the occasion of any of its intended magnificence.

👑 👑 👑

Marshal Pétain's reaction to the *Führer's* "generous gesture" had been, in the main, cool. Much as the vain old man adored this sort of ceremony, it did not seem quite fitting that the victor of Verdun should parade himself before the tomb of Napoleon and there receive, at the hands of the German conquerors of France, the body of the Great Frenchman's son. To render the prospect of the ceremony a little more attractive to the diffident Marshal, it was hinted that Hitler himself might be present at the Invalides. This was a possibility which quickened the old man's pulses, for to stand as an equal beside the most powerful man in Europe, for all the world to see, was an idea which appealed to the Marshal's sense of self-glorification. It was understood that he might, after all, honor the solemn occasion with his illustrious presence.

On December 13 the pro-German minister Pierre Laval arrived at Vichy in order to ensure that the Marshal attend the ceremony in Paris on the fifteenth. That afternoon Pétain was warned that his journey to Paris might lead to his being forced to sign an unacceptable treaty with Hitler, or in the event of his refusal to sign it, to his kidnaping and the assumption of power in Vichy by Laval. The apprehensive Marshal promptly refused to go to Paris, and he had Laval arrested that very night.

Swift German intervention procured the almost immediate release of their puppet, but the stubborn Marshal refused to have him back as a minister. By this stand Pétain at last set his limits on collaboration with the enemy. The Franco-German friendship, so recently proclaimed at Montoire, seemed suddenly to have soured. On the night of December 14 the train carrying the coffin which was to have been the symbol of this Franco-German *entente* rattled into Paris. It was rather like the guest of honor arriving the day after the party.

Soon after one on the morning of December 15 the remains were placed on an artillery wagon and escorted by a detachment of German soldiers from the Gare de l'Est to the Invalides. The cortege rattled through the snow-strewn streets of the deserted city, past the blank façades of the shuttered houses, unheeded and unmourned. The churn of wheels and the scrunch of boots were the only sounds in all the cold gray stillness of the uninterested city.

Arriving at the Invalides, Reichstadt's cortege was met by Abetz, the German ambassador, and the coffin then carried by German soldiers into the courtyard. There stood two rows of municipal guards, holding flaming torches, in whose wind-tossed light were discernible the anxious faces of General Laure (representing Pétain), Admiral Darlan, and an assortment of high officials. Abetz, handing the coffin over to these representatives of Vichy France, made a short formal speech about the *Führer's* gift, and then, to the throbbing of drums, followed the coffin into the Dome. Here waited a group of die-hard collaborators and some hastily assembled members of the Bonaparte family. Conspicuous by their absence were the parents of this still-born scheme, Hitler and Pétain.

The coffin, covered by a great tricolor flag, was placed on the steps of the High Altar, and Mass celebrated. With the aid of dramatic lighting and pungent smells (one witness claims that a whole kilo of incense was burning in a container of such vast size that the congregation felt like Lilliputians), some sort of magnificence was achieved. But it was a hollow magnificence. The coldness of the proceedings was due less to the bitterness of the winter's night than to the absence of any real feeling of Franco-German comradeship. The whole meaning of the ceremony seemed to have changed; it appeared more like the funeral of Hitler's and Pétain's Montoire policy.

The return of Napoleon's son to Paris, instead of consecrating the new alliance, marked the virtual end of the idea of France's integration in Germany's New Order. Public opinion in France became, from that time onward, increasingly anti-German. It was almost as if Napoleon had returned to rally his country once more.

They put Reichstadt's coffin in the Chapelle Saint Jerome—one of the small chapels surrounding the huge circular crypt in which the body of the Great Napoleon is housed. And there, beneath the gilded dome of the Invalides, they remain to this day. The father lies in his monumental porphyry sarcophagus, the son in his slight copper casket. They are destined, these two, who had known each other, in life, for only three short years, to lie beside each other, in death, for all eternity.

BIBLIOGRAPHY

ABELL, LUCIA, *Recollections of the Emperor Napoleon,* J. Murray, London, 1844.

ANONYMOUS, *Uncensored Recollections,* E. Nash & Grayson, Ltd., London, 1924.

ABRANTES, LAURE SAINT-MARTIN JUNOT, DUCHESSE D', *Memoires,* 12 vols., Mame Delaunay, Paris, 1835 and later editions.

ANTOMMARCHI, FRANCESCO A., *The Last Days of Napoleon,* 2 vols., H. Colburn, London, 1826.

ASHE, WALLER, and EDGELL, THE HONORABLE E. V. WYATT, CAPTAIN, *The Story of the Zulu Campaign,* S. Low, Marston, Searle & Rivington, London, 1880.

ATTERIDGE, ANDREW HILLIARD, *Joachim Murat, Marshal of France and King Of Naples,* Brentano's, New York, 1911.

AUBREY, OCTAVE, *The King of Rome,* J. B. Lippincott, Philadelphia, 1932.

——, *St. Helena,* J. B. Lippincott, Philadelphia, 1936.

——, *Eugenie, Empress of the French,* J. B. Lippincott, Philadelphia, 1931.

AUJOL, JEAN LOUIS, *Le Proces Benoist-Mechin,* A. Michel, Paris, 1948.

BALMAIN, ALEKSANDRE ANTONOVICH, COUNT, *Napoleon in Captivity,* The Century Co., New York, 1927.

BARING-GOULD, SABINE, *The Life of Napoleon Bonaparte,* Methuen & Co., London, 1908.

BARLEE, ELLEN, *The Life of the Prince Imperial of France,* Griffith & Farran, London, 1880.

BERTAUT, JULES, *Le Menage Murat,* Le Livre Contemporain, Paris, 1958.

BERTRAND, HENRI GRATIEN, COMTE, *Cahiers de Sainte-Helene,* Sulliver, Paris, 1949.

BICKNELL, ANNA, *Life in the Tuileries Under the Second Empire,* The Century Co., New York, 1895.

BINGHAM, DENIS, THE HONORABLE CAPTAIN, *The Marriages of the Bonapartes,* Longmans, Green and Co., London, 1882.

BOIGNE, CHARLOTTE LOUISE ELEONORE ADELAIDE, COMTESSE D', *Memories of the Comtesse De Boigne,* C. Scribner's Sons, New York, 1907-8.

BOURGOING, JEAN DE, BARON, *Le Fils de Napoleon; Roi de Rome, Prince de Parme, Duc de Reichstadt,* Payot, Paris, 1932.

BOURRIENNE, LOUIS ANTOINE FAUVELET DE, *Memoirs of Napoleon Bonaparte,* 6 vols., C. Scribner's Sons, New York, 1906.

CAHUET, ALBERIC, *Retours de Sainte-Helene,* Fasquelle, Paris, 1932.

CARETTE, MME. A., *Recollections of the Court of the Tuileries,* D. Appleton & Co., New York, 1889.

CAREY, AGNES, *The Empress Eugenie in Exile,* The Century Co., New York, 1920.

CARLTON, WM. NEWNHAM CHATTIN, *Pauline, Favorite Sister of Napoleon,* Harper & Bros., New York, 1930.

CASTELOT, ANDRE, *L'Aiglon, Napoleon Deux*, Le Livre Contemporain, Paris, 1959.

CASTILLON DU PERRON, MARGUERITE, *Princess Mathilde*, W. Heinemann, London, 1956.

CHEETHAM, FRANK H., *Louis Napoleon and the Genesis of the Second Empire*, John Lane Co., New York, 1909.

COLE, HUBERT, *Josephine*, W. Heinemann, London, 1962.

CONSTANT, LOUIS C. W., *Memoirs of Constant, First Valet de Chambre of the Emperor*, C. Scribner's Sons, New York, 1895.

COPE, VINCENT ZACHARY, *A Versatile Victorian*, Harvey and Blythe, London, 1951.

CORLEY, THOMAS A. B., *Democratic Despot, A Life of Napoleon III*, Barrie & Rockliff, London, 1961.

COWLEY, HENRY WELLESLEY, BARON, *The Paris Embassy During the Second Empire*, T. Butterworth, Ltd., London, 1928.

CRESTON, DORMER, *In Search of Two Characters*, MacMillan & Co., Ltd., London, 1946.

D'AUVERGNE, EDMUND BASIL, *Napoleon the Third*, E. Nash & Grayson, London, 1929.

DECAUX, ALAIN, *Letizia, Mere de L'Empereur*, A. Fayard, Paris, 1959.

DES GARETS, MARIE (DE LARMINAT) DE GARNIER, CONTESSE, *Souvenirs d'une Demoiselle d'Honneur: L'Imperatrice Eugenie en Exile*, Calmann-Levy, Paris, 1929.

————, *Souvenirs d'une Demoiselle d'Honneur: Aupres de L'Imperatrice Eugenie*, Calmann-Levy, Paris, 1928.

DIDIER, EUGENE LEMOINE, *The Life and Letters of Madame Bonaparte*, C. Scribner's Sons, New York, 1879.

DU CAMP, MAXIME, *Souvenirs d'un Demi-Siecle*, Hachette, Paris, 1949.

DUCREST, GEORGETTE, *Memoirs of the Empress Josephine*, H. S. Nichols & Co., London, 1894.

DUMONT, GEORGES H., *La Dynastie Belge*, Elsevier, Brussels, 1959.

DURAND, MADAME, *Napoleon and Marie Louise; A Memoir*, Sampson, Low, Marston, Searle and Rivington, London, 1886.

ESPITALIER, ALBERT, *Napoleon and King Murat*, John Lane Co., New York, 1912.

EUGENIE, EMPRESS CONSORT OF NAPOLEON III, *Lettres Familieres de l'Imperatrice Eugenie*, 2 vols., Le Divan, Paris, 1935.

EVANS, THOMAS WILTBERGER, *Memoirs of Dr. Thomas W. Evans*, D. Appleton & Co., New York, 1905.

FABRE-LUCE, ALFRED, *Journal de la France 1939–1944*, Les Editions Du Cheval, Geneva, 1946.

FERRI-PISANI, CAMILLE, *Prince Napoleon in America, 1861*, Indiana University Press, Bloomington, 1959.

FILON, PIERRE MARIE AUGUSTIN, *Memoirs of the Prince Imperial*, W. Heinemann, London, 1913.

————, *Recollections of the Empress Eugenie*, Funk & Wagnalls, New York, 1921.

FLEISHMANN, HECTOR, *Napoleon III and the Women He Loved*, Holden & Hardingham, London, 1915.

———, *An Unknown Son of Napoleon*, John Lane Co., New York, 1914.

FLEURY, MAURICE, COMTE, *Memoirs of the Empress Eugenie*, D. Appleton & Co., New York, 1920.

FORBES, ARCHIBALD, *Souvenirs of Some Continents*, Harper & Bros., New York, 1885.

———, *Memories and Studies of War and Peace*, Cassell & Co., London, 1895.

FORSHUFVUD, STEN, *Who Killed Napoleon?*, Hutchinson, London, 1961.

FORSYTH, WILLIAM, *History of the Captivity of Napoleon at St. Helena*, 3 vols., Harper & Bros., 1853.

FRASER, SIR WILLIAM AUGUSTUS, BART., *Napoleon III (My Recollections)*, Sampson, Low, Marston & Co., Ltd., 1896.

FREMEAUX, PAUL, *The Drama of St. Helena*, D. Appleton & Co., New York, 1910.

FRENCH, G., MAJOR, *Lord Chelmsford and the Zulu War*, John Lane—The Bodley Head, London, 1939.

GEER, WALTER, *Napoleon and His Family*, Brentano's, New York, 1927-29.

GONCOURT, JULES AND EDMOND DE, *The Goncourt Journals*, Doubleday, Doran & Co., New York, 1937.

GOOCH, GEORGE PEABODY, *The Second Empire*, Longmans, London, 1960.

GOURGAUD, GASPARD, BARON GENERAL, *The St. Helena Journal, 1815-1818*, John Lane, London, 1932.

GREVILLE, CHARLES CAVENDISH FULKE, *The Greville Diary*, Doubleday Page & Co., Garden City, 1927.

GREVILLE, HENRY WILLIAM, *Leaves From the Diary of Henry Greville*, Smith, Elder & Co., London, 1883-1905.

GUEDALLA, PHILLIP, *The Second Empire*, G. P. Putnam's Sons, New York, 1922.

———, *The Hundred Days*, G. P. Putnam's Sons, New York, 1934.

GUEST, IVOR, *Napoleon III In Engand*, British Technical and General Press, London, 1952.

HARRISON, RICHARD, SIR GENERAL, *Recollections of a Life in the British Army*, Smith, Elder & Co., London, 1908.

HEGERMAN-LINDENCRONE, LILLIE (GREENOUGH) MOULTON, *In the Courts of Memory*, Harper & Bros., New York, 1912.

HOLDEN, W. H., *The Pearl from Plymouth*, British Technical and General Press, London, 1950.

———, *Second Empire Medley*, British Technical and General Press, London, 1952.

HORTENSE, QUEEN CONSORT OF LOUIS, KING OF HOLLAND, *The Memoirs of Queen Hortense*, 2 vols., Cosmopolitan Book Corp., New York, 1927.

HOUSSAYE, HENRY, *1815, Waterloo*, F. Hudson Publishing Co., Kansas City, 1905.

IMBERT DE SAINT-AMAND, ARTHUR LEON BARON, *The Court of Empress Josephine*, C. Scribner's Sons, New York, 1901.

IRISSON D'HERISSON, MAURICE, *The Prince Imperial*, P. Ollendorff, Paris, 1890.

JERROLD, BLANCHARD, *The Life of Napoleon III*, 4 vols., Longmans, Green & Co., London, 1874–82.

JOHN, KATHERINE, *The Prince Imperial*, Putnam, London, 1939.

JOINVILLE, FRANCOIS FERDINAND PHILIPPE LOUIS MARIE D'ORLEANS, PRINCE DE, *Memoirs of The Prince De Joinville*, Macmillan & Co., New York, 1895.

KEMBLE, JAMES, *Napoleon Immortal*, J. Murray, London, 1959.

KUHN, JOACHIM, *Pauline Bonaparte*, Hutchinson, London, 1937.

LAS CASES, EMMANUEL, COMTE DE, *Memorial de Sainte-Helene*, H. Colburn & Co., London, 1823.

LEGGE, EDWARD, *The Empress Eugenie and Her Son*, Dodd Meade & Co., New York, 1916.

——, *The Comedy and Tragedy of the Second Empire*, Harper & Bros. New York, 1911.

——, *The Empress Eugenie, 1870–1910*, Harper & Bros., New York, 1910.

LEVY, ARTHUR, *Napoleon Intime d'Apres des Documents Nouveaux*, Calmann-Levy, Paris, 1932.

LOCKHART, JOHN GIBSON, *The History of Napoleon Buonaparte*, E. P. Dutton & Co., Inc., New York, 1930.

LOLIEE, FREDERIC AUGUSTE, *Les Femmes Du Second Empire*, F. Juven, Paris, 1906.

——, *The Life of an Empress (Eugenie de Montijo)*, E. Nash, London, 1908.

MALMESBURY, JAMES HOWARD DAVIS, 3RD EARL OF, *Memoirs of an Ex-minister*, Scribner & Welford, New York, 1885.

MASSON, FREDERIC, *Napoleon A Sainte-Helene, 1815–1821*, P. Ollendorff, Paris, 1912.

——, *Napoleon et sa Famille*, P. Ollendorff, Paris, 1900–19.

——, *Napoleon and the Fair Sex*, J. B. Lippincott Co., Philadelphia, 1894.

——, *Napoleon and His Coronation*, Leipsic, T. F. Unwin, London, 1911.

——, *Napoleon at Home*, J. B. Lippincott Co., Philadelphia, 1894.

MENEVAL, CLAUDE FRANCOIS, BARON DE, *Memoirs of Napoleon Bonaparte*, P. F. Collier & Co.,

——, *The Empress Josephine*, J. B. Lippincott Co., Philadelphia, 1912.

MERCY-ARGENTEAU, MARIE CLOTHILDE ELISABETH LOUISE (DE CARAMAN-CHIMAY) COMTESSE DE, *The Last Love of an Emperor*, Doubleday, Page & Co., New York, 1926.

MITFORD, BERTRAM, *Through the Zulu Country*, Kegan, Paul, Trench & Co., London, 1883.

MOLE, LOUIS MATHIEU, COMTE, *The Life and Memoirs of Count Mole*, Hutchinson & Co., London, 1923.

MOLYNEAUX, WILLIAM CHARLES FRANCIS, *Campaigning in South Africa and Egypt*, Macmillan & Co., New York, 1896.

MONTBEL, GUILLAUME ISIDORE BARON, COMTE DE, *Le Duc De Reichstadt*, J. Auge (etc.), Paris, 1836.

MURAT, CAROLINE LATITIA, PRINCESS, *My Memoirs*, G. P. Putnam's Sons, New York, 1910.

Bibliography

NAPOLEON I, EMPEROR OF THE FRENCH, *Correspondance de Napoleon I^{er,}* 5 vols., H. Plon, J. Dumaine, Paris, 1858–70.

———, EMPEROR OF THE FRENCH, *Napoleon's Letters to Josephine,* H. F. Hall, editor, E. P. Dutton & Co., New York, 1901.

———, EMPEROR OF THE FRENCH, *Letters of Napoleon,* J. M. Thompson, editor, B. Blackwell, Oxford, 1934.

———, EMPEROR OF THE FRENCH, *Napoleon's Letters to Marie Louise,* Farrar & Rinehart, Inc., New York, 1935.

———, EMPEROR OF THE FRENCH, *The Confidential Correspondence of Napoleon Bonaparte with His Brother Joseph,* D. Appleton & Co., New York, 1856.

NAPOLEON, JOSEPH CHARLES PAUL BONAPARTE, PRINCE, *Napoleon and His Detractors,* W. H. Allen, London, 1888.

NICOLSON, HAROLD, *Sainte-Beuve,* Doubleday, Garden City, 1957.

O'DONOGHUE, ELINOR MARY (ODDIE, E. M., [pseud.]), *Napoleon II, King of Rome, Prince of Parma, Duke of Reichstadt,* S. Low, Marston & Co., Ltd., London, 1932.

———, *Marie Louise, Empress of France, Duchess of Parma,* C. Scribner's Sons, New York, 1931.

———, *The Bonapartes in the New World,* E. Mathews & Marrot, Ltd., London, 1932.

O'MERA, BARRY EDWARD, *Napoleon at St. Helena,* R. Bentley & Son., Cambridge, 1888.

PALEOLOGUE, GEORGES MAURICE, *Les Entretiens de l'Imperatice Eugenie,* Plon, Paris, 1928.

PROKESCH-OSTEN, COMTE DE, *Les Temoins de l'Epopee,* Librairie Plon, Paris, 1934.

RAVAGE, MARCUS ELI, *Empress Innocence,* A. A. Knopf, New York, 1931.

REMUSAT, CLAIR ELISABETH GRAVIER DE VERGENNES, COMTESSE DE, *Memoirs de Madame de Remusat,* 3 vols., D. Appleton & Co., New York, 1888.

ROSE, JOHN HOLLAND, *The Life of Napoleon I,* Harcourt, Brace & Co., New York, 1924.

———, *The Personality of Napoleon,* G. P. Putnam's Sons, New York, 1912.

ROSEBERY, ARCHIBALD PHILLIP PRIMROSE, 5TH EARL OF, *Napoleon, the Last Phase,* Harper & Bros., New York, 1900.

ST. DENIS, LOUIS ETIENNE, *Souvenirs du Mameluck Ali,* Payot, Paris, 1926.

SAVANT, JEAN (editor), *Napoleon in His Time,* Nelson, New York, 1958.

SENCOURT, ROBERT ESMONDE, *The Life of Empress Eugenie,* E. Benn, Ltd., London, 1931.

SERGEANT, PHILLIP WALSINGHAM, *The Burlesque Napoleon,* T. W. Laurie, London, 1905.

SHAW, CLEMENT, *Letizia Bonaparte (Madame Mere),* The Viking Press, New York, 1928.

SIMPSON, FREDERICK ARTHUR, *The Rise of Louis Napoleon,* Longmans, Green & Co., New York, 1925.

SMYTH, ETHEL MARY, DAME, *As Time Went On,* Longmans, Green & Co., New York, 1936.

———, *Impressions That Remained*, Longmans, Green & Co., New York, 1919.

———, *Streaks of Life*, Longmans, Green & Co., New York, 1921.

STIRLING, MONICA, *A Pride of Lions*, Collins, London, 1961.

THACKERAY, WM. MAKEPEACE, *The Second Funeral of Napoleon*, John W. Lovell Co., New York, 1883.

THIERRY, AUGUSTINE, *Le Prince Imperial*, B. Grasset, Paris, 1935.

THOMPSON, JAMES MATTHEW, *Louis Napoleon and the Second Empire*, Blackwell, Oxford, 1954.

———, *Napoleon Bonaparte, His Rise and Fall*, Blackwell, Oxford, 1952.

TISDALL, EVELYN ERNEST P., *The Prince Imperial*, Jarrolds, London, 1959.

TSCHUDI, CLARA, *Napoleon's Mother*, P. Reclam Jun, Leipzig, 1898.

TURQUAN, JOSEPH, *The Empress Josephine*, John Lane Co., New York, 1913.

———, *The Sisters of Napoleon*, T. F. Unwin, London, 1908.

TYRNER-TYRNAUER, A. R., *Lincoln and the Emperors*, Harcourt, Brace & World, New York, 1962.

VANDAM, ALBER DRESDEN, *An Englishman in Paris*, D. Appleton & Co., New York, 1893.

VICTORIA, QUEEN OF GREAT BRITAIN, *The Letters of Queen Victoria*, 3 vols., Longmans, Green & Co., New York, 1926-28.

———, *More Leaves from the Journal of a Life in the Highlands*, J. W. Lovell, New York, 1884.

———, *Further Letters of Queen Victoria*, T. Butterworth, London, 1938.

VIEL-CASTEL, HORACE, COMTE DE, *Memoires du Horace de Viel-Castel*, 6 vols., Chez Tous Les Libraires, Paris, 1883-4.

VIZETELLA, ERNEST ALFRED, *The Court of The Tuileries*, Chatto & Windus, London, 1912.

WELLESLEY, VICTOR, SIR, & SENCOURT, ROBERT, *Conversations With Napoleon III*, E. Benn, Ltd., London, 1934.

WERTH, ALEXANDER, *France 1940-1955*, R. Hale, London, 1956.

WERTHEIMER, EDUARD VON, *The Duke of Reichstadt*, J. Lane Co., New York, 1905.

WILLIAMS, HUGH NOEL, *The Women Bonapartes*, 2 vols., C. Scribner's Sons, New York, 1909.

WILSON, ROBERT MCNAIR, *Josephine, The Portrait of a Woman*, Eyre & Spottiswoode, Ltd., London, 1930.

———, *The King of Rome*, D. Appleton & Co., New York, 1933.

———, *Napoleon's Mother*, J. B. Lippincott Co., Philadelphia, 1933.

WOLFF, HENRY DRUMMOND, SIR, *Rambling Recollections*, 2 vols., Macmillan & Co., Ltd., London, 1908.

WOOD, EVELYN, SIR, *From Midshipman to Field Marshall*, 2 vols., Methues & Co., London, 1906.

WRIGHT, CONSTANCE, *Daughter to Napoleon*, Holt, Rinehart & Winston, New York, 1961.

Newspapers and Periodicals

Graphic, Histoires de l'Histoire, Le Figaro, London Illustrated News, London Times, Morning Post, Neues Weiner Tagblatt, Paris Soir, Punch, Standard, Volks-Zeitung.

INDEX

Abbatucci, Marie, 373
Alba, Duke of, 387
Alexander, Czar of Russia, 144; pension to Catherine of Württemberg, 146
Aosta, Duke of, 371
d'Attainville, Madame (later Countess Bacciochi), 385
Augusta, Princess of Bavaria, engagement and marriage to Eugène de Beauharnais, 74

Bacciochi, Felix, marriage to Elisa Bonaparte, 26; in Corsica, 28; with Lucien Bonaparte, 62
Bacciochi, Frédéric, 145; 212
Bacciochi, Count Marius, 256
Bacciochi, Napoléone, 80; becomes Countess Camerata, 201; to Vienna; 202; to Italy, 202
Barras, 20; 21
Bartolini-Baldelli, Marchesa, 223; 269
Beatrice, Princess, 352; 362
de Beauharnais, Vicomte Alexandre, 20
de Beauharnais, Eugène, aide-de-camp to Napoleon I, 30; Vice-Chancellor, 72; Viceroy of Italy, 72; successor to throne of Italy, 72; adopted by Napoleon I and made Prince of France, 74; marriage to Augusta of Bavaria, 74; created Duke of Leuchtenberg, 179; death, 196; Fig. XX
de Beauharnais, Hortense, opposition to mother's remarriage, 23; marriage to Louis Bonaparte, 48; Queen of Holland, 80; separation from Louis, 123; bears son to Charles de Flahaut, 125; created Duchess of St.-Leu, 144; settles in Augsburg, 178; to Switzerland, 197; to Paris, 199; to England, 200; return to Switzerland, 200; death, 217; Fig. X
de Beauharnais, Josephine, see Josephine, Empress
de Beauharnais, Stéphanie, marriage to Grand Duke of Baden, 75
Bélanger, Marguerite, 277
Bertrand, Count, 162; 172
Bismarck, 306; 311; Fig XXXVII
Bombelles, Count, 226
Bonaparte, Caroline, 3; sent to the school of Madame Campan, 31; marriage to Murat (civil) 45; church marriage, 49; given title of Imperial Highness, 64; given duchies of Berg and Cleves, 85; Regent of Naples, 131; forced to flee, 152; becomes "Comtesse de Lipona," 175; death, 213; Fig. XIV
Bonaparte, Catherine, 287
Bonaparte, Charles (son of Lucien), Prince of Canino, marries Zénaïde, 194; death, 300
Bonaparte, Charles Patterson (son of "Bo"), 349; Secretary of U.S. Navy, 380; U.S. Attorney General, 380; marriage to Ellen Channing Day, 380
Bonaparte, Charles (son of Prince Napoleon), 387
Bonaparte, Charlotte (daughter of Lucien and Christine), "Lolotte," sent to Paris, 108; marriage to Prince Gabrielli, 174
Bonaparte, Charlotte (daughter of Joseph and Julie), 177; marriage to Napoleon-Louis, 194; death, 222
Bonaparte, Christine, to Spain with father, 63; marriage to Count de Posse, 174
Bonaparte, Elisa, to girls' school of St. Cyr, 9; return to Corsica, 13; marriage, 26; cultivates Fontanes, 52; given title of Imperial Highness, 64; created Princess of Piombino, 79; reforms, 79; adds Tuscany to domains (Grand Duchess), 129; forced to flee, 136; death, 176; Fig. VII
Bonaparte, Princess Eugenie, 384
Bonaparte, Jérôme, at Mombello, 30; comes to live with Napoleon I at Tuileries, 44; lands in Norfolk, Va., 56; meets Elizabeth Patterson, 57; marriage, 58; sails to Lisbon and leaves wife, 59; made King of Westphalia, 86; marries Catherine of Württemberg, 87; goes to join Napoleon I in Russia, resigns, 129; conquered and routed from Westphalia, 134; made Count de Montfort, 174; in Trieste, 174; refused permission to send agent to Vienna, 201; visits Hortense in Switzerland, 213; marriage to Marchesa Bartolino-Baldelli, 223; death and funeral, 268
Bonaparte, Jérôme Napoleon (son of Elizabeth Patterson and Jerome),

birth, 59; "Bo", 189; to Rome, 190;
return to America, 190; to Harvard,
192; to Europe, 192; marries Susan
May Williams, 195; returns to France,
252; leaves, 254; death, 348; Fig. XVI
Bonaparte, Jérôme-Napoleon (son of
Jérôme and Catherine of Württemberg), 145; 226
Bonaparte, Jerome-Napoleon (son of
Jerome Patterson Bonaparte), 380
Bonaparte, Jerome Patterson (son of
"Bo" and Susan), birth, 215; Crimea,
252; 270; 271; to England, 323; 349;
380; Fig. XXXIII
Bonaparte, Joseph, 3; study in Italy, 8;
marriage to Julie Clary, 15; ap-
pointed French Ambassador to
Rome, 28; returns to Paris, 31; made
member of Corps Legislatif and Am-
bassador Extraordinary, 50; made
Prince of Empire, 63; becomes King
of Naples, 76; King of Spain and the
Indies, 96; relieved of command in
Spain, returns to Mortefontaine, 132;
appointed Lt.-Gen. of Empire, 137;
to America, 177; returns to Europe,
210; death, 225; Fig. VII
Bonaparte, Princess Laetitia (daughter of
Plon-Plon) 371; 372; 386
Bonaparte, Laura-Clémentine, 387
Bonaparte, Letizia Ramolino, Madame
Mère, marriage, 3; thriftiness, 11, 32,
40, 76; flees to Calvi, 16; to France,
16; opposition to Napoleon's marriage, 29; comes to Paris, 39; given
title of Son Altesse Impériale, Madame Mère de l'Empereur; 75; visit
to Napoleon at Elba, 141; to Rome,
171, 172; death in Rome, 212; return
of body to Ajaccio, 212; Fig. IV
Bonaparte, Louis, to France with Napoleon I, 10; appointed aide-de-camp
and personal secretary to Napoleon,
17; made Colonel in Fifth Dragoons,
43; marriage to Hortense, 48; made
prince of Empire, 63; made King of
Holland, 80; abdicates, 123; to Gratz,
127; to Switzerland, 134; return to
Paris, 134; Rome, 174; death, 225;
Fig. XI
Bonaparte, Prince Louis (son of Plon-
Plon) 362; 371; 376; 379
Bonaparte, Louis-Lucien (son of Lucien),
marriage, 216; 324; 329; guardian of
Prince Imperial, 330; 331; 343; 344;
350; 361; 376; 381
Bonaparte, Louise-Eugenie, 380
Bonaparte, Lucien, study at Military College, 8; rebellious letter to Joseph,
13; speech to Revolutionary Club in
Toulon, 14; marriage to Christine
Boyer, 16; arrest, 17; visits mother in
Marseilles, 17; appointed Commissioner of Army of North, assistant to
Fréron, 17; consigned to Corsica, 30;
appointed French Commissioner, 30;
elected Corsican deputy to the Council of Five Hundred in Paris, 32;
made Minister of Interior, 42; appointed Ambassador to Spain, 50;
proposes Napoleon marry Infanta
Isabella, 50; return to France, 50;
takes Alexandrine Jouberthon as mistress, 51; son by mistress, 51; marriage to Alexandrine, 51; forced to
Italy, 52; prince of Canino, 78; attempts to emigrate to America, taken
to Malta, then to England, 109; in-
tercession with Castlereagh for
Joseph in Spain, 127; return to Rome,
143; in Rome, 173; refused passport
to Vienna, 201; death, 225; Fig. IX
Bonaparte, Princess Marie, 381
Bonaparte, Princess Mathilde, 3; birth,
175; marriage, 222; to Paris, 223; to
Florence, 223; separation from husband, 224; 231; 258; 279; 281; 283; 307;
321; 322; 323; 336; 341; 342; 354; 362;
371; 372; 374; 381; Fig. XXXI
Bonaparte, Prince Napoleon (Plon-Plon,
son of Jerome and Catherine of
Württemberg) 192; 228; in France,
228; ambassador to Spain, 231; 241;
Crimean War, 252; to Paris, 253;
marriage, 265; 270; 272; 279; 291; 303;
resigns and goes to Switzerland, 304;
309; 310; to England, 320; Switzerland, 321; 333; 337; 343; 345; 362;
369; 370; death, 372; Fig. XXXII
Bonaparte, Prince Napoleon (son of
Prince Victor), 387
Bonaparte, Napoleon-Charles (oldest son
of Louis and Hortense), 81
Bonaparte, Napoleon Francis Charles
Joseph (Napoleon II, King of
Rome), birth, 121; created Emperor,
154; stripped of titles of King of
Rome, Napoleon II, Prince of Parma,
169; given title of Duke of Reichstadt, 169; receives news of father's
death, 186; description, 203; illness,
206; death, autopsy, titles restored,
209; body to Paris, 391; Fig. XXIV
Bonaparte, Napoleon-Louis (second son
of Louis and Hortense), taken to
Rome by father, 174; marries Char-

lotte Bonaparte, 194; death, 199; Fig. VI

Bonaparte, Pauline, 3; courted by Fréron, 18; married to General Victor Leclerc, 29; goes to San Domingo, 53; return to France, 53; marries Prince Borghese, 54; Princess and Duchess of Guastalla, 83; illness, 130; visits Elba, 142; cultivates British, 173; legally separated from Prince Borghese, 173; will, 197; death, 197; Figs. XII and XIII

Bonaparte, Pierre (fourth son of Lucien) birth, 143; 299; shoots Victor Noir, 305; 317; 324; 330

Bonaparte, Roland, 331

Bonaparte, Prince Victor, 362; 364; 368; 371; 372; 376; 386; Fig. XL

Bonaparte, Zénaïde, 177; marries cousin Charles, 194

Bonaparte-Wyse de Solms, Marie, 255

Borghese, Prince Camillo, 54

Bourrienne, 34; 38

Buonaparte, Carlo, marriage, 4; *procureur de roi,* 5; to France, 6; death, 7

Camerata, Count, marriage to Napoléone Bacciochi, 201

Camerata, Count (son of Napoléone Bacciochi) 249

Canova, 54

Carey, Captain, 356; 360

Castel, Viel, 251; 252; 259; 267; 270; 299; 301

de Castiglione, Countess, 276

Catherine of Württemberg, Princess, marriage to Jerome Bonaparte, 87; 146; death, 211

Cecchi, Maria, 216

de Chambaudouin, Madame, 53

Charles, Hippolyte, 33

Chelmsford, Lord, 355

Clary, Désirée, Queen of Sweden, sister of Julie Clary, 16

Clary, Julie, marriage to Joseph Bonaparte, 15; 221; death, 225

Clavel, 212

Clémentine, Princess, 378

Clotilde, Princess of Sardinia, marriage, 265; return to Italy, 321; 371; 378; death, 379; Fig. XXXII

Constant, 33

Corvisart, 73; 120

David, Fig. I

David, Jerome, 269

Day, Ellen Channing, 349

Demidov, Anatole, marriage to Mathilde, 222; death, 342

Demorny, Charles Auguste Joseph Louis, son of Hortense de Beauharnais and Charles de Flahaut, birth, 125 (see de Morny, Duke)

Dénuelle, Charles Léon, son of Napoleon I and Eléonore Dénuelle, 90, (see Léon, Count)

Dénuelle, Eléonore, "Proof of Potency," 90; 156

Disraeli, 354

Duchâtel, Madame, 65

Durand, Madame, 122

Edgar, Mrs. Newbolt, nee Appleton, Caroline LeRoy, married to Jerome Patterson Bonaparte, 349

Emmanuel II, King Victor, 295; 321

Empress Eugenie (Eugenie de Montijo), 240; marriage, 243; 272; to Scotland, 277; return to France, 277; 287; 288; 293; 294; Suez Canal, 297; 309; 312; flees palace, 313; to England, 314; visits Emperor, 318; returns to England, 319; 326; 351; 352; 359; 366; 370; 375; 382; 387; Figs. XXIX, XXX, XXXV and XLI

Fesch, Joseph, 5

Filon, 295; 319; 322; 328; 335; 345; 382; 385

de Flahaut, Charles, natural son of Tallyrand, lover of Hortense, 124; marriage to Margaret Elphinstone, 179

de' Fontanes, Louis, 42

de Forbin, Auguste, 84

de Foresta, Alix, 387

Fouché, 50; 93; 136; 153

Fourés, Madame, 34

Fourés, Lt., 34

Franz Joseph, Emperor of Austria, 392

Fréron, Commissioner-Extraordinary for Southern France, 54

Freud, Sigmund, 381

Gladstone, 329

golden bees, emblem of Napoleon, 69

Gourgand, Baron, 161

Hitler, Adolf, 391

Hugenschmidt, Dr., 276

Isabey, 164

Jefferson, Thomas, 72

Josephine, Empress, first meeting with Napoleon and background, 20; marriage, 22; in Milan, 27; buys Malmaison, 41; proposes marriage of Hortense and Louis, 47; secretly married by church to Napoleon, 67; crowned Empress, 67; divorced by Napoleon, 105, meets Czar Alexander, 144; death, 145; Figs. XVIII and XIX

Junot, 75

Junot, Madame (Laure Permon), 15; 43; 44; 45; 53; 59; 84; 86; 93; 143

Jouberthon, Alexandrine, mistress of Lucien, 51; has son by Lucien, 51; marriage, 51

Kirkpatrick, William, maternal grandfather of Empress Eugenie, 239

de Labenne, Count Louis, 227

de Larminat, Marie, 362; 366

de Las Cases, Count, 161; 172

Laval, Pierre, 391; 393

Leclerc, General Victor, marriage to Pauline, 29; divisional commander of Army of Italy, 43; regains San Domingo, 53; dies of yellow fever, 53

Léon, Count, in London, 219; attempt at duel, 219; 255; 303; Fig. XXV

Lespérat, 79

de Lesseps, Ferdinand, 295

Letessier, Elisa, 249

Louis XVI, 6

Louis-Philippe, King Louis XVIII, 147; 175; 198; 219; 228

Lowe, Sir Hudson, 98

MacDonald, General, 176

MacMahon, Marshal, 308

Marie Antoinette, 6

Marie Louise, Empress of France, description and marriage to Napoleon I, 111; appointed Regent, 137; leaves Paris, 138; goes to Schönbrunn, 140; breaks with Napoleon, 150; made Duchess of Parma, Piacenza, Guastalla, 169; liaison with Neipperg, 170; marriage to Count Bombelles, 226; death, 226; Figs. XXI and XXII

Masson, Frédéric, 341; 369; 379

Maximilian, Emperor of Mexico, 294

Méneval, 157

de Mercy-Argenteau, Countess, 296

Metternich, 3; 146; 198; 208

de Mouchy, Duke, 302

Montenuovo, Count, 170

Montenuovo, Countess, 170

de Montholon, Count, 162

de Montijo, Paca, Duchess of Alba, 239; 240; 276

de Morny, Duke, birth, 125; 245; with Madame Le Hon, 245; minister of Interior, 246; resigns, 246; Pres. of Legislative Chamber, 247; ambassador to Russia, 247; 262; marriage, 263; 279; death, 284; Fig. XXXVIII

Murat, Achille (son of Caroline & Joachim Murat), 193; marries Catherine Byrd Willis, 193; Fig. VI

Murat, Achille (son of Lucien Murat) 301; 317; 381

Murat, Anna, 194; 257; 280; 301; 350; 362; 385

Murat, Caroline, 250; 270; 286; 317; 323; 331; 350; 351; 365; 381

Murat, "Chino" 350; 354

Murat, Joachim, at Mombello, 29; marriage to Caroline Bonaparte (civil), 45; church marriage, 49; made King of Naples, 98; joins Napoleon in Russia, 131; betrayal of Napoleon, 135; defeat at Tolentino, 152; death, 176; Fig. XV

Murat, Joachim (son of Lucien), 301; 350; 361; 381

Murat, Letizia, Fig. VI

Murat, Louise, Fig. VI

Murat, Lucien, to America, 193; marriage to Caroline Fraser, 194; to France, 231; 300; death, 350; Figs. VI and XXXIV

Napoleon I, Emperor 1764–1821, birth, 3; school in France, 6; with Lucien in France, 8; puts Elisa in St. Cyr, 9; takes Louis to France, 10; back to Corsica, 13; brings family to France, 14; description, 15; publishes Le Souper de Beaucaire, 15; put in command of artillery at Toulon, 15; "13 Vendemiaire," 15; promoted to Commander in Chief of Army of Interior, 15; meets Josephine, 20; marriage, 22; moves family to Mombello, 27; gives Elisa dowry, 28; family leaves Mombello, 29; returns to Paris, 31; goes on Egyptian campaign, 33; threatens divorce, 34; affair with Madame Fourés, 34; return to France, 35; arrival in Paris, 35; made First Consul, 37; Italian campaign, 46; Code Civil, Concordant with Pope, peace with Austria, England, Spain, Holland, treaties with Russia, 46; Consul for Life, 46; forces Jerome to give up Elizabeth Patterson, 59; declares himself Emperor of the French, 63; secretly married by church to Josephine, 67; crowned Emperor, 67; crowns himself King of Italy, 71; victories at Jena, 74; defeats Russian Army at Friedland, 88; decision to divorce, 100; meets Czar Alexander at Tilsit, separates from Josephine, 105; marries Marie Louise, 111; annexes Holland, 123; takes command of Grande Armee, 125; defeat, 131; 134; Campaign of 1814, 138; abdication, 140; to Elba, 140; escapes Elba, 147; draws up new constitution, 152; leaves for battle, 153; Waterloo, 154; abdicates in favor of son, 154; leaves to go to America, 157; exile at St. Helena, 161; recommendations to family, 181; will, 182; death 183; autopsy, 184; burial at St. Helena, 185; remains removed to Paris, 220; Figs. II, III, V, VI

Napoleon III, Charles Louis-Napoleon, birth, 82; education, 180; expelled from Rome, 199; to Paris, 199; to England, 200; return to Switzerland, 200; becomes pretender, 210; romance with Mathilde, 214; attempts to re-establish empire, 214; sent in exile to America, 214; lands at Norfolk, 215; return to Switzerland, 217; to England, 217; imprisoned in France, 220; writing in prison, 227; escape to London, 227; to Paris, 229; proclaimed President, 230; establishes 2nd Empire, 233; marriage, 243; attempt on life, 263; 264; Italian campaign, 264; ill health, 278; declares war on Prussia, 307; to War, 307; defeat, 308; captivity, 311; to England, 324; restoration plans, 333; death, 335; will, 337; 340; Figs. VI, XXVII, XXVIII, XXXV, XXXVI and XXXVII

von Neipperg, Count, 149; 169; 226

Nicholas, Czar, 222

Nieuwerkerque, Count de, 224; 281; 284; 299

Noir, Victor (Yvan Salmon), 305

Orsini, 264

d'Orx, Count Eugene, 227

Patterson, Elizabeth, meets Jerome Bonaparte, 56; marriage, 58; bears son in England, 59; obtains divorce, 133; to Paris, 175; to Rome with son, 189; eccentricity, 216; to France, 252; sues for share of estate, 271; death, 350; Fig. XVII

Patterson, William, objects to daughter's marriage, 57; agrees to marriage, 58

Pearl, Cora, 320

Permon, Laure (see Madame Junot)

Pétain, Marshal, 391

Pichon, 58

Pietri, 337; 386

Popelin, Claudius, 341; 372; 374

Potocki, Count, 221

Prince Imperial, Napoleon, Eugene Louis Jean Joseph, birth, 260; early life, 288; operation, 290; to war with father, 307; to Belgium, 310; to England, 317; Royal Military Academy, 332; 335; 351; to Africa, 354; death, 359; 361; Figs. XXXV, XXXVI, and XXXIX

Primoli, Count, 374; 382; 384

de Ricci, Marie-Anne, second wife of Count Alexandre Walewski, 248; 267; 287; 322

Roccagiovine, Marchioness (Julie Bonaparte), 282

Rochefort, Henri, 305; 306

Ruffin, Justine, 330

Sainte-Beuve, Charles Augustus, 282

Savage, Annette, 178

Talleyrand, 99; 146; 350

Thiebault, Aimée, 164

Trochu, General, 309; 327

Troubetskoi, Princess Sophie, marriage to de Morny, 263; 286

Vergeot, Alexandrine, 227

Victoria, Queen, 248; 258; 360; 362; 366

Walewska, Marie, mistress of Napoleon I, 91; visits Napoleon at Elba, 141; 247

Walewski, Count Alexandre, 91; marriage to Caroline Montague, 247; son by Rachel, 247; ambassador to London, 248; Foreign Minister, 249; 266; 280; Fig. XXVI

Walewski, Antoine, 248

Watkyns, Charlotte, 352